TENNYSON
–·–
IN MEMORIAM

Fair ship, that from the Italian shore
Sailest the glassy oceanplains,
With my lost Arthur's loved remains,
Spread thy full wings & waft him o'er.

So draw him home

Convoy thy charge to those that mourn.
In vain for him. A happy speed
Ruffle thy All day strain all thy cords, & lead
Thro' prosperous floods his holy urn.

All night no ruder air perplex
Thy sliding keel, till Phosphor, bright
As our pure love, thro' early light
Shall glimmer on the dewy decks

The earliest surviving manuscript of section *9*, the first written section,
in Houghton Library, Harvard University MS Eng 952 (16), f.19

TENNYSON
IN MEMORIAM

EDITED BY
SUSAN SHATTO
AND
MARION SHAW

CLARENDON PRESS · OXFORD
1982

Oxford University Press, Walton Street, Oxford OX2 6DP

London Glasgow New York Toronto
Delhi Bombay Calcutta Madras Karachi
Kuala Lumpur Singapore Hong Kong Tokyo
Nairobi Dar es Salaam Cape Town
Melbourne Auckland
and associate companies in
Beirut Berlin Ibadan Mexico City

Published in the United States by
Oxford University Press, New York

British Library Cataloguing in Publication Data
Tennyson, Alfred
Tennyson's In memoriam.
I. Title   II. Shatto, Susan   III. Shaw,
Marion
821'.8   PR5562
ISBN 0-19-812747-2

Set by Hope Services, Abingdon
and printed at the University Press, Oxford
by Eric Buckley
Printer to the University

PREFACE

In 1897 Lady Catherine Simeon and Hallam, Lord Tennyson, gave Trinity College, Cambridge a major manuscript of *In Memoriam*, on the condition (in accordance with Tennyson's own wishes) that 'no copy of it nor of any part of it is ever made, nor made public'.[1] Further Tennyson manuscripts, including a notebook containing the earliest written sections of *In Memoriam*, were given by Hallam Tennyson to Trinity College in 1924. But again the gift was made on the condition that the manuscripts never be copied or quoted.

This interdict made impossible a definitive edition of any of Tennyson's poems. Christopher Ricks, in his important edition of the poems (1969), admits to the handicap the restriction imposed. Although he was able to consult the manuscripts at Trinity, he was not allowed to copy, let alone publish, any of the variants or any cancelled or hitherto unpublished line, stanza, or poem.

But the removal of the interdict in 1969 has enabled scholars to make public a detailed examination of the manuscripts and to provide full-scale editions of Tennyson's poems.

This edition of *In Memoriam* is the first collation of all the known manuscripts, of the privately printed Trial issue, and of the editions (or impressions) of the poem up to, and including, 1884. The relationships of the manuscripts have been established, and the bearing of the manuscripts upon the development of the poem is discussed. The growth of the poem is reconstructed from the evidence of the manuscripts, from the letters and reminiscences of Tennyson's contemporaries, and from Tennyson's own statements. The dates of composition of the sections are established when sufficient evidence is available. Nine further poems, which Tennyson originally intended to form part of *In Memoriam* but later rejected, are collated and annotated in the same way as the published text.

The Commentary describes the process of composition of the sections, so far as this is evidenced in the manuscripts. The notes incorporate the remarks of the poet himself, of his family and friends, and a selection of those of other editors and commentators. The significant variants — those which alter the meaning, however slightly — are, where it is appropriate, annotated in the same way as the published text.

[1] Letter from Catherine Simeon to the Master of Trinity College, 9 December 1897 (Trinity College Add. MS a.187[1]).

Marion Shaw conceived the idea for this edition. Susan Shatto is responsible for the text, the textual apparatus, and the introduction. The editors are jointly responsible for the Commentary and 'The Growth of the Poem'.

The University of Edinburgh   SUSAN SHATTO
The University of Hull   MARION SHAW

ACKNOWLEDGMENTS

This edition owes much to the generosity and help of many institutions and individuals. We are pleased to acknowledge our indebtedness to the following institutions which have allowed us to examine their Tennyson manuscripts and printed texts and have given permission to quote from them: Trinity College Library, Cambridge; the Houghton Library, Harvard University; the Tennyson Research Centre, Lincoln Central Library; the Henry E. Huntington Library; the Fitzwilliam Museum, Cambridge University; Cambridge University Library; the Beinecke Rare Book and Manuscript Library, Yale University; the Tennyson Collection, University College Cardiff Library; and the Bodleian Library. We are very grateful to the librarians and staff of these libraries.

We are greatly indebted to the Tennyson Trustees, who, through Lord Tennyson, have given permission to quote from the manuscripts for which they hold the copyright. We also wish to thank Richard L. Purdy and John Sparrow, who have given permission to quote from their manuscripts. Portions of this edition have appeared in articles by Dr Shatto published in *Notes and Queries, Victorian Poetry*, and *The Library*. We are grateful to the editors of these journals for permission to reprint.

For permission to reproduce the illustrations, we wish to thank The Master and Fellows of Trinity College, Cambridge (Plates II, III); the Librarian of the Houghton Library, Harvard University (Plates I, IV); the Director of the Lincolnshire Library Services (Plate V); and the Tennyson Trustees.

Many friends and colleagues have generously given assistance and advice. James Binns helped us with classical references in the Commentary. Aidan Day and Philip L. Elliott, Jr. pointed out many interesting items among the material in the Tennyson Research Centre; Laurence Elvin helped and advised one of the editors in the use of the material in the Tennyson Research Centre; Philip Gaskell gave us advice on textual matters; Jack Kolb answered a number of queries about Arthur Hallam; Cecil Lang gave us information from Tennyson's unpublished letters; R.B. Martin shared with us information collected during the preparation of his biography of Tennyson; Joseph Sendry discussed with us his own conclusions about the manuscripts and drew our attention to the Moxon MS; Paul Turner read the Commentary with meticulous care and offered us much valuable advice; John Yearwood helped us in our work on the manuscripts at Trinity College.

We are very gratified by the interest of Arthur Pollard, who encouraged and promoted the project from its inception, and we would finally like to acknowledge the late T.J.B. Spencer, whose continued help and advice were of inestimable worth.

The generosity of The Leverhulme Trust, through the University of Hull, has provided free time for one of the editors towards the completion of this edition.

TABLE OF CONTENTS

LIST OF PLATES

REFERENCES

1. *Manuscripts*

H.Lpr.	'Harvard Loose paper' Houghton Library, Harvard University bMS Eng 952.1 (98), (99), (100), (101), (102), (103), (104)
H.Nbk.	'Harvard Notebook' Houghton Library, Harvard University MS Eng 952 (10), (16), (17), (18), (19)
Heath MS	Fitzwilliam Museum, Cambridge University, John M. Heath Commonplace Book
Hn.Nbk.	'Huntington Notebook' Henry E. Huntington Library HM 1321, and MS in the possession of Richard L. Purdy, New Haven, Conn.
L.MS	'Lincoln MS' Tennyson Research Centre, Lincoln Central Library
Moxon MS	Houghton Library, Harvard University MS Eng 601.66 (24)
Prayer Book MS	Tennyson Research Centre, Lincoln Central Library
Sparrow MSS *(18)*, *(19)*, *(59)*	MSS in the possession of John Sparrow, Oxford
T.MS	'Trinity MS' Trinity College, Cambridge MS O.15.13
T.Nbk.	'Trinity Notebook' Trinity College, Cambridge MS O.15.17
Beinecke MS	Beinecke Rare Book and Manuscript Library, Yale University, MS Tinker 2044

2. *Printed texts*

Trial	'Trial issue' The private printing which appeared in March 1850
1850A	London: Edward Moxon
1850B	'Second Edition'. London: Edward Moxon
1850C	'Third Edition'. London: Edward Moxon
1851A	'Fourth Edition'. London: Edward Moxon
1851B	'Fifth Edition'. London: Edward Moxon
1855	'Sixth Edition'. London: Edward Moxon

1856	'Seventh Edition'. London: Edward Moxon
1859	'Eighth Edition'. London: Edward Moxon
1860	'Ninth Edition'. London: Edward Moxon
1861	'Tenth Edition'. London: Edward Moxon
1862A	'Eleventh Edition'. London: Edward Moxon
1862B	'Twelfth Edition'. London: Edward Moxon
1863A	'Thirteenth Edition'. London: Edward Moxon
1863B	'Fourteenth Edition'. London: Edward Moxon
1864	'Fifteenth Edition'. London: Edward Moxon
1865A	'Sixteenth Edition'. London: Edward Moxon
1865B	'Seventeenth Edition'. London: Edward Moxon
1866	'Eighteenth Edition'. London: Edward Moxon
1867	'Nineteenth Edition'. London: Edward Moxon
1868	'Twentieth Edition'. London: Edward Moxon
1869	(separate edition). London: Strahan
1870	(separate edition). London: Strahan
1872	(separate edition). London: Strahan
1874	(separate edition). London: Henry S. King
1875	(separate edition). London: Henry S. King
1877	(separate edition). London: Henry S. King
1878	(separate edition). London: C. Kegan Paul
1880	(separate edition). London: C. Kegan Paul
1881	(separate edition). London: C. Kegan Paul
1883	(separate edition). London: C. Kegan Paul
1884A	in *The Works*. London: Macmillan (January)
1884B	in *The Works*. London: Macmillan (April)

3. *Symbols used in the textual apparatus and in the Commentary*

T.MS– 1850A–	A dash after a MS or printed text signifies that the reading or section which first appears in that MS or printed text appears in all subsequent MSS and texts.
8a–d	Signifies a stanza which, although occurring in MS, was not included in the printed texts.
24∧25	Signifies a line which, although occurring in MS, was not included in the printed texts.
∧ or ∧	Carets around a word or words signify addition or substitution in MS.
[~~illegible word~~]	Signifies that crossing out or erasure in MS has made a word unreadable.
[*intentional blank*]	Signifies a missing word, line, or lines in MS.
alternative reading	Signifies a word or words interlineated without the deletion of the original reading.

ABBREVIATIONS FOR NAMES AND WORKS
FREQUENTLY CITED

(The place of publication of all books cited is London unless stated otherwise.)

Add. Poem i–ix — Seven additional sections omitted before publication, and two other poems on A.H. Hallam in the *In Memoriam* stanza

Allingham's *Diary* — *William Allingham, A Diary*, edited by H. Allingham and D. Radford (1907)

Beeching — *'In Memoriam', with an analysis and notes,* by H.C. Beeching (1900)

Bradley — A.C. Bradley, *A Commentary on Tennyson's 'In Memoriam'* (1901; third edition, 1910, reprinted, 1915)

Brand, *Popular Antiquities* — John Brand, *Observations on Popular Antiquities, including the whole of Mr Bourne's 'Antiquitates Vulgares'* (1810). A copy inscribed 'Alfred Tennyson' is in Tennyson Research Centre

Chapman — Elizabeth Rachel Chapman, *A Companion to 'In Memoriam'* (1888)

Charles Tennyson — Charles Tennyson, *Alfred Tennyson* (1949; reissued with alterations, 1968)

Collins — *'In Memoriam', 'The Princess', and 'Maud',* edited by John Churton Collins (1902)

Collins, *Cornhill* — John Churton Collins, 'A New Study of Tennyson', in *Cornhill Magazine*, No. XLI (January 1880), 36–50, the copy containing Tennyson's marginal notes (Tennyson Research Centre)

Cook and Wedderburn — *The Complete Works of John Ruskin*, edited by E.T. Cook and Alexander Wedderburn, 39 vols. (1903–12)

Emily's Diary — The MS diary of Emily, Lady Tennyson, 2 vols. (Tennyson Research Centre)

Eversley — *The Works of Alfred, Lord Tennyson*, edited by Hallam, Lord Tennyson, Eversley Edition, 9 vols. (1907–8)

Gatty (1900) — Alfred Gatty, *A Key to Tennyson's 'In Memoriam'* (1881; fourth edition, 1894, reprinted, 1900)

Gatty

—— idem ('a new and revised edition', 1882), the copy containing Tennyson's marginal notes (Tennyson Research Centre)

Genung

John F. Genung, *Tennyson's 'In Memoriam', Its Purpose and Its Structure. A Study* (1884)

H.T.

Hallam Tennyson

Harrison

James Harrison, 'Tennyson and Evolution', in *Durham University Journal*, LXIV, New Series, XXXIII (December 1971), 26–31

Hundred Wonders of the World

Sir Richard Phillips (the 'Rev C.C. Clarke'), *The Hundred Wonders of the World, and of the Three Kingdoms of Nature, Described According to the Best and Latest Authorities* (twelfth edition, enlarged and improved, 1821), a copy of which is in Tennyson's library (Tennyson Research Centre)

I.M.

In Memoriam

Jacobs

Joseph Jacobs, *Tennyson and 'In Memoriam', An Appreciation and a Study* (1892)

Knowles

Tennyson's extempore comments on *In Memoriam*, as recorded in 1870-1 by James Knowles; printed *literatim* by Gordon Ray in *Tennyson Reads 'Maud'*, Sedgewick Memorial Lecture (Vancouver, 1968), Appendix I, 37–42

Knowles, *Nineteenth Century*

James Knowles, 'Aspects of Tennyson: II (A Personal Reminiscence)', in *Nineteenth Century*, XXXIII (1893), 164–88

Materials

[Hallam Tennyson], *Materials for a Life of A.T.*, 4 vols. [1895]. The privately-printed early stage of *Memoir*. Originally there were thirty-two sets. Tennyson Research Centre has several sets, one of which contains Hallam Tennyson's revisions and deletions in pencil and in ink

MS *Materials*

Ten MS volumes (Tennyson Research Centre) from which were printed *Materials*. The volumes (32.5 cm × 20 cm) are mostly in the hand of Audrey Tennyson, Tennyson's daughter-in-law, and contain

	her transcripts of letters and printed material, and passages dictated to her by her husband. There are also many items pinned in or pasted down to the leaves. Hallam Tennyson has made numerous interlineations and deletions
Mattes	Eleanor Bustin Mattes, *'In Memoriam': The Way of a Soul* (New York, 1951)
Memoir	Hallam, Lord Tennyson, *Alfred, Lord Tennyson: A Memoir By His Son*, 2 vols. (1897)
Memories of the Tennysons	H.D. Rawnsley, *Memories of the Tennysons* (Glasgow, 1900)
Motter	T.H. Vail Motter, *The Writings of Arthur Hallam, Now First Collected and Edited* (New York, 1943)
Mustard	Wilfred P. Mustard, *Classical Echoes in Tennyson* (1904)
OED	*Oxford English Dictionary*
Potter	George Reuben Potter, 'Tennyson and the Biological Theory of Mutability in Species', in *Philological Quarterly*, XVI (1937), 321–43
PMLA	*Publications of the Modern Language Association*
Remains	*Remains, in Verse and Prose, of Arthur Henry Hallam* [edited by Henry Hallam], (1834)
Ricks	*The Poems of Tennyson*, edited by Christopher Ricks, Longmans' Annotated English Poets (1969)
Robertson	Frederick W. Robertson, *Analysis of Mr Tennyson's 'In Memoriam'* (1862; sixth edition, 1875)
Rutland	William R. Rutland, 'Tennyson and the Theory of Evolution', in *Essays and Studies*, XXVI (1940), 7–29
Shannon	Edgar Finley Shannon, Jr., *Tennyson and the Reviewers* (Cambridge, Mass., 1952)
Shepherd	[R.H. Shepherd], *Tennysoniana* (1866; second edition, revised and enlarged, 1879)
Some Unpublished Poems	*Some Unpublished Poems by Arthur Henry Hallam*, edited by Sir Charles Tennyson and F.T. Baker, *Victorian*

	Poetry, Supplement to III (Summer 1965)
T.	Tennyson (otherwise unattributed comments by T. and by H.T. are from *Eversley*)
TRC	Tennyson Research Centre
Tennyson and His Friends	*Tennyson and His Friends*, edited by Hallam, Lord Tennyson (1911)
Turner	Paul Turner, *Tennyson*, Routledge Author Guides (1976)
Ward	Wilfrid Ward, *Aubrey de Vere, A Memoir* (1904)

Page references do not carry the initial p. or pp. unless they are internal references to this edition or unless the reference stands on its own in brackets.

INTRODUCTION

The Manuscripts

The major manuscripts of *In Memoriam* are two tall, narrow notebooks written in Tennyson's small, neat hand. T.MS (including five leaves which have become detached: H.Lpr.100, H.Lpr.103, Sparrow MS(*18*), Sparrow MS(*19*)) contains 71 sections published by Tennyson, five sections originally intended for inclusion in the sequence but not published by Tennyson, and 'On a Mourner'. L.MS contains 114 sections published by Tennyson, two sections originally intended for inclusion but not published by Tennyson, and the Epilogue.

Tennyson inscribed both notebooks with the same date, November 1842. This is the *terminus ad quem* for T.MS and the *terminus a quo* for L.MS, for T.MS represents an earlier stage than L.MS in the composition of the sequence: it contains (including the detached leaves) forty-one fewer sections than L.MS; the arrangement of the sections is not so close to the published arrangement as is that of L.MS; and the texts of the sections are not so close to the texts published in **1850A** as are those of L.MS. L.MS includes all the sections in T.MS except five.

Most of the leaves in both manuscripts have only one section written on recto and/or verso. Both manuscripts have only a few sections which are much revised: T.MS has three, and L.MS has seven sections and the Epilogue. Most of the sections in both manuscripts are fair copies or have only one word revised.

A manuscript which antedates T.MS and L.MS is a notebook (T.Nbk.) inscribed (by Hallam Tennyson) '1833–35'. It contains eight sections: *30, 9, 17* (headed 'II'), *18* (headed 'III'), *31* and *32* — which are written as one section drafted twice — *85* (ten stanzas only), and *28*. Sections *9, 17,* and *18* are written on adjacent leaves and are numbered as a sequence. T.Nbk. is the earliest surviving manuscript of a group of sections. It is the same 'manuscript-book' which Hallam Tennyson described as containing 'the first written sections of *In Memoriam*'. He made many attempts to identify correctly the sections in T.Nbk., but his five lists (loose sheet in TRC; MS *Materials*, I 152; *Materials*, I 127–8; *Memoir*, I 109; *Eversley*, III 187) have errors and discrepancies, and none is reliable.[1]

Another holograph manuscript which antedates T.MS and L.MS is a notebook (Hn.Nbk.) the leaves of which have become dispersed.

---

[1] See Shatto, '"The first written sections of *In Memoriam*"', *Notes and Queries*, ns 25 (June 1978), 233–7.

Of the leaves which survive, two contain fifteen sections. On one leaf are eleven sections (*41, 42, 68, 66, 61, 75, 30, 78, 44, 45, 74*), and on the other are four (*9, 17, 18, 21*). Hn.Nbk. provides the earliest surviving drafts of eleven sections. The drafts of *9, 17, 18*, and *30* show a later stage of composition than those in T.Nbk.

The only other manuscripts of consequence are two transcripts by other hands for which the originals do not survive. The one is a common-place book (Heath MS) kept by John Heath, a friend of Tennyson. Heath MS is broadly contemporary with T.Nbk. and has all but one (*28*) of the sections which appear in T.Nbk., in addition to *19*. The sections appear in the following order: *9, 17, 18, 85* (eleven stanzas), *30, 31, 19*. These were transcribed at different times by John Heath, but Tennyson himself has written *17*.1-7 and has made verbal revisions in *9* and *17*. The other is a transcript by Emily Sellwood (H.Lpr.101) of seventeen sections, of which twelve (*1*.1-4, *33, 34, 36, 46, 48, 51, 60, 73, 91, 105, 112*) do not appear in any earlier surviving manuscript.

In comparison with the manuscripts already described, those which remain to be considered − sixteen holographs containing from one section to four sections − are less important. As mentioned above, four of the manuscripts (H.Lpr.100, H.Lpr.103, Sparrow MS(*18*), Sparrow MS(*19*)) were originally leaves in T.MS and doubtless came towards the front of the notebook. Among them, the detached leaves contain *3, 9, 18, 19, 21, 22*, and *The path by which I walkt alone* (Add. Poem i).

Three fragments (H.Nbk.16, H.Nbk.17, H.Lpr.98) are related in respect to *9*. H.Nbk.16 contains the earliest surviving draft of this section, and H.Nbk.17 (which also contains *3, 17, 18*.1-4) and H.Lpr.98 descend from it. The draft of *9* in T.Nbk. descends from H.Lpr.98. Another leaf (H.Nbk.10) contemporary with these three contains an early version of *18*.

Three manuscripts (H.Nbk.19, H.Lpr.102, H.Lpr.104) probably date from 1849-50 because they contain sections, or parts of sections, which were added to the sequence in **1850A**: H.Nbk.19 contains *96, 97*; H.Lpr.102 contains *124, 128*; H.Lpr.104 contains *7* and also an incomplete section not published by Tennyson, *Speak to me from the stormy sky!*.

There are two leaves (H.Lpr.99, Sparrow MS(*59*)) which show *59* in an early and in a late stage of composition.

There is one leaf (H.Nbk.18) which contains the earliest surviving draft of *131*. Another (Moxon MS), in an autograph album belonging to the wife of Tennyson's publisher, contains *31*. On the face of an envelope (Beinecke MS) is written the only surviving manuscript of *39*. The inside front board of a notebook contains the Introductory stanzas, 13-16 (Prayer Book MS), the only lines of the Introductory stanzas which survive in holograph.

In addition to the above holographs of sections published by Tennyson, there is one leaf (Cambridge University Library MS add. 6346) containing *He was too good and kind and sweet* (Add. Poem viii), a poem about Arthur Hallam in the *In Memoriam* stanza which was probably intended at one time for inclusion in the sequence but which was never published by Tennyson.[1]

The diagrams following this section illustrate how the surviving manuscripts relate to each other and to the printed texts. Diagram D includes the now lost fair copy of L.MS transcribed 'for the press' by Mrs Coventry Patmore (see p. 18), and also the now lost proofs of **Trial** corrected by G.S. Venables (see pp. 20-1). It can be seen that most of the manuscripts derive from Tennyson's now lost drafts. This supports other evidence which indicates that the majority of Tennyson's manuscripts of sections of *In Memoriam* no longer survive: no manuscripts are known for eight of the sections (*8, 106, 114, 116, 119, 120, 121, 129*) and for the Introductory stanzas (excepting lines 13-16); although 90 per cent of the sections in both T.MS and L.MS are fair copies or nearly so, T.MS (including the detached leaves) contains forty-one sections and L.MS contains forty which occur in no earlier known manuscripts; moreover, several sections in T.MS which are fair copies are very different from the versions (also fair copies) in L.MS (*29, 44, 52, 71, 80, 81, 82*); the earliest manuscript of twelve of the sections is a transcript by Emily Sellwood (H.Lpr.101). This evidence establishes that the surviving manuscripts of *In Memoriam* constitute only a small portion of the original number.

The following table lists the manuscripts in their presumed chronological order.[2] Dates have been ascribed to them for usually more than one of the following reasons which are listed in order of their reliability (for example, a dating on the basis of adjacent material should be cautiously considered):

(1) A date is inscribed (T.Nbk., Heath MS, H.Nbk.10, T.MS, L.MS).
(2) Relationship to another manuscript which can be dated with reasonable certainty (H.Lpr.98, H.Lpr.101, Sparrow MS(*18*), Sparrow MS(*19*), H.Lpr.100, H.Lpr.103).
(3) Watermark having a date (H.Nbk.16, H.Nbk.17, Hn.Nbk.).
(4) The manuscript has sections (or stanzas) which were first printed in **1850A** (H.Nbk.19, H.Lpr.102, H.Lpr.104).

---

[1] A holograph notebook (Tinker 2041), which has been temporarily mislaid by the Beinecke Rare Book and Manuscript Library, contains drafts of *9* (ff.4^v-5^r) and 'From sorrow sorrow yet is born' (f.9^r). The editors have been unable to examine this notebook, or copies of it.

[2] H.Lpr.99, Sparrow MS(*59*), and Prayer Book MS have not been included in the list because there is no evidence on which to base a conjecture about their dates.

(5) Biographical details (H.Lpr.101).
(6) The date of composition of the adjacent material is known or can be conjectured with reasonable certainty (H.Nbk.16, H.Nbk.17, H.Nbk.18, Hn.Nbk., Moxon MS, Cambridge University Library MS add. 6346).

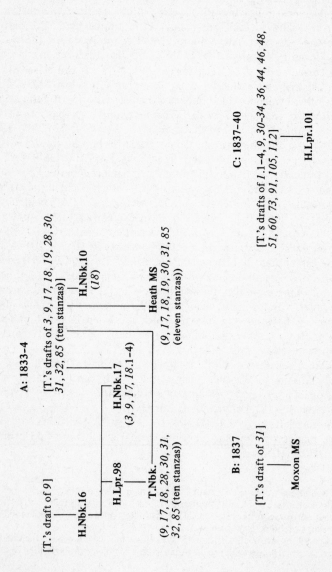

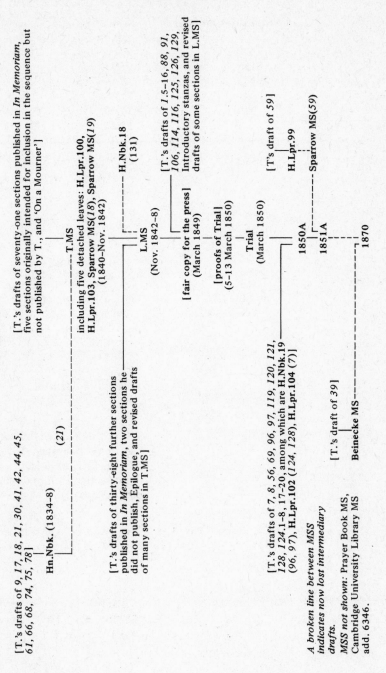

D: 1834–70

[T.'s drafts of seventy-one sections published in *In Memoriam*, five sections originally intended for inclusion in the sequence but not published by T., and 'On a Mourner']

T.MS including five detached leaves: **H.Lpr.100, H.Lpr.103,** Sparrow MS(*18*), Sparrow MS(*19*) (1840–Nov. 1842)

H.Nbk.18 (*131*)

[T.'s drafts of *1.5–16, 88, 91, 106, 114, 116, 125, 126, 129,* Introductory stanzas, and revised drafts of some sections in L.MS]

[T's draft of 59]

H.Lpr.99

Sparrow MS(*59*)

L.MS (Nov. 1842–8)

[fair copy for the press] (March 1849)

[proofs of Trial] (5–13 March 1850)

Trial (March 1850)

1850A

1851A

1870

[T.'s drafts of *9, 17, 18, 21, 30, 41, 42, 44, 45, 61, 66, 68, 74, 75, 78*]

Hn.Nbk. (1834–8)

(*21*)

[T.'s drafts of thirty-eight further sections published in *In Memoriam*, two sections he did not publish, Epilogue, and revised drafts of many sections in T.MS]

[T.'s drafts of *7, 8, 56, 69, 96, 97, 119, 120, 121, 128, 124.1–8, 17–20,* among which are **H.Nbk.19** (*96, 97*), **H.Lpr.102** (*124, 128*), **H.Lpr.104** (*7*)]

[T.'s draft of *39*]

Beinecke MS

A broken line between MSS indicates now lost intermediary drafts.

MSS not shown: Prayer Book MS, Cambridge University Library MS add. 6346.

Presumed Chronology of the Manuscripts

Date	Manuscript	Sections
1833–4	H.Nbk.16	*9*
	H.Lpr.98	*9*
	H.Nbk.10	*18*.1–4, 13–20
	H.Nbk.17	*9, 3, 17, 18*.1–4
	T.Nbk.	*30, 9, 17, 18, 31* and *32, 85, 28*
	Heath MS	*9, 17, 18, 85, 30, 31, 19*
1834–8	Hn.Nbk.	*41, 42, 68, 66, 61, 75, 30, 78, 44, 45, 74, 9, 17, 18, 21*
1837	Moxon MS	*31*
1837–40	H.Lpr.101	*9, 1.*1–4, *31, 32, 60, 73, 112, 91, 105, 51, 33, 34, 36, 44, 46, 48, 30*
1840–Nov. 1842	T.MS and the five following detached leaves:	(Sixty-seven sections published in *In Memoriam*, four sections not published by Tennyson, and 'On a Mourner')
	H.Lpr.100	*3, 9*
	H.Lpr.103	*22, 21, The path by which I walkt alone* (Add. Poem i)
	Sparrow MS(*18*)	*18*
	Sparrow MS(*19*)	*19*
Nov. 1842–8	L.MS	(One hundred and fourteen sections published in *In Memoriam*, Epilogue, and two sections not published by Tennyson)
1848	H.Nbk.18	*131*
	Cambridge University Library MS add. 6346	*He was too good and kind and sweet* (Add. Poem viii)
1849–50	H.Nbk.19	*96, 97*
1850	H.Lpr.102	*124, 128*
	H.Lpr.104	*7, Speak to me from the stormy sky!* (Add. Poem ix)
1868	Beinecke MS	*39*

Dating the Sections

1. The use of manuscript evidence

The manuscripts are more useful in establishing the order in which the sections were composed than in providing evidence about when they were composed. Unfortunately, however, for the majority of sections the manuscripts provide the only clue to the date of composition. The manuscripts containing many sections (Hn.Nbk., H.Lpr.101, T.MS, L.MS) can be ascribed only to a period during which Tennyson is presumed to have written in them. It would be simple to date a section according to the dates ascribed to the manuscript in which it appears for the first time. But this procedure would be misleading because for most sections drafts showing the early stages of composition do not survive. Tennyson usually destroyed the first drafts after he had transcribed fair copies. In general, the manuscripts which can be ascribed to a period during which Tennyson is presumed to have written in them are useful in that they provide (for the sections they contain) a *terminus ad quem*, but rarely an actual date of composition.

2. Criteria used for dating

The dates of composition of five sections (*9, 19, 39, 95, 121*) and the Introductory stanzas and the Epilogue can be established with certainty for one or more of the following reasons:

a) A draft of the section has a date attached to it (*9*).
b) The date of composition has been recorded (or implied) by Tennyson, Hallam Tennyson, or a friend (Introductory stanzas, *9, 19, 39, 95, 121*, Epilogue).

The date of composition of six further sections (*17, 18, 28, 30, 31, 32*) and ten stanzas of *85* can be established with certainty because they appear in T.Nbk. Hallam Tennyson described this manuscript as containing 'the first written sections'. His inscription in T.Nbk., '1833-35', indicates the period of composition of the sections it contains.

The dates of composition of *131* and *He was too good and kind and sweet* (Add. Poem viii) can be conjectured on the basis of adjacent material. This is not usually a reliable means of dating because Tennyson was in the habit of re-using old notebooks, and two adjacent poems may in fact have been composed at widely different times. But in respect to *131* and *He was too good and kind and sweet*, the manuscript evidence does strongly suggest that these poems were composed at the same time as the adjacent material.

There are four sections in L.MS which survive in no earlier manuscript and which are located after the Epilogue (*124*.9-16,21-4, *127*, *130, 131*). This suggests that these sections were added to L.MS after the Epilogue (composed 1844-5) and that they may well have been (but were not necessarily) composed after 1845.

The dates of composition of other sections can be sometimes conjectured with the help of two kinds of internal evidence:

a) Close verbal similarities to a book which Tennyson is known to have first read at a specific time (for example, *Principles of Geology* in 1837, *Vestiges of the Natural History of Creation* in 1844, *Festus* in 1846).

b) Allusions to an event in Tennyson's life of which the date is known.

The headnotes in the Commentary give information on dating only when the date of composition is certain or when sufficient evidence is available to support a reasonable conjecture.

The Growth of the Poem, 1833-1870

Stage A: 1833-1840

On 1 October 1833 Henry Elton wrote to Tennyson at Somersby Rectory to announce the death of his nephew, Arthur Hallam:

At the desire of a most afflicted family, I write to you, because they are unequal, from the abyss of grief into which they have fallen, to do it themselves.

Your friend, Sir, and my much loved nephew, Arthur Hallam, is no more — it has pleased God, to remove him from this his first scene of Existence, to that better World, for which he was Created —

He died at Vienna on his return from Buda, by Apoplexy — and I believe his Remains come by sea from Trieste —.[1]

The next few weeks were productive ones for Tennyson. By no means paralysed by his grief, he drew upon the experience of it to write a number of poems.[2] One of these, 'Fair ship, that from the Italian

---

[1] The letter (TRC) is dated and postmarked 1 October 1833. Hallam Tennyson prints an edited version and states that Tennyson received the letter on 1 October (*Memoir*, I 105).

[2] 'Ulysses', 'Tithon', 'Tiresias', and 'On a Mourner' are all known to have been composed in October 1833. By the end of the year he had written the first version of 'Oh! that 'twere possible', and 'Youth'. He was also working on 'Morte d'Arthur'. He had written 'Hark! the dogs howl!', which Hallam Tennyson described as 'the germ of "In Memoriam"' (*Memoir*, I 107). This description is misleading in respect to the sequence of sections as a whole, but several of the images were indeed developed later in various sections.

shore' (section *9* of *In Memoriam*), was composed on 6 October.[1] Its subject was suggested by a phrase in Henry Elton's letter: 'I believe his Remains come by sea from Trieste'.

By early 1834 he had composed two companion-pieces to *9*: 'Thou comest, much wept for' (*17*), and "Tis well; 'tis something' (*18*). These poems have the same stanza form as *9* (a quatrain of iambic tetrameters with enclosed rhyme), and the same number of stanzas (five), and they develop the subject of *9*: *17* describes the safe arrival of the ship, and *18* describes the burial of the body. They further resemble *9* in that they seem to have been suggested by a report of the actual events surrounding the death of Hallam. Hallam's father wrote to Tennyson on 30 December 1833:

It may remove some anxiety from the minds of yourself & others to know that the mortal part of our dearest Arthur will be interred at Clevedon on Friday . . . My first thought was not to write to you till all was over − But you may have been apprehensive for the safety of the vessel − I did not expect her arrival so soon.

(TRC; printed in *Memoir*, I 106)

The letter would not have reached Tennyson until the first days of the new year.[2] It seems likely that *17* and *18* were occasioned by this letter, and they may well have been composed soon after Tennyson received it.[3]

Henry Hallam wrote again in February to ask Tennyson to contribute to a short memoir of his son by way of a preface to a privately printed volume of Arthur's prose and poetry: 'I must rely on his contemporaries & most intimate friends to furnish me with part of my materials . . . Perhaps you would do something − I should desire to have the character of his mind, his favourite studies & pursuits, his habits & views, delineated' (TRC; printed in *Memoir*, I 108). Tennyson replied on 14 February:

That you intend to print some of my friend's remains (tho' only for private circulation) has given me greater pleasure than anything I have experienced for a length of time. I attempted to draw up a memoir of his life and character, but I failed to do him justice. I failed even to please myself. I could scarcely have pleased you. I hope to be able at a future period to concentrate whatever powers I may possess on the construction of some tribute to those high speculative endowments

[1] In Heath MS *9* is dated 6 October 1833. H.Lpr.98 is inscribed by Hallam Tennyson: 'The first section of *In Memoriam* that was written down 1833'. In 1870-1, Tennyson told James Knowles that *9* was 'the first written'.
[2] The funeral took place on 3 January. Tennyson did not attend.
[3] The earliest surviving drafts of both sections are on adjacent leaves in a notebook (H.Nbk.17) having other poems known to have been composed in 1833.

and comprehensive sympathies which I ever loved to contemplate; but at present, tho' somewhat ashamed at my own weakness, I find the object yet is too near me to permit of any very accurate delineation.

(*Eversley*, III 258)

The 'memoir of his life and character' which Tennyson refers to as having been attempted no longer survives. He did not mention any of the poems he had already composed on the death of Hallam, probably because they were not the kind of material Henry Hallam was asking for. Nor does he seem to have yet envisaged that three of these poems (*9, 17,* and *18*) would eventually develop into the 'tribute to those high speculative endowments and comprehensive sympathies' which he intended to construct at 'a future period'.

During 1834 he composed at least five further sections: *28, 30, 31* and *32* (these two were written initially as one poem), and ten stanzas of *85*.[1] Along with *9, 17,* and *18*, these appear in T.Nbk., which is inscribed by Hallam Tennyson '1833-35' and 'Read to Fitz & Spedding − 35'.[2] This important and interesting manuscript deserves to be called the real 'germ of *In Memoriam*' for two reasons. Firstly, it shows Tennyson arranging sections in groups (*9, 17,* and *18* are arranged sequentially, the second two being headed 'II' and 'III'); already present in his mind is the idea of a collection of related poems. Secondly, the sections themselves are the nucleii of further growth in the sequence. Sections *9, 17,* and *18* were to be expanded into the series of ten 'ship' sections (*9-18*). Similarly, *28* and *30* are the first composed of the seven sections (*28, 29, 30; 78; 104, 105, 106*) describing the three Christmases which serve to mark (as Tennyson stated in 1883) the divisions of the sequence (*Memoir*, I 305).[3] Sections *31* and *32* were first written as one poem of five stanzas, drafted twice (see Plate I). The division of this poem into two initiated the series of sections (*31-6*) on the subject of immortality as symbolized by Christ. The ten stanzas of *85* show the poet, within a year of Hallam's death, recovering from his sorrow and looking for new companionship. Later Tennyson added twenty more stanzas elaborating on his need for social intercourse and for one new friend in particular. This theme of the subsuming of personal grief in social concern is developed in other sections of the published sequence.

[1] Probably also composed at this time was 'A cloud is drawn across the sky', an early version of *3* in H.Nbk.17.

[2] Tennyson and FitzGerald visited Spedding at Mirehouse in 1835 (*Memoir*, I 151).

[3] In 1870-1, however, he explained to Knowles that there are 'nine natural groups or divisions': *1-8; 9-20; 20-7; 28-49; 50-8; 59-71; 72-98; 99-103; 104-31* (*Nineteenth Century*, 182).

Most of the sections in T.Nbk. appear in the commonplace book (Heath MS) of Tennyson's Cambridge friend, John Heath.[1] Heath probably copied them from Tennyson's own drafts (some of Heath's transcripts have additions and revisions in Tennyson's hand), but none of the sections is copied from T.Nbk. Such transcripts of Tennyson's poems 'were widely circulated about Cambridge' during Tennyson's years there (1827-31) and for several years later (*Memoir*, I 201).[2] The transcripts in Heath MS were made over a period of years,[3] and some of them were in turn transcribed by others (see pp. 310-11).

After T.Nbk., Tennyson seems to have next assembled his sections in a folio-size notebook (Hn.Nbk.) in which he also copied poems which would be eventually published in 1842. The leaves of Hn.Nbk. have become dispersed, but two surviving ones have between them four of the eight sections known to have been composed during 1833-4 and eleven further sections. Evidence suggests that the new sections (*21, 41, 42, 44, 45, 61, 66, 68, 74, 75, 78*) were composed between 1834-8.[4] Ten of the fifteen sections are arranged in pairs: *17* and *18*; *41* and *42*; *44* and *45*; *30* and *78* (two sections on Christmas); and *18* and *21* (two sections set at the graveside).

Later than Hn.Nbk., but not descendant from it or from any other known manuscript, is a transcript by Emily Sellwood of seventeen sections (H.Lpr.101), of which twelve (*1*.1-4, *33, 34, 36, 46, 48, 51, 60, 73, 91, 105, 112*) do not appear in any earlier surviving manuscript. The transcript dates almost certainly from 1837-40 when Emily was engaged to Tennyson. No evidence survives to indicate whether she transcribed from a notebook containing all the sections, or (what is more likely) from several loose sheets having one or more sections.

Stage B: T.MS (1840-1842)

By this stage in the development of the poem, Tennyson had composed at least thirty-one sections. He had probably composed many more. Doubtless he had a large number of sections written in various note-

---

[1] Heath MS lacks *28* but contains *19*, which is not in T.Nbk.

[2] Charles Merivale wrote to Frederick Tennyson on 20 May 1832: 'I have begun writing out Alfred's MSS in a very neat book. Poets who won't publish put their friends to a great deal of trouble' (from a typed transcript in Sir Charles Tennyson's notebooks (TRC; vol. 3) in preparation for *Alfred Tennyson*).

[3] Heath may have transcribed *9* during his visit to Somersby at Christmas 1833 (see headnote to *30*). Section *19*, which comes towards the end of Heath MS, was written at Tintern Abbey (*Eversley*, III 229), probably in 1839 when Tennyson visited Wales.

[4] The poems in the other surviving leaves of this now lost notebook are known to have been composed in 1833-8. For a note on these leaves (now in the Henry E. Huntington Library), see pp. 311-12.

books and on individual sheets of writing-paper. It is likely that in 1840
he began to copy these sections into a long, narrow notebook (T.MS).
By Christmas 1841 he had transcribed into T.MS a large number of
sections, as Edmund Lushington records:

> The number of the memorial poems had rapidly increased since I had
> seen the poet, his book containing many that were new to me. Some I
> heard him repeat before I had seen them in writing, others I learnt to
> know first from the book itself which he kindly allowed me to look
> through without stint. I remember one particular night . . . He began
> to recite the poem that stands sixth in 'In Memoriam', 'One writes,
> that "Other friends remain"' . . . On one other occasion he came and
> showed me a poem he had just composed, saying he liked it better
> than most he had done lately, this was No.LI, 'Do we indeed desire
> the dead'.
>
> *(Memoir*, I 202-3)[1]

T.MS (including five leaves which have become detached: H.Lpr.100,
H.Lpr.103, Sparrow MS(*18*), and Sparrow MS(*19*)) contains seventy-
three sections published by Tennyson, and five sections which are
known to have been originally intended for inclusion in the sequence
but which Tennyson omitted before the poem was published. In
addition, 'On a Mourner' appears on the last leaf.[2] From the placement
of the sections in T.MS it seems that Tennyson's practice was usually
to copy only one section on to the recto of each leaf, leaving the lower
half and the verso of the leaf blank. This method of transcription would
leave plenty of space to incorporate new sections at appropriate places
in the notebook. (The leaves of L.MS also give evidence that they were
filled up in the same way.) This procedure is perhaps what Tennyson
was alluding to when (in 1870-1) he commented on the composition
of the poem to James Knowles: 'The general way of its being written
was so queer that if there were a blank space, I would put in a poem.'
Allowing for this degree of flexibility, the arrangement of T.MS
suggests that it was originally intended to be a fair copy of a sequence
complete in itself, and thus to be Tennyson's final intention with respect
to a 'tribute' to Arthur Hallam. Just as L.MS for the most part represents
the poem published in 1850, T.MS represents the poem Tennyson
might have published in, say, 1843.

The order of the sections generally approximates to the published

---

[1] Section 6 is not now in T.MS, but evidence indicates that several leaves are
missing from the front of the notebook.

[2] The poem is given this title in T.MS, but the appearance of the ink and the
style of the hand indicate that Tennyson added the title many years after he
transcribed the poem.

order. There are, however, a number of obvious differences. In the first place, most of the sections between 2 and 23 are absent, including seven (3, 9, 17, 18, 19, 21, 22) of the thirty-one sections which appear in manuscripts which antedate T.MS. All but one (17) of these seven sections are to be found on five leaves which once belonged to the front of T.MS: H.Lpr.100 (having 3 and 9), H.Lpr.103 (having The path by which I walkt alone (Add. Poem i), 22, and 21), Sparrow MS(18), and Sparrow MS(19). The first four complete sections now in T.MS (38, 23, 24, 25) would logically follow these (and possibly other) detached sections from the front of the manuscript to form a group of sections linked by the image of a journey.

A second obvious difference between T.MS and the published sequence is in the conclusion. The sections between 23 and 85 in T.MS are arranged for the most part according to the published order, but after 85 many of the sections are absent and the order of those that are present differs significantly from the published order. Yet the sections from 85 onwards are ordered with as much care as the preceding sections and, like most of them, fall into distinct groups. After 85 come 102, 104, 105, 91–4, 88, 108, 112, 111.21–4, Young is the grief I entertain (Add. Poem iii), Are these the far-famed Victor Hours (Add. Poem iv), 128, 117, 126, I keep no more a lone distress (Add. Poem v), 125, 57, 'On a Mourner', and 123, respectively. The first seven sections after 85 make two groups (102, 104, 105 and 91–4) which, except for being transposed, were not otherwise rearranged in the published sequence. The next two sections, 88 and 108, present opposing aspects of sorrow. Section 108 is a prelude to three sections on the character of Arthur Hallam (112, 111.21–4, and Young is the grief I entertain). Then follows, all on one page, a series of three sections on the subject of Time (Are these the far-famed Victor Hours, 128, and 117). On the verso of the leaf having this series is 126, which was originally intended to precede 'The Victor Hours' (see headnote 126–8). Section 125 also comes on the verso of a leaf (f.44) and seems to have been an after-thought with respect to the conclusion of the sequence. The section which may have been originally intended to conclude the sequence is I keep no more a lone distress (f.44^r). This section, which Eversley describes as 'originally No. LVII', was replaced by 57.

Both the location of 57 at the end of T.MS, and the subject-matter of the section suggest that it was intended to conclude the entire T.MS sequence. On the leaf following 57 is 'On a Mourner'. This poem, which was not published until 1865, seems to have been intended as the envoi to the sequence.

Tennyson was dissatisfied, however, with this conclusion. As he later told James Knowles, he thought 57 'too sad for an ending'. Having decided this, he apparently composed *123* (originally five stanzas instead of three) and copied it on to the verso of the leaf having 'On a Mourner'. Section *123* repudiates the tone and thought of *57*. It is possible that *123* may have been intended to replace *57* as the concluding section of the sequence, but *123* seems more suited to a beginning than to an ending. The likelihood is that at this point, Tennyson decided not to publish the T.MS sequence but to carry on composing sections in order to bring the sequence to a more hopeful conclusion.

Throughout its compilation Tennyson had shown T.MS to his friends. The most influential of these was James Spedding, who had taken the place of Arthur Hallam as Tennyson's literary adviser (*Materials*, I 117). Spedding studied T.MS thoroughly – probably on several occasions – making pencil annotations.[1] He no doubt discussed the sequence with Tennyson whenever they met. Tennyson's revisions and additions were often in direct response to Spedding's criticisms. Sometimes he even wrote on top of Spedding's note to make them. A specific recommendation Spedding made was that Tennyson should omit three sections: *Young is the grief I entertain, Are these the far-famed Victor Hours*, and *I keep no more a lone distress* (Add. Poems iii, iv, v).[2] Spedding's advice may well have played an important part in Tennyson's decision to undertake a substantial revision of the poem. This was done, however, not in T.MS but in L.MS.

Stage C: L.MS (1842–1848)

Tennyson apparently left off T.MS and began writing in L.MS in the same month, November 1842, for both manuscripts are inscribed with this date. L.MS has 114 sections, in addition to two ('*O Sorrower for the faded leaf*' and *Let Death and Memory keep the face*) (Add. Poems vi and vii) which were omitted from the published sequence, and the Epilogue.[3] Forty-two sections (as well as '*O Sorrower*' and *Let Death and Memory*) do not appear in any earlier manuscript, but they were not necessarily composed after November 1842.[4]

---

[1] Most of Spedding's pencil annotations have been cut out of T.MS by Hallam Tennyson. For the surviving annotations (which are not allowed to be quoted), see the notes on *13*.15, *43*.9–12, *44*.4, *46*.5, *57*.8a–d, *78*.16, *81*.1–5, *108*.15–16, *112*.5–8, and *Young is the grief I entertain*, headnote.

[2] Tennyson is reported to have observed of these sections: 'The following poems were omitted from "In Memoriam" when I published, because I thought them redundant' (*Memoir*, I 306; *Eversley*, III 205). The original version of this passage reads: '... (because Spedding and I thought them redundant)' (*Materials*, II 15). A copy of this volume in TRC shows Hallam Tennyson's deletion of 'Spedding and'.

[3] Tennyson gave this no title. This edition follows Genung in using the term 'Epilogue'.

[4] For example, at least four sections had been composed in time to be included

Like T.MS, L.MS was apparently intended initially to be a fair-copy of the sequence and to represent, again, Tennyson's final intentions. The arrangement of the sections approximates closely that of the published sequence. Nevertheless, there are significant differences. The most important of these concerns the conclusion. The long epithalamion towards the end of L.MS (the Epilogue, composed 1844-5 as a counterpart to 'On a Mourner') is followed by five sections (*123, 130, 124, 127, 131*) of which all but *123* were probably composed after 1845. This group of sections is the part of L.MS which least corresponds to the order of the published sequence. Also, of the sections which do not appear in L.MS, all but four (*7, 8, 39, 59*) are towards the end of the poem: *88* (in T.MS), *91* (in T.MS), *96, 97, 106, 114, 116, 119, 120, 121, 125* (in T.MS), *126* (in T.MS), *128* (in T.MS), *129*. Six of these sections (*96, 97, 119, 120, 121, 128*) appear for the first time (in their entirety) in the first edition (**1850A**). These facts seem to indicate that in revising the sequence for publication, Tennyson again focused his attention on the last part of the poem.

Tennyson's dissatisfaction with the poem at this time is recorded in a letter to his Aunt Russell: 'With respect to the non publication of those poems w^h you mention, it is partly occasioned by the considerations you speak of, & partly by my sense of their present imperfectness perhaps they will not see the light till I have ceased to be. I cannot tell, but I have no wish to send them out yet' (Beinecke MS).[1]

He expressed the same melancholy sentiments in a letter to G.S. Venables, written from Barmouth in July 1844:

You had better keep the MSS which you mention till I see you. I suppose I must myself have slipt it behind your books to keep it out of peoples way, for I scarcely liked everyone who came in to overhaul those poems & moreover the volume itself was not fit to be seen, foul with the rust dust & mildew of innumerable moons.
(Dept. of Special Collections, Spencer Library, University of Kansas)

By January 1845 he had given L.MS to at least two of his close friends to read, and by mid-summer he had read it aloud to at least two more. A letter written by Edward FitzGerald on 29 January to W.B. Donne reveals that not only FitzGerald but also Spedding had already read L.MS: 'A.T. has near a volume of poems — elegiac — in memory of Arthur Hallam. Don't you think the world wants other notes than

---

in T.MS, and yet none appears in the leaves which survive. One section, *86*, is known to have been composed in 1839. Another section, *95*, was apparently written between 1841 and the summer of 1842.

[1] *Memoir*, I 243 assigns this letter to 1847, but the original is undated. The postscript and other evidence strongly indicate that the letter belongs to 1844.

elegiac now? Lycidas is the utmost length an elegiac should reach. But Spedding praises: and I suppose the elegiacs will see daylight, public daylight, one day' (*Letters of Edward Fitzgerald*, edited by William Aldis Wright, 2 vols. (1894), I 187). FitzGerald wrote again to Donne in February and expressed further opinions (characteristically deprecatory) on Tennyson's elegies:

We have surely had enough of men reporting their sorrows: especially when one is aware all the time that the poet wilfully protracts what he complains of, magnifies it in the Imagination, puts it into all the shapes of Fancy: and yet we are to condole with him, and be taught to ruminate our losses & sorrows in the same way. I felt that if Tennyson had got on a horse & ridden 20 miles, instead of moaning over his pipe, he would have been cured of his sorrows in half the time. As it is, it is about 3 years before the Poetic Soul walks itself out of darkness & Despair into Common Sense.[1]

On 17 April Aubrey De Vere called on the poet in London and found him at first 'much out of spirits. He cheered up soon, and read me some beautiful Elegies . . . I went to the House of Commons and heard a good speech from Sir. G. Grey — went back to Tennyson, who "crooned" out his magnificent Elegies till one in the morning' (Ward, 71). Such readings became frequent occurrences during the spring and summer:

I went to him very late each night, and he read many of the poems to me or discussed them with me till the early hours of the morning. The tears often ran down his face as he read, without the slightest apparent consciousness of them on his part. The pathos and grandeur of these poems were to me greatly increased by the voice which rather intoned than recited them, and which, as was obvious, could not possibly have given them utterance in any manner not thus musical. Sometimes towards the close of a stanza his voice dropped; but I avoided the chance of thus losing any part of the meaning by sitting beside him, and glancing at the pieces he read. They were written in a long and narrow manuscript book, which assisted him to arrange the poems in due order by bringing many of them at once before his eye.[2]

(*Memoir*, I 293)

[1] The letter, postmarked 28 February 1845, is printed in *A Fitzgerald Friendship*, edited by N.C. Hannay (New York, 1932), 10. FitzGerald's reference to '3 years . . .' is, of course, an allusion to the internal chronology of the poem.

[2] This passage is part of an account written when de Vere was more than eighty years old. He recalls that the readings described took place soon before the poem was published, but they seem obviously to belong to the period of his London visit in 1845. Hallam Tennyson seems to be mistaken in ascribing the readings to 1850 (*Memoir*, I 287), for Tennyson would doubtless then have had a copy of *Trial* to read from, rather than L.MS.

Later on in the summer, Tennyson showed L.MS to Edmund Lushington. Lushington's account of the occasion reveals that by this time Tennyson had composed the Epilogue.[1] Moreover, Lushington suggests one of the reasons why, having completed the sequence, Tennyson made no attempt to prepare it for publication:

> He had then completed many of the cantos in 'In Memoriam' and was engaged on 'The Princess', of which I had heard nothing before. He read or showed me the first part, beyond which it had then hardly advanced. He said to me, 'I have brought in your marriage at the end of "In Memoriam"', and then showed me those poems of 'In Memoriam' which were finished and which were a perfectly novel surprise to me.
>
> (*Memoir*, I 203)[2]

With one long poem nearing completion, Tennyson had started work on another, one which he had actually begun several years before. He had already read the 'University of Women' to de Vere in April and May before he read it to Lushington in the summer (Ward, 71, 74). By the following winter, January 1846, he had completed Part II of the poem.[3] The next year (1847) he wrote to tell his publisher, Edward Moxon, that he was 'putting the last touches to the "Princess". I trust there will still be time when I come up to get the book out by Christmas' (*Materials*, I 319). The poem was published in December 1847. So between 1845 and 1847 Tennyson was giving his attention predominantly to the composition and publication of *The Princess*.

In the spring of 1848, following the publication of the second edition, he journeyed to Ireland at the invitation of de Vere. During this visit he may have composed *131*, the section which comes last in L.MS.[4] It seems probable that the other sections which in L.MS come after the Epilogue (*124*.9–16, 21–4, *127*, *130*)[5] were also composed around this time. Tennyson discussed his progress on the poem in a letter to de Vere in November 1849 (quoted on p. 20). He refers to his visit to Ireland and implies ('I do not know whether I have done anything new . . . since you saw them') that during or shortly before that visit he had been at work on the sequence.

---

[1] On the dating of the Epilogue, see the headnote.

[2] Tennyson obviously would not have referred to the sequence as *In Memoriam*, for this was not suggested as a title until 1850.

[3] Letter from Elizabeth Barrett to Robert Browning, 31 January 1846, in *Letters* (1899), I 444.

[4] For the attribution of *131* to 1848, see the explanation by Joseph Sendry given in the headnote to that section.

[5] Section *123* also comes after the Epilogue but was composed, of course, much earlier (it is in T.MS). It was doubtless transcribed into L.MS around the same time as the other four sections.

In December (1848) or January (1849), Tennyson showed L.MS to his publisher:[1]

Moxon, when on a vist to Alfred, asked if he had been writing anything of late, with a view to issuing a vol. for him. On which Alfred said emphatically 'No.' Moxon then said surely you have not been idle? Alfred said he had been writing for his own relief & private satisfaction some things that the public would have no interest in, and would not care to see. Moxon asked to see the Ms. It was 'In Memoriam'. Moxon was delighted, &, to Alfreds utter astonishment, offered to publish it and to hand him a cheque to a/c on the spot. If my memory serves me I think the amt. was £300.

(An account by Charles Tennyson Turner, as reported by A.J. Symington
in a letter to Hallam Tennyson, 11 January 1894; TRC)

Stage D: Preparation for the press (1849–1850)

As a result of Moxon's offer, Tennyson made preparations during 1849 for the publication of the L.MS sequence. In late January he saw de Vere and promised him (as de Vere wrote on 24 January) 'to *print* at least his exquisite Elegies, and let his friends have a few copies' (Ward, 154). In February the future of the elegies was jeopardized when L.MS was nearly lost. Tennyson had been staying with George Venables in Mitre Court, The Temple. He left the elegies behind in Venables's chambers, and from Bonchurch on 28 February he wrote to Coventry Patmore to ask him to search for the manuscript:[2]

I went up to my room yesterday to get my book of Elegies: you know what I mean, a long, butcher-ledger-like book. I was going to read one or two to an artist here: I could not find it. I have some obscure remembrance of having lent it to you: if so, all is well: if not, will you go to my old chambers and institute a rigorous inquiry? I was coming up to-day to look after it, but as the weather is so furious I have yielded to the wishes of my friends to stop till tomorrow. I shall be, I expect, in town to-morrow at 25 M.P., when I shall be glad to see you.[3]

[1] Charles Tennyson (p. 240) states that this meeting took place in December 1849. This assumption seems partly based on Hallam Tennyson's incorrect dating of Tennyson's letter from Bonchurch quoted below and discussed in the following note.

[2] On 14 January 1849 Tennyson wrote to his sister, Emily Jesse, from 2 Mitre Court Buildings (transcript of letter in TRC). Patmore's account, written many years after the event, errs in recalling that he collected L.MS from Mornington Place. Tennyson was returning to Mornington Place the next day, so he would not have asked Patmore to retrieve the manuscript for him when he could do it himself. It would have been sensible, however, to ask Patmore to collect the manuscript from Mitre Court on his way to work at the British Museum, so saving Tennyson the journey when he returned to London the next day.

[3] Basil Champneys, *Memoirs and Correspondence of Coventry Patmore*, 2 vols. (1900), 1, 179–80. The letter is dated 'Feb. 28th 1850' by both Champneys

Patmore recovered the manuscript which Tennyson 'had left in a closet where he was used to keep some of his provisions' (*Memoir*, I 297).[1] Tennyson then asked Mrs Patmore to make a fair-copy of L.MS.[2] She completed the task within the month, for on 2 April Tennyson read aloud to Palgrave from her transcript:

Tennyson offered to read me certain poems he had written about Arthur, which his friends 'seemed to approve.' He then brought forth a bundle of beautifully copied verse: the name 'In Memoriam' I do not think he used; and read several pieces. One was No. CIII, 'On that last night . . . ,' which friends had specially admired: others from the early series describing the ship sailing 'from the Italian shore' (No. IX): and that, I think, where parents or sweetheart await a son's or a lover's return.   (*Memoir*, II 486)[3]

Patmore retained L.MS, for on 18 August he showed it to William Allingham, who recorded an account of the occasion:

He went on to tell me: 'I have in this room perhaps the greatest literary treasure in England — the manuscript of Tennyson's *next poem*. It is written in a thing like a butcher's account-book. He left it behind him in his lodging when he was up in London and wrote to me to go and look for it. He had no other copy, and he never remembers his verses. I found it by chance, in a drawer; if I had been a little later it would probably have been sold to a butter-shop.' Before I went away Patmore took out this MS. book from a cabinet and turned over the leaves before my longing eyes, but Tennyson had told him not to show it to

---

and Hallam Tennyson (*Memoir*, I 297). This date has been proved incorrect. The letter itself (Beinecke Rare Book and Manuscript Library) shows that Tennyson did not inscribe the year but only the day of the month and the day of the week, 'Wednesday morning'. February 28 fell on Thursday in 1850 but on Wednesday in 1849 (see Joseph Sendry, 'The *In Memoriam* Manuscripts: Some Solutions to the Problems', *Harvard Library Bulletin*, XXI (April 1973), 210. The expression 'Butcher's Book', or 'Butcher's Account Book', to describe such tall, narrow notebooks as T.MS and L.MS, seems to have been coined by FitzGerald.

[1] For Patmore's mistaken assumption that the manuscript he retrieved was the one which Tennyson later gave to Sir John Simeon (*Memoir*, I 297) and which was afterwards given to Trinity College, Cambridge, see Sendry, 'The *In Memoriam* Manuscripts: Some Solutions to the Problems', 212–13. Patmore and Hallam Tennyson both believed that there was only one 'Butcher's Book' of *In Memoriam*.

[2] Mrs Patmore acted as his amanuensis again in 1857 when she spent 'many days copying out old Welsh ballads from unpublished Manuscripts in the British Museum.' Emily Tennyson wrote to thank her for her 'beautifully written' copies (Charles Tennyson, 302;*Memoirs and Correspondence of Coventry Patmore*, II 309).

[3] That the 'bundle of beautifully copied verse' was Mrs Patmore's fair-copy was first remarked upon by Sendry, 'The *In Memoriam* Manuscripts: Some Solutions to the Problems', 211. Palgrave's use of 'bundle' suggests that the transcript was made on loose sheets rather than in a notebook.

anybody. Mrs. Patmore had copied it out for the press, and T. gave her the original.[1]   (Allingham's *Diary*, 55)

L.MS was still in Patmore's hands on 2 November when (again in spite of Tennyson's request not to show it to anyone) he showed it to W.M. Rossetti, who recorded in the *PRB Journal*: 'I saw Tennyson's MS. book of elegies on young Hallam, which are to be published some day'.[2] Later that month, Tennyson told de Vere that he had not yet begun to revise the elegies for publication (even though they had been copied for the press in August). He wrote to de Vere at some time between mid-November (1849) and February (1850):

With respect to the 'Elegies', I cannot say that I have turned my attention to them lately. I do not know whether I have done anything new in that quarter since you saw them, but I believe I am going to print them, and then I need not tell you that you will be perfectly welcome to a copy, on the condition that when the book is published, this avant-courier of it shall be either sent back to me, or die the death by fire in Curragh Chase. I shall print about twenty-five copies, and let them out among friends under the same condition of either return or cremation.

(*Memoir*, I 282)[3]

Stage E: The Trial Issue (March 1850)

The private issue (**Trial**)[4] to which Tennyson refers appeared in March 1850, a month after the publication of the third edition of *The Princess*. It introduces many changes from L.MS. Tennyson must have made the revisions between mid-November 1849 and March 1850. The revisions, for the most part, would have been made in Mrs Patmore's copy before it was sent to the printer. Patmore still retained L.MS, and this is probably one of the reasons why Tennyson revised the copy instead of the original.

Neither Mrs Patmore's copy nor the proofs survive. The proofs are mentioned, however, in the journals of G.S. Venables.[5]

[1] At a later date L.MS was returned to the Tennyson family.

[2] *Præraphaelite Diaries and Letters*, edited by William Michael Rossetti (1900), 227.

[3] The letter, which is not dated in *Memoir*, has been conjectured to date from 'soon after 13 November 1849' on the basis of internal evidence by W.D. Paden, 'A Note on the Variants of *In Memoriam* and *Lucretius*', *Library*, VIII (1953), 260). Other evidence strongly suggests that the letter may well date from February 1850. In any case, the letter sounds very like what de Vere reports Tennyson as having told him in January 1849 (see p. 18). It is quite possible that Tennyson forgot that he had already told de Vere of his plans.

[4] Tennyson and Hallam Tennyson referred to such early copies as 'proof-sheets' (*Memoir*, II 383).

[5] National Library of Wales, Aberystwyth. The editors are grateful to John O. Waller for bringing this account to their attention.

March 5 Called on A.T. at Lincoln's Inn Fields & looked over the new edition of The Princess. Agreed to correct the sheets of the Elegies.
March 7 Corrected the first sheets of the Elegies, called on A.T. about them, & then took them to the printer's.
March 10 After breakfast worked for three hours correcting A.T.'s proof sheets . . . The poems very beautiful.
March 12 The remaining sheets came from the printers.
March 13 Finished correcting the proofs & sent them to A.T. F.L. [Franklin Lushington] & [Harry] Hallam came in to look at them.

Tennyson 'always liked to see his poems in print some months and sometimes some years before publication, "for," as he said, "poetry looks better, more convincing, in print"' (*Memoir*, I 190). The earliest record of a copy of **Trial** is given by William Michael Rossetti in the *PRB Journal* on 21 March 1850:[1] 'I went to Patmore's . . . He has got one out of some half-dozen copies of Tennyson's Elegies that have been printed strictly for private perusal; the publication of the work being postponed for some while, till about Christmas' (*Præraphaelite Diaries and Letters*, 267). Patmore gave the same details to William Allingham a few weeks later. On 17 April he wrote to Allingham: 'His elegies are printed. I have one of the *only* half dozen copies at present in existence. He talks of publishing them next Christmas.'[2] Patmore understood that only six copies had been printed, but Tennyson had told de Vere that he would print 'about twenty-five'. There is no reason to suppose that the number actually printed was other than that proposed by Tennyson. (Three copies are known to survive.) Patmore was probably mistaken about the number of copies,[3] just as he was mistaken in assuming that the poem would not be published until Christmas.

Trial appeared with no title-page.[4] It introduced, however, a dedication which (for the most part) was to be retained in all subsequent editions: 'IN MEMORIAM | A.H.H. | OBIIT SEPT. MDCCCXXXIII.'.[5] It adds nine sections not in L.MS, giving a total of 119 sections. It also adds eleven stanzas (here referred to as the 'Introductory stanzas') at the beginning of the sequence. The addition of these stanzas is perhaps the most important change from L.MS.

The stanzas are set apart from the sequence itself by being placed before the dedication and by having a date of composition, 1849,

---

[1] *Eversley*, III 195 states in error: 'It was not until May 1850 that *In Memoriam* was printed and given to a few friends.'

[2] *Memoirs and Correspondence of Coventry Patmore*, II 173.

[3] Paden suggests that Patmore's estimate is 'an enthusiastic understatement' ('A Note on the Variants of *In Memoriam* and *Lucretius*', 260, n.6).

[4] The TRC copy has a half-title and title (facsimiles of those in **1850A**) which were tipped in when the copy was rebound in 1891 (see Appendix A.2).

[5] The published editions omit 'Sept.'.

printed after the last line. This arrangement is retained in all subsequent editions of the poem published during Tennyson's life-time. The tone of the Introductory stanzas is apologetic and Christian. They may well have been added, as E.B. Mattes observes, in order to reassure Emily Sellwood about the quality of Tennyson's faith. Indeed, it is likely, as Mattes suggests, that the copy of the Elegies which Tennyson sent to Emily Sellwood in March 1850 was a copy of **Trial** and not, as Willingham Rawnsley records, a manuscript.[1]

The friends to whom Tennyson sent copies of **Trial** were apparently invited to offer their criticisms, for one of the three surviving copies contains the annotations of Aubrey de Vere.[2] Of the twenty-five changes suggested by de Vere, Tennyson adopted only a few. He made verbal revisions in seven places and revisions in capitalization and punctuation in four places (see p. 324). The revisions were introduced into the published text over a long period of time: the earliest appears in **1850A** and the last in **1875**.

Stage F: The first, second, and third editions (June–August 1850)

The Elegies were published by Moxon anonymously on 1 June 1850, but the identity of the author was announced the same day in *Publisher's Circular* (XIII 190): 'Tennyson (A.) – In Memoriam. By Alfred Tennyson. Fcp. 8 vo. pp. 210, cloth, 6s.' Although his authorship of the poem became widely known almost immediately, his name never appeared on the title-page of any single-volume edition of the poem in his lifetime. The title of the volume, *In Memoriam*, had been suggested by Emily Sellwood.[3] She was doubtless inspired by the inscription which first appeared in **Trial**: 'IN MEMORIAM |A.H.H....'. Up to this time, Tennyson and his friends had usually referred to the sequence of sections as the 'Elegies'. It is not known if he ever envisaged 'Elegies' as a title to the sequence,[4] but he did tell de Vere that he once thought of entitling

[1] Mattes, 91, 92, 99 n.9. Rawnsley's statement (in *Memories of the Tennysons*, 123) is based on hearsay, as he was only four or five years old in 1850. Moreover, if indeed the Introductory stanzas were composed partly in order to influence Emily Sellwood, Tennyson would have sent a copy of **Trial** (which has the stanzas) rather than L.MS (which does not).

[2] Beinecke, Tinker 2065, (see Appendix A.2). Tennyson has inscribed the inside front board 'A de Vere', and above this an unidentified hand has written 'From the library of Aubrey de Vere'. The annotations are definitely in the hand of de Vere. The hand is considered unidentified, however, by W.D. Paden, who also doubts that this is the copy which Tennyson sent de Vere in the early spring of 1850. Paden discusses this copy in 'A Note on the Variants of *In Memoriam* and *Lucretius*', 261–2.

[3] James O. Hoge, *The Letters of Emily, Lady Tennyson* (University Park and London, 1974), 181, Letter 143.

[4] 'Elegies' is stamped on the spine of a loose-leaf notebook (Prayer Book MS) in TRC.

it 'Fragments of an Elegy' (*Memoir*, I 293), and he also sometimes referred to it as 'The Way of the Soul' (*Memoir*, I 393).

The first edition (actually the second issue),[1] **1850A**, adds ten sections (*7, 8, 56, 69, 96, 97, 119, 120, 121, 128*) and *124*.1-8 and 17-20 to the poem printed in **Trial**, bringing the total number of sections to 129. Three of the ten (*56, 69, 128*) had appeared in T.MS (*128*.9-24 only) and L.MS (*56, 69*), but were omitted from **Trial**. The other seven sections were possibly (but not necessarily) composed between March and May 1850. At least one was apparently composed in 1849, according to the account of Willingham Rawnsley: 'My earliest remembrance of him is of his visiting my parents at Shiplake, before 1850, when I was turned out of my little room in order that he might have a place of his own to smoke in. He was then still working on "In Memoriam", and it was in this little room of mine that he wrote the "Hesper Phosphor" canto' [*121*] (*Memories of the Tennysons*, 121).

Several of the new sections form companion pieces (*7* and *119, 56* and *120*), and several seem to have been added in order to elaborate or to anticipate an idea (*56, 69, 96, 97, 120, 121, 128*). To *124*, **1850A** adds three new stanzas (1-8, 17-20) which amplify and modify the thought of this section. There are also many changes in diction and in punctuation (see p. 325). The 5,000 copies of **1850A** were sold out within a few weeks of publication. The second edition (strictly, the third issue), **1850B**, came out in the middle of July, and the third edition (the fourth issue), **1850C**, in August.[2]

Stage G: Further major revisions (1851-1870)

The fourth edition (strictly, the second edition), **1851A**, was published in January 1851.[3] It introduces a new section, *59*, as a 'pendant' to *3* (*Eversley*, III 242). Many years later (1870-1), Tennyson commented to James Knowles on this section: 'Added afterwards but one of the old poems nevertheless.' Some internal evidence suggests that *59* may have been composed in 1842 or before (see note *59*.8a-h).

Between **1855** and **1869** Tennyson introduced about thirty changes in diction. He was also, of course, always tinkering with punctuation. In **1870** he added *39* as a companion-piece to *2*. He had composed *39* in April 1868 (*Memoir*, II 53), but it was not included in the poem

---

[1] The first three so-called 'editions' are, strictly, reissues of **Trial**. This is explained in detail in Appendix A.2.

[4] Charles Tennyson, 248; Samson Low, *A Catalogue of Books Published in the United Kingdom During the Year 1850*, 23.

[3] Samson Low, *A Catalogue of Books Published in the United Kingdom During the Year 1851*, 27.

until **1870** because the draft of it had slipped into the back of a writing desk and had become, apparently, lost or forgotten.[1]

The addition of *39* gave *In Memoriam* 131 sections. The only further significant changes in the subsequent editions of the poem up to and including **1884B** are changes in diction in eleven places. Although Tennyson did not add any more sections after **1870**, he toyed with the idea of doing so, as he told James Knowles in 1870-1: 'I think of adding another poem — a speculative one bringing out the thoughts of the higher Pantheism and showing that all the arguments are about as good on one side as the other — & thus throw man back more & more on the primitive impulses & feelings.'

Tennyson may have been inspired to add a section on this subject by the short poem 'The Higher Pantheism' which he had composed in December 1867 and published in 1869. His sketch of the proposed section suggests that he might have intended it to elaborate the thought of *124*, or at least to be located among the last sections of the poem.

On the basis of this reconstruction of the development of *In Memoriam*, it is possible to make a few general statements about the growth of the poem from the composition of the first written section on 6 October 1833 to the addition to the published sequence in **1870** of the last written section. There is no reason to disbelieve Tennyson's statement that he did not write the sections 'with any view of weaving them into a whole, or for publication, until I found that I had written so many' (*Eversley*, III 204). Within a year of Hallam's death, however, he had at least begun to compose pairs and triplets of sections. The sections which were written during the earlier stages of composition tend to be located in the first half or first two-thirds of the sequence, and the sections which were written during the later stages of composition are more often than not located towards the latter part of the sequence. In other words, the composition of the poem broadly corresponds to the development of the 'different moods of sorrow' within the poem itself.[2] Tennyson's original intention with respect to a 'tribute' to Hallam seems to be represented in the sequence of about seventy-five sections which he had completed by the autumn of 1842 (T.MS). His dissatisfaction with the conclusion of this sequence was the principal cause of his composing further sections in order to extend it in a more hopeful course of thought. Many of the sections which were added last (in **Trial, 1850A, 1851A,** and **1870**) are either companion-pieces or

---

[1] A note by Sir Charles Tennyson in vol. 8 of his notebooks (TRC), in preparation for *Alfred Tennyson*.

[2] Tennyson remarked of *In Memoriam*: 'The different moods of sorrow as in a drama are dramatically given' (*Eversley*, III 204).

elaborations or anticipations of sections previously included in the sequence. This suggests that once Tennyson had decided upon publication, he was chiefly concerned to tighten and formalize the structure of the sequence.

Palgrave's 'In Memoriam': A Postscript

In 1885, Macmillan published *Lyrical Poems by Alfred Lord Tennyson*, selected and annotated by Francis T. Palgrave. This contained a selection of forty-two sections from *In Memoriam*, in this order: *85, 10, 11, 13, 14, 18, 19, 38, 57, 58, 74, 90, 91, 115, 116, 119, 123, 2, 6, 20, 27, 28, 31, 32, 33, 36, 40, 50, 51, 54, 60, 64, 69, 86, 94, 97, 99, 100, 101, 78, 106, 131.* (Palgrave actually numbered the sections from *71* to *112* to accord with the arrangement of the whole volume.) After Tennyson's death, Palgrave wrote (*Memoir*, II 503) that the sections included from *In Memoriam* 'follow a list which he gave me'. This information is not given in the selection itself. There, Palgrave assumes responsibility for what is included, explaining (p. 262) that his guiding wish has been to give 'first the songs most directly setting forth the personal love and sorrow which inspired this great lyrical elegy, and then those, or some of those, in which the same motive-theme is developed in figures, or connected with the aspects of nature and of religious thought'.

There can be no doubt, however, that at the very least, Tennyson knew and approved of Palgrave's selection.

Depersonalizing the poem: verbal revisions

The most significant revisions Tennyson made during the composition of the poem are, of course, those which relate to the arrangement of the sections. These are described in the appropriate places in the Commentary. In respect to verbal revisions within the sections themselves, there is evidence of one interesting tendency. This is Tennyson's deliberate attempt to obscure and make less personal the references to himself and to Arthur Hallam. Below is a table of such revisions. An arrow between the revision and the final reading signifies 'changed to'. For example, the first item means that the personal pronoun *his* was changed to the article *the* which was changed to *a*, the final reading.

7.4   his hand H.Lpr.104 *1st reading* → the hand H.Lpr.104 *2nd reading* → a hand **1850A**

7.5   The hand H.Lpr.104 → A hand **1850A**

23.3   I move alone T.MS *1st reading* → alone alone T.MS *2nd reading*

24.10   Hath stretch'd [made T.MS] my former joy L.MS-**1850C** → Makes former gladness loom **1851A**

24.11   my present state T.MS → the present state L.MS

30.20   We kist each other T.Nbk.-Hn.Nbk. *1st reading*, H.Lpr.101-
          L.MS *1st reading* → And silence follow'd Hn.Nbk. *2nd reading*,
          L.MS *2nd reading*

43.13   And therefore that our love was true T.MS, L.MS → And thus
          our love, for ever new **Trial** → And love will [would **1850A-
          1851B**] last as pure and whole **1855**

51.7   my secret shame H.Lpr.101, T.MS *1st reading*? → some hidden
          shame T.MS *2nd reading*

54.1,13 I T.MS → we L.MS

85.51   my mind T.Nbk., Heath MS → the mind L.MS

89.15   With me to suck the cool L.MS → To drink the cooler air **Trial**

92.3   my brain T.MS → the brain L.MS

93.13   Stoop soul & touch me: wed me: hear T.MS, L.MS *1st reading*
          → Descend & touch & enter: hear L.MS *2nd reading*

95.36   His living soul L.MS-1870 → The living soul **1872**

95.37. mine in his L.MS-1870 → mine in this **1872**

The 'Elegies': Some Formal Influences

1. The Latin elegiac poets

Tennyson usually referred to *In Memoriam* before it was published as
his 'Elegies'. Since the beginning of the sixteenth century the term
'elegy' has come to mean in English 'a poem of lamentation or regret',
and from the sixteenth century onwards, poets composed funeral
elegies on occasions of private and public bereavement. In composing
his poems on Arthur Hallam, Tennyson clearly had this tradition in
mind. But there was another and an older tradition which he used as a
model and of which he must have intended his 'Elegies' to be reminiscent.

The exact meaning of ἐλεγεία ('elegy') is obscure. It is possible that
its original meaning was simply 'a song sung to a flute'. In fifth-century
Greece it was understood to mean 'a song of mourning', but the earliest
Greek elegies which survive (seventh century and sixth century BC)
treat not so much of death as of war and love. The elegies of the
Alexandrian period (third century BC) have as their subject love only,
and these were the poems which the Roman elegists — Gallus, Catullus,
Propertius, Tibullus, and Ovid — took as their models. Their amatory
elegies have two characteristic features: a great variety of subjects all
treated in the same metre (alternating dactylic hexameters and penta-
meters), the metre now called 'elegiac'; and the subjective and self-

conscious analysis of complex emotions. For example, the ninety-two elegies by Propertius, the leading Roman elegist, are addressed mostly to a lady whom he calls 'Cynthia', and within the same metre they deal with such subjects as his constancy in love; his standing outside her house at night lamenting that he has been excluded; his sleepless nights as he lies in bed thinking of her; her birthday; her appearance to him in a dream after she has died; and the immortality that he and his mistress will achieve on account of his poems. In treating these subjects, the poet conveys his shifting moods and continually examines his own emotions and those of his mistress. Tibullus and Ovid similarly wrote highly personal love elegies on a wide range of subjects and all in the same metre.

It is well known that Tennyson's 'Elegies' are characterized by the poet's analytical description of his emotions and by his extreme self-consciousness. They are not in the measure called 'elegiac' (which has never been successfully adopted by the English poets), but they are all in one measure (a quatrain of iambic tetrameters with enclosed rhyme), and they are as varied in mood and situation as are the classical elegies. Several stock situations and attitudes which belong to the minor poetic genres used by the elegiac poets are adapted by Tennyson for his own elegiac purpose. For example, sections 7 and 119 — the admired companion-pieces on the poet standing outside Arthur Hallam's house in Wimpole Street — are adaptations of the genre (*paraclausithyron*) in which the poet-lover stands outside the house of his mistress at night and laments that the door is bolted against him. Poems by Catullus, Horace, Propertius, and Tibullus depict the hapless lover addressing the door (which sometimes talks back) and blaming it for his being locked out (see headnote to 7).

The series of sections (9-17) addressed to the ship which brings home the body of Arthur Hallam is modelled on one of the genres for which rules were laid down in the schools of rhetoric, the *propemptikon*, or farewell to the departing traveller. Section 9 illustrates an important element of the *propemptikon*, the invocation for a safe journey. Sections 14 and 17 illustrate a genre sometimes included in a *propemptikon*, the *prosphonetikon*, or speech of welcome to a traveller who has just arrived. Sections 15 and 16 illustrate one of the commonplaces of these genres, the expression of anxiety for the safety of the traveller during the journey (see headnote to 9-18).

Section 107, which commemorates the birthday of Arthur Hallam, is a reminiscence (as Bradley noticed) of the celebration by the fireside during a winter day described by Horace in *Odes*, I 9. It is also a type of *genethliakon*, or birthday ode. Such poems usually commemorate the birthday of a living person, but if Tennyson had needed a model for his poem he could have found one in Statius, *Silvae*, II 7, which com-

memorates the birthday of Lucan, who had been dead for some years.[1]
A characteristic of the *genethliakon* is that it depicts celebrations
which are appropriate to the person being honoured. So the birthday
ode by Tibullus for Messalla (I 7) praises the triumphs and achieve-
ments of the conqueror, and the elegy by Propertius for the birthday
of his mistress (III 10) looks forward to the day's festivities and the
consummation of the anniversary rites when he and his mistress retire.
Tennyson's poem on Hallam's birthday similarly describes how the
celebrations are appropriate to Hallam's character:

> Be cheerful-minded, talk and treat
> Of all things ev'n as he were by;
>
> We keep the day. With festal cheer,
> With books and music, surely we
> Will drink to him, whate'er he be,
> And sing the songs he loved to hear.
>   (19-24)

Another kind of celebration is the subject of the Epilogue, which
describes the marriage of Tennyson's sister, Cecilia, to his friend,
Edmund Lushington. This long poem is closely modelled on the genre
of the nuptial song, or *epithalamion*, of which the classic example is
Catullus LXI (see headnote to Epilogue).

There are other sections of *In Memoriam* which illustrate common-
places familiar in classical literature. The sections in which the poet lies
restlessly in bed and experiences visions and dreams (*67-71*) are
reminiscent of the situation of the sleepless or fitfully sleeping lover
which is recurrent in elegies (for example, the well known dream elegy
by 'Lygdamus' included in the poems of Tibullus, III 4; and Ovid,
Amores, I 2). Section *89*, which describes Arthur Hallam escaping
from the heat and cares of London to enjoy the rural pleasures of
Somersby Rectory, recalls the classical theme of the happy man who
retires from the anxious life of the city ('Beatus ille qui procul negotiis')
to a cool and quiet country spot (Horace, *Epodes*, II; cf. also *Odes*,
I 17; Martial, XII 18). Sections *10, 18, 21,* and *I keep no more a lone
distress* (Add. Poem v) allude to several commonplaces about burial,
the ritual of which was so important in the ancient world: that it is
better to be buried on earth than to have one's body lost in the sea;
better to be buried among one's family than in a distant land; and

---

[1] In 1883 Tennyson denied knowing even 'one line of Statius' (*Memoir*, I
305), but he quotes Statius himself in his notes to *33* in *Eversley*. It seems unlikely
that he should never have read such a well-known poet.

better to be buried in a quiet spot than by the roadside where passers-by may dishonour the tomb.

In many classical books of poems (for example, the elegies of Tibullus and Ovid's *Amores*) the arrangement is governed by a principle of *variatio*. Short poems having the same theme, subject, or literary form are carefully arranged in relation to each other. Sometimes similar poems are grouped together; sometimes they are widely separated so that the later one recalls the earlier; sometimes the same theme or subject is treated from different points of view. The reader's impression of a collection of poems arranged in this way is one of both variety and structural unity. The effect of an individual poem is, moreover, enhanced when it is appreciated in relation to corresponding poems.

As has already been described in 'The Growth of the Poem', this kind of arrangement is a feature which characterizes the development of *In Memoriam* from its earliest stages. From the trio of ship poems (*9, 17, 18*) composed in 1833-4, to the yew-tree poem (*39*) added to the sequence in **1870** as a companion-piece to *2*, Tennyson was guided by the principle of *variatio*. Indeed, in his final preparations for publications, *variatio* seems to have been his chief concern.[1] Most of the sections which were added to the sequence from **Trial** onwards are either companion-pieces or they are elaborations and anticipations of ideas in sections previously included in the sequence.

Of the numerous groups of sections which comprise *In Memoriam*, the ones which come immediately to mind are those on the ship and the burial (*9-19*), Christmas (*28-30, 78, 104-6*), Spring (*38, 86, 88, 115, 116*), departure from Somersby (*100-3*), immortality (*31-6*), the state of the soul after death (*40-7*), communion with the dead (*90-5*), the character of Arthur Hallam (*109-14*), and those which Hallam Tennyson referred to as concerning 'Evolution' (*55, 56, 118, 123*). Moreover, there are several pairs of sections which treat the same subject from a different point of view, for example: the sections on the yew tree (*2, 39*), on Sorrow (*3, 59*), on the anniversary of Hallam's death (*72, 99*), and on the poet outside the door of 67 Wimpole Street (*7, 119*). And, of course, the Introductory stanzas (composed 1849) are intended as a conscious contrast to the Epilogue (composed 1844-5).

2. Epicedia

The classical principle of *variatio* governs the arrangement only of small groups of poems within a collection. The larger framework of *In Memoriam* is modelled on that of a major classical genre, the *epicedion* or funeral lament. Among the shorter *epicedia* are the elegies of Catullus

---

[1] A.C. Bradley was the first critic to note that the entire sequence, for the most part, falls into groups and pairs of sections.

on the death of his brother (CI, LXV, LXVIII); the ode by Horace for Quintilius (I 24); the elegy of Ovid for his fellow poet Tibullus (*Amores*, III 9); and the elegy by Propertius on the death of a young nobleman of promise (III 18). Some longer poems of this type include the six *epicedia* of Statius on the loss of relatives and friends (*Silvae*, II 1, 6; III 3; V 1, 3, 5), and the 'Consolation to Livia' commonly ascribed to Ovid.

Epicedia always contain a number of commonplace ideas which can be conveniently adduced from such works as the three *Consolationes* of Seneca, the well-known letter of condolence from Sulpicius to Cicero (*ad Fam.* IV 5), and the Ovidian 'Consolation to Livia'. *In Memoriam* illustrates many of the stock arguments: all men must die; it is better to have been happy for a short time than never to have been happy at all; it is better to control sorrow than to indulge it; time will ease the sorrow, but reason should do so first; it is vain to grieve on our own account or on that of the dead, who cannot be recalled to life; the dead are happy, indeed, they are probably happier than the living; the dead would not wish us to grieve for them. *In Memoriam* also contains virtually all the conventions of the *epicedion*: a description of the chief mourner as overwhelmed by grief in the initial stages of bereavement; the reply of the poet to those who dare to prescribe conditions of mourning; a description of the manner of death; a description of the funeral and the distress of the mourners at the pyre or tomb; the poet's exaggerated praise of the deceased (including a description of his physical appearance, his demeanour, and his manner of speech), and his lamentation that so much virtue has died with him; the mourner's regrets that he is left behind and his looking forward to joining the deceased; his grief at the end of all physical contact with the deceased; the acknowledgment that, although the existence of an afterlife is not a matter of absolute certainty, it is nevertheless likely that the deceased will be received into some mode of further existence; a description of this reception of the deceased by the worthies who have preceded him; the mourner's desire to communicate with the deceased; the apparition of the deceased to the mourner in a dream or waking vision and the comfort it brings.

The location of an *epicedion* is usually the funeral pyre or the tomb, and the poem concludes with a reference to the mourners' departure: the poet urges the other mourners to cease grieving and to come away. It is interesting to notice that the T.MS sequence, which represents the completed sequence of sections as Tennyson originally conceived it, concludes with section 57, the subject of which is a final farewell as the poet and a fellow-mourner (the conventional figure of a young woman, who might here be identified with Tennyson's sister Emily) depart from the grave. In the last stanza Tennyson has even alluded to the famous farewell of Catullus to his brother: 'frater, ave atque vale' (CI):

> I hear it now, and o'er and o'er,
> Eternal greetings to the dead;
> And 'Ave, Ave, Ave,' said,
> 'Adieu, adieu' for evermore.

Having concluded the sequence with this section, Tennyson then decided (as he later told James Knowles), that this was 'too sad for an ending'. It lacks those elements of the *epicedion* which are intended to console the mourner: the prospect of the afterlife, the happiness there of the deceased, and the comfort which this offers to the bereaved. These are the elements which Tennyson added to the poem after he decided to reject the T.MS sequence as his final intention and to carry on composing sections in order to extend the sequence in more hopeful modes of thought. Of course, English poets before Tennyson had modelled their funeral poems on those of the classical poets, and especially on a variant of the *epicedion* which descends from the Greek bucolic poets. Three of their poems in particular — Idyll I of Theocritus, the 'Lament for Bion' attributed to Moschus, and the 'Lament for Adonis' by Bion — have come to be known as 'pastoral elegies', although they were regarded by the ancients as 'idylls' (εἰδύλλια: 'little poems', commonly translated 'little pictures'). This is the genre adapted by Virgil (Daphnis becomes a star in *Eclogues* V), and introduced into English poetry by Sidney in the 'Old' *Arcadia*, IV 75, and by Spenser in his three pastoral elegies, 'November' in *The Shepheards Calender*, 'Astrophel' (for Sir Philip Sidney), and 'Daphnaida'. Following the example set by Milton in 'Lycidas', many of the eighteenth-century poets attempted the pastoral elegy, and Gay even satirized it in *The Shepherd's Week*, 'Friday; or, the Dirge'. In the nineteenth century Shelley's 'Adonais' incorporated many details from the pastoral tradition.

There are several traces of this tradition in *In Memoriam*. The most obvious examples are the occasional references to the graveside flowers and to the poet's 'pipes' and 'songs'. In *21*, the poet presents himself as a shepherd piping by the grave, and in *23*, the past happiness of the friends is described in terms of an Arcadian landscape. The pastoralism of *21* offended two early commentators: Bradley felt that it had 'a jarring effect', and Collins considered it 'very unworthy of Tennyson'. Sections *3* and *72* are examples of the pastoral convention of Nature's manifesting grief for the death of her favourite by reversing her natural processes. The stellification of Hallam at the end of the poem is an example of the convention introduced by Virgil and imitated in many English pastoral elegies, notably in 'Lycidas' and 'Adonais'.

A feature of many *epicedia* (for example, the notably regular ones of
Statius) and their English descendents (for example, 'Lycidas') is the
prominent and self-conscious role of the poet, who is either the chief
mourner or the consoler of a friend or patron (in which case the *epicedion*
is, strictly, a *consolatio*). He may apologize to the other mourners
because his songs are feeble and unworthy and because his talent has
deteriorated since the death of the loved one. He may confess that
although in the past he has been able to console others for their losses,
he now finds it difficult to turn his mourning into verse when the loss is
his own. The self-conscious role of the poet in *In Memoriam* has often
been remarked upon. Throughout the poem the interest of the poet
centres upon his own grief and his ability to express it through song. On
the few occasions when he acknowledges the grief of others for Arthur
(as in *57* and *I keep no more a lone distress* (Add. Poem v)), he considers
their grief to be of secondary importance to his own. In this respect
In Memoriam is an *epicedion* as distinct from a *consolatio*.[1] Tennyson
could have been concerned to console the others who had as much
claim upon the affections of Arthur Hallam as he had — Hallam's
betrothed, his parents, his other close friends. Typically, however, he
was concerned to console only himself, as he told his publisher in 1848
when he admitted that he had been writing the 'Elegies' 'for his own
relief and private satisfaction' (*Materials*, II 39).

The Text

The text of this edition is that of the poem in the one-volume edition of
the *Works* published by Macmillan in April 1884 (henceforward referred
to as **1884B**). This is a reprint with slight corrections of the edition
published earlier that year, in January (**1884A**). Hallam Tennyson
records that his father 'carefully revised' his poems for the one-volume
edition published in 1884 (*Memoir*, II 310). He doubtless refers to
1884A which, so far as concerns *In Memoriam*, introduces one verbal
change (*prophet* for *prophets* at *87*.8), and twenty-five changes in
punctuation, seven of which concern the punctuation of quoted
speeches.[2] The text of *In Memoriam* in **1884A** has two misprints:
lifelong for *livelong* at *89. 31* and *June* for *June*, at *97*.11. These are
corrected in **1884B**.[3]

---

[1] He did compose a *consolatio* for James Spedding, 'To J.S.' (1832) on the death
of his brother, a poem which illustrates many of the commonplaces of the genre.

[2] A passage of direct speech was set in inverted commas for the first time
in *102*.9–12. In several passages of direct speech which run through two or more
stanzas, inverted commas were introduced at the beginning of each new stanza
(*21*.17, *37*.5, 13, 17, 21, *85*.81, *89*.41).

[3] Tennyson's correction in ink of *lifelong* is in a copy of **1884A** in TRC.

An alternative text which needs to be considered is the text of the poem in the edition of the *Works* prepared by Hallam Tennyson with annotations by the poet supplemented by Hallam's and included in Macmillan's Eversley Library (9 vols., 1907-8; reprinted, 1908-13). *Eversley* introduces one change in the **1884B** text: *walls*; for *walls*: at *67.4*. Either this is a change made by the poet's son or it is an error made by the printing-house. In either case it is not authoritative. Moreover, in certain instances (in some copies) the impression of the terminal punctuation in *Eversley* is imperfect or invisible.

In the present edition, the spelling and punctuation of the chosen text have not been altered. Tennyson was himself scrupulous in these matters, as the significant variants and minor variants show. In **1850A** he abandoned the old spelling *landskip* as having become archaic or seeming affected, for the now more familiar *landscape*. He changed *Shakespeare* (*61.12*) in Hn.Nbk. and T.MS to *Shakespere* in L.MS (the spelling 'Shakspere' was promoted by Charles Knight), and finally to *Shakspeare* (the spelling promoted by Malone) from **Trial** onwards. He altered past verb-forms, changing - *'t* to - *'d* (as in *hush'd* for *hush't*).[1] He also took care to retain forms like *tho'*, *thro'*, *bring'st*, and *ruin'd*.[2]

In the transcription of readings from the manuscripts, this edition does not retain Tennyson's use of the long 's'. This edition numbers the sections with arabic numerals partly because they are easier to read than Roman numerals (introduced when the poem was first printed), and partly because Tennyson used arabic numerals in his manuscripts.

---

[1] In later years, however, he commented: 'I like the *t*- the strong perfect in verbs ending in *s, p,* and *x*- past, slipt, vext' (*Eversley*, V 468).

[2] These have been changed to *though, through, bringest, ruined,* etc. in Ricks's edition, in accordance with the principles laid down for the Longmans' Annotated English Poets.

IN MEMORIAM

But vaster. We are fools and slight;
  We mock thee when we do not fear: 30
  But help thy foolish ones to bear;
Help thy vain worlds to bear thy light.

Forgive what seem'd my sin in me;
  What seem'd my worth since I began;
  For merit lives from man to man,   35
And not from man, O Lord, to thee.

Forgive my grief for one removed,
  Thy creature, whom I found so fair.
  I trust he lives in thee, and there
I find him worthier to be loved.   40

Forgive these wild and wandering cries,
  Confusions of a wasted youth;
  Forgive them where they fail in truth,
And in thy wisdom make me wise.

                    1849

[Introductory stanzas]

Strong Son of God, immortal Love,
　Whom we, that have not seen thy face,
　By faith, and faith alone, embrace,
Believing where we cannot prove;

Thine are these orbs of light and shade;　　　　5
　Thou madest Life in man and brute;
　Thou madest Death; and lo, thy foot
Is on the skull which thou hast made.

Thou wilt not leave us in the dust:
　Thou madest man, he knows not why,　　　　10
　He thinks he was not made to die;
And thou hast made him: thou art just.

Thou seemest human and divine,
　The highest, holiest manhood, thou:
　Our wills are ours, we know not how;　　　　15
Our wills are ours, to make them thine.

Our little systems have their day;
　They have their day and cease to be:
　They are but broken lights of thee,
And thou, O Lord, art more than they.

We have but faith: we cannot know;
　For knowledge is of things we see;
　And yet we trust it comes from thee,
A beam in darkness: let it grow.

Let knowledge grow from more to more,　　　　25
　But more of reverence in us dwell;
　That mind and soul, according well,
May make one music as before,

[Introductory stanzas] 13-16 *(only) in* Prayer Book MS; **Trial, 1850A-;** *not in*
T.MS, L.MS *Dated* 1849 *from* **Trial** *onwards*
　　13-16] *an early draft in* Prayer Book MS:
　　　　　　　　Thou seemest human & divine
　　　　　　　　　Thou madest man without, within:
　　　　　　　　　Yet who shall say thou madest sin
　　　　　　　　For who shall say 'it is not mine'

IN MEMORIAM.

LONDON:
EDWARD MOXON, DOVER STREET.
1850.

The title-page of the first edition (actual size)

ERRATUM

...6 and its facing page [Introductory stan...
...ly positioned and should be reversed.

IN MEMORIAM A. H. H.

OBIIT MDCCCXXXIII.

1

I held it truth, with him who sings
    To one clear harp in divers tones,
    That men may rise on stepping-stones
Of their dead selves to higher things.

But who shall so forecast the years   5
    And find in loss a gain to match?
    Or reach a hand thro' time to catch
The far-off interest of tears?

Let Love clasp Grief lest both be drown'd,
    Let darkness keep her raven gloss: 10
    Ah, sweeter to be drunk with loss,
To dance with death, to beat the ground,

Than that the victor Hours should scorn
    The long result of love, and boast,
    'Behold the man that loved and lost,   15
But all he was is overworn.'

2

Old Yew, which graspest at the stones
    That name the under-lying dead,
    Thy fibres net the dreamless head,
Thy roots are wrapt about the bones.

The seasons bring the flower again,   5
    And bring the firstling to the flock;
    And in the dusk of thee, the clock
Beats out the little lives of men.

_1_] 1-4 _(only), in_ H.Lpr.101, T.MS, L.MS; **Trial, 1850A-**
    5-16] _Not in_ H.Lpr.101, T.MS, L.MS   ₁11 Ah,] **1850B-; Ah! Trial-1850A**
16 was] **1850A-;** loves **Trial**

_2_] L.MS, **Trial, 1850A-;** _not in_ T.MS

O not for thee the glow, the bloom,
    Who changest not in any gale,   10
    Nor branding summer suns avail
To touch thy thousand years of gloom:

And gazing on thee, sullen tree,
    Sick for thy stubborn hardihood,
    I seem to fail from out my blood   15
And grow incorporate into thee.

3

O Sorrow, cruel fellowship,
    O Priestess in the vaults of Death,
    O sweet and bitter in a breath,
What whispers from thy lying lip?

'The stars,' she whispers, 'blindly run;   5
    A web is wov'n across the sky;
    From out waste places comes a cry,
And murmurs from the dying sun:

'And all the phantom, Nature, stands —
    With all the music in her tone,   10
    O hollow echo of my own, —
A hollow form with empty hands.'

And shall I take a thing so blind,
    Embrace her as my natural good;
    Or crush her, like a vice of blood,   15
Upon the threshold of the mind?

    9 O] L.MS, 1850B-; O! Trial-1850A   10 gale,] 1851A-; gale L.MS; gale!
Trial-1850C   13 thee,] 1851A-; the L.MS 2nd reading-1850C; thy L.MS
1st reading

3] 5-8 (only), in H.Nbk.17; H.Lpr.100 (a detached leaf from T.MS), L.MS, Trial,
1850A-
    1-4] Not in H.Nbk.17   1 fellowship,] 1850B-; fellowship L.MS; fellowship!
H.Lpr.100, Trial-1850A   2 Death,] 1850B-; Death L.MS; Death! H.Lpr.100,
Trial-1850A   5-8] See early fragment from H.Nbk.17 in Commentary
9-16] Not in H.Nbk.17   9 'And all] L.MS (And . . .), Trial-; Because H.Lpr.
100   10 the] H.Lpr.100, L.MS, 1851B-; her Trial-1851A   16 a-d]
Deleted in H.Lpr.100:
            But Sorrow cares not for my frown
            And Sorrow says 'we must not part
            For if I die upon thy heart
            Then my dead weight will draw thee down.'

4

To Sleep I give my powers away;
  My will is bondsman to the dark;
  I sit within a helmless bark,
And with my heart I muse and say:

O heart, how fares it with thee now,   5
  That thou should'st fail from thy desire,
  Who scarcely darest to inquire,
'What is it makes me beat so low?'

Something it is which thou hast lost,
  Some pleasure from thine early years.   10
  Break, thou deep vase of chilling tears,
That grief hath shaken into frost!

Such clouds of nameless trouble cross
  All night below the darken'd eyes;
  With morning wakes the will, and cries,   15
'Thou shalt not be the fool of loss.'

5

I sometimes hold it half a sin
  To put in words the grief I feel;
  For words, like Nature, half reveal
And half conceal the Soul within.

But, for the unquiet heart and brain,   5
  A use in measured language lies;
  The sad mechanic exercise,
Like dull narcotics, numbing pain.

In words, like weeds, I'll wrap me o'er,
  Like coarsest clothes against the cold: 10
  But that large grief which these enfold
Is given in outline and no more.

4] L.MS, Trial, 1850A-; *not in* T.MS

5] L.MS, Trial, 1850A-; *not in* T.MS
  7 sad] Trial-; set L.MS

6

One writes, that 'Other friends remain,'
   That 'Loss is common to the race' —
   And common is the commonplace,
And vacant chaff well meant for grain.

That loss is common would not make   5
   My own less bitter, rather more:
   Too common! Never morning wore
To evening, but some heart did break.

O father, wheresoe'er thou be,
   Who pledgest now thy gallant son;   10
   A shot, ere half thy draught be done,
Hath still'd the life that beat from thee.

O mother, praying God will save
   Thy sailor, — while thy head is bow'd,
   His heavy-shotted hammock-shroud   15
Drops in his vast and wandering grave.

Ye know no more than I who wrought
   At that last hour to please him well;
   Who mused on all I had to tell,
And something written, something thought;   20

Expecting still his advent home;
   And ever met him on his way
   With wishes, thinking, 'here to-day,'
Or 'here to-morrow will he come.'

O somewhere, meek, unconscious dove,   25
   That sittest ranging golden hair;
   And glad to find thyself so fair,
Poor child, that waitest for thy love!

For now her father's chimney glows
   In expectation of a guest;   30
   And thinking 'this will please him best,'
She takes a riband or a rose;

6] L.MS, Trial, 1850A-; *not in* T.MS
   10 Who] 1855-; That L.MS-1851B   25 O] L.MS, 1850B-; O! Trial-1850A

For he will see them on to-night;
　　And with the thought her colour burns;
　　And, having left the glass, she turns   35
Once more to set a ringlet right;

And, even when she turn'd, the curse
　　Had fallen, and her future Lord
　　Was drown'd in passing thro' the ford,
Or kill'd in falling from his horse.   40

O what to her shall be the end?
　　And what to me remains of good?
　　To her, perpetual maidenhood,
And unto me no second friend.

7

Dark house, by which once more I stand
　　Here in the long unlovely street,
　　Doors, where my heart was used to beat
So quickly, waiting for a hand,

A hand that can be clasp'd no more —   5
　　Behold me, for I cannot sleep,
　　And like a guilty thing I creep
At earliest morning to the door.

He is not here; but far away
　　The noise of life begins again,   10
　　And ghastly thro' the drizzling rain
On the bald street breaks the blank day.

8

A happy lover who has come
　　To look on her that loves him well,

7] H.Lpr.104, 1850A-; *not in* T.MS, L.MS, Trial
　　　3 Doors,] 1850A-; Door, H.Lpr.104   4] 1850A-; So quickly waiting for
the hand H.Lpr.104 *2nd reading*; In expectation of his hand H.Lpr.104 *1st reading*
5 A] 1850A-; The H.Lpr.104   7 And] 1850A-; But H.Lpr. 104   11
drizzling] 1850A-; dripping H.Lpr.104

8] 1850A-; *not in* T.MS, L.MS, Trial

Who 'lights and rings the gateway bell,
And learns her gone and far from home;

He saddens, all the magic light   5
    Dies off at once from bower and hall,
    And all the place is dark, and all
The chambers emptied of delight:

So find I every pleasant spot
    In which we two were wont to meet,   10
    The field, the chamber and the street,
For all is dark where thou art not.

Yet as that other, wandering there
    In those deserted walks, may find
    A flower beat with rain and wind,   15
Which once she foster'd up with care;

So seems it in my deep regret,
    O my forsaken heart, with thee
    And this poor flower of poesy
Which little cared for fades not yet.   20

But since it pleased a vanish'd eye,
    I go to plant it on his tomb,
    That if it can it there may bloom,
Or dying, there at least may die.

9

Fair ship, that from the Italian shore
    Sailest the placid ocean-plains
    With my lost Arthur's loved remains,
Spread thy full wings, and waft him o'er.

So draw him home to those that mourn   5
    In vain; a favourable speed

---

3 'lights] 1855–; lights 1850A–1851B

9] H.Nbk.16, H.Nbk.17 (1–6 only, because after Ruffle T. stopped writing), H.Lpr.98, Heath MS, T.Nbk., Hn.Nbk., H.Lpr.101, H.Lpr.100 (a detached leaf from T.MS), L.MS, Trial, 1850A–
    2 placid] H.Nbk.16 2nd reading–; glassy H.Nbk.16 1st reading   5–8]
H.Nbk.16 2nd reading, revised– (some later differences in spelling and punctuation are in Minor Variants);

Ruffle thy mirror'd mast, and lead
Thro' prosperous floods his holy urn.

All night no ruder air perplex
    Thy sliding keel, till Phosphor, bright   10
    As our pure love, thro' early light
Shall glimmer on the dewy decks.

Sphere all your lights around, above;
    Sleep, gentle heavens, before the prow;
    Sleep, gentle winds, as he sleeps now,   15
My friend, the brother of my love;

My Arthur, whom I shall not see
    Till all my widow'd race be run;
    Dear as the mother to the son,
More than my brothers are to me.   20

10

I hear the noise about thy keel;
    I hear the bell struck in the night:
    I see the cabin-window bright;
I see the sailor at the wheel.

Thou bring'st the sailor to his wife,   5
    And travell'd men from foreign lands;

Convoy thy charge to those that mourn
In vain for him. A happy speed
    -are tight,
All day strain all thy cords, & lead
Thro' prosperous floods his holy urn!
               H.Nbk.16 *1st reading*

So draw him home
Draw thy dear freight to those that mourn
    In vain. A favourable speed
    Ruffle thy mirrored mast, & lead
Thro' prosperous floods his holy urn!
               H.Nbk.16 *2nd reading*

Heath MS *agrees with the revised 2nd reading. The revision in line 5 is in Tennyson's hand*   7-20] *Not in* H.Nbk.17   13 lights] Heath MS (lights:), T.Nbk.-; light H.Nbk.16; light, H.Lpr.98   15 winds,] Hn.Nbk., T.Nbk. *and* L.MS (winds), H.Lpr.101, H.Lpr.100, Trial-; waves, H.Nbk.16-Heath MS   17 Arthur,] H.Lpr.98, H.Lpr.101, H.Lpr.100, 1850B-; Arthur-, H.Nbk.16; Arthur T.Nbk., Hn.Nbk., L.MS; Arthur! Trial, 1850A

10] L.MS, **Trial, 1850A-**; *not in* T.MS

And letters unto trembling hands;
And, thy dark freight, a vanish'd life.

So bring him: we have idle dreams:
  This look of quiet flatters thus
  Our home-bred fancies: O to us,
The fools of habit, sweeter seems

To rest beneath the clover sod,
  That takes the sunshine and the rains,
  Or where the kneeling hamlet drains
The chalice of the grapes of God;

Than if with thee the roaring wells
  Should gulf him fathom-deep in brine;
  And hands so often clasp'd in mine,
Should toss with tangle and with shells.

10

15

20

11

Calm is the morn without a sound,
  Calm as to suit a calmer grief,
  And only thro' the faded leaf
The chestnut pattering to the ground:

Calm and deep peace on this high wold,
  And on these dews that drench the furze,
  And all the silvery gossamers
That twinkle into green and gold:

Calm and still light on yon great plain
  That sweeps with all its autumn bowers,
  And crowded farms and lessening towers,
To mingle with the bounding main:

Calm and deep peace in this wide air,
  These leaves that redden to the fall;

5

10

---

8 thy dark freight,] L.MS *2nd reading-*; dearer yet, L.MS *1st reading*
O] L.MS *2nd reading-*; that L.MS *1st reading*

11] L.MS, **Trial, 1850A-**; *not in* T.MS
  4 chestnut] L.MS, **1870-**; chesnut **Trial-1869**   6 these] L.MS *2nd reading-*; the L.MS *1st reading*   14 These] L.MS *2nd reading-*; And L.MS *1st reading*

11

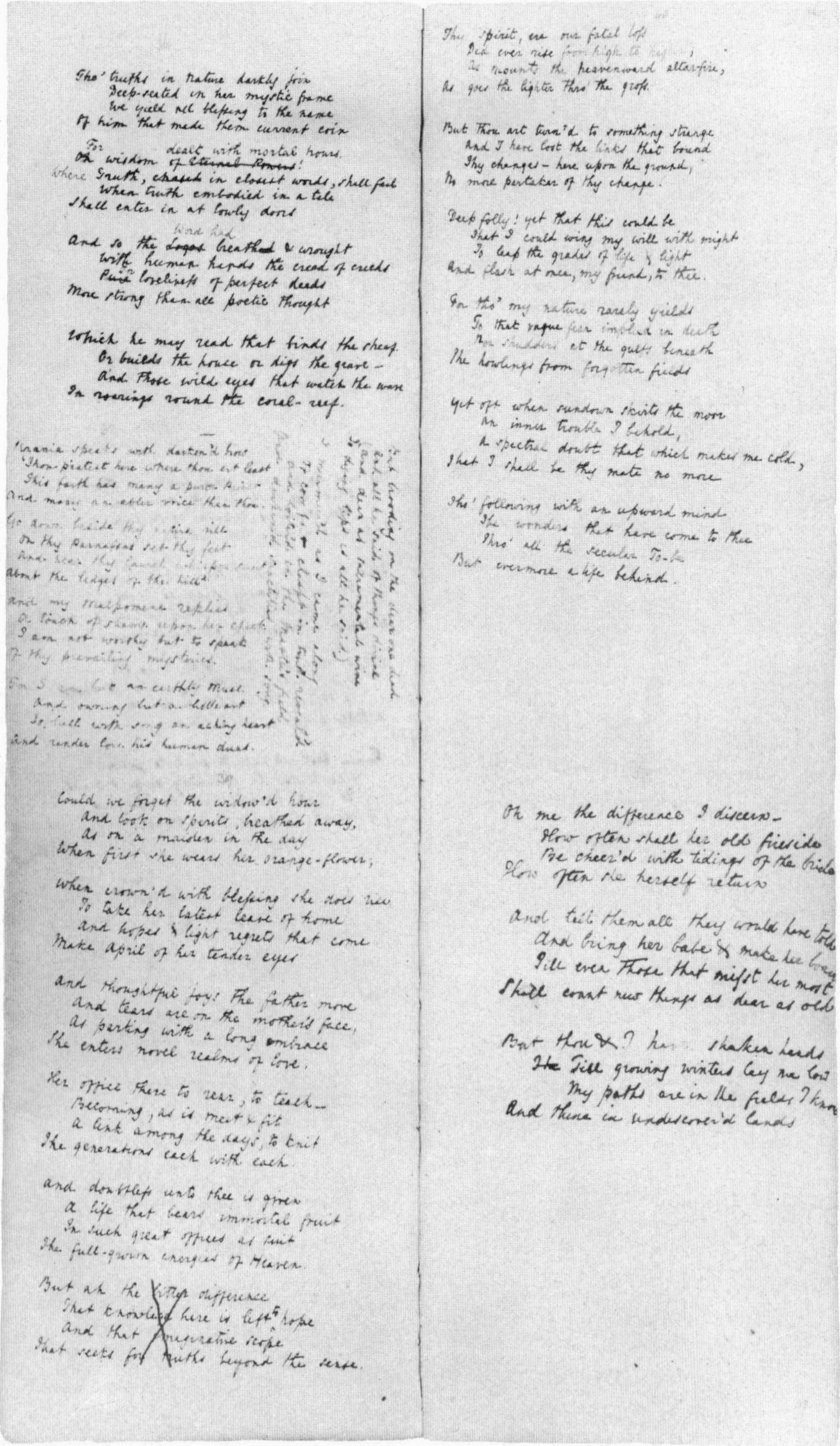

Tho' truths in nature darkly join
Deep-seated in her mystic frame
We yield all blessing to the name
Of him that made them current coin

For wisdom dealt with mortal powers
Oh wisdom of Eternal [?]
Where Truth, chased in closet words, shall fail
When truth embodied in a tale
Shall enter in at lowly doors

And so the Word had breath & wrought
With human hands the creed of creeds
Pure loveliness of perfect deeds
More strong than all poetic thought

Which he may read that binds the sheaf
Or builds the house or digs the grave —
And those wild eyes that watch the wave
In roarings round the coral-reef.

Urania speaks with darkening brow
'Thou pratest here where thou art least
This faith has many a purer priest
And many an abler voice than thou.

Go down beside thy native rill
On the Parnassus set thy feet
And hear thy laurel whisper sweet
About the ledges of the hill.'

And my Melpomene replies
A touch of shame upon her cheek
I am not worthy but to speak
Of thy prevailing mysteries

For I am but an earthly Muse
And owning but a little art
To lull with song an aching heart
And render human dust.

Could we forget the widow'd hour
And look on spirits breathed away,
As on a maiden in the day
When first she wears her orange-flower;

When crown'd with blessing she doth rise
To take her latest leave of home
And hopes & light regrets that come
Make April of her tender eyes

And thoughtful joy! The father move
And tears are on the mother's face,
At parting with a long embrace
She enters novel realms of love.

Her office there to rear, to teach —
Becoming, as is meet & fit
A link among the days, to knit
The generations each with each.

And doubtless unto thee is given
A life that bears immortal fruit
In such great offices as suit
The full-grown energies of Heaven

But ah the [?] difference
That troubles here is left [?] hope
And that [?] scope
That seeks for Truth beyond the sense.

Thy spirit, ere our fatal loss
Did ever rise from high to higher
As mounts the heavenward altar-fire,
As goes the lighter thro' the gross

But thou art turn'd to something strange
And I have lost the links that bound
Thy changes — here upon the ground,
No more partaker of thy change.

Deep folly! yet that this could be
That I could wing my will with might
To leap the grades of life & light
And flash at once, my friend, to thee.

For tho' my nature rarely yields
To that vague fear implied in death
Nor shudders at the gulfs beneath
The howlings from forgotten fields

Yet oft when sundown skirts the moor
An inner trouble I behold,
A spectral doubt that which makes me cold,
That I shall be thy mate no more

Tho' following with an upward mind
The wonders that have come to thee
Thro' all the secular to-be
But evermore a life behind.

Oh me the difference I discern —
How often shall her old fireside
Be cheer'd with tidings of the bride
How often she herself return

And tell them all they would have told
And bring her babe & make her [?]
I'll ever those that miss'd her most
Shall count new things as dear as old

But thou & I have shaken hands
Till growing winters lay me low
My paths are in the fields I know
And thine in undiscover'd lands

Plate II Sections *36*, *37*, *40*, *41*, in Trinity College, Cambridge MS 0.15.13, ff.15[v], 16[r]

And in my heart, if calm at all,   15
If any calm, a calm despair:

Calm on the seas, and silver sleep,
    And waves that sway themselves in rest,
    And dead calm in that noble breast
Which heaves but with the heaving deep.   20

12

Lo, as a dove when up she springs
    To bear thro' Heaven a tale of woe,
    Some dolorous message knit below
The wild pulsation of her wings;

Like her I go; I cannot stay;   5
    I leave this mortal ark behind,
    A weight of nerves without a mind,
And leave the cliffs, and haste away

O'er ocean-mirrors rounded large,
    And reach the glow of southern skies,   10
    And see the sails at distance rise,
And linger weeping on the marge,

And saying; 'Comes he thus, my friend?
    Is this the end of all my care?'
    And circle moaning in the air: 15
'Is this the end? Is this the end?'

And forward dart again, and play
    About the prow, and back return
    To where the body sits, and learn
That I have been an hour away.   20

13

Tears of the widower, when he sees
    A late-lost form that sleep reveals,

12] L.MS, Trial, 1850A–; *not in* T.MS
   1 Lo,] 1850B–; Lo! L.MS–1850A

13] T.MS (1–16 *only*), L.MS, Trial, 1850A–

And moves his doubtful arms, and feels
Her place is empty, fall like these;

Which weep a loss for ever new,   5
  A void where heart on heart reposed;
  And, where warm hands have prest and closed,
Silence, till I be silent too.

Which weep the comrade of my choice,
  An awful thought, a life removed,   10
  The human-hearted man I loved,
A Spirit, not a breathing voice.

Come Time, and teach me, many years,
  I do not suffer in a dream;
  For now so strange do these things seem,   15
Mine eyes have leisure for their tears;

My fancies time to rise on wing,
  And glance about the approaching sails,
  As tho' they brought but merchants' bales,
And not the burthen that they bring.   20

14

If one should bring me this report,
  That thou hadst touch'd the land to-day,
  And I went down unto the quay,
And found thee lying in the port;

And standing, muffled round with woe,   5
  Should see thy passengers in rank
  Come stepping lightly down the plank,
And beckoning unto those they know;

And if along with these should come
  The man I held as half-divine;   10
  Should strike a sudden hand in mine,
And ask a thousand things of home;

15 For] L.MS–; But T.MS do these things] L.MS–; does this thing T.MS
17–20] *Not in* T.MS

14] L.MS, **Trial, 1850A**–; *not in* T.MS

And I should tell him all my pain,
  And how my life had droop'd of late,
  And he should sorrow o'er my state   15
And marvel what possess'd my brain;

And I perceived no touch of change,
  No hint of death in all his frame,
  But found him all in all the same,
I should not feel it to be strange.   20

15

To-night the winds begin to rise
  And roar from yonder dropping day:
  The last red leaf is whirl'd away,
The rooks are blown about the skies;

The forest crack'd, the waters curl'd,   5
  The cattle huddled on the lea;
  And wildly dash'd on tower and tree
The sunbeam strikes along the world:

And but for fancies, which aver
  That all thy motions gently pass   10
  Athwart a plane of molten glass,
I scarce could brook the strain and stir

That makes the barren branches loud;
  And but for fear it is not so,
  The wild unrest that lives in woe   15
Would dote and pore on yonder cloud

That rises upward always higher,
  And onward drags a labouring breast,
  And topples round the dreary west,
A looming bastion fringed with fire.   20

15] L.MS, Trial, 1850A-; not in T.MS
   1 begin] L.MS, 1855-; began Trial-1851B (error)

16

What words are these have fall'n from me?
  Can calm despair and wild unrest
  Be tenants of a single breast,
Or sorrow such a changeling be?

Or doth she only seem to take   5
  The touch of change in calm or storm;
  But knows no more of transient form
In her deep self, than some dead lake

That holds the shadow of a lark
  Hung in the shadow of a heaven?   10
  Or has the shock, so harshly given,
Confused me like the unhappy bark

That strikes by night a craggy shelf,
  And staggers blindly ere she sink?
  And stunn'd me from my power to think   15
And all my knowledge of myself;

And made me that delirious man
  Whose fancy fuses old and new,
  And flashes into false and true,
And mingles all without a plan?   20

17

Thou comest, much wept for: such a breeze
  Compell'd thy canvas, and my prayer
  Was as the whisper of an air
To breathe thee over lonely seas.

16] L.MS, **Trial,** 1850A-; *not in* T.MS
    20 And mingles all] L.MS *2nd reading-*; In all his words L.MS *1st reading*

17] H.Nbk.17, T.Nbk., Heath MS, Hn.Nbk., L.MS, **Trial,** 1850A-; *not in* T.MS
    1-7] Heath MS *has these lines, including the revisions, in Tennyson's hand*
    2-3] L.MS (. . . canvas . . .), **Trial–**;
    Was on thee, hollowing all the sail. [thee T.Nbk.; thee . . . sail Heath MS
    My prayer was, likewise, as a gale   [was . . . gale T.Nbk., Heath MS
                    H.Nbk.17 *1st reading*, T.Nbk.,
                    Heath MS *1st reading*

For I in spirit saw thee move   5
Thro' circles of the bounding sky,
Week after week: the days go by:
Come quick, thou bringest all I love.

Henceforth, wherever thou may'st roam,
My blessing, like a line of light,   10
Is on the waters day and night,
And like a beacon guards thee home.

So may whatever tempest mars
Mid-ocean, spare thee, sacred bark;
And balmy drops in summer dark   15
Slide from the bosom of the stars.

So kind an office hath been done,
Such precious relics brought by thee;
The dust of him I shall not see
Till all my widow'd race be run.   20

        Was on thee, hollowing all the sail.
        My prayer was also like a gale
                H.Nbk.17 *2nd reading*

        Compelled the canvas & my prayer
        Was as the whisper of an air
                Heath MS *2nd reading*

        Compell'd the canvass, . . .
                Hn.Nbk.

7-8 the . . . love.] Trial-; 'The . . . love.' H.Nbk.17; 'the . . . T.Nbk.; The . . . love
Heath MS; The . . . Hn.Nbk.; 'The . . . L.MS   10 like] H.Nbk.17 *1st reading*,
T.Nbk.-; as H.Nbk.17 *2nd reading*   12 guards] L.MS-; leads H.Nbk.17-
Hn.Nbk.   13-16] H.Nbk.17 *has instead these lines:*
        May never adverse wind incline
          Thee moving swift thy burnisht sides
          From port to port in glassy tides
          Whose loudest motion comes from thine
19-20] L.MS-;
          More than my brothers are to me   [me, Hn.Nbk.
          Dear as the mother to the son.
                H.Nbk.17, Hn.Nbk.

          Dear as a brother is to me
          Dear as the mother to the son.   [son Heath MS
                T.Nbk., Heath MS
(Heath MS *has an error in transcription:* ~~mother~~ brother)

18

'Tis well; 'tis something; we may stand
    Where he in English earth is laid,
    And from his ashes may be made
The violet of his native land.

'Tis little; but it looks in truth   5
    As if the quiet bones were blest
    Among familiar names to rest
And in the places of his youth.

Come then, pure hands, and bear the head
    That sleeps or wears the mask of sleep,   10
    And come, whatever loves to weep,
And hear the ritual of the dead.

Ah yet, ev'n yet, if this might be,
    I, falling on his faithful heart,
    Would breathing thro' his lips impart   15
The life that almost dies in me;

That dies not, but endures with pain,
    And slowly forms the firmer mind,
    Treasuring the look it cannot find,
The words that are not heard again.   20

18] H.Nbk.10 (13–20, 1-4 *only; see headnote in Commentary*), H.Nbk.17 (1–4 *only*), T.Nbk., Heath MS, Hn.Nbk., Sparrow MS(18) (*a detached leaf from* T.MS), L.MS, **Trial**, 1850A–
    1] H.Nbk.17- (*except for, in some cases, minor variants*); And yet 'tis something here to stand H.Nbk.10 (*in which this line opens the final stanza of the early version of the section*)   5-20] *Not in* H.Nbk.17   5-12] *Not in* H.Nbk.10   13] L.MS (. . . yet – ev'n yet – . . . be –), **Trial** (Ah! yet – . . . yet – . . .), 1850A (Ah! . . .), 1850B–;
        Oh yet that – tho' it cannot be –
                            H.Nbk.10

    Ah yet – ev'n yet – if this may be –   [be Heath MS, Sparrow MS(18)
                    T.Nbk., Heath MS, Hn.Nbk.,
                    Sparrow MS(18)
15 Would] Heath MS *2nd reading*, Hn.Nbk. *and* Sparrow MS(18) (Would,), L.MS–; Could H.Nbk.10; Will, T.Nbk., Heath MS *1st reading*   20 that] L.MS–; which H.Nbk.10–Sparrow MS(18)

19

The Danube to the Severn gave
   The darken'd heart that beat no more;
   They laid him by the pleasant shore,
And in the hearing of the wave.

There twice a day the Severn fills;   5
   The salt sea-water passes by,
   And hushes half the babbling Wye,
And makes a silence in the hills.

The Wye is hush'd nor moved along,
   And hush'd my deepest grief of all,   10
   When fill'd with tears that cannot fall,
I brim with sorrow drowning song.

The tide flows down, the wave again
   Is vocal in its wooded walls;
   My deeper anguish also falls,   15
And I can speak a little then.

20

The lesser griefs that may be said,
   That breathe a thousand tender vows,
   Are but as servants in a house
Where lies the master newly dead;

Who speak their feeling as it is,   5
   And weep the fulness from the mind:
   'It will be hard,' they say, 'to find
Another service such as this.'

My lighter moods are like to these,
   That out of words a comfort win;   10
   But there are other griefs within,
And tears that at their fountain freeze;

For by the hearth the children sit
   Cold in that atmosphere of Death,

19] Heath MS, Sparrow MS(19) (*a detached leaf from* T.MS), L.MS, **Trial, 1850A–**

20] L.MS, **Trial, 1850A–**; *not in* T.MS

And scarce endure to draw the breath,   15
Or like to noiseless phantoms flit:

But open converse is there none,
So much the vital spirits sink
To see the vacant chair, and think,
'How good! how kind! and he is gone.'   20

21

I sing to him that rests below,
And, since the grasses round me wave,
I take the grasses of the grave,
And make them pipes whereon to blow.

The traveller hears me now and then,   5
And sometimes harshly will he speak:
'This fellow would make weakness weak,
And melt the waxen hearts of men.'

Another answers, 'Let him be,
He loves to make parade of pain,   10
That with his piping he may gain
The praise that comes to constancy.'

A third is wroth: 'Is this an hour
For private sorrow's barren song,
When more and more the people throng   15
The chairs and thrones of civil power?

'A time to sicken and to swoon,
When Science reaches forth her arms
To feel from world to world, and charms
Her secret from the latest moon?'   20

20] **Trial**–; How good how kind and he is gone. L.MS

21] Hn.Nbk. (1–8 *only*), H.Lpr.103 (*a detached leaf from* T.MS), L.MS, **Trial**, 1850A–
6 sometimes] H.Lpr.103–; pausing Hn.Nbk.   8 a–d] Hn.Nbk., H.Lpr.103 (*where it is deleted*):
        Yet I as soon would use [preach H.Lpr.103] a creed
          Whose hatred [baseness H.Lpr.103] levels humankind
          Or help a canker'd heart [an old man's vice H.Lpr.103] to find
        Low motives for a noble deed.

Behold, ye speak an idle thing:
    Ye never knew the sacred dust:
    I do but sing because I must,
And pipe but as the linnets sing:

And one is glad; her note is gay,   25
    For now her little ones have ranged;
    And one is sad; her note is changed,
Because her brood is stol'n away.

22

The path by which we twain did go,
    Which led by tracts that pleased us well,
    Thro' four sweet years arose and fell,
From flower to flower, from snow to snow:

And we with singing cheer'd the way,   5
    And, crown'd with all the season lent,
    From April on to April went,
And glad at heart from May to May:

But where the path we walk'd began
    To slant the fifth autumnal slope,   10
    As we descended following Hope,
There sat the Shadow fear'd of man;

Who broke our fair companionship,
    And spread his mantle dark and cold,
    And wrapt thee formless in the fold,   15
And dull'd the murmur on thy lip,

9-28] *Not in* Hn.Nbk.   25 And one is glad;] 1855-; And unto one H.Lpr.
103-1851B   27 And one is sad;] 1855-; And unto one H.Lpr.103-1851B

22] H.Lpr.103 (*a detached leaf from* T.MS), L.MS, Trial, 1850A-
    3 four] Trial-; three H.Lpr.103, L.MS   4 a-d] *deleted in* H.Lpr.103
and transferred to 23.21-4:
                And many an old Philosophy
                On Argive heights divinely sang
                And round us all the thicket rang
                To many a flute of Arcady
6 lent,] L.MS (lent), Trial-; sent H.Lpr.103   8 glad at heart] L.MS-; gaily
stept H.Lpr.103   9 where] H.Lpr.103 *2nd reading*-; when H.Lpr.103 *1st
reading*   10 To slant the fifth] Trial-; It's fourth ~~Aut~~ long H.Lpr.103; Its
fourth long L.MS   11] L.MS (. . . Hope), Trial-; And we came down it high
in hope H.Lpr.103   13 our] L.MS-; the H.Lpr.103   14 his] H.Lpr.103
2nd reading-; a H.Lpr.103 *1st reading*   15 the] L.MS-; its H.Lpr.103

And bore thee where I could not see
　　Nor follow, tho' I walk in haste,
　　And think, that somewhere in the waste
The Shadow sits and waits for me.   20

23

Now, sometimes in my sorrow shut,
　　Or breaking into song by fits,
　　Alone, alone, to where he sits,
The Shadow cloak'd from head to foot,

Who keeps the keys of all the creeds,   5
　　I wander, often falling lame,
　　And looking back to whence I came,
Or on to where the pathway leads;

And crying, How changed from where it ran
　　Thro' lands where not a leaf was dumb;   10
　　But all the lavish hills would hum
The murmur of a happy Pan:

When each by turns was guide to each,
　　And Fancy light from Fancy caught,
　　And Thought leapt out to wed with Thought   15
Ere Thought could wed itself with Speech;

And all we met was fair and good,
　　And all was good that Time could bring,
　　And all the secret of the Spring
Moved in the chambers of the blood;   20

And many an old philosophy
　　On Argive heights divinely sang,
　　And round us all the thicket rang
To many a flute of Arcady.

23] T.MS, L.MS, **Trial,** 1850A–
　　 1 Now,] L.MS (Now), **Trial–**; And T.MS   3 Alone, alone,] T.MS *2nd*
reading (alone alone), L.MS (Alone alone), **Trial–**; I move alone T.MS *1st reading*
6] T.MS *2nd reading* (*no commas*), L.MS (. . . lame), **Trial–**; The secret oft I
falter lame T.MS *1st reading*   7 And] T.MS *2nd reading–*; In T.MS *1st reading*

24

And was the day of my delight
　　As pure and perfect as I say?
　　The very source and fount of Day
Is dash'd with wandering isles of night.

If all was good and fair we met,   5
　　This earth had been the Paradise
　　It never look'd to human eyes
Since our first Sun arose and set.

And is it that the haze of grief
　　Makes former gladness loom so great?   10
　　The lowness of the present state,
That sets the past in this relief?

Or that the past will always win
　　A glory from its being far;
　　And orb into the perfect star   15
We saw not, when we moved therein?

25

I know that this was Life, — the track
　　Whereon with equal feet we fared;
　　And then, as now, the day prepared
The daily burden for the back.

But this it was that made me move   5
　　As light as carrier-birds in air;
　　I loved the weight I had to bear,
Because it needed help of Love:

24] T.MS, L.MS, **Trial**, 1850A-
　　3 The very source and fount] 1850A-; We know the very Lord T.MS-**Trial**
6 been] T.MS *2nd reading*-; seem'd T.MS *1st reading*　　8] 1875-; Since
Adam left his garden yet. T.MS-1874 (. . . yet T.MS)　　10 Makes former
gladness loom] 1851A-; Hath made my former joy T.MS; Hath stretch'd my
former joy L.MS-1850C　　11 the] L.MS-; my T.MS　　12 this] L.MS-;
such T.MS

25] T.MS, L.MS, **Trial**, 1850A-
　　4 burden] **Trial**-; burthen T.MS, L.MS

Nor could I weary, heart or limb,
    When mighty Love would cleave in twain   10
    The lading of a single pain,
And part it, giving half to him.

26

Still onward winds the dreary way;
    I with it; for I long to prove
    No lapse of moons can canker Love,
Whatever fickle tongues may say.

And if that eye which watches guilt   5
    And goodness, and hath power to see
    Within the green the moulder'd tree,
And towers fall'n as soon as built —

Oh, if indeed that eye foresee
    Or see (in Him is no before)   10
    In more of life true life no more
And Love the indifference to be,

Then might I find, ere yet the morn
    Breaks hither over Indian seas,
    That Shadow waiting with the keys,   15
To shroud me from my proper scorn.

27

I envy not in any moods
    The captive void of noble rage,
    The linnet born within the cage,
That never knew the summer woods:

9 could] L.MS, Trial-; was T.MS

26] L.MS, Trial, 1850A-; *not in* T.MS
    5 which] Trial-; that L.MS   11] L.MS *2nd reading,* Trial (. . . more,),
1850A-; In Being that it is no more L.MS *1st reading*   12 And] L.MS *2nd
reading-;* In L.MS *1st reading*   13 Then] 1851B-; So L.MS-1851A   14
Indian] 1850A-; Eastern L.MS, Trial   16 shroud] 1855-; cloak L.MS-1851B

27] L.MS, Trial, 1850A-; *not in* T.MS

I envy not the beast that takes   5
   His license in the field of time,
   Unfetter'd by the sense of crime,
To whom a conscience never wakes;

Nor, what may count itself as blest,
   The heart that never plighted troth   10
   But stagnates in the weeds of sloth;
Nor any want-begotten rest.

I hold it true, whate'er befall;
   I feel it, when I sorrow most;
   'Tis better to have loved and lost   15
Than never to have loved at all.

28

The time draws near the birth of Christ:
   The moon is hid; the night is still;
   The Christmas bells from hill to hill
Answer each other in the mist.

Four voices of four hamlets round,   5
   From far and near, on mead and moor,
   Swell out and fail, as if a door
Were shut between me and the sound:

Each voice four changes on the wind,
   That now dilate, and now decrease,   10
   Peace and goodwill, goodwill and peace,
Peace and goodwill, to all mankind.

This year I slept and woke with pain,
   I almost wish'd no more to wake,
   And that my hold on life would break   15
Before I heard those bells again:

13 hold it true, whate'er] L.MS *2nd reading*-; [*illegible words*] *1st reading*

28] T.Nbk., T.MS, L.MS, **Trial, 1850A**-
   1 The time draws] T.MS-; It draweth near T.Nbk.   4 in] T.Nbk., L.MS-;
thro'' T.MS   6 From far and] L.MS-; Some far, some T.Nbk. *and* T.MS
(*which has no comma*)   7 Swell out and] L.MS-; Voices that T.Nbk.;
They rise and T.MS   8-9] *Missing in* T.Nbk. *because part of leaf is cut out*
15-16] L.MS (. . . again . . .), **Trial** (. . . again.), 1850A-;

But they my troubled spirit rule,
For they controll'd me when a boy;
They bring me sorrow touch'd with joy,
The merry merry bells of Yule.   20

29

With such compelling cause to grieve
As daily vexes household peace,
And chains regret to his decease,
How dare we keep our Christmas-eve;

Which brings no more a welcome guest   5
To enrich the threshold of the night
With shower'd largess of delight
In dance and song and game and jest?

Yet go, and while the holly boughs
Entwine the cold baptismal font,   10
Make one wreath more for Use and Wont,
That guard the portals of the house;

I almost thought my heart would break
To hear those merry bells again
                    T.Nbk.

And that my hold of life would break
Before I heard those bells again
                    T.MS

29] T.MS, L.MS, **Trial, 1850A–**
False start (which is deleted) in T.MS
          My sister with such cause to grieve
              As that which drains our days of peace
              And fetters thought to his decease –
          How dare we keep our Christmas-Eve?
    2 daily] T.MS *2nd reading–*; that which T.MS *1st reading*   4 How dare
we keep our] L.MS–; We scarce can keep this T.MS   5–7] L.MS–;
              The last brought here a welcome guest
              And showering largess of delight
              Enriched the threshold of the night
                    T.MS
8 In] L.MS–; With T.MS   8 a–d]
              But this – to keep it like the last
              To keep it even for his sake
              Lest one more link should seem to break
              And Death sweep all into the Past
                    T.MS
9 Yet go, and] L.MS (... go &,), **Trial–**; So be it &, T.MS

Old sisters of a day gone by,
　　Gray nurses, loving nothing new;
　　Why should they miss their yearly due　　15
Before their time? They too will die.

30

With trembling fingers did we weave
　　The holly round the Christmas hearth;
　　A rainy cloud possess'd the earth,
And sadly fell our Christmas-eve.

At our old pastimes in the hall　　5
　　We gambol'd, making vain pretence
　　Of gladness, with an awful sense
Of one mute Shadow watching all.

We paused: the winds were in the beech:
　　We heard them sweep the winter land;　　10
　　And in a circle hand-in-hand
Sat silent, looking each at each.

Then echo-like our voices rang;
　　We sung, tho' every eye was dim,
　　A merry song we sang with him　　15
Last year: impetuously we sang:

We ceased: a gentler feeling crept
　　Upon us: surely rest is meet:
　　'They rest,' we said, 'their sleep is sweet,'
And silence follow'd, and we wept.　　20

Our voices took a higher range;
　　Once more we sang: 'They do not die

30] T.Nbk., Heath MS, Hn.Nbk., H.Lpr.101, T.MS, L.MS, **Trial, 1850A-**
　　7] T.Nbk. *2nd reading (no comma)*, Heath MS, Hn.Nbk.-L.MS (*all have no comma*), **Trial-**; Despite of that restraining sense T.Nbk. *1st reading*　　20
And silence follow'd,] Hn.Nbk. *2nd reading*, L.MS *2nd reading (no comma)*,
Trial-; We kist each other T.Nbk., Heath MS (kiss'd), Hn.Nbk. *1st reading* (kisst),
H.Lpr.101, T.MS, L.MS *1st reading* (kisst)　　22-32 'They . . . veil.' . . . born.]
Trial, 1850B-; 'They . . . veil . . . born. T.Nbk.; they . . . veil. . . . born Heath MS,
H.Lpr.101; They . . . veil . . . . born. Hn.Nbk., T.MS; they . . . veil. . . . born.
L.MS; 'They . . . veil. . . . born.' **1850A**

Nor lose their mortal sympathy,
Nor change to us, although they change;

'Rapt from the fickle and the frail   25
With gather'd power, yet the same,
Pierces the keen seraphic flame
From orb to orb, from veil to veil.'

Rise, happy morn, rise, holy morn,
Draw forth the cheerful day from night: 30
O Father, touch the east, and light
The light that shone when Hope was born.

31

When Lazarus left his charnel-cave,
And home to Mary's house return'd,
Was this demanded — if he yearn'd
To hear her weeping by his grave?

'Where wert thou, brother, those four days?'   5
There lives no record of reply,
Which telling what it is to die
Had surely added praise to praise.

From every house the neighbours met,
The streets were fill'd with joyful sound,   10

24] T.Nbk. *2nd reading– (except for, in some cases, minor variants)*; Tho' burning
up from change to change. T.Nbk. *1st reading*   32 Hope] T.Nbk.– (hope),
but Hn.Nbk. *reads* ~~truth~~ Hope

31] T.Nbk. *has two drafts* (a, b) *of 31 and 32 written as one section (see Plate I).*
T.Nbk.a *is deleted. Both* T.Nbk.a *and* T.Nbk.b *have 31*.1–8 *(only)*, Heath MS,
Moxon MS, H.Lpr.101, T.MS, L.MS, **Trial, 1850A–**   1–3]
                When rose the corpse from out his cave,
                Did Mary ask of him she loved,
                If any time the spirit moved
                                    T.Nbk.a
1 his] Moxon MS–; the T.Nbk.b, Heath MS   4 by] L.MS–; at T.Nbk.a–T.MS
5–8]   Or told he what it is to die
                An answer adding praise to praise?
                Where wert thou, brother, those four days?
                There lives no record of reply.
                                    T.Nbk.a
8] Heath Ms– (. . . praise L.MS); Had filled the measure of her praise. T.Nbk.b
9–16] *Not in* T.Nbk.a, b   10 fill'd] Heath MS (filled), Moxon MS, T.MS–;
lined H.Lpr.101 *(error in transcription?)*

A solemn gladness even crown'd
The purple brows of Olivet.

Behold a man raised up by Christ!
The rest remaineth unreveal'd;
He told it not; or something seal'd   15
The lips of that Evangelist.

32

Her eyes are homes of silent prayer,
    Nor other thought her mind admits
    But, he was dead, and there he sits,
And he that brought him back is there.

Then one deep love doth supersede   5
    All other, when her ardent gaze
    Roves from the living brother's face,
And rests upon the Life indeed.

All subtle thought, all curious fears,
    Borne down by gladness so complete,   10
    She bows, she bathes the Saviour's feet
With costly spikenard and with tears.

Thrice blest whose lives are faithful prayers,
    Whose loves in higher love endure;
    What souls possess themselves so pure,   15
Or is there blessedness like theirs?

13 raised up] H.Lpr.101-; upraised Heath MS, Moxon MS

32] T.Nbk. *has two drafts* (a, b) *of 31 and 32 written as one section (see Plate I).* T.Nbk.a *(which is deleted) has 32.5-16 (only),* T.Nbk.b *has 32.1-12 (only),* H.Lpr.101, T.MS, L.MS, **Trial, 1850A-**
    1-4] *Not in* T.Nbk.a   1 are] H.Lpr.101-; were T.Nbk.b   2] H.Lpr.
101-; She musing moved not lips or hands. T.Nbk.b   3 But,] H.Lpr.101-
L.MS *(all read* But), **Trial-**; For T.Nbk.b sits,] H.Lpr.101-L.MS *(all read* sits),
Trial-; stands T.Nbk.b   5 Then one deep love doth] H.Lpr.101-; One
deeper love did T.Nbk.a; Then one deep love did T.Nbk.b   7 Roves] H.Lpr.
101-; Roved T.Nbk.a, b   8 rests upon] H.Lpr.101-; rested on T.Nbk.a, b
11 bows,] H.Lpr.101 *and* T.MS (bows), L.MS-; bowed, T.Nbk.a, b she] T.Nbk.a,
b, L.MS-; & H.Lpr.101, T.MS   bathes] H.Lpr.101-; bathed T.Nbk.a, b   13-16]
Not in T.Nbk.b   13 Thrice blest] H.Lpr.101, **Trial-**; Happy, T.Nbk.a;
Thrice-blest T.MS, L.MS   15 What] H.Lpr.101-; No T.Nbk.a   16 Or]
H.Lpr.101-; Nor T.Nbk.a

33

O thou that after toil and storm
    Mayst seem to have reach'd a purer air,
    Whose faith has centre everywhere,
Nor cares to fix itself to form,

Leave thou thy sister when she prays,   5
    Her early Heaven, her happy views;
    Nor thou with shadow'd hint confuse
A life that leads melodious days.

Her faith thro' form is pure as thine,
    Her hands are quicker unto good: 10
    Oh, sacred be the flesh and blood
To which she links a truth divine!

See thou, that countest reason ripe
    In holding by the law within,
    Thou fail not in a world of sin,   15
And ev'n for want of such a type.

34

My own dim life should teach me this,
    That life shall live for evermore,
    Else earth is darkness at the core,
And dust and ashes all that is;

This round of green, this orb of flame,   5
    Fantastic beauty; such as lurks
    In some wild Poet, when he works
Without a conscience or an aim.

What then were God to such as I?
    'Twere hardly worth my while to choose   10

33] H.Lpr.101, T.MS, L.MS, **Trial, 1850A–**
    6 early] 1850A–; local H.Lpr.101–**Trial** (*Hallam Tennyson has written* early *in the margin of* T.MS)   10 Her hands are quicker unto] **Trial–**; Nor could thy vision bring her H.Lpr.101–L.MS   11 Oh,] **Trial–**; So H.Lpr.101–L.MS
12 divine!] **Trial–**; divine. H.Lpr.101, T.MS; divine L.MS

34] H.Lpr.101, T.MS, L.MS, **Trial, 1850A–**
    1] 1850A–; My own dark heart can teach me this H.Lpr.101, T.MS *1st reading*; My own dim life can teach me this, T.MS *2nd reading* (this), L.MS, **Trial**

Of things all mortal, or to use
A little patience ere I die;

'Twere best at once to sink to peace,
  Like birds the charming serpent draws,   15
  To drop head-foremost in the jaws
Of vacant darkness and to cease.

35

Yet if some voice that man could trust
  Should murmur from the narrow house,
  'The cheeks drop in; the body bows;
Man dies: nor is there hope in dust:'

Might I not say? 'Yet even here,   5
  But for one hour, O Love, I strive
  To keep so sweet a thing alive:'
But I should turn mine ears and hear

The moanings of the homeless sea,
  The sound of streams that swift or slow   10
  Draw down Aeonian hills, and sow
The dust of continents to be;

And Love would answer with a sigh,
  'The sound of that forgetful shore
  Will change my sweetness more and more,   15
Half-dead to know that I shall die.'

O me, what profits it to put
  An idle case? If Death were seen
  At first as Death, Love had not been,
Or been in narrowest working shut,   20

Mere fellowship of sluggish moods,
  Or in his coarsest Satyr-shape
  Had bruised the herb and crush'd the grape,
And bask'd and batten'd in the woods.

35] T.MS, L.MS, **Trial, 1850A–**
  1 man] L.MS–;men T.MS   11] T.MS *2nd reading and* L.MS (*no comma*),
Trial–; For millions of millenniums, sow T.MS *1st reading*   17 O me,]
1850B–; O me! T.MS–1850A

36

Tho' truths in manhood darkly join,
Deep-seated in our mystic frame,
We yield all blessing to the name
Of Him that made them current coin;

For Wisdom dealt with mortal powers,   5
Where truth in closest words shall fail,
When truth embodied in a tale
Shall enter in at lowly doors.

And so the Word had breath, and wrought
With human hands the creed of creeds   10
In loveliness of perfect deeds,
More strong than all poetic thought;

Which he may read that binds the sheaf,
Or builds the house, or digs the grave,
And those wild eyes that watch the wave   15
In roarings round the coral reef.

37

Urania speaks with darken'd brow:
'Thou pratest here where thou art least;
This faith has many a purer priest,
And many an abler voice than thou.

'Go down beside thy native rill,   5
On thy Parnassus set thy feet,

36] H.Lpr.101, T.MS, L.MS, Trial, 1850A–
     1 manhood] 1850A–; nature H.Lpr.101; Nature T.MS–Trial   2 our]
1850A–; her H.Lpr.101–Trial   5–6] L.MS– (*except, in some cases, for
punctuation and capitalization; see Minor Variants*);
     Oh wisdom of eternal Powers! [Eternal T.MS
          Truth chased in closest words shall fail [Truth, . . . words, . . . T.MS
                    H.Lpr.101, T.MS *1st reading*

For wisdom dealt with mortal hours.
     Where Truth, in closest words, shall fail
                    T.MS *2nd reading*
9 And so the Word had breath,] T.MS *2nd reading and* L.MS (*no comma*), Trial–;
And so the Logos breathed H.Lpr.101, T.MS *1st reading*   11 In] T.MS *2nd
reading*–; Pure H.Lpr.101, T.MS *1st reading*

37] T.MS, L.MS, Trial, 1850A–

And hear thy laurel whisper sweet
About the ledges of the hill.'

And my Melpomene replies,
    A touch of shame upon her cheek: 10
    'I am not worthy ev'n to speak
Of thy prevailing mysteries;

'For I am but an earthly Muse,
    And owning but a little art
    To lull with song an aching heart,   15
And render human love his dues;

'But brooding on the dear one dead,
    And all he said of things divine,
    (And dear to me as sacred wine
To dying lips is all he said),   20

'I murmur'd, as I came along,
    Of comfort clasp'd in truth reveal'd;
    And loiter'd in the master's field,
And darken'd sanctities with song.'

                    38

With weary steps I loiter on,
    Tho' always under alter'd skies
    The purple from the distance dies,
My prospect and horizon gone.

No joy the blowing season gives,   5
    The herald melodies of spring,
    But in the songs I love to sing
A doubtful gleam of solace lives.

If any care for what is here
    Survive in spirits render'd free,   10
    Then are these songs I sing of thee
Not all ungrateful to thine ear.

11 ev'n] 1855–; but T.MS–1851B   16 human love his] L.MS–; love his
human T.MS   19 to me as sacred] 1855–; as sacramental T.MS–1851B

38] T.MS, L.MS, Trial, 1850A–
    11 of] T.MS 2nd reading–; to T.MS 1st reading

39

Old warder of these buried bones,
   And answering now my random stroke
   With fruitful cloud and living smoke,
Dark yew, that graspest at the stones

And dippest toward the dreamless head,   5
   To thee too comes the golden hour
   When flower is feeling after flower;
But Sorrow — fixt upon the dead,

And darkening the dark graves of men, —
   What whisper'd from her lying lips?   10
   Thy gloom is kindled at the tips,
And passes into gloom again.

40

Could we forget the widow'd hour
   And look on Spirits breathed away,
   As on a maiden in the day
When first she wears her orange-flower!

When crown'd with blessing she doth rise   5
   To take her latest leave of home,
   And hopes and light regrets that come
Make April of her tender eyes;

And doubtful joys the father move,
   And tears are on the mother's face,   10
   As parting with a long embrace
She enters other realms of love;

Her office there to rear, to teach,
   Becoming as is meet and fit
   A link among the days, to knit   15
The generations each with each;

39] Beinecke MS, 1870-; *not in* T.MS-1869

40] T.MS, L.MS, **Trial, 1850A-**
   5 doth] L.MS-; does T.MS   9 doubtful] L.MS-; thoughtful T.MS   12
other] 1850A-; novel T.MS-Trial

And, doubtless, unto thee is given
  A life that bears immortal fruit
  In those great offices that suit
The full-grown energies of heaven.   20

Ay me, the difference I discern!
  How often shall her old fireside
  Be cheer'd with tidings of the bride,
How often she herself return,

And tell them all they would have told,   25
  And bring her babe, and make her boast,
  Till even those that miss'd her most
Shall count new things as dear as old:

But thou and I have shaken hands,
  Till growing winters lay me low;   30
  My paths are in the fields I know,
And thine in undiscover'd lands.

41

Thy spirit ere our fatal loss
  Did ever rise from high to higher;
  As mounts the heavenward altar-fire,
As flies the lighter thro' the gross.

But thou art turn'd to something strange,   5
  And I have lost the links that bound
  Thy changes; here upon the ground,
No more partaker of thy change.

19 those great offices that suit] 1877-; such great offices as suit T.MS-1875   20
a-d] *deleted in* T.MS:
            But ah the bitter difference
            That knowledge here is left to hope
            And that imaginative scope
            That seeks for truths beyond the sense.
21 Ay me,] L.MS *and* Trial (Ay me!), 1850A-; Oh me T.MS   30 Till] T.MS
2nd reading-; The T.MS *1st reading*

41] Hn.Nbk., T.MS, L.MS, **Trial**, 1850A-
  4 flies] L.MS-; goes Hn.Nbk., T.MS   8 a-d] *deleted in* Hn.Nbk:
            How far, how far gone upward now?
            Too far for me to catch the while
            The sweetness of thy proper smile
            Thro' those new splendours of thy brow!

Deep folly! yet that this could be —
   That I could wing my will with might   10
   To leap the grades of life and light,
And flash at once, my friend, to thee.

For tho' my nature rarely yields
   To that vague fear implied in death;
   Nor shudders at the gulfs beneath,   15
The howlings from forgotten fields;

Yet oft when sundown skirts the moor
   An inner trouble I behold,
   A spectral doubt which makes me cold,
That I shall be thy mate no more,   20

Tho' following with an upward mind
   The wonders that have come to thee,
   Thro' all the secular to-be,
But evermore a life behind.

42

I vex my heart with fancies dim:
   He still outstript me in the race;
   It was but unity of place
That made me dream I rank'd with him.

And so may Place retain us still,   5
   And he the much-beloved again,
   A lord of large experience, train
To riper growth the mind and will:

And what delights can equal those
   That stir the spirit's inner deeps,   10
   When one that loves but knows not, reaps
A truth from one that loves and knows?

10 I could] Hn.Nbk. *2nd reading*-; God would Hn.Nbk. *1st reading*   19
which] T.MS *alternative reading*, L.MS-; that Hn.Nbk., T.MS *1st reading*

42] Hn.Nbk., T.MS, L.MS, **Trial**, 1850A-
   10] T.MS *and* L.MS (*no comma*), **Trial**-; That stir the spirit thro' it's deeps
Hn.Nbk.

43

If Sleep and Death be truly one,
　And every spirit's folded bloom
　Thro' all its intervital gloom
In some long trance should slumber on;

Unconscious of the sliding hour,　　　　　5
　Bare of the body, might it last,
　And silent traces of the past
Be all the colour of the flower:

So then were nothing lost to man;
　So that still garden of the souls　　　10
　In many a figured leaf enrolls
The total world since life began;

And love will last as pure and whole
　As when he loved me here in Time,
　And at the spiritual prime　　　　　15
Rewaken with the dawning soul.

44

How fares it with the happy dead?
　For here the man is more and more;

43] T.MS (1-8, *a version of* 13-16, *but not* 9-12), L.MS (1-8, *the* T.MS *version
of* 13-16 *revised but deleted*, 9-12, *the revision of* 13-16 *written again*), Trial,
1850A-
　　7-8] 1850A-;
　　　　　And only memories of the Past　　[past Trial
　　　　Be scent & colour to the flower　　[and Trial flower. L.MS
　　　　　　　　T.MS, L.MS, Trial　　[　　flower: Trial
9-12] *Not in* T.MS　　　10 So] 1855-; But L.MS-1851B　　　13] 1855-;
And therefore that our love was true T.MS, L.MS; And thus our love, for ever
new, Trial; And love would last as pure and whole 1850A-1851B　　　14-16]
1850A-;
　　　　　　　　Would live thro' all & pure & whole
　　　　　　　　Within the bosom of the soul
　　　　　　Lie, lapt till dawn, like golden dew.
　　　　　　　　　　　　T.MS

　　　　　　　　Would last thro' all & pure & whole
　　　　　　　　Within the centre of the soul
　　　　　　Lie lapt till dawn like golden dew.
　　　　　　　　　　L.MS *2nd reading (1st reading has no
　　　　　　　　　　punctuation)*, Trial

44] Hn.Nbk., H.Lpr.101, T.MS, L.MS, Trial, 1850A-

But he forgets the days before
God shut the doorways of his head.

The days have vanish'd, tone and tint,   5
   And yet perhaps the hoarding sense
   Gives out at times (he knows not whence)
A little flash, a mystic hint;

And in the long harmonious years
   (If Death so taste Lethean springs),   10
   May some dim touch of earthly things
Surprise thee ranging with thy peers.

If such a dreamy touch should fall,
   O turn thee round, resolve the doubt;
   My guardian angel will speak out   15
In that high place, and tell thee all.

45

The baby new to earth and sky,
   What time his tender palm is prest
   Against the circle of the breast,
Has never thought that 'this is I:'

But as he grows he gathers much,   5
   And learns the use of 'I,' and 'me,'
   And finds 'I am not what I see,
And other than the things I touch.'

---

3 days] L.MS-; day Hn.Nbk.-T.MS   4 doorways of] L.MS-; doors within
Hn.Nbk.-T.MS   5-8] L.MS-;
          The days of many a tone & tint
             Have ceased to haunt the hoarding sense.
             Yet comes, he hardly knows from whence
          A flash from these, a mystic hint.
                   Hn.Nbk.

          The days have vanisht tone & tint
             Yet send from out the hoarding sense
             At times (he hardly knows from whence)
          A little flash, a mystic hint
                 H.Lpr.101, T.MS
13 such] Hn.Nbk. 2nd reading-; ever Hn.Nbk. 1st reading

45] Hn.Nbk., T.MS, L.MS, Trial, 1850A-
   8 And] L.MS-; But Hn.Nbk., T.MS

So rounds he to a separate mind
    From whence clear memory may begin,   10
    As thro' the frame that binds him in
His isolation grows defined.

This use may lie in blood and breath,
    Which else were fruitless of their due,
    Had man to learn himself anew   15
Beyond the second birth of Death.

46

We ranging down this lower track,
    The path we came by, thorn and flower,
    Is shadow'd by the growing hour,
Lest life should fail in looking back.

So be it: there no shade can last   5
    In that deep dawn behind the tomb,
    But clear from marge to marge shall bloom
The eternal landscape of the past;

A lifelong tract of time reveal'd;
    The fruitful hours of still increase;   10
    Days order'd in a wealthy peace,
And those five years its richest field.

O Love, thy province were not large,
    A bounded field, nor stretching far;
    Look also, Love, a brooding star,   15
A rosy warmth from marge to marge.

10 From whence clear] T.MS-; And thence his Hn.Nbk.   12 grows] T.MS-;
is Hn.Nbk.   14] T.MS *and* L.MS (*no comma*), Trial-; And Life were pilfer'd
of her due Hn.Nbk.   15 man . . . himself] T.MS-; men . . . themselves
Hn.Nbk.

46] H.Lpr.101, T.MS, L.MS, **Trial**, 1850A-
    1-4] L.MS *2nd reading- (except for, in some cases, minor variants*);
        In travelling thro' this lower clime   [thro L.MS
        With reason our memorial power
        Is shadow'd by the growing hour   [shadowed H.Lpr.101
        Lest this should be too much for time. [time L.MS
                         H.Lpr.101, T.MS, L.MS *1st reading*
5 So be it:] L.MS *2nd reading-*; Yet surely H.Lpr.101, T.MS, L.MS *1st reading*
8 landscape] 1850A-; landskip H.Lpr.101-Trial   12 five L.MS *2nd reading-*;
four H.Lpr.101, T.MS, L.MS *1st reading*   13 O Love, thy] L.MS *2nd reading*,
Trial *and* 1850A (O Love! thy), 1850B-; O me Love's H.Lpr.101, T.MS, L.MS
1st reading (. . . me, . . .)

47

That each, who seems a separate whole,
　　Should move his rounds, and fusing all
　　The skirts of self again, should fall
Remerging in the general Soul,

Is faith as vague as all unsweet:　　　　　　5
　　Eternal form shall still divide
　　The eternal soul from all beside;
And I shall know him when we meet:

And we shall sit at endless feast,
　　Enjoying each the other's good:　　　　　10
　　What vaster dream can hit the mood
Of Love on earth? He seeks at least

Upon the last and sharpest height,
　　Before the spirits fade away,
　　Some landing-place, to clasp and say,　　15
'Farewell! We lose ourselves in light.'

48

If these brief lays, of Sorrow born,
　　Were taken to be such as closed
　　Grave doubts and answers here proposed,
Then these were such as men might scorn:

Her care is not to part and prove;　　　　　5
　　She takes, when harsher moods remit,
　　What slender shade of doubt may flit,
And makes it vassal unto love:

And hence, indeed, she sports with words,
　　But better serves a wholesome law,　　　10

47] L.MS, Trial, 1850A-; *not in* T.MS
　　1 who] L.MS *2nd reading-*; which L.MS *1st reading*　　　2 his] L.MS *2nd reading-*; its L.MS *1st reading*　　　3 self again,] 1850A-; self, again L.MS, Trial
5] L.MS *2nd reading-*; Such faith as vague and all unsweet: L.MS *1st reading*
11 vaster] L.MS *2nd reading-*; dimmer L.MS *1st reading*

48] H.Lpr.101, T.MS, L.MS, Trial, 1850A-
　　1 brief] L.MS-; light H.Lpr.101, T.MS　　　7 slender shade] T.MS *2nd reading-*; random ghost H.Lpr.101, T.MS *1st reading*

And holds it sin and shame to draw
The deepest measure from the chords:

Nor dare she trust a larger lay,
    But rather loosens from the lip
    Short swallow-flights of song, that dip   15
Their wings in tears, and skim away.

49

From art, from nature, from the schools,
    Let random influences glance,
    Like light in many a shiver'd lance
That breaks about the dappled pools:

The lightest wave of thought shall lisp,   5
    The fancy's tenderest eddy wreathe,
    The slightest air of song shall breathe
To make the sullen surface crisp.

And look thy look, and go thy way,
    But blame not thou the winds that make   10
    The seeming-wanton ripple break,
The tender-pencil'd shadow play.

Beneath all fancied hopes and fears
    Ay me, the sorrow deepens down,
    Whose muffled motions blindly drown   15
The bases of my life in tears.

50

Be near me when my light is low,
    When the blood creeps, and the nerves prick
    And tingle; and the heart is sick,
And all the wheels of Being slow.

49] T.MS, L.MS, Trial, 1850A–
    6 tenderest] L.MS 2nd reading–; lightest T.MS, L.MS 1st reading   7
slightest] L.MS–; lightest T.MS   12 The] L.MS–; And T.MS   13] T.MS
2nd reading (beneath . . .), L.MS–; Aye me! beneath all hopes & fears T.MS 1st
reading

Be near me when the sensuous frame   5
    Is rack'd with pangs that conquer trust;
    And Time, a maniac scattering dust,
And Life, a Fury slinging flame.

Be near me when my faith is dry,
    And men the flies of latter spring,   10
    That lay their eggs, and sting and sing
And weave their petty cells and die.

Be near me when I fade away,
    To point the term of human strife,
    And on the low dark verge of life   15
The twilight of eternal day.

51

Do we indeed desire the dead
    Should still be near us at our side?
    Is there no baseness we would hide?
No inner vileness that we dread?

Shall he for whose applause I strove,   5
    I had such reverence for his blame,
    See with clear eye some hidden shame
And I be lessen'd in his love?

I wrong the grave with fears untrue:
    Shall love be blamed for want of faith?   10
    There must be wisdom with great Death:
The dead shall look me thro' and thro'.

Be near us when we climb or fall:
    Ye watch, like God, the rolling hours
    With larger other eyes than ours,   15
To make allowance for us all.

50] L.MS, **Trial,** 1850A-; *not in* T.MS
  1 my light] L.MS *2nd reading-;* the pulse L.MS *1st reading*

51] H.Lpr.101, T.MS, L.MS, **Trial,** 1850A-
  7] T.MS *2nd reading-;* See with clear sight my secret shame H.Lpr.101, T.MS
1st reading (See with clear sight [illegible words])

52

I cannot love thee as I ought,
   For love reflects the thing beloved;
   My words are only words, and moved
Upon the topmost froth of thought.

'Yet blame not thou thy plaintive song,'   5
   The Spirit of true love replied;
   'Thou canst not move me from thy side,
Nor human frailty do me wrong.

'What keeps a spirit wholly true
   To that ideal which he bears?   10
   What record? not the sinless years
That breathed beneath the Syrian blue:

'So fret not, like an idle girl,
   That life is dash'd with flecks of sin.
   Abide: thy wealth is gather'd in,   15
When Time hath sunder'd shell from pearl.'

53

How many a father have I seen,
   A sober man, among his boys,
   Whose youth was full of foolish noise,
Who wears his manhood hale and green:

And dare we to this fancy give,   5
   That had the wild oat not been sown,
   The soil, left barren, scarce had grown
The grain by which a man may live?

52] T.MS, L.MS, Trial, 1850A–
   3] L.MS (no comma), Trial–; My words are words & lightly moved T.MS
5 'Yet] L.MS–; Oh T.MS   8 human] T.MS 2nd reading–; casual T.MS 1st
reading   9–11] L.MS– (except for, in some cases, minor variants);
                What record keeps a spirit true
                To that ideal which he bears?
                No — not the thirty sinless years
                              T.MS
16 Time hath sunder'd] 1850A–; years have rotted T.MS–Trial

53] T.MS, L.MS, Trial, 1850A–
   5 fancy] 1850C–; doctrine T.MS–1850B   7 scarce had] 1850C–; had not
T.MS–1850B

Or, if we held the doctrine sound
   For life outliving heats of youth,   10
   Yet who would preach it as a truth
To those that eddy round and round?

Hold thou the good: define it well:
   For fear divine Philosophy
   Should push beyond her mark, and be   15
Procuress to the Lords of Hell.

54

Oh yet we trust that somehow good
   Will be the final goal of ill,
   To pangs of nature, sins of will,
Defects of doubt, and taints of blood;

That nothing walks with aimless feet;   5
   That not one life shall be destroy'd,
   Or cast as rubbish to the void,
When God hath made the pile complete;

That not a worm is cloven in vain;
   That not a moth with vain desire   10
   Is shrivell'd in a fruitless fire,
Or but subserves another's gain.

Behold, we know not anything;
   I can but trust that good shall fall
   At last — far off — at last, to all,   15
And every winter change to spring.

So runs my dream: but what am I?
   An infant crying in the night:

9 Or, if] **1883–**; Or if T.MS; Oh if L.MS; Oh! if **Trial, 1850A**; Oh, if **1850B–1882**
12 those] **1850A–**; lives T.MS–Trial   16 Procuress] **Trial–**; A pandar T.MS,
L.MS

54] T.MS, L.MS, **Trial, 1850A–**
   1 we] L.MS–; I T.MS   12 a–d] *deleted in* T.MS:
                 For hope at awful distance set
                   Oft whispers of a kindlier plan
                   Tho never prophet came to man
                 Of such a revelation yet.
13 Behold,] **1850B–**; Behold T.MS, L.MS; Behold! **Trial, 1850A** we] L.MS–;
I T.MS   14 I can but trust] L.MS–; But that I would T.MS

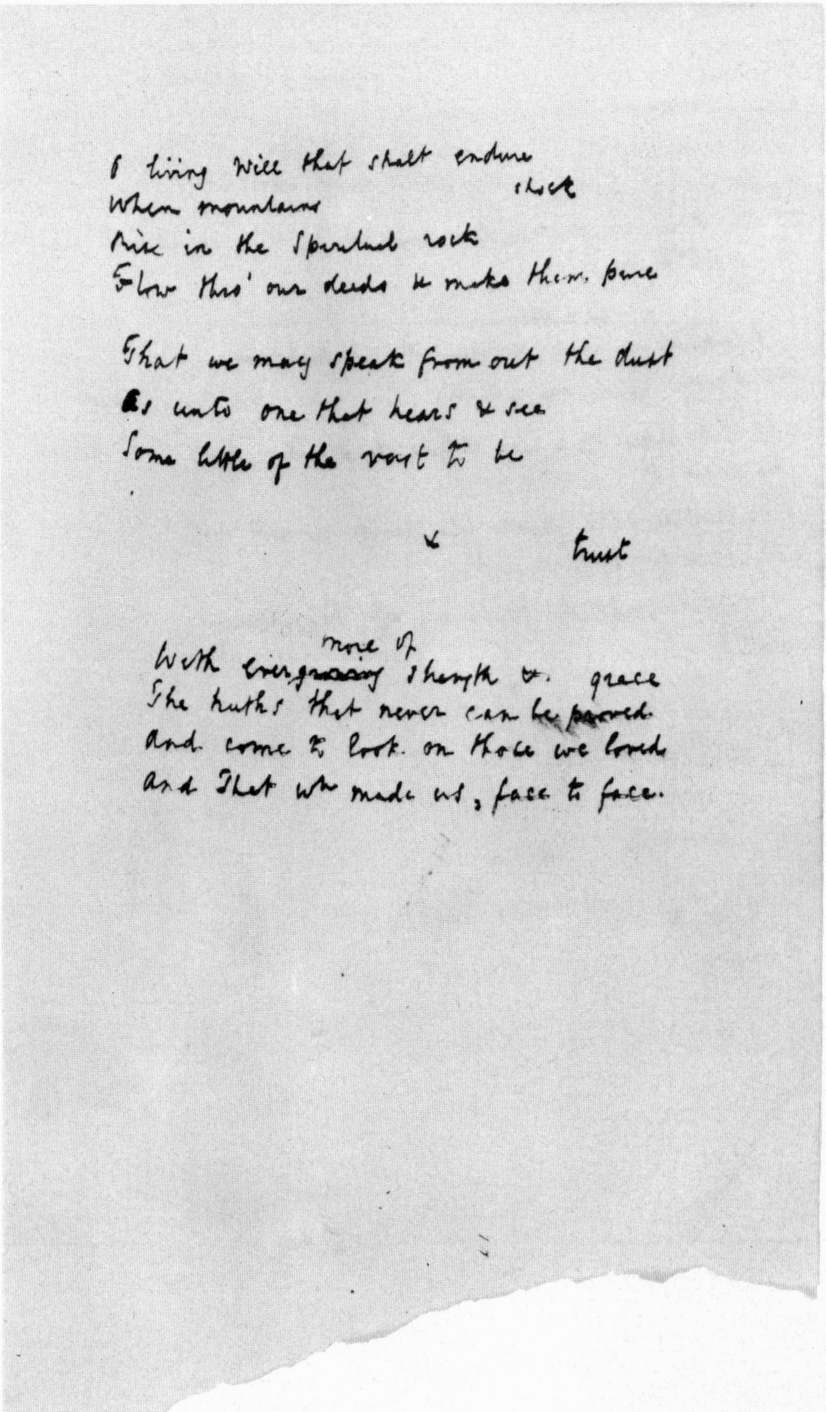

O living will that shalt endure
When mountains   shock
Rise in the Spiritual rock
Flow thro' our deeds & make them pure

That we may speak from out the dust
As unto one that hears & sees
Some little of the vast to be

                    &   trust

                    more of
With evergrowing strength &. grace
The truths that never can be proved
And come to look on those we loved
And That who made us, face to face.

Plate III Section *131* in Houghton Library, Harvard University MS Eng 952 (18), f.3ᵛ

Plate IV Epilogue, lines 57-108, in Tennyson Research Centre, Lincoln MS, f.86ᴿ

Now sign your names, which shall be read,
  Mute symbols of a blissful morn,
  By village eyes as yet unborn;
The names are signed & overhead

Begin the clash & clang that tells
  The joy to every wandering breeze;
  The blind wall rocks, & on the trees
The dead leaf trembles to the bells.

O happy hour & happier hours
  Await them, many a merry face
  ~~invites them you~~, maidens of the place,
That pelt us in the porch with flowers

O happy hour, behold the bride
  With him to whom her hand I gave.
  They leave the porch, they pass the grave,
That has to-day its sunny side.

To-day the grave is bright for me
  For them the light of life increased,
  ~~who flew to cheer the morning feast~~
  ~~~~

Let all my genial spirits advance
  To meet & greet a whiter sun.
  My drooping memory will not shun
The foaming grape of eastern France.

It circles round: the fancy plays,
  The hearts are warm'd, the faces bloom,
  We drinking health to bride & groom
We wish them store of happy days.

Nor count me all to blame if I
  Conjecture of a stiller guest,
  Perchance, perchance among the rest,
And, tho' in silence, wishing joy

A passing fancy, let it be:
  However wrought, their joy will grow
  Beyond the pride; but they must go.
They rest to-night beside the sea.

But they must go: the time draws on:
  Farewell, & yet they lingering.
  And those white-favour'd horses wait;
They rise, but linger: it is late:
Farewell: we kiss, & they are gone.

A shade falls on us like the dark
  From little cloudlets on the grass,
  But ~~sweeps~~ away as out we pass,
We listen'd & we drank the park:
To range the woods, to roam the park,
We pace the stubbly fare of sheaves,
We watch the brimming river steal
And half the golden woodland reel
Athwart the smoke of burning leaves.

Discussing how their courtship grew,
  And talk of others that are wed,
  And how she look'd & what he said,
And back we come at fall of dew.

Again the feast, the speech, the glee,
  The shade of passing thought, the wealth
  Of words & wit, the double health,
And that, the three-times-three,
And last the dance; till I retire.

Dumb is that tower which spake so loud,
  And high in heaven the streaming cloud,
And on the down a rising fire.

An infant crying for the light:
And with no language but a cry.   20

55

The wish, that of the living whole
  No life may fail beyond the grave,
  Derives it not from what we have
The likest God within the soul?

Are God and Nature then at strife,   5
  That Nature lends such evil dreams?
  So careful of the type she seems,
So careless of the single life;

That I, considering everywhere
  Her secret meaning in her deeds,   10
  And finding that of fifty seeds
She often brings but one to bear,

I falter where I firmly trod,
  And falling with my weight of cares
  Upon the great world's altar-stairs   15
That slope thro' darkness up to God,

I stretch lame hands of faith, and grope,
  And gather dust and chaff, and call
  To what I feel is Lord of all,
And faintly trust the larger hope.   20

56

'So careful of the type?' but no.
  From scarped cliff and quarried stone
  She cries, 'A thousand types are gone:
I care for nothing, all shall go.

'Thou makest thine appeal to me: 5
  I bring to life, I bring to death:

55] L.MS, Trial, 1850A-; not in T.MS

56] L.MS, 1850A-; not in T.MS, Trial
  1 but no.] L.MS 2nd reading (but no!), 1850A-; not so L.MS 1st reading

The spirit does but mean the breath:
I know no more.' And he, shall he,

Man, her last work, who seem'd so fair,
  Such splendid purpose in his eyes,   10
  Who roll'd the psalm to wintry skies,
Who built him fanes of fruitless prayer,

Who trusted God was love indeed
  And love Creation's final law —
  Tho' Nature, red in tooth and claw   15
With ravine, shriek'd against his creed —

Who loved, who suffer'd countless ills,
  Who battled for the True, the Just,
  Be blown about the desert dust,
Or seal'd within the iron hills?   20

No more? A monster then, a dream,
  A discord. Dragons of the prime,
  That tare each other in their slime,
Were mellow music match'd with him.

O life as futile, then, as frail!   25
  O for thy voice to soothe and bless!
  What hope of answer, or redress?
Behind the veil, behind the veil.

57

Peace; come away: the song of woe
  Is after all an earthly song:
  Peace; come away: we do him wrong
To sing so wildly: let us go.

Come; let us go: your cheeks are pale;   5
  But half my life I leave behind:

9] L.MS *2nd reading (no commas)*, 1850A-; Shall he that seem'd so grand & fair
L.MS *1st reading*   11 wintry] 1850A-; Sabbath L.MS   12 fruitless]
1850A-; praise & L.MS   15 in] 1850A-; with L.MS   16 With ravine,
shriek'd] 1850A-; And ravin cried L.MS   18] 1850A-; Who yearn'd for
True & Good & Just, L.MS   23 tare] 1850A-; tore L.MS

57] T.MS, L.MS, Trial, 1850A-
  5 Come;] L.MS-1851B (Come,), 1855-; Peace — T.MS

Methinks my friend is richly shrined;
But I shall pass; my work will fail.

Yet in these ears, till hearing dies,
   One set slow bell will seem to toll   10
   The passing of the sweetest soul
That ever look'd with human eyes.

I hear it now, and o'er and o'er,
   Eternal greetings to the dead;
   And 'Ave, Ave, Ave,' said,   15
'Adieu, adieu' for evermore.

58

In those sad words I took farewell:
   Like echoes in sepulchral halls,
   As drop by drop the water falls
In vaults and catacombs, they fell;

And, falling, idly broke the peace   5
   Of hearts that beat from day to day,
   Half-conscious of their dying clay,
And those cold crypts where they shall cease.

The high Muse answer'd: 'Wherefore grieve
   Thy brethren with a fruitless tear?   10
   Abide a little longer here,
And thou shalt take a nobler leave.'

8 a-d]   So might it last & guard thy dust
                  For ever! O I would for this, *revised to*
                  For ever! would indeed for this,
                  My skill were greater than it is!
                  But let it be. the years are just.
                                T.MS

58] L.MS, **Trial, 1850A–;** *not in* T.MS
   8 a-h] *Deleted in* L.MS
                  The grave Muse answer'd Go not yet *revised to*
                  The high Muse answer'd Wherefore grieve
                  A speechless child can move the heart
                  But thine my friend is nobler Art.
                I lent thee force & pay the debt.
                Why wouldst thou make thy brethren grieve
                  Depart not with an idle tear
                  But wait: there comes a stronger year
                When thou shalt take a nobler leave.
9–12] *Added in margin of* L.MS

59

O Sorrow, wilt thou live with me
No casual mistress, but a wife,
My bosom-friend and half of life;
As I confess it needs must be;

O Sorrow, wilt thou rule my blood,   5
Be sometimes lovely like a bride,
And put thy harsher moods aside,
If thou wilt have me wise and good.

My centred passion cannot move,
Nor will it lessen from to-day;   10
But I'll have leave at times to play
As with the creature of my love;

And set thee forth, for thou art mine,
With so much hope for years to come,
That, howsoe'er I know thee, some   15
Could hardly tell what name were thine.

59] H.Lpr.99, Sparrow MS(59), 1851A–; *not in* T.MS–1850C
   1 wilt] Sparrow MS(59)–; would'st H.Lpr.99   4 a–d]
                  I cannot put thee forth again
                  Nor lose thee in the cloud of change
                  The Times that grow to something strange
                  The faces & the minds of men
                                    H.Lpr.99
6 like] Sparrow MS(59)–; as H.Lpr.99   7 harsher] Sparrow MS(59)–; deeper
H.Lpr.99   8 wilt] Sparrow MS(59)–; would'st H.Lpr.99   8 a–h]
                  Use other means than sobbing breath
                  And other charms than misted eyes
                  And broodings on the change that lies
                  Shut in the second-birth of death

                  Nor shalt thou only wear the rue
                  But there are daisies on the grave
                  And sweeter blooms which thou shalt have
                  Not ⟨dasht with⟩ ∧ dipt ∧ tears but dasht with dew.
                                    H.Lpr.99
9 centred] Sparrow MS(59) (center'd), 1851A–; deepset H.Lpr.99   10]
H.Lpr.99 *reads* Be less to-morrow than today   11] *In* H.Lpr.99 T. *originally*
wrote
                  But sometimes I'll take leave
He broke off before completing the line and revised it to
                  But I'll have leave at times to play
13 for thou art mine,] Sparrow MS(59) ((for thou art mine)), 1851A–; so trim
and fine H.Lpr.99   15] H.Lpr.99 *reads* That tho' I know thee well yet some

60

He past; a soul of nobler tone:
  My spirit loved and loves him yet,
  Like some poor girl whose heart is set
On one whose rank exceeds her own.

He mixing with his proper sphere,
  She finds the baseness of her lot,
  Half jealous of she knows not what,
And envying all that meet him there.

The little village looks forlorn;
  She sighs amid her narrow days,
  Moving about the household ways,
In that dark house where she was born.

The foolish neighbours come and go,
  And tease her till the day draws by:
  At night she weeps, 'How vain am I!
How should he love a thing so low?'

61

If, in thy second state sublime,
  Thy ransom'd reason change replies
  With all the circle of the wise,
The perfect flower of human time;

And if thou cast thine eyes below,
  How dimly character'd and slight,
  How dwarf'd a growth of cold and night,
How blanch'd with darkness must I grow!

Yet turn thee to the doubtful shore,
  Where thy first form was made a man;
  I loved thee, Spirit, and love, nor can
The soul of Shakspeare love thee more.

60] H.Lpr.101, T.MS, L.MS, **Trial, 1850A–**

61] Hn.Nbk., T.MS, L.MS, **Trial, 1850A–**
  4] T.MS *2nd reading (no punctuation)*, L.MS (. . . time.), **Trial–**; The flower
& quintessence of Time. Hn.Nbk., T.MS *1st reading* (Time)   12 Shakspeare]
Trial–; Shakespeare Hn.Nbk., T.MS; Shakespere L.MS

62

Tho' if an eye that's downward cast
    Could make thee somewhat blench or fail,
    Then be my love an idle tale,
And fading legend of the past;

And thou, as one that once declined,   5
    When he was little more than boy,
    On some unworthy heart with joy,
But lives to wed an equal mind;

And breathes a novel world, the while
    His other passion wholly dies,   10
    Or in the light of deeper eyes
Is matter for a flying smile.

63

Yet pity for a horse o'er-driven,
    And love in which my hound has part,
    Can hang no weight upon my heart
In its assumptions up to heaven;

And I am so much more than these,   5
    As thou, perchance, art more than I,
    And yet I spare them sympathy,
And I would set their pains at ease.

So mayst thou watch me where I weep,
    As, unto vaster motions bound,   10
    The circuits of thine orbit round
A higher height, a deeper deep.

64

Dost thou look back on what hath been,
    As some divinely gifted man,

62] T.MS, L.MS, **Trial, 1850A-**
    3 Then] 1851A-; So T.MS-1850C

63] T.MS, L.MS, **Trial, 1850A-**
    8 I would] T.MS *2nd reading-*; will to T.MS *1st reading*

64] L.MS, **Trial, 1850A-**; *not in* T.MS

Whose life in low estate began
And on a simple village green;

Who breaks his birth's invidious bar,   5
　　And grasps the skirts of happy chance,
　　And breasts the blows of circumstance,
And grapples with his evil star;

Who makes by force his merit known
　　And lives to clutch the golden keys,   10
　　To mould a mighty state's decrees,
And shape the whisper of the throne;

And moving up from high to higher,
　　Becomes on Fortune's crowning slope
　　The pillar of a people's hope,   15
The centre of a world's desire;

Yet feels, as in a pensive dream,
　　When all his active powers are still,
　　A distant dearness in the hill,
A secret sweetness in the stream,   20

The limit of his narrower fate,
　　While yet beside its vocal springs
　　He play'd at counsellors and kings,
With one that was his earliest mate;

Who ploughs with pain his native lea   25
　　And reaps the labour of his hands,
　　Or in the furrow musing stands;
'Does my old friend remember me?'

65

Sweet soul, do with me as thou wilt;
　　I lull a fancy trouble-tost
　　With 'Love's too precious to be lost,
A little grain shall not be split.'

6 skirts] **Trial-**; skirt L.MS   21 limit] L.MS *2nd reading-*; limits L.MS
1st reading   22 its vocal] L.MS *2nd reading* (it's . . .), **Trial-**; his native
L.MS *1st reading*

65] T.MS, L.MS, **Trial, 1850A-**
2 fancy] L.MS-; spirit T.MS

And in that solace can I sing,   5
    Till out of painful phases wrought
    There flutters up a happy thought,
Self-balanced on a lightsome wing:

Since we deserved the name of friends,
    And thine effect so lives in me,   10
    A part of mine may live in thee
And move thee on to noble ends.

66

You thought my heart too far diseased;
    You wonder when my fancies play
    To find me gay among the gay,
Like one with any trifle pleased.

The shade by which my life was crost,   5
    Which makes a desert in the mind,
    Has made me kindly with my kind,
And like to him whose sight is lost;

Whose feet are guided thro' the land,
    Whose jest among his friends is free,   10
    Who takes the children on his knee,
And winds their curls about his hand:

He plays with threads, he beats his chair
    For pastime, dreaming of the sky;
    His inner day can never die,   15
His night of loss is always there.

67

When on my bed the moonlight falls,
    I know that in thy place of rest

6 phases] L.MS-; changes T.MS

66] Hn.Nbk., T.MS, L.MS, Trial, 1850A-
    9] L.MS 2nd reading-; Like one gone blind within the land Hn.Nbk. (land:),
T.MS, L.MS 1st reading

67] T.MS, L.MS, Trial, 1850A-

By that broad water of the west,
There comes a glory on the walls:

Thy marble bright in dark appears,   5
  As slowly steals a silver flame
  Along the letters of thy name,
And o'er the number of thy years.

The mystic glory swims away;
  From off my bed the moonlight dies;   10
  And closing eaves of wearied eyes
I sleep till dusk is dipt in gray:

And then I know the mist is drawn
  A lucid veil from coast to coast,
  And in the dark church like a ghost   15
Thy tablet glimmers to the dawn.

                    68

When in the down I sink my head,
  Sleep, Death's twin-brother, times my breath;
  Sleep, Death's twin-brother, knows not Death,
Nor can I dream of thee as dead:

I walk as ere I walk'd forlorn,   5
  When all our path was fresh with dew,
  And all the bugle breezes blew
Reveillée to the breaking morn.

But what is this? I turn about,
  I find a trouble in thine eye,   10
  Which makes me sad I know not why,
Nor can my dream resolve the doubt:

   3 broad water] Trial-; great River T.MS; broad river L.MS   5 marble]
T.MS 2nd reading-; tab[let] T.MS 1st reading   15 dark church] 1855-;
chancel T.MS-1851B

68] Hn.Nbk. (1-4, 9-16 only), T.MS (two drafts: T.MSa agrees with Hn.Nbk.
except for 15; T.MSb adds 5-8), L.MS, Trial, 1850A-
   5-8] Not in Hn.Nbk., T.MSa   9] T.MSb and L.MS (no comma), Trial-;
Again with thee I wander out Hn.Nbk., T.MSa (out:)   10 I find a] T.MSb-;
But there is Hn.Nbk., T.MSa

But ere the lark hath left the lea
  I wake, and I discern the truth;
  It is the trouble of my youth   15
That foolish sleep transfers to thee.

69

I dream'd there would be Spring no more,
  That Nature's ancient power was lost:
  The streets were black with smoke and frost,
They chatter'd trifles at the door:

I wander'd from the noisy town,   5
  I found a wood with thorny boughs:
  I took the thorns to bind my brows,
I wore them like a civic crown:

I met with scoffs, I met with scorns
  From youth and babe and hoary hairs: 10
  They call'd me in the public squares
The fool that wears a crown of thorns:

They call'd me fool, they call'd me child:
  I found an angel of the night;
  The voice was low, the look was bright;   15
He look'd upon my crown and smiled:

He reach'd the glory of a hand,
  That seem'd to touch it into leaf:
  The voice was not the voice of grief,
The words were hard to understand.   20

13] L.MS–; But when the bird is in the tree Hn.Nbk., T.MSa, T.MSb (tree,)   15
trouble] T.MSa–; sorrow Hn.Nbk

69] L.MS, 1850A–; not in T.MS, Trial
   2 That Nature's ancient] 1850A–; I dream'd that Nature's L.MS   10
youth and babe] 1850A–; babe & youth L.MS   14 I found an angel] 1850A–;
There came a Vision L.MS   15 look was] 1850A–; eyes were L.MS

70

I cannot see the features right,
   When on the gloom I strive to paint
   The face I know; the hues are faint
And mix with hollow masks of night;

Cloud-towers by ghostly masons wrought,   5
   A gulf that ever shuts and gapes,
   A hand that points, and palled shapes
In shadowy thoroughfares of thought;

And crowds that stream from yawning doors,
   And shoals of pucker'd faces drive;   10
   Dark bulks that tumble half alive,
And lazy lengths on boundless shores;

Till all at once beyond the will
   I hear a wizard music roll,
   And thro' a lattice on the soul   15
Looks thy fair face and makes it still.

71

Sleep, kinsman thou to death and trance
   And madness, thou hast forged at last

70] L.MS (*two drafts*, L.MSa, L.MSb), Trial, 1850A-; *not in* T.MS
   1 see] L.MSb-; get L.MSa   5 Cloud-towers] L.MSa, Trial-; A fort L.MSb
7 A hand that points, and] L.MSb (... points & ...), Trial-; A long long train of
L.MSa   8 In shadowy] L.MSb-; That sweep the L.MSa   8 a-d]
     Revolving spheres & weltering waves,
       And gusts of sand and foam and snow
       That down a dreary margin go,
       And lamps that wink at yawning graves
                  L.MSb
9] Trial-; High shadows crossing dreary moors; L.MSa; [*intentional blank*] L.MSb
16] L.MSa, Trial-; Look thy fair eyes & make it still. L.MSb

71] T.MS, L.MS, Trial, 1850A-
   1-2] 1850A-;
     Old things are clear in waking trance
      And thou, O Sleep, hast made at last
            T.MS

   Kinsman of madness, waking trance   [trance, Trial
   And Death, O Sleep, thou hast forged at last [death, O Sleep! Trial
           L.MS, Trial

A night-long Present of the Past
In which we went thro' summer France.

Hadst thou such credit with the soul?   5
Then bring an opiate trebly strong,
Drug down the blindfold sense of wrong
That so my pleasure may be whole;

While now we talk as once we talk'd
Of men and minds, the dust of change,   10
The days that grow to something strange,
In walking as of old we walk'd

Beside the river's wooded reach,
The fortress, and the mountain ridge,
The cataract flashing from the bridge,   15
The breaker breaking on the beach.

72

Risest thou thus, dim dawn, again,
And howlest, issuing out of night,
With blasts that blow the poplar white,
And lash with storm the streaming pane?

Day, when my crown'd estate begun   5
To pine in that reverse of doom,
Which sicken'd every living bloom,
And blurr'd the splendour of the sun;

4 summer] L.MS-; sunny T.MS went] T.MS, 1850A-; paced L.MS, Trial   5
Hadst] L.MS-; Hast T.MS   6-7] 1855- (*in respect of* 6), Trial- (*in respect of* 7);
So can'st thou not put back & blight
The sense that something is not right
T.MS
So bring an opiate treble-strong   [treble-strong, Trial-1850C
Drug down the blindfold sense of wrong, [wrong Trial-
L.MS, Trial-1850C
Then bring an opiate treble-strong,
. . .
1851A, 1851B
8] 1851A-; That thus my pleasure might be whole. T.MS-1850C (whole L.MS;
whole; 1850A-C)   14-15] L.MS (*no commas*), Trial-;
The meadow set with summer flags
The cataract clashing from the crags,
T.MS
72] L.MS, Trial, 1850A-; *not in* T.MS
8 blurr'd] L.MS *2nd reading*-; suck'd L.MS *1st reading* of] Trial-; from L.MS

Who usherest in the dolorous hour
    With thy quick tears that make the rose   10
    Pull sideways, and the daisy close
Her crimson fringes to the shower;

Who might'st have heaved a windless flame
    Up the deep East, or, whispering, play'd
    A chequer-work of beam and shade   15
Along the hills, yet look'd the same.

As wan, as chill, as wild as now;
    Day, mark'd as with some hideous crime,
    When the dark hand struck down thro' time,
And cancell'd nature's best: but thou,   20

Lift as thou may'st thy burthen'd brows
    Thro' clouds that drench the morning star,
    And whirl the ungarner'd sheaf afar,
And sow the sky with flying boughs,

And up thy vault with roaring sound   25
    Climb thy thick noon, disastrous day;
    Touch thy dull goal of joyless gray,
And hide thy shame beneath the ground.

73

So many worlds, so much to do,
    So little done, such things to be,
    How know I what had need of thee,
For thou wert strong as thou wert true?

The fame is quench'd that I foresaw,   5
    The head hath miss'd an earthly wreath:
    I curse not nature, no, nor death;
For nothing is that errs from law.

We pass; the path that each man trod
    Is dim, or will be dim, with weeds: 10

16 Along the hills, yet] 1855-; From hill to hill & L.MS; From hill to hill, yet
Trial-1851B

73] H.Lpr.101, T.MS, L.MS, **Trial, 1850A-**
    6 hath] L.MS-; has H.Lpr.101, T.MS

What fame is left for human deeds
In endless age? It rests with God.

O hollow wraith of dying fame,
Fade wholly, while the soul exults,
And self-infolds the large results   15
Of force that would have forged a name.

74

As sometimes in a dead man's face,
To those that watch it more and more,
A likeness, hardly seen before,
Comes out — to some one of his race:

So, dearest, now thy brows are cold,   5
I see thee what thou art, and know
Thy likeness to the wise below,
Thy kindred with the great of old.

But there is more than I can see,
And what I see I leave unsaid,   10
Nor speak it, knowing Death has made
His darkness beautiful with thee.

75

I leave thy praises unexpress'd
In verse that brings myself relief,
And by the measure of my grief
I leave thy greatness to be guess'd;

13 wraith] T.MS-; wreath H.Lpr.101

74] Hn.Nbk., T.MS, L.MS, Trial, 1850A-
    3-4] T.MS- (except for, in some cases, minor variants);
                    A likeness comes, scarce-seen before
              Unto some other of his race
                                        Hn.Nbk.
5] Hn.Nbk. (no commas), L.MS (no terminal comma), Trial-; So now thy mossy
brain is cold T.MS 1st reading; So dearest now thy brain is cold T.MS 2nd reading
6 art,] T.MS (art), L.MS-; wert Hn.Nbk.   9 But] T.MS-; And Hn.Nbk.
11 knowing] T.MS 2nd reading-; seeing Hn.Nbk., T.MS 1st reading

75] Hn.Nbk. (stanzas in this order: 1-12, and 17-20 which is deleted; 13-16, and
17-20 revised), T.MS, L.MS, Trial, 1850A-

What practice howsoe'er expert   5
    In fitting aptest words to things,
    Or voice the richest-toned that sings,
Hath power to give thee as thou wert?

I care not in these fading days
    To raise a cry that lasts not long,   10
    And round thee with the breeze of song
To stir a little dust of praise.

Thy leaf has perish'd in the green,
    And, while we breathe beneath the sun,
    The world which credits what is done   15
Is cold to all that might have been.

So here shall silence guard thy fame;
    But somewhere, out of human view,
    Whate'er thy hands are set to do
Is wrought with tumult of acclaim.   20

76

Take wings of fancy, and ascend,
    And in a moment set thy face
    Where all the starry heavens of space
Are sharpen'd to a needle's end;

Take wings of foresight; lighten thro'   5
    The secular abyss to come,
    And lo, thy deepest lays are dumb
Before the mouldering of a yew;

And if the matin songs, that woke
    The darkness of our planet, last,   10
    Thine own shall wither in the vast,
Ere half the lifetime of an oak.

8 Hath] L.MS-; Has Hn.Nbk., T.MS   9 these] L.MS-; our Hn.Nbk., T.MS
11] Hn.Nbk. *2nd reading-*; And with the breeze of lyric song Hn.Nbk. *1st reading*
17 So here] Hn.Nbk. *deleted*, T.MS-; Here then Hn.Nbk. *revised*

76] T.MS, L.MS, Trial, 1850A-
    3 starry heavens] **Trial**-; milky girths T.MS, L.MS   7 And] L.MS-; But
T.MS   8 Before] T.MS *has intentional blank later filled in with* Before
10 our] T.MS *2nd reading-*; the T.MS *1st reading*

Ere these have clothed their branchy bowers
With fifty Mays, thy songs are vain;
And what are they when these remain   15
The ruin'd shells of hollow towers?

77

What hope is here for modern rhyme
To him, who turns a musing eye
On songs, and deeds, and lives, that lie
Foreshorten'd in the tract of time?

These mortal lullabies of pain   5
May bind a book, may line a box,
May serve to curl a maiden's locks;
Or when a thousand moons shall wane

A man upon a stall may find,
And, passing, turn the page that tells   10
A grief, then changed to something else,
Sung by a long-forgotten mind.

But what of that? My darken'd ways
Shall ring with music all the same;
To breathe my loss is more than fame,   15
To utter love more sweet than praise.

78

Again at Christmas did we weave
The holly round the Christmas hearth;
The silent snow possess'd the earth,
And calmly fell our Christmas-eve:

13 clothed] T.MS *alternative reading*, L.MS-; changed T.MS *1st reading* bowers]
T.MS *2nd reading*, L.MS (bowers,), **Trial-**; towers T.MS *1st reading*   14 With
fifty] **Trial-**; A hundred T.MS, L.MS

77] T.MS, L.MS, **Trial, 1850A-**
     6] **1850A-**; May be the lining of a box T.MS *1st reading*; May bind a book or
line a box T.MS *2nd reading*, L.MS, **Trial** (book, box,)   7 May] **1850A-**;
Or T.MS-**Trial**   13 darken'd ways] L.MS, **Trial** (darkened . . .), **1850A-**;
mortal days T.MS *1st reading*; darkend days T.MS *2nd reading*

78] Hn.Nbk.(1-16 *only*), T.MS, L.MS, **Trial, 1850A-**

The yule-clog sparkled keen with frost, 5
  No wing of wind the region swept,
  But over all things brooding slept
The quiet sense of something lost.

As in the winters left behind,
  Again our ancient games had place, 10
  The mimic picture's breathing grace,
And dance and song and hoodman-blind.

Who show'd a token of distress?
  No single tear, no mark of pain:
  O sorrow, then can sorrow wane? 15
O grief, can grief be changed to less?

O last regret, regret can die!
  No — mixt with all this mystic frame,
  Her deep relations are the same,
But with long use her tears are dry. 20

79

'More than my brothers are to me,' —
  Let this not vex thee, noble heart!
  I know thee of what force thou art
To hold the costliest love in fee.

But thou and I are one in kind, 5
  As moulded like in Nature's mint;
  And hill and wood and field did print
The same sweet forms in either mind.

For us the same cold streamlet curl'd
  Thro' all his eddying coves; the same 10
  All winds that roam the twilight came
In whispers of the beauteous world.

At one dear knee we proffer'd vows,
  One lesson from one book we learn'd,

14 mark] 1855–; type Hn.Nbk.–1851B   16 be changed to] L.MS *2nd reading*–; become the Hn.Nbk., T.MS, L.MS *1st reading*; decline L.MS *alternative reading*   17–20] *Not in* Hn.Nbk.   20 But] L.MS–; Tho' T.MS

79] T.MS, L.MS, **Trial, 1850A**–

Ere childhood's flaxen ringlet turn'd   15
To black and brown on kindred brows.

And so my wealth resembles thine,
    But he was rich where I was poor,
    And he supplied my want the more
As his unlikeness fitted mine.   20

80

If any vague desire should rise,
    That holy Death ere Arthur died
    Had moved me kindly from his side,
And dropt the dust on tearless eyes;

Then fancy shapes, as fancy can,   5
    The grief my loss in him had wrought,
    A grief as deep as life or thought,
But stay'd in peace with God and man.

I make a picture in the brain;
    I hear the sentence that he speaks;   10
    He bears the burthen of the weeks
But turns his burthen into gain.

His credit thus shall set me free;
    And, influence-rich to soothe and save,
    Unused example from the grave   15
Reach out dead hands to comfort me.

81

Could I have said while he was here,
    'My love shall now no further range;

---

16 kindred] 1850A-; brother T.MS *2nd reading*, L.MS, **Trial**; either T.MS *1st reading*   17 And] L.MS-; Even T.MS wealth] T.MS *2nd reading*-; mould T.MS *1st reading*

80] T.MS, L.MS, **Trial**, 1850A-
    10] L.MS-; I see him in familiar ways T.MS   11 the burthen of the weeks] L.MS-; about a weight of days T.MS   14 And, influence-rich] L.MS (And . . .), **Trial**-; And rich in force T.MS

81] T.MS, L.MS, **Trial**, 1850A-

There cannot come a mellower change,
For now is love mature in ear.'

Love, then, had hope of richer store: 5
What end is here to my complaint?
This haunting whisper makes me faint,
'More years had made me love thee more.'

But Death returns an answer sweet:
'My sudden frost was sudden gain,   10
And gave all ripeness to the grain,
It might have drawn from after-heat.'

82

I wage not any feud with Death
For changes wrought on form and face;
No lower life that earth's embrace
May breed with him, can fright my faith.

Eternal process moving on,   5
From state to state the spirit walks;
And these are but the shatter'd stalks,
Or ruin'd chrysalis of one.

Nor blame I Death, because he bare
The use of virtue out of earth: 10
I know transplanted human worth
Will bloom to profit, otherwhere.

3 There cannot come a] L.MS-; Oh! now there comes no T.MS   5 Love,
then,] L.MS (Love then . . .), Trial-; If Love T.MS   8 a-d
                    Scarce in my love can I rejoice
                    By that conjectured loss dismay'd,
                    Like some blind boy whose life is made
                    Dejected by his mother's voice.
                                        T.MS
          (Below Dejected by his is written A sorrow thro'.)
9] L.MS (. . . sweet.), Trial-; Yet mighty Death speaks out at once. T.MS   12
after-heat.'] L.MS-; future Suns.' T.MS

82] T.MS, L.MS, Trial, 1850A-
     6 From state to state] L.MS-; Thro' other states T.MS   7 shatter'd]
L.MS-; ruin'd T.MS   8 ruin'd] L.MS, 1850C-; shatter'd T.MS; ruined
Trial-1850B   10 out of] Trial; from the T.MS, L.MS   12 Will] L.MS-;
Must T.MS

For this alone on Death I wreak
   The wrath that garners in my heart;
   He put our lives so far apart   15
We cannot hear each other speak.

83

Dip down upon the northern shore,
   O sweet new-year delaying long;
   Thou doest expectant nature wrong;
Delaying long, delay no more.

What stays thee from the clouded noons,   5
   Thy sweetness from its proper place?
   Can trouble live with April days,
Or sadness in the summer moons?

Bring orchis, bring the foxglove spire,
   The little speedwell's darling blue,   10
   Deep tulips dash'd with fiery dew,
Laburnums, dropping-wells of fire.

O thou, new-year, delaying long,
   Delayest the sorrow in my blood,
   That longs to burst a frozen bud   15
And flood a fresher throat with song.

84

When I contemplate all alone
   The life that had been thine below,
   And fix my thoughts on all the glow
To which thy crescent would have grown;

I see thee sitting crown'd with good,   5
   A central warmth diffusing bliss

83] T.MS, L.MS, **Trial, 1850A**–
   5-8, 9-12] *Transposed in* T.MS   5-6] T.MS *2nd reading* (. . . noons --),
L.MS-;   Dark nights, dim morrows, clouded noons—
              Art thou too stay'd within thy place?
                      T.MS *1st reading*

84] L.MS, **Trial, 1850A**-; *not in* T.MS

In glance and smile, and clasp and kiss,
On all the branches of thy blood;

Thy blood, my friend, and partly mine;
    For now the day was drawing on,   10
    When thou should'st link thy life with one
Of mine own house, and boys of thine

Had babbled 'Uncle' on my knee;
    But that remorseless iron hour
    Made cypress of her orange flower,   15
Despair of Hope, and earth of thee.

I seem to meet their least desire,
    To clap their cheeks, to call them mine.
    I see their unborn faces shine
Beside the never-lighted fire.   20

I see myself an honour'd guest,
    Thy partner in the flowery walk
    Of letters, genial table-talk,
Or deep dispute, and graceful jest;

While now thy prosperous labour fills   25
    The lips of men with honest praise,
    And sun by sun the happy days
Descend below the golden hills

With promise of a morn as fair;
    And all the train of bounteous hours   30
    Conduct by paths of growing powers,
To reverence and the silver hair;

Till slowly worn her earthly robe,
    Her lavish mission richly wrought,
    Leaving great legacies of thought,   35
Thy spirit should fail from off the globe;

What time mine own might also flee,
    As link'd with thine in love and fate,
    And, hovering o'er the dolorous strait
To the other shore, involved in thee,   40

Arrive at last the blessed goal,
    And He that died in Holy Land

Would reach us out the shining hand,
And take us as a single soul.

What reed was that on which I leant?   45
Ah, backward fancy, wherefore wake
The old bitterness again, and break
The low beginnings of content.

85

T.Nbk

This truth came borne with bier and pall,
I felt it, when I sorrow'd most,
'Tis better to have loved and lost,
Than never to have loved at all —

O true in word, and tried in deed,   5
Demanding, so to bring relief
To this which is our common grief,
What kind of life is that I lead;

And whether trust in things above
Be dimm'd of sorrow, or sustain'd;   10
And whether love for him have drain'd
My capabilities of love;

Your words have virtue such as draws
A faithful answer from the breast,
Thro' light reproaches, half exprest,   15
And loyal unto kindly laws.

My blood an even tenor kept,
Till on mine ear this message falls,
That in Vienna's fatal walls
God's finger touch'd him, and he slept.   20

The great Intelligences fair
That range above our mortal state,

---

47 break] L.MS *2nd reading-*; shake L.MS *1st reading*

85] T.Nbk. *and* Heath MS (1-4, 49-52, 57-76, 97-108; Heath MS *has also* 41-4),
T.MS (93-120 *only*), L.MS, **Trial, 1850A-**
    1-92] *Not in* T.MS, *but evidence indicates a missing leaf (see Appendix A.1)*
5-48] *Not in* T.Nbk.   5-40] *Not in* Heath MS

In circle round the blessed gate,
Received and gave him welcome there;

And led him thro' the blissful climes,   25
    And show'd him in the fountain fresh
    All knowledge that the sons of flesh
Shall gather in the cycled times.

But I remain'd, whose hopes were dim,
    Whose life, whose thoughts were little worth,   30
    To wander on a darken'd earth,
Where all things round me breathed of him.

O friendship, equal-poised control,
    O heart, with kindliest motion warm,
    O sacred essence, other form,   35
O solemn ghost, O crowned soul!

Yet none could better know than I,
    How much of act at human hands
    The sense of human will demands
By which we dare to live or die.   40

Whatever way my days decline,
    I felt and feel, tho' left alone,
    His being working in mine own,
The footsteps of his life in mine;

A life that all the Muses deck'd   45
    With gifts of grace, that might express
    All-comprehensive tenderness,
All-subtilising intellect:

And so my passion hath not swerved
    To works of weakness, but I find   50
    An image comforting the mind,
And in my grief a strength reserved.

Likewise the imaginative woe,
    That loved to handle spiritual strife,
    Diffused the shock thro' all my life,   55
But in the present broke the blow.

41 days decline,] L.MS (. . . decline), **Trial**–; life incline Heath MS   45–8]
Not in Heath MS   51 the] L.MS–; my T.Nbk., Heath MS   53–56] *Not
in* T.Nbk., Heath MS

My pulses therefore beat again
　　For other friends that once I met;
　　Nor can it suit me to forget
The mighty hopes that make us men.　　　60

I woo your love: I count it crime
　　To mourn for any overmuch;
　　I, the divided half of such
A friendship as had master'd Time;

Which masters Time indeed, and is　　　65
　　Eternal, separate from fears:
　　The all-assuming months and years
Can take no part away from this:

But Summer on the steaming floods,
　　And Spring that swells the narrow brooks,　　　70
　　And Autumn, with a noise of rooks,
That gather in the waning woods,

And every pulse of wind and wave
　　Recalls, in change of light or gloom,
　　My old affection of the tomb,　　　75
And my prime passion in the grave:

My old affection of the tomb,
　　A part of stillness, yearns to speak:
　　'Arise, and get thee forth and seek
A friendship for the years to come.　　　80

'I watch thee from the quiet shore;
　　Thy spirit up to mine can reach;
　　But in dear words of human speech
We two communicate no more.'

57 My pulses therefore] L.MS-; These mortal pulses T.Nbk., Heath MS   59
can] L.MS-; doth T.Nbk., Heath MS   61-4] *In* T.Nbk. *this stanza appears*
three times: between 60 *and* 65; *between* 104 *and* 105 *(where it is deleted); and*
following 108. *So* 61-4 *is the concluding stanza of the section as it appears in*
T.Nbk. *and in* Heath MS. *In respect of* 61, *the draft following* 60 *agrees with the*
final reading; the draft following 104 *reads*
　　　　　　　　　　And yet I love you — count it crime
The draft following 108 *reads*
　　　　　　　　　　But yet I love you — count it crime
In respect of 62-4, *see minor variants*　　74 or] L.MS-; & T.Nbk., Heath MS
77-96] *Not in* T.Nbk., Heath MS

And I, 'Can clouds of nature stain   85
    The starry clearness of the free?
    How is it? Canst thou feel for me
Some painless sympathy with pain?'

And lightly does the whisper fall;
    ''Tis hard for thee to fathom this;   90
    I triumph in conclusive bliss,
And that serene result of all.'

So hold I commerce with the dead;
    Or so methinks the dead would say;
    Or so shall grief with symbols play   95
And pining life be fancy-fed.

Now looking to some settled end,
    That these things pass, and I shall prove
    A meeting somewhere, love with love,
I crave your pardon, O my friend;   100

If not so fresh, with love as true,
    I, clasping brother-hands, aver
    I could not, if I would, transfer
The whole I felt for him to you.

For which be they that hold apart   105
    The promise of the golden hours?
    First love, first friendship, equal powers,
That marry with the virgin heart.

Still mine, that cannot but deplore,
    That beats within a lonely place,   110
    That yet remembers his embrace,
But at his footstep leaps no more,

My heart, tho' widow'd, may not rest
    Quite in the love of what is gone,
    But seeks to beat in time with one   115
That warms another living breast.

93 commerce] L.MS−; commune T.MS   97 Now] T.MS−; Yet T.Nbk., Heath
MS some] T.MS−; a T.Nbk., Heath MS   104 whole] T.MS−; all, T.Nbk.,
Heath MS   105 which be they] T.MS−; who are those T.Nbk., Heath MS
109-20] *Not in* T.Nbk., Heath MS

Ah, take the imperfect gift I bring,
Knowing the primrose yet is dear,
The primrose of the later year,
As not unlike to that of Spring.   120

86

Sweet after showers, ambrosial air,
That rollest from the gorgeous gloom
Of evening over brake and bloom
And meadow, slowly breathing bare

The round of space, and rapt below   5
Thro' all the dewy-tassell'd wood,
And shadowing down the horned flood
In ripples, fan my brows and blow

The fever from my cheek, and sigh
The full new life that feeds thy breath   10
Throughout my frame, till Doubt and Death,
Ill brethren, let the fancy fly

From belt to belt of crimson seas
On leagues of odour streaming far,
To where in yonder orient star   15
A hundred spirits whisper 'Peace.'

87

I past beside the reverend walls
In which of old I wore the gown;
I roved at random thro' the town,
And saw the tumult of the halls;

86] L.MS, **Trial, 1850A-**; *not in* T.MS
     1 ambrosial] L.MS *2nd reading-*; delicious L.MS *1st reading*   3 evening
over brake and bloom] L.MS (Evening . . .), 1850A-; evening, over brake, and
bloom, **Trial**   4 meadow,] L.MS, 1850A-; meadow; **Trial**   5 space,]
Trial-; space L.MS below] L.MS, 1850A-; below, **Trial**   8 ripples,] L.MS,
1850A-; ripples; **Trial**   11 Throughout] L.MS *2nd reading-*; Thro' L.MS
1st reading

87] L.MS, **Trial, 1850A-**; *not in* T.MS

And heard once more in college fanes   5
   The storm their high-built organs make,
   And thunder-music, rolling, shake
The prophet blazon'd on the panes;

And caught once more the distant shout,
   The measured pulse of racing oars   10
   Among the willows; paced the shores
And many a bridge, and all about

The same gray flats again, and felt
   The same, but not the same; and last
   Up that long walk of limes I past   15
To see the rooms in which he dwelt.

Another name was on the door:
   I linger'd; all within was noise
   Of songs, and clapping hands, and boys
That crash'd the glass and beat the floor;   20

Where once we held debate, a band
   Of youthful friends, on mind and art,
   And labour, and the changing mart,
And all the framework of the land;

When one would aim an arrow fair,   25
   But send it slackly from the string;
   And one would pierce an outer ring,
And one an inner, here and there;

And last the master-bowman, he,
   Would cleave the mark. A willing ear   30
   We lent him. Who, but hung to hear
The rapt oration flowing free

From point to point, with power and grace
   And music in the bounds of law,
   To those conclusions when we saw   35
The God within him light his face,

6-7] L.MS *2nd reading* (. . . highbuilt . . . *no commas*), **Trial-**;
            The silver anthem trilling wake
            And that melodious thunder shake
                                    L.MS *1st reading*
8 prophet] 1884A-; prophets L.MS-1883   20 beat] 1850A-; smote L.MS,
Trial   25 When] L.MS *2nd reading-*; And L.MS *1st reading*

And seem to lift the form, and glow
  In azure orbits heavenly-wise;
  And over those ethereal eyes
The bar of Michael Angelo.   40

88

Wild bird, whose warble, liquid sweet,
  Rings Eden thro' the budded quicks,
  O tell me where the senses mix,
O tell me where the passions meet,

Whence radiate: fierce extremes employ   5
  Thy spirits in the darkening leaf,
  And in the midmost heart of grief
Thy passion clasps a secret joy:

And I — my harp would prelude woe —
  I cannot all command the strings;   10
  The glory of the sum of things
Will flash along the chords and go.

89

Witch-elms that counterchange the floor
  Of this flat lawn with dusk and bright;
  And thou, with all thy breadth and height
Of foliage, towering sycamore;

How often, hither wandering down,   5
  My Arthur found your shadows fair,
  And shook to all the liberal air
The dust and din and steam of town:

He brought an eye for all he saw;
  He mixt in all our simple sports;   10

39 ethereal] **Trial-**; seraphic L.MS

88] T.MS, **Trial, 1850A-**; *not in* L.MS
    6 darkening] **1855-**; dusking T.MS-1851B   7 heart] **Trial-**; pith T.MS

89] L.MS, **Trial, 1850A-**; *not in* T.MS
    7 shook] L.MS *2nd reading-*; flung L.MS *1st reading*

They pleased him, fresh from brawling courts
And dusty purlieus of the law.

O joy to him in this retreat,
   Immantled in ambrosial dark,
   To drink the cooler air, and mark   15
The landscape winking thro' the heat:

O sound to rout the brood of cares,
   The sweep of scythe in morning dew,
   The gust that round the garden flew,
And tumbled half the mellowing pears!   20

O bliss, when all in circle drawn
   About him, heart and ear were fed
   To hear him, as he lay and read
The Tuscan poets on the lawn:

Or in the all-golden afternoon   25
   A guest, or happy sister, sung,
   Or here she brought the harp and flung
A ballad to the brightening moon:

Nor less it pleased in livelier moods,
   Beyond the bounding hill to stray,   30
   And break the livelong summer day
With banquet in the distant woods;

Whereat we glanced from theme to theme,
   Discuss'd the books to love or hate,
   Or touch'd the changes of the state,   35
Or threaded some Socratic dream;

But if I praised the busy town,
   He loved to rail against it still,
   For 'ground in yonder social mill
We rub each other's angles down,   40

---

12 dusty] L.MS, **Trial, 1855-**; dusky 1850A–1851B   15 To drink the cooler
air,] **Trial-**; With me to suck the cool L.MS   16 landscape] 1850A–; landskip
L.MS, **Trial**   25 all-golden] L.MS *2nd reading-*; golden L.MS *1st reading*
35 touch'd] L.MS *2nd reading-*; grazed L.MS *1st reading*   36 threaded]
L.MS *2nd reading-*; handled L.MS *1st reading*   Socratic] L.MS *2nd reading-*;
Platonic L.MS *1st reading*

'And merge' he said 'in form and gloss
   The picturesque of man and man.'
   We talk'd: the stream beneath us ran,
The wine-flask lying couch'd in moss,

Or cool'd within the glooming wave;   45
   And last, returning from afar,
   Before the crimson-circled star
Had fall'n into her father's grave,

And brushing ankle-deep in flowers,
   We heard behind the woodbine veil   50
   The milk that bubbled in the pail,
And buzzings of the honied hours.

90

He tasted love with half his mind,
   Nor ever drank the inviolate spring
   Where nighest heaven, who first could fling
This bitter seed among mankind;

That could the dead, whose dying eyes   5
   Were closed with wail, resume their life,
   They would but find in child and wife
An iron welcome when they rise:

'Twas well, indeed, when warm with wine,
   To pledge them with a kindly tear,   10
   To talk them o'er, to wish them here,
To count their memories half divine;

But if they came who past away,
   Behold their brides in other hands;
   The hard heir strides about their lands,   15
And will not yield them for a day.

Yea, tho' their sons were none of these,
   Not less the yet-loved sire would make
   Confusion worse than death, and shake
The pillars of domestic peace.   20

90] L.MS, **Trial,** 1850A-; *not in* T.MS
  20 a–d] *deleted in* L.MS:

Ah dear, but come thou back to me:
  Whatever change the years have wrought,
  I find not yet one lonely thought
That cries against my wish for thee.

91

When rosy plumelets tuft the larch,
  And rarely pipes the mounted thrush;
  Or underneath the barren bush
Flits by the sea-blue bird of March;

Come, wear the form by which I know   5
  Thy spirit in time among thy peers;
  The hope of unaccomplish'd years
Be large and lucid round thy brow.

When summer's hourly-mellowing change
  May breathe, with many roses sweet,   10
  Upon the thousand waves of wheat,
That ripple round the lonely grange;

Come: not in watches of the night,
  But where the sunbeam broodeth warm,
  Come, beauteous in thine after form,   15
And like a finer light in light.

92

If any vision should reveal
  Thy likeness, I might count it vain
  As but the canker of the brain;
Yea, tho' it spake and made appeal

          Alas — but could I gaze on him
            Reclothed with human life from dust,
            My friend should share my latest crust,
          Tho' famine tore me limb from limb.

91] H.Lpr.101, T.MS, **Trial, 1850A**-; *not in* L.MS, *but evidence suggests it has been cut out (see Appendix A.1).*

92] T.MS, L.MS, **Trial, 1850A**-
    1 If any] L.MS *2nd reading*-; Yet if a T.MS, L.MS *1st reading*   3 the brain;] L.MS *(no punctuation)*, **Trial**-; my brain: T.MS

To chances where our lots were cast   5
   Together in the days behind,
   I might but say, I hear a wind
Of memory murmuring the past.

Yea, tho' it spake and bared to view
   A fact within the coming year;   10
   And tho' the months, revolving near,
Should prove the phantom-warning true,

They might not seem thy prophecies,
   But spiritual presentiments,
   And such refraction of events   15
As often rises ere they rise.

93

I shall not see thee. Dare I say
   No spirit ever brake the band
   That stays him from the native land
Where first he walk'd when claspt in clay?

No visual shade of some one lost,   5
   But he, the Spirit himself, may come
   Where all the nerve of sense is numb;
Spirit to Spirit, Ghost to Ghost.

O, therefore from thy sightless range
   With gods in unconjectured bliss,   10
   O, from the distance of the abyss
Of tenfold-complicated change,

Descend, and touch, and enter; hear
   The wish too strong for words to name;
   That in this blindness of the frame   15
My Ghost may feel that thine is near.

5 where] **Trial–;** when T.MS, L.MS   13 thy] L.MS–; *thy* T.MS

93] T.MS, L.MS, **Trial, 1850A–**
   7 Where all the nerve of sense is] T.MS *2nd reading–;* Where sense is deaf &
blind & T.MS *1st reading*   13] L.MS *2nd reading (no commas . . .enter: . . .),*
Trial–; Stoop soul & touch me: wed me: hear T.MS, L.MS *1st reading*   15
blindness] T.MS *2nd reading–;* darkness T.MS *1st reading*   16] L.MS (. . .
ghost . . .), **Trial–;** *My* soul may feel that thou art near. T.MS *1st reading; My*
ghost may feel that thine is near. T.MS *2nd reading*

94

How pure at heart and sound in head,
   With what divine affections bold
   Should be the man whose thought would hold
An hour's communion with the dead.

In vain shalt thou, or any, call   5
   The spirits from their golden day,
   Except, like them, thou too canst say,
My spirit is at peace with all.

They haunt the silence of the breast,
   Imaginations calm and fair,   10
   The memory like a cloudless air,
The conscience as a sea at rest:

But when the heart is full of din,
   And doubt beside the portal waits,
   They can but listen at the gates,   15
And hear the household jar within.

95

By night we linger'd on the lawn,
   For underfoot the herb was dry;
   And genial warmth; and o'er the sky
The silvery haze of summer drawn;

And calm that let the tapers burn   5
   Unwavering: not a cricket chirr'd:
   The brook alone far-off was heard,
And on the board the fluttering urn:

And bats went round in fragrant skies,
   And wheel'd or lit the filmy shapes   10
   That haunt the dusk, with ermine capes
And woolly breasts and beaded eyes;

94] T.MS, L.MS, **Trial, 1850A–**
    3 be the man] L.MS–; that man be T.MS   thought] **Trial–**; thoughts T.MS,
L.MS   4 dead.] L.MS–; dead! T.MS   8 My . . . all.] **Trial–**; 'My . . .
all.' T.MS; My . . . all L.MS

95] L.MS, **Trial, 1850A–**; *not in* T.MS

While now we sang old songs that peal'd
    From knoll to knoll, where, couch'd at ease,
    The white kine glimmer'd, and the trees   15
Laid their dark arms about the field.

But when those others, one by one,
    Withdrew themselves from me and night,
    And in the house light after light
Went out, and I was all alone,   20

A hunger seized my heart; I read
    Of that glad year which once had been,
    In those fall'n leaves which kept their green,
The noble letters of the dead:

And strangely on the silence broke   25
    The silent-speaking words, and strange
    Was love's dumb cry defying change
To test his worth; and strangely spoke

The faith, the vigour, bold to dwell
    On doubts that drive the coward back,   30
    And keen thro' wordy snares to track
Suggestion to her inmost cell.

So word by word, and line by line,
    The dead man touch'd me from the past,
    And all at once it seem'd at last   35
The living soul was flash'd on mine,

And mine in this was wound, and whirl'd
    About empyreal heights of thought,
    And came on that which is, and caught
The deep pulsations of the world,   40

Aeonian music measuring out
    The steps of Time — the shocks of Chance —
    The blows of Death. At length my trance
Was cancell'd, stricken thro' with doubt.

Vague words! but ah, how hard to frame   45
    In matter-moulded forms of speech,

36 The] 1872-; His L.MS-1870   37 this] 1872-; his L.MS-1870

Or ev'n for intellect to reach
Thro' memory that which I became:

Till now the doubtful dusk reveal'd
   The knolls once more where, couch'd at ease,   50
   The white kine glimmer'd, and the trees
Laid their dark arms about the field:

And suck'd from out the distant gloom
   A breeze began to tremble o'er
   The large leaves of the sycamore,   55
And fluctuate all the still perfume,

And gathering freshlier overhead,
   Rock'd the full-foliaged elms, and swung
   The heavy-folded rose, and flung
The lilies to and fro, and said   60

'The dawn, the dawn,' and died away;
   And East and West, without a breath,
   Mixt their dim lights, like life and death,
To broaden into boundless day.

96

You say, but with no touch of scorn,
   Sweet-hearted, you, whose light-blue eyes
   Are tender over drowning flies,
You tell me, doubt is Devil-born.

I know not: one indeed I knew   5
   In many a subtle question versed,
   Who touch'd a jarring lyre at first,
But ever strove to make it true:

Perplext in faith, but pure in deeds,
   At last he beat his music out.   10

96] H.Nbk.19, 1850A-; *not in* T.MS, L.MS, **Trial**
   1 You say, but] H.Nbk.19 *2nd reading (no comma)*, 1850A-; Dear Lady
H.Nbk.19 *1st reading*   2 Sweet-hearted, you,] H.Nbk.19 *2nd reading (no
hyphen*), 1850A-; Sweethearted maid H.Nbk.19 *1st reading*   3 flies,]
H.Nbk.19 *2nd reading-*; eyes, H.Nbk.19 *1st reading*   4 You tell me,] 1850A-;
You say that H.Nbk.19   10 At last he] H.Nbk.19 *2nd reading-*; Till he had
H.Nbk.19 *1st reading*

There lives more faith in honest doubt,
    Believe me, than in half the creeds.

He fought his doubts and gather'd strength,
    He would not make his judgment blind,
    He faced the spectres of the mind   15
And laid them: thus he came at length

To find a stronger faith his own;
    And Power was with him in the night,
    Which makes the darkness and the light,
And dwells not in the light alone,   20

But in the darkness and the cloud,
    As over Sinaï's peaks of old,
    While Israel made their gods of gold,
Altho' the trumpet blew so loud.

97

My love has talk'd with rocks and trees;
    He finds on misty mountain-ground
    His own vast shadow glory-crown'd;
He sees himself in all he sees.

Two partners of a married life —   5
    I look'd on these and thought of thee
    In vastness and in mystery,
And of my spirit as of a wife.

These two — they dwelt with eye on eye,
    Their hearts of old have beat in tune,   10
    Their meetings made December June,
Their every parting was to die.

15 faced] H.Nbk.19 *2nd reading*-; met H.Nbk.19 *1st reading*   17 find]
H.Nbk.19 *2nd reading*-; make H.Nbk.19 *1st reading*   19 makes] H.Nbk.19
2nd reading-; made H.Nbk.19 *1st reading*

97] H.Nbk.19 (*two drafts* (H.Nbk.a, H.Nbk.b): H.Nbk.a *has lines in this order:*
9-12, 33, 18-20, 13-16, 21-4, 29, 31, 30, 32, 25-8, 33-6; H.Nbk.b *lacks* 1-4
but has the other lines in the published order), 1850A-; *not in* T.MS, L.MS, **Trial**
    1-4] *Not in* H.Nbk.a,b   5-8] *Not in* H.Nbk.a   5 married] 1850A-;
common H.Nbk.b   6 look'd on these and] 1850A-; saw them & I H.Nbk.b
8 spirit as of a] 1850A-; soul as of thy H.Nbk.b   9-12] *Above this stanza in*
H.Nbk.a *is the isolated line (a false start?):* Long married souls, dear friend, are we
Both drafts have a version of this stanza:

Their love has never past away;
The days she never can forget
Are earnest that he loves her yet,   15
Whate'er the faithless people say.

Her life is lone, he sits apart,
He loves her yet, she will not weep,
Tho' rapt in matters dark and deep
He seems to slight her simple heart.   20

He thrids the labyrinth of the mind,
He reads the secret of the star,
He seems so near and yet so far,
He looks so cold: she thinks him kind.

She keeps the gift of years before,   25
A wither'd violet is her bliss:
She knows not what his greatness is,
For that, for all, she loves him more.

For him she plays, to him she sings
Of early faith and plighted vows;   30
She knows but matters of the house,
And he, he knows a thousand things.

Her faith is fixt and cannot move,
She darkly feels him great and wise,
She dwells on him with faithful eyes,   35
'I cannot understand: I love.'

They madly drank [These two have drunk H.Nbk.b] each other's breath
    With breast to breast in early years [years. H.Nbk.b]
    They met with passion and with tears
    Their every parting was a death [death. H.Nbk.b]
13 Their] H.Nbk.b-; His H.Nbk.a past] 1850A-; died H.Nbk.a,b   17]
1850A-; Her faith is fixt & cannot move H.Nbk.a,b (. . . rove.)   20 heart.]
1850A-; love H.Nbk.a,b   24 she thinks him] H.Nbk.b-; & is so H.Nbk.a
1st reading; she knows so H.Nbk.a 2nd reading   25 keeps the gift of]
H.Nbk.b-; dwells upon the H.Nbk.a   26 A wither'd violet is] H.Nbk.b-; To
think he loves her H.Nbk.a   27 knows] H.Nbk.b-; knowing H.Nbk.a   28
For that, for all,] H.Nbk.b (. . . all . . .), 1850A-; And yet for that H.Nbk.a
30] H.Nbk.b (. . . faith, . . . vows-), 1850A-; She looks upon his ample brows
H.Nbk.a   32 he,] H.Nbk.b-; thinks H.Nbk.a   33] H.Nbk.a and H.Nbk.b
2nd reading (no comma), 1850A-; His thoughts in vaster orbits move H.Nbk.b
1st reading   34 darkly feels him] H.Nbk.b-; feels him, darkly H.Nbk.a

98

You leave us: you will see the Rhine,
And those fair hills I sail'd below,
When I was there with him; and go
By summer belts of wheat and vine

To where he breathed his latest breath,   5
That City. All her splendour seems
No livelier than the wisp that gleams
On Lethe in the eyes of Death.

Let her great Danube rolling fair
Enwind her isles, unmark'd of me: 10
I have not seen, I will not see
Vienna; rather dream that there,

A treble darkness, Evil haunts
The birth, the bridal; friend from friend
Is oftener parted, fathers bend   15
Above more graves, a thousand wants

Gnarr at the heels of men, and prey
By each cold hearth, and sadness flings
Her shadow on the blaze of kings:
And yet myself have heard him say,   20

That not in any mother town
With statelier progress to and fro
The double tides of chariots flow
By park and suburb under brown

98] L.MS, **Trial, 1850A~**; *not in* T.MS
   2-3] L.MS *2nd reading* (*no comma*), **Trial-**;
                  And watch the impetuous current flow
                  That once I watch'd with him; & go
                                    L.MS *1st reading*
12 rather dream] L.MS *2nd reading-*; but methinks L.MS *1st reading*   13-16]
L.MS *2nd reading* (. . . evil . . . bridal, . . .), **Trial-**;
                  In tenfold frequence evil haunts
                     The threshold, oftener friend from friend
                  Is pluck'd asunder, parents bend
                  Above their dead, a thousand wants
                                    L.MS *1st reading*
20] **Trial-**; And Death is lord; albeit they say L.MS *1st reading*; And Pain is lord;
albeit they say L.MS *2nd reading*

Of lustier leaves; nor more content,   25
   He told me, lives in any crowd,
   When all is gay with lamps, and loud
With sport and song, in booth and tent,

Imperial halls, or open plain;
   And wheels the circled dance, and breaks   30
   The rocket molten into flakes
Of crimson or in emerald rain.

99

Risest thou thus, dim dawn, again,
   So loud with voices of the birds,
   So thick with lowings of the herds,
Day, when I lost the flower of men;

Who tremblest thro' thy darkling red   5
   On yon swoll'n brook that bubbles fast
   By meadows breathing of the past,
And woodlands holy to the dead;

Who murmurest in the foliaged eaves
   A song that slights the coming care,   10
   And Autumn laying here and there
A fiery finger on the leaves;

Who wakenest with thy balmy breath
   To myriads on the genial earth,
   Memories of bridal, or of birth,   15
And unto myriads more, of death.

26] **Trial–**; Sits on the foreheads of the crowd, L.MS *1st reading*; They tell me, lives in any crowd, L.MS *2nd reading*   28 booth and] **Trial–**; booth or L.MS   30 And] **Trial–**; As L.MS *1st reading*; While L.MS *alternative reading* 32] *Afterthought in* L.MS *following* 32
               As once I watch'd them at his side
               And heard him breathe a broken line
               From that strong hearted Florentine
               O vana gloria! thus he cried.

99] L.MS (*two drafts:* L.MSa, *on f.55^V, has* 1–4, 9–20 *only, and it is deleted;* L.MSb, *on f.66^V, adds* 5–8), Trial, 1850A–; *not in* T.MS
   5–8] *Not in* L.MSa   6 swoll'n] **Trial–**; wild L.MSb   9–10] L.MSb (. . . care), **Trial–**;   Who risest not as one that grieves
               In silence for a world of care,
               L.MSa

O wheresoever those may be,
Betwixt the slumber of the poles,
To-day they count as kindred souls;
They know me not, but mourn with me.   20

100

I climb the hill: from end to end
Of all the landscape underneath,
I find no place that does not breathe
Some gracious memory of my friend;

No gray old grange, or lonely fold,   5
Or low morass and whispering reed,
Or simple stile from mead to mead,
Or sheepwalk up the windy wold;

Nor hoary knoll of ash and haw
That hears the latest linnet trill,   10
Nor quarry trench'd along the hill
And haunted by the wrangling daw;

Nor runlet tinkling from the rock;
Nor pastoral rivulet that swerves
To left and right thro' meadowy curves,   15
That feed the mothers of the flock;

But each has pleased a kindred eye,
And each reflects a kindlier day;
And, leaving these, to pass away,
I think once more he seems to die.   20

101

Unwatch'd, the garden bough shall sway,
The tender blossom flutter down,

19 they count as] L.MSb-; I count them L.MSa

100] L.MS, **Trial, 1850A-**; *not in* T.MS
    1 I climb the hill:] **1855-**; I wake, I rise: L.MS-1851B   2 landscape]
1850A-; landskip L.MS, **Trial**   12 wrangling] **Trial-**; jangling L.MS   13
runlet tinkling] **Trial-**; fountain sparkling L.MS

101] L.MS, **Trial, 1850A-**; *not in* T.MS

Unloved, that beech will gather brown,
This maple burn itself away;

Unloved, the sun-flower, shining fair,   5
  Ray round with flames her disk of seed,
  And many a rose-carnation feed
With summer spice the humming air;

Unloved, by many a sandy bar,
  The brook shall babble down the plain,   10
  At noon or when the lesser wain
Is twisting round the polar star;

Uncared for, gird the windy grove,
  And flood the haunts of hern and crake;
  Or into silver arrows break   15
The sailing moon in creek and cove;

Till from the garden and the wild
  A fresh association blow,
  And year by year the landscape grow
Familiar to the stranger's child;   20

As year by year the labourer tills
  His wonted glebe, or lops the glades;
  And year by year our memory fades
From all the circle of the hills.

102

We leave the well-beloved place
  Where first we gazed upon the sky;
  The roofs, that heard our earliest cry,
Will shelter one of stranger race.

We go, but ere we go from home,   5
  As down the garden-walks I move,

---

3 that beech] L.MS *2nd reading*-;those elms L.MS *1st reading*   19] L.MS
2nd reading and **Trial** (... landskip ...), 1850A-; And all the landskip slowly
grow L.MS *1st reading*

102] T.MS, L.MS, **Trial**, 1850A-
  2 gazed] L.MS-; lookt T.MS

Two spirits of a diverse love
Contend for loving masterdom.

One whispers, 'Here thy boyhood sung
    Long since its matin song, and heard   10
    The low love-language of the bird
In native hazels tassel-hung.'

The other answers, 'Yea, but here
    Thy feet have stray'd in after hours
    With thy lost friend among the bowers.   15
And this hath made them trebly dear.'

These two have striven half the day,
    And each prefers his separate claim,
    Poor rivals in a losing game,
That will not yield each other way.   20

I turn to go: my feet are set
    To leave the pleasant fields and farms;
    They mix in one another's arms
To one pure image of regret.

103

On that last night before we went
    From out the doors where I was bred,
    I dream'd a vision of the dead,
Which left my after-morn content.

Methought I dwelt within a hall,   5
    And maidens with me: distant hills
    From hidden summits fed with rills
A river sliding by the wall.

The hall with harp and carol rang.
    They sang of what is wise and good   10
    And graceful. In the centre stood
A statue veil'd, to which they sang;

---

7 Two spirits] T.MS *2nd reading*-; I've spirits T.MS *1st reading*   20 yield]
T.MS *2nd reading*-; give T.MS *1st reading*

103] L.MS, **Trial, 1850A**-; *not in* T.MS

And which, tho' veil'd, was known to me,
  The shape of him I loved, and love
  For ever: then flew in a dove   15
And brought a summons from the sea:

And when they learnt that I must go
  They wept and wail'd, but led the way
  To where a little shallop lay
At anchor in the flood below;   20

And on by many a level mead,
  And shadowing bluff that made the banks,
  We glided winding under ranks
Of iris, and the golden reed;

And still as vaster grew the shore   25
  And roll'd the floods in grander space,
  The maidens gather'd strength and grace
And presence, lordlier than before;

And I myself, who sat apart
  And watch'd them, wax'd in every limb;   30
  I felt the thews of Anakim,
The pulses of a Titan's heart;

As one would sing the death of war,
  And one would chant the history
  Of that great race, which is to be.   35
And one the shaping of a star;

Until the forward-creeping tides
  Began to foam, and we to draw
  From deep to deep, to where we saw
A great ship lift her shining sides.   40

The man we loved was there on deck,
  But thrice as large as man he bent
  To greet us. Up the side I went,
And fell in silence on his neck:

Whereat those maidens with one mind   45
  Bewail'd their lot; I did them wrong:

41 there on] L.MS *2nd reading*-; on the L.MS *1st reading*

'We served thee here,' they said, 'so long,
And wilt thou leave us now behind?'

So rapt I was, they could not win
An answer from my lips, but he
Replying, 'Enter likewise ye
And go with us:' they enter'd in.

And while the wind began to sweep
A music out of sheet and shroud,
We steer'd her toward a crimson cloud
That landlike slept along the deep.

104

The time draws near the birth of Christ;
The moon is hid, the night is still;
A single church below the hill
Is pealing, folded in the mist.

A single peal of bells below,
That wakens at this hour of rest
A single murmur in the breast,
That these are not the bells I know.

Like strangers' voices here they sound,
In lands where not a memory strays,
Nor landmark breathes of other days,
But all is new unhallow'd ground.

105

To-night ungather'd let us leave
This laurel, let this holly stand:
We live within the stranger's land,
And strangely falls our Christmas eve.

104] T.MS, L.MS, **Trial**, 1850A–
2 hid,] L.MS (hid:), **Trial**–; out: T.MS   10 lands] L.MS *2nd reading*–;
fields T.MS, L.MS *1st reading*   11 other] L.MS–; older T.MS

105] H.Lpr.101, T.MS, L.MS, **Trial**, 1850A–
1-2] 1863–;   The holly by the cottage-case
To-night ungather'd shall it stand
H.Lpr.101

Our father's dust is left alone   5
  And silent under other snows:
  There in due time the woodbine blows,
The violet comes, but we are gone.

No more shall wayward grief abuse
  The genial hour with mask and mime;   10
  For change of place, like growth of time,
Has broke the bond of dying use.

Let cares that petty shadows cast,
  By which our lives are chiefly proved,
  A little spare the night I loved,   15
And hold it solemn to the past.

But let no footstep beat the floor,
  Nor bowl or wassail mantle warm:
  For who would keep an ancient form
Thro' which the spirit breathes no more?   20

Be neither song, nor game, nor feast;
  Nor harp be touch'd, nor flute be blown;
  No dance, no motion, save alone
What lightens in the lucid east

Of rising worlds by yonder wood.   25
  Long sleeps the summer in the seed;
  Run out your measured arcs, and lead
The closing cycle rich in good.

106

Ring out, wild bells, to the wild sky,
  The flying cloud, the frosty light:

This holly by the cottage-eave
  To-night ungather'd shall it stand [Tonight L.MS
                T.MS, L.MS

This holly by the cottage-eave,
  To night, ungather'd, shall it stand:
               Trial-1862
22 Nor] T.MS-; No H.Lpr.101   23 no] Trial-; nor H.Lpr.101-L.MS   28
good.] L.MS-; good! H.Lpr.101, T.MS

106] Trial, 1850A-; not in T.MS, L.MS
  1 Ring out, wild bells,] 1870-; Ring out wild bells Trial-1869

The year is dying in the night;
Ring out, wild bells, and let him die.

Ring out the old, ring in the new,   5
Ring, happy bells, across the snow:
The year is going, let him go;
Ring out the false, ring in the true.

Ring out the grief that saps the mind,
For those that here we see no more;   10
Ring out the feud of rich and poor,
Ring in redress to all mankind.

Ring out a slowly dying cause,
And ancient forms of party strife;
Ring in the nobler modes of life,   15
With sweeter manners, purer laws.

Ring out the want, the care, the sin,
The faithless coldness of the times;
Ring out, ring out my mournful rhymes,
But ring the fuller minstrel in.   20

Ring out false pride in place and blood,
The civic slander and the spite;
Ring in the love of truth and right,
Ring in the common love of good.

Ring out old shapes of foul disease;   25
Ring out the narrowing lust of gold;
Ring out the thousand wars of old,
Ring in the thousand years of peace.

Ring in the valiant man and free,
The larger heart, the kindlier hand;   30
Ring out the darkness of the land,
Ring in the Christ that is to be.

107

It is the day when he was born,
A bitter day that early sank

107] L.MS, **Trial, 1850A-;** *not in* T.MS

Behind a purple-frosty bank
Of vapour, leaving night forlorn.

The time admits not flowers or leaves   5
    To deck the banquet. Fiercely flies
    The blast of North and East, and ice
Makes daggers at the sharpen'd eaves,

And bristles all the brakes and thorns
    To yon hard crescent, as she hangs   10
    Above the wood which grides and clangs
Its leafless ribs and iron horns

Together, in the drifts that pass
    To darken on the rolling brine
    That breaks the coast. But fetch the wine,   15
Arrange the board and brim the glass;

Bring in great logs and let them lie,
    To make a solid core of heat;
    Be cheerful-minded, talk and treat
Of all things ev'n as he were by;   20

We keep the day. With festal cheer,
    With books and music, surely we
    Will drink to him, whate'er he be,
And sing the songs he loved to hear.

108

I will not shut me from my kind,
    And, lest I stiffen into stone,
    I will not eat my heart alone,
Nor feed with sighs a passing wind:

What profit lies in barren faith,   5
    And vacant yearning, tho' with might
    To scale the heaven's highest height,
Or dive below the wells of Death?

108] T.MS, L.MS, **Trial, 1**850A–
    4 Nor] T.MS, **Trial-**; And L.MS   6 yearning,] **Trial-**; yearnings T.MS;
yearning L.MS

What find I in the highest place,
  But mine own phantom chanting hymns?   10
  And on the depths of death there swims
The reflex of a human face.

I'll rather take what fruit may be
  Of sorrow under human skies:
  'Tis held that sorrow makes us wise,   15
Whatever wisdom sleep with thee.

109

Heart-affluence in discursive talk
  From household fountains never dry;
  The critic clearness of an eye,
That saw thro' all the Muses' walk;

Seraphic intellect and force   5
  To seize and throw the doubts of man;
  Impassion'd logic, which outran
The hearer in its fiery course;

High nature amorous of the good,
  But touch'd with no ascetic gloom;   10
  And passion pure in snowy bloom
Thro' all the years of April blood;

A love of freedom rarely felt,
  Of freedom in her regal seat
  Of England; not the schoolboy heat,   15
The blind hysterics of the Celt;

And manhood fused with female grace
  In such a sort, the child would twine
  A trustful hand, unask'd, in thine,
And find his comfort in thy face;   20

16] T.MS *2nd reading-*; Yet how much wisdom sleeps with thee. T.MS *1st reading*

109] L.MS, Trial, 1850A-; *not in* T.MS
  1 Heart-affluence] Trial-; Heart effluence L.MS

All these have been, and thee mine eyes
   Have look'd on: if they look'd in vain,
   My shame is greater who remain,
Nor let thy wisdom make me wise.

110

Thy converse drew us with delight,
   The men of rathe and riper years:
   The feeble soul, a haunt of fears,
Forgot his weakness in thy sight.

On thee the loyal-hearted hung,   5
   The proud was half disarm'd of pride,
   Nor cared the serpent at thy side
To flicker with his double tongue.

The stern were mild when thou wert by,
   The flippant put himself to school   10
   And heard thee, and the brazen fool
Was soften'd, and he knew not why;

While I, thy nearest, sat apart,
   And felt thy triumph was as mine;
   And loved them more, that they were thine,   15
The graceful tact, the Christian art;

Nor mine the sweetness or the skill,
   But mine the love that will not tire,
   And, born of love, the vague desire
That spurs an imitative will.   20

21-2] L.MS *2nd reading–* (*except for, in some cases, minor variants*);
    All these have vanish'd from mine eyes.
    All these have been, & if in vain
                L.MS *1st reading*

110] L.MS, **Trial, 1850A–;** *not in* T.MS
   7 cared] **Trial–;** loved L.MS   8 double] **1855–;** treble **L.MS–1851B**
13 nearest,] **1875–;** dearest, **L.MS–1874**   16 art;] L.MS *2nd reading* (art:),
Trial–; heart: L.MS *1st reading*   17 Nor] **1864–1874, 1877–;** Not **L.MS–
1863, 1875**

111

The churl in spirit, up or down
    Along the scale of ranks, thro' all,
    To him who grasps a golden ball,
By blood a king, at heart a clown;

The churl in spirit, howe'er he veil   5
    His want in forms for fashion's sake,
    Will let his coltish nature break
At seasons thro' the gilded pale:

For who can always act? but he,
    To whom a thousand memories call,   10
    Not being less but more than all
The gentleness he seem'd to be,

Best seem'd the thing he was, and join'd
    Each office of the social hour
    To noble manners, as the flower   15
And native growth of noble mind;

Nor ever narrowness or spite,
    Or villain fancy fleeting by,
    Drew in the expression of an eye,
Where God and Nature met in light;   20

And thus he bore without abuse
    The grand old name of gentleman,
    Defamed by every charlatan,
And soil'd with all ignoble use.

112

High wisdom holds my wisdom less,
    That I, who gaze with temperate eyes

111] T.MS (21-24 *only*), L.MS, **Trial, 1850A–**
    1-20] *Not in* T.MS   2 scale] L.MS *2nd reading–*; scales L.MS *1st reading*
3 him who grasps] 1855–; who may grasp L.MS-1851B   13 Best seem'd the
thing he was,] 1855–; So wore his outward best, L.MS-1851B   21 And thus
he bore] L.MS–; He best might bear T.MS   22 gentleman,] **Trial**–; 'gentleman'
T.MS; gentleman L.MS   23 Defamed] L.MS–; Profaned T.MS

112] H.Lpr.101, T.MS, L.MS, **Trial, 1850A–**

On glorious insufficiencies,
Set light by narrower perfectness.

But thou, that fillest all the room   5
    Of all my love, art reason why
    I seem to cast a careless eye
On souls, the lesser lords of doom.

For what wert thou? some novel power
    Sprang up for ever at a touch,   10
    And hope could never hope too much,
In watching thee from hour to hour,

Large elements in order brought,
    And tracts of calm from tempest made,
    And world-wide fluctuation sway'd   15
In vassal tides that follow'd thought.

113

'Tis held that sorrow makes us wise;
    Yet how much wisdom sleeps with thee
    Which not alone had guided me,
But served the seasons that may rise;

For can I doubt, who knew thee keen   5
    In intellect, with force and skill
    To strive, to fashion, to fulfil —
I doubt not what thou wouldst have been:

A life in civic action warm,
    A soul on highest mission sent,   10
    A potent voice of Parliament,
A pillar steadfast in the storm,

5-8] T.MS *2nd reading and* L.MS (*no commas*), **Trial-**;
            For souls, the lesser lords of doom [lesser-lords T.MS
            Are worth all praise from young & old
            Tho those are quick to judge that hold
            Completion in a little room.
                                        H.Lpr.101, T.MS *1st reading*
9 For what wert] T.MS *2nd reading-*; Such wert not H.Lpr.101, T.MS *1st reading*

113] L.MS, **Trial**, 1850A-; *not in* T.MS

Should licensed boldness gather force,
  Becoming, when the time has birth,
  A lever to uplift the earth   15
And roll it in another course,

With thousand shocks that come and go,
  With agonies, with energies,
  With overthrowings, and with cries,
And undulations to and fro.   20

114

Who loves not Knowledge? Who shall rail
  Against her beauty? May she mix
  With men and prosper! Who shall fix
Her pillars? Let her work prevail.

But on her forehead sits a fire: 5
  She sets her forward countenance
  And leaps into the future chance,
Submitting all things to desire.

Half-grown as yet, a child, and vain —
  She cannot fight the fear of death.   10
  What is she, cut from love and faith,
But some wild Pallas from the brain

Of Demons? fiery-hot to burst
  All barriers in her onward race
  For power. Let her know her place;   15
She is the second, not the first.

A higher hand must make her mild,
  If all be not in vain; and guide
  Her footsteps, moving side by side
With wisdom, like the younger child: 20

For she is earthly of the mind,
  But Wisdom heavenly of the soul.

17 thousand] 1855-; many L.MS-1851B

114] **Trial, 1850A-**; *not in* T.MS, L.MS

O, friend, who camest to thy goal
So early, leaving me behind,

I would the great world grew like thee,   25
Who grewest not alone in power
And knowledge, but by year and hour
In reverence and in charity.

115

Now fades the last long streak of snow,
Now burgeons every maze of quick
About the flowering squares, and thick
By ashen roots the violets blow.

Now rings the woodland loud and long,   5
The distance takes a lovelier hue,
And drown'd in yonder living blue
The lark becomes a sightless song.

Now dance the lights on lawn and lea,
The flocks are whiter down the vale,   10
And milkier every milky sail
On winding stream or distant sea;

Where now the seamew pipes, or dives
In yonder greening gleam, and fly
The happy birds, that change their sky   15
To build and brood; that live their lives

From land to land; and in my breast
Spring wakens too; and my regret
Becomes an April violet,
And buds and blossoms like the rest.   20

27 by year and] 1855-; from hour to Trial-1851B

115] L.MS, Trial, 1850A-; *not in* T.MS
    3 flowering] L.MS *2nd reading*-; greening L.MS *1st reading*   6 lovelier]
L.MS-1874, 1877-; living 1875   7 living] L.MS-1874, 1877-; livelier 1875
16 that] L.MS *2nd reading*-; & L.MS *1st reading*

116

Is it, then, regret for buried time
   That keenlier in sweet April wakes,
   And meets the year, and gives and takes
The colours of the crescent prime?

Not all: the songs, the stirring air,   5
   The life re-orient out of dust,
   Cry thro' the sense to hearten trust
In that which made the world so fair.

Not all regret: the face will shine
   Upon me, while I muse alone;   10
   And that dear voice, I once have known,
Still speak to me of me and mine:

Yet less of sorrow lives in me
   For days of happy commune dead;
   Less yearning for the friendship fled,   15
Than some strong bond which is to be.

117

O days and hours, your work is this
   To hold me from my proper place,
   A little while from his embrace,
For fuller gain of after bliss:

That out of distance might ensue   5
   Desire of nearness doubly sweet;
   And unto meeting when we meet,
Delight a hundredfold accrue,

For every grain of sand that runs,
   And every span of shade that steals,   10
   And every kiss of toothed wheels,
And all the courses of the suns.

116] **Trial, 1850A-;** *not in* T.MS, L.MS
   11-12 And that dear voice, I once have known, / Still] **1855-;** The dear, dear
voice that I have known / Will **Trial-1851B**

117] T.MS, L.MS, **Trial, 1850A-**

118

Contemplate all this work of Time,
   The giant labouring in his youth:
   Nor dream of human love and truth,
As dying Nature's earth and lime;

But trust that those we call the dead   5
   Are breathers of an ampler day
   For ever nobler ends. They say,
The solid earth whereon we tread

In tracts of fluent heat began,
   And grew to seeming-random forms,   10
   The seeming prey of cyclic storms,
Till at the last arose the man;

Who throve and branch'd from clime to clime,
   The herald of a higher race,
   And of himself in higher place,   15
If so he type this work of time

Within himself, from more to more;
   Or, crown'd with attributes of woe
   Like glories, move his course, and show
That life is not as idle ore,   20

But iron dug from central gloom,
   And heated hot with burning fears,
   And dipt in baths of hissing tears,
And batter'd with the shocks of doom

To shape and use. Arise and fly   25
   The reeling Faun, the sensual feast;
   Move upward, working out the beast,
And let the ape and tiger die.

118] L.MS, **Trial, 1850A**-; *not in* T.MS
   1 all] L.MS *2nd reading*-; thou L.MS *1st reading*   9] **Trial**-; In fields of
fluid fire began, L.MS *1st reading*; In tracts of fluent fire began, L.MS *2nd reading*
18 Or,] **1850B**-; And, L.MS–1850A

119

Doors, where my heart was used to beat
So quickly, not as one that weeps
I come once more; the city sleeps;
I smell the meadow in the street;

I hear a chirp of birds; I see   5
Betwixt the black fronts long-withdrawn
A light-blue lane of early dawn,
And think of early days and thee,

And bless thee, for thy lips are bland,
And bright the friendship of thine eye;   10
And in my thoughts with scarce a sigh
I take the pressure of thine hand.

120

I trust I have not wasted breath:
I think we are not wholly brain,
Magnetic mockeries; not in vain,
Like Paul with beasts, I fought with Death;

Not only cunning casts in clay: 5
Let Science prove we are, and then
What matters Science unto men,
At least to me? I would not stay.

Let him, the wiser man who springs
Hereafter, up from childhood shape   10
His action like the greater ape,
But I was *born* to other things.

121

Sad Hesper o'er the buried sun
And ready, thou, to die with him,

119] 1850A-; *not in* T.MS, L.MS, Trial

120] 1850A-; *not in* T.MS, L.MS, Trial
  12 *born]* 1872-; born 1850A-1870

121] 1850A-; *not in* T.MS, L.MS, Trial

Thou watchest all things ever dim
And dimmer, and a glory done:

The team is loosen'd from the wain,   5
  The boat is drawn upon the shore;
  Thou listenest to the closing door,
And life is darken'd in the brain.

Bright Phosphor, fresher for the night,
  By thee the world's great work is heard   10
  Beginning, and the wakeful bird;
Behind thee comes the greater light:

The market boat is on the stream,
  And voices hail it from the brink;
  Thou hear'st the village hammer clink,   15
And see'st the moving of the team.

Sweet Hesper-Phosphor, double name
  For what is one, the first, the last,
  Thou, like my present and my past,
Thy place is changed; thou art the same.   20

122

Oh, wast thou with me, dearest, then,
  While I rose up against my doom,
  And yearn'd to burst the folded gloom,
To bare the eternal Heavens again,

To feel once more, in placid awe,   5
  The strong imagination roll
  A sphere of stars about my soul,
In all her motion one with law;

If thou wert with me, and the grave
  Divide us not, be with me now,   10
  And enter in at breast and brow,
Till all my blood, a fuller wave,

122] L.MS, **Trial, 1850A–**; *not in* T.MS
  3 yearn'd] **1850B–**; strove L.MS–1850A

Be quicken'd with a livelier breath,
    And like an inconsiderate boy,
    As in the former flash of joy,   15
I slip the thoughts of life and death;

And all the breeze of Fancy blows,
    And every dew-drop paints a bow,
    The wizard lightnings deeply glow,
And every thought breaks out a rose.   20

123

There rolls the deep where grew the tree.
    O earth, what changes hast thou seen!
    There where the long street roars, hath been
The stillness of the central sea.

The hills are shadows, and they flow   5
    From form to form, and nothing stands;
    They melt like mist, the solid lands,
Like clouds they shape themselves and go.

But in my spirit will I dwell,
    And dream my dream, and hold it true;   10
    For tho' my lips may breathe adieu,
I cannot think the thing farewell.

17 breeze] L.MS *2nd reading-*; storm L.MS *1st reading*

123] T.MS, L.MS, **Trial, 1850A-**
    2 hast thou] T.MS-1859, 1864-; thou hast **1860-1863**   4 a-d] *deleted*
in T.MS   Like days & hours the cycles fleet,
                    The deep seas pass away like steam.
                    But Love hath such a real dream
                    It cannot pass, it is so sweet.
5 and they flow] T.MS *1st reading*, L.MS-; flowing by T.MS *2nd reading*   8
go.] T.MS *1st reading*, L.MS-; fly T.MS *2nd reading*   8 a-d]
                But in my love will I rejoice
                Nor should my song of love be mute
                Tho' Earth should shake beneath my foot,
                And Heaven's axle break with noise
                            T.MS
9 But] L.MS-; And T.MS will I] L.MS-; I will T.MS

124

That which we dare invoke to bless;
  Our dearest faith; our ghastliest doubt;
  He, They, One, All; within, without;
The Power in darkness whom we guess;

I found Him not in world or sun,   5
  Or eagle's wing, or insect's eye;
  Nor thro' the questions men may try,
The petty cobwebs we have spun:

If e'er when faith had fall'n asleep,
  I heard a voice 'believe no more'   10
  And heard an ever-breaking shore
That tumbled in the Godless deep;

A warmth within the breast would melt
  The freezing reason's colder part,
  And like a man in wrath the heart   15
Stood up and answer'd 'I have felt.'

No, like a child in doubt and fear:
  But that blind clamour made me wise;
  Then was I as a child that cries,
But, crying, knows his father near;   20

And what I am beheld again
  What is, and no man understands;
  And out of darkness came the hands
That reach thro' nature, moulding men.

124] L.MS *and* Trial (9-16, 21-4 *only*), H.Lpr.102, 1850A-; *not in* T.MS
    1-8] *Not in* L.MS, Trial   10-12] L.MS *2nd reading- (except for, in some
cases, minor variants*);
                    And doubt began 'believe no more'
                    I heard upon the crumbling shore
                    The long roll of the Godless deep.
                                        L.MS *1st reading*
17-20] *Not in* L.MS, Trial   21 what I am] 1859-; the inner eye L.MS, Trial;
what I seem H.Lpr.102-1856   22-3] H.Lpr.102-;
                    The form which no one understands,
                    And glimpses of the shadowy hands [hands, Trial
                                        L.MS, Trial

125

Whatever I have said or sung,
   Some bitter notes my harp would give,
   Yea, tho' there often seem'd to live
A contradiction on the tongue,

Yet Hope had never lost her youth;   5
   She did but look through dimmer eyes;
   Or Love but play'd with gracious lies,
Because he felt so fix'd in truth:

And if the song were full of care,
   He breathed the spirit of the song;   10
   And if the words were sweet and strong
He set his royal signet there;

Abiding with me till I sail
   To seek thee on the mystic deeps,
   And this electric force, that keeps   15
A thousand pulses dancing, fail.

126

Love is and was my Lord and King,
   And in his presence I attend
   To hear the tidings of my friend,
Which every hour his couriers bring.

Love is and was my King and Lord,   5
   And will be, tho' as yet I keep

125] T.MS, **Trial,** 1850A-; *not in* L.MS
   3 Yea,] T.MS *2nd reading* (Yea), **Trial**-; And T.MS *1st reading*   5 had
never lost her] T.MS *2nd reading*-; was ever hale in T.MS *1st reading*   6]
Trial-1863 (... thro' ...), 1864-; And did but borrow dimmer eyes T.MS *1st
reading*; And did but look thro' dimmer eyes T.MS *2nd reading*   7 Or] T.MS
2nd reading-; And T.MS *1st reading* gracious] T.MS *2nd reading*-; graceful T.MS
1st reading   9 song] T.MS *2nd reading*-; lay T.MS *1st reading* of care,]
T.MS *2nd reading* (*no comma*), **Trial**-; & strong T.MS *1st reading*   11 words]
T.MS *2nd reading*-; lay T.MS *1st reading* sweet] **Trial**-; full T.MS

126] T.MS, **Trial,** 1850A-; *not in* L.MS
   1] T.MS *2nd reading* (... king), **Trial**-; Love is my Lord & Love my king
T.MS *1st reading*   4 a-d] *Deleted in* T.MS
          Love is my king, nor here alone
          But where I see the distance loom
          For on the field behind the tomb
          There rest the shadows of his throne.

Within his court on earth, and sleep
Encompass'd by his faithful guard,

And hear at times a sentinel
Who moves about from place to place,   10
And whispers to the worlds of space,
In the deep night, that all is well.

127

And all is well, tho' faith and form
Be sunder'd in the night of fear;
Well roars the storm to those that hear
A deeper voice across the storm,

Proclaiming social truth shall spread,   5
And justice, ev'n tho' thrice again
The red fool-fury of the Seine
Should pile her barricades with dead.

But ill for him that wears a crown,
And him, the lazar, in his rags: 10
They tremble, the sustaining crags;
The spires of ice are toppled down,

And molten up, and roar in flood;
The fortress crashes from on high,
The brute earth lightens to the sky,   15
And the great Æon sinks in blood,

And compass'd by the fires of Hell;
While thou, dear spirit, happy star,
O'erlook'st the tumult from afar,
And smilest, knowing all is well.

9 a] T.MS *2nd reading*-; the T.MS *1st reading*   10 Who] 1855-; That
T.MS-1851B   11 worlds] 1855-; vast T.MS-1851B   12] 1855-; A
distant notice 'All is well' T.MS *1st reading*; Among the worlds, that all is well.
T.MS *2nd reading*-1851B

127] L.MS, Trial, 1850A-; *not in* T.MS
    6 ev'n] L.MS *2nd reading*-; yea, L.MS *1st reading* thrice] 1850A-; once L.MS,
Trial   7 red fool-fury] Trial-; red-capt harlot L.MS   9 But ill for him]
1850B-; Woe to the head L.MS *1st reading*; But Woe to him L.MS *2nd reading*,
Trial *and* 1850A (woe)   14 fortress] Trial-; mountain L.MS   16 great]
1851A-; vast L.MS-1850C   18 happy star,] 1850A-; from afar L.MS, Trial
19 O'erlook'st] Trial-; Look'st o'er L.MS from afar,] 1850A-; like a star L.MS,
Trial (star,)

128

The love that rose on stronger wings,
   Unpalsied when he met with Death,
   Is comrade of the lesser faith
That sees the course of human things.

No doubt vast eddies in the flood   5
   Of onward time shall yet be made,
   And throned races may degrade;
Yet O ye mysteries of good,

Wild Hours that fly with Hope and Fear,
   If all your office had to do   10
   With old results that look like new;
If this were all your mission here,

To draw, to sheathe a useless sword,
   To fool the crowd with glorious lies,
   To cleave a creed in sects and cries,   15
To change the bearing of a word,

To shift an arbitrary power,
   To cramp the student at his desk,
   To make old bareness picturesque
And tuft with grass a feudal tower;   20

Why then my scorn might well descend
   On you and yours. I see in part
   That all, as in some piece of art,
Is toil cöoperant to an end.

128] T.MS (9-24 only), H.Lpr.102 (5-24 only), 1850A-; not in L.MS, Trial
  1-4] Not in T.MS, H.Lpr.102   5-8] Not in T.MS   8 mysteries]
1850B-; ministers H.Lpr.102, 1850A   14-15] 1850A-;
        To split a creed in barren sects,
        Heap simple goodness with neglects,
               T.MS

        To choke a creed with mythic lies,
        Or cleave it into sects & cries,
             H.Lpr.102
16 To] 1850A-; Or T.MS, H.Lpr.102   18 cramp] T.MS alternative reading,
1850A-; bow T.MS 1st reading   19 bareness] 1850B-; baseness T.MS-1850A
21 Why] H.Lpr.102-; Oh T.MS well descend] T.MS alternative reading, 1850A-;
largely blend T.MS 1st reading   22 On] H.Lpr.102-; With T.MS   23
piece] H.Lpr.102-; work T.MS   24 cöoperant]H.Lpr.102-; cöoperate T.MS

129

Dear friend, far off, my lost desire,
   So far, so near in woe and weal;
   O loved the most, when most I feel
There is a lower and a higher;

Known and unknown; human, divine;   5
   Sweet human hand and lips and eye;
   Dear heavenly friend that canst not die,
Mine, mine, for ever, ever mine;

Strange friend, past, present, and to be;
   Loved deeplier, darklier understood;   10
   Behold, I dream a dream of good,
And mingle all the world with thee.

130

Thy voice is on the rolling air;
   I hear thee where the waters run;
   Thou standest in the rising sun,
And in the setting thou art fair.

What art thou then? I cannot guess;   5
   But tho' I seem in star and flower

129] **Trial, 1850A-;** *not in* **T.MS, L.MS**
   2 So far,] **1850A-;** Sweet friend, **Trial**   3 O loved the most,] **1855-;**
Dear friend, loved most **Trial;** O, loved the most **1850A-1851B**   5 divine;]
1855-; divine! **Trial-1851B**   6 hand and lips] **1850A-;** voice, and hand
Trial   8 Mine, mine,] **1850A-;** My friend, **Trial** ever mine;] **1855-;** ever
mine! **Trial-1851B**   11-12] **1850A-1851B** (. . . good), **1855-;**
                Let me not lose my faith in good
                Lest I make less my love for thee.
                                        Trial

130] **L.MS, Trial, 1850A-;** *not in* **T.MS**
   1 on] **L.MS** *2nd reading-;* in **L.MS** *1st reading*   4 setting] **L.MS** *2nd*
reading-; flowers **L.MS** *1st reading*   4 a-h] *Deleted in* **L.MS**
                No more I yearn no longer grieve:
                   I walk the meadows & rejoice
                   And prosper, compass'd by thy voice
                For ever. Strange that I should live

                To say such wondrous things of thee!
                   I know the beauty which thou wast
                   Thy single sweetness in the Past
                Yet art thou oft as God to me.

To feel thee some diffusive power,
I do not therefore love thee less:

My love involves the love before;
My love is vaster passion now;   10
Tho' mix'd with God and Nature thou,
I seem to love thee more and more.

Far off thou art, but ever nigh;
I have thee still, and I rejoice;
I prosper, circled with thy voice;   15
I shall not lose thee tho' I die.

131

O living will that shalt endure
When all that seems shall suffer shock,
Rise in the spiritual rock,
Flow thro' our deeds and make them pure,

That we may lift from out of dust   5
A voice as unto him that hears,
A cry above the conquer'd years
To one that with us works, and trust,

With faith that comes of self-control,
The truths that never can be proved   10
Until we close with all we loved,
And all we flow from, soul in soul.

13 Far off thou art,] Trial-; O thou far off L.MS   15 circled] Trial-; compassd L.MS

131] H.Nbk.18, L.MS, Trial, 1850A-; *not in* T.MS
2] L.MS (. . . seems, . . .), Trial-; When mountains [*intentional blank*] shock H.Nbk.18   5 lift] L.MS-; speak H.Nbk.18 of] L.MS, 1850B-; the H.Nbk.18, Trial, 1850A   6] L.MS *2nd reading* (. . . hears;), Trial-; As unto one that hears & see H.Nbk.18; A voice as unto one that hears; L.MS *1st reading*   7] L.MS-; Some little of the vast to be H.Nbk.18   8] L.MS, Trial-1850C (. . . trust), 1851A-; [*intentional blank*] & [*intentional blank*] trust H.Nbk.18   9] L.MS, Trial-1850C (. . . self-control), 1851A-; With evergrowing strength [*intentional blank containing &*] grace H.Nbk.18 *1st reading*; With ever more of strength [*intentional blank containing &*] grace H.Nbk.18 *2nd reading*   11-12] L.MS (. . . loved . . .), Trial-;
          And come to look on those we loved
          And That wh made us, face to face.
          H.Nbk.18

[Epilogue]

O true and tried, so well and long,
    Demand not thou a marriage lay;
    In that it is thy marriage day
Is music more than any song.

Nor have I felt so much of bliss   5
    Since first he told me that he loved
    A daughter of our house; nor proved
Since that dark day a day like this;

Tho' I since then have number'd o'er
    Some thrice three years: they went and came,   10
    Remade the blood and changed the frame,
And yet is love not less, but more;

No longer caring to embalm
    In dying songs a dead regret,
    But like a statue solid-set,   15
And moulded in colossal calm.

Regret is dead, but love is more
    Than in the summers that are flown,
    For I myself with these have grown
To something greater than before;   20

Which makes appear the songs I made
    As echoes out of weaker times,
    As half but idle brawling rhymes,
The sport of random sun and shade.

But where is she, the bridal flower,   25
    That must be made a wife ere noon?

[*Epilogue*]] L.MS, **Trial, 1850A–**; *not in* T.MS
    2] L.MS *2nd reading* (. . . lay?), **Trial–**; Why ask of me a marriage lay? L.MS
1st reading   7] L.MS *2nd reading–*; Her elder sister: no, nor proved L.MS
1st reading   10] they went and came,] L.MS *2nd reading–*; have seen go
them go [*sic*] L.MS *1st reading*   11] L.MS *2nd reading* (. . . frame:), **Trial–**;
With change of blossom, fruit & snow; L.MS *1st reading*   21 appear] L.MS
2nd reading–; me deem L.MS *1st reading*   24 a–d] *Deleted in* L.MS
                For if the wisest rule, to rest
                In Him is wisest; all are His:
                And so we leave whatever is
                To Him the wisest & the Best.

She enters, glowing like the moon
Of Eden on its bridal bower:

On me she bends her blissful eyes
 And then on thee; they meet thy look   30
 And brighten like the star that shook
Betwixt the palms of paradise.

O when her life was yet in bud,
 He too foretold the perfect rose.
 For thee she grew, for thee she grows   35
For ever, and as fair as good.

And thou art worthy; full of power;
 As gentle; liberal-minded, great,
 Consistent; wearing all that weight
Of learning lightly like a flower.   40

But now set out: the noon is near,
 And I must give away the bride;
 She fears not, or with thee beside
And me behind her, will not fear.

For I that danced her on my knee,   45
 That watch'd her on her nurse's arm,
 That shielded all her life from harm
At last must part with her to thee;

Now waiting to be made a wife,
 Her feet, my darling, on the dead;   50
 Their pensive tablets round her head,
And the most living words of life

Breathed in her ear. The ring is on,
 The 'wilt thou' answer'd, and again
 The 'wilt thou' ask'd, till out of twain   55
Her sweet 'I will' has made you one.

Now sign your names, which shall be read,
 Mute symbols of a joyful morn,
 By village eyes as yet unborn;
The names are sign'd, and overhead   60

41 now set out:] L.MS *2nd reading*-; we must go: L.MS *1st reading* 56 you]
1872-; ye L.MS-1870   58 joyful] **Trial**-; blissful L.MS

Begins the clash and clang that tells
The joy to every wandering breeze;
The blind wall rocks, and on the trees
The dead leaf trembles to the bells.

O happy hour, and happier hours   65
Await them. Many a merry face
Salutes them — maidens of the place,
That pelt us in the porch with flowers.

O happy hour, behold the bride
With him to whom her hand I gave.   70
They leave the porch, they pass the grave
That has to-day its sunny side.

To-day the grave is bright for me.
For them the light of life increased,
Who stay to share the morning feast,   75
Who rest to-night beside the sea.

Let all my genial spirits advance
To meet and greet a whiter sun;
My drooping memory will not shun
The foaming grape of eastern France.   80

It circles round, and fancy plays,
And hearts are warm'd and faces bloom,
As drinking health to bride and groom
We wish them store of happy days.

65] L.MS *2nd reading-*; Come out: a day of happy hours L.MS *1st reading*   66
Await them.] L.MS *2nd reading* (... them:), **Trial-**; Awaits you: L.MS *1st reading*
67 Salutes them —] **Trial-**; Will greet you, L.MS *1st reading*; Salute them L.MS
2nd reading   68 That] L.MS *2nd reading-*; They L.MS *1st reading*   69]
L.MS *2nd reading* (... hour! ...), **Trial-**; Return with him: return a bride L.MS
1st reading   70 her] L.MS *2nd reading-*; thy L.MS *1st reading*   71]
L.MS *2nd reading* (... porch: ... grave,), **Trial-**; Step lightly by the sunny
grave, L.MS *1st reading*   72 That] L.MS *2nd reading-*; It L.MS *1st reading*
73-6] L.MS *2nd reading* (*no hyphens or punctuation*), **Trial-**;
             For all is light & life increased
             For you & so for us today
             Albeit you leave us here: but stay
             A little: Share the morning feast.
                              L.MS *1st reading*
81 and] L.MS *2nd reading-*; The L.MS *1st reading*   82 And] L.MS *2nd
reading-*; The L.MS *1st reading* and] L.MS *2nd reading-*; the L.MS *1st reading*

Nor count me all to blame if I   85
   Conjecture of a stiller guest,
   Perchance, perchance, among the rest,
And, tho' in silence, wishing joy.

But they must go, the time draws on,
   And those white-favour'd horses wait;   90
   They rise, but linger; it is late;
Farewell, we kiss, and they are gone.

A shade falls on us like the dark
   From little cloudlets on the grass,
   But sweeps away as out we pass   95
To range the woods, to roam the park,

Discussing how their courtship grew,
   And talk of others that are wed,
   And how she look'd, and what he said,
And back we come at fall of dew.   100

Again the feast, the speech, the glee,
   The shade of passing thought, the wealth
   Of words and wit, the double health,
The crowning cup, the three-times-three,

And last the dance; — till I retire: 105
   Dumb is that tower which spake so loud,

86 a stiller] L.MS *2nd reading*-; another L.MS *1st reading*   87 Perchance,
perchance,] L.MS *2nd reading (no commas)*, Trial-; As here unseen L.MS *1st
reading*   88 a–d] *Deleted in* L.MS
        A passing fancy, let it be:
        However wish'd, their joy will grow
        Beyond the wish: but they must go:
        They rest to-night beside the sea.
89] L.MS *2nd reading* (. . . go: . . . on:), Trial-; Farewell — & yet they linger on:
L.MS *1st reading*   91 rise, but linger;] L.MS *2nd reading* (. . . linger:),
Trial-1850C (rise . . . linger,), 1851A-; rise, but go not: L.MS *1st reading*   94
grass,] L.MS *2nd reading*-; sun, L.MS *1st reading*   95–6] L.MS *2nd reading*-;
        But out we go, we walk, we run,
        We loiter in & out the park:
                L.MS *1st reading*
96 a–d] *Deleted in* L.MS
        We pace the stubble bare of sheaves,
        We watch the brimming river steal
        And half the golden woodland reel
        Athwart the smoke of burning leaves.
97 Discussing] L.MS *2nd reading*-; We talk of L.MS *1st reading*   98 And
talk] L.MS *2nd reading*-; We speak L.MS *1st reading*   104 The crowning
cup,] L.MS *2nd reading*-; And close on that, L.MS *1st reading*

And high in heaven the streaming cloud,
And on the downs a rising fire:

And rise, O moon, from yonder down,
    Till over down and over dale   110
    All night the shining vapour sail
And pass the silent-lighted town,

The white-faced halls, the glancing rills,
    And catch at every mountain head,
    And o'er the friths that branch and spread   115
Their sleeping silver thro' the hills;

And touch with shade the bridal doors,
    With tender gloom the roof, the wall;
    And breaking let the splendour fall
To spangle all the happy shores   120

By which they rest, and ocean sounds,
    And, star and system rolling past,
    A soul shall draw from out the vast
And strike his being into bounds,

And, moved thro' life of lower phase,   125
    Result in man, be born and think,
    And act and love, a closer link
Betwixt us and the crowning race

Of those that, eye to eye, shall look
    On knowledge; under whose command   130

---

109 down,] L.MS *2nd reading* (down), **Trial-**; downs L.MS *1st reading*   110]
L.MS *2nd reading-*; And over tower & grove & vale L.MS *1st reading*   112
pass] L.MS *1st reading*, **Trial-**; cross L.MS *2nd reading* town,] L.MS *2nd reading-*;
towns, L.MS *1st reading*   113] L.MS *2nd reading* (white faced halls . . .),
Trial-; And cross with gloom with glancing rills, L.MS *1st reading*   114 catch]
L.MS *2nd reading-*; touch L.MS *1st reading*   117 touch with shade the]
L.MS *2nd reading-*; oer the blessed L.MS *1st reading*   118] L.MS *2nd
reading* (. . . roof . . . wall,), **Trial-**; And pausing fall in sparks of dew, L.MS *1st
reading*   119 fall] L.MS *2nd reading-*; thro' L.MS *1st reading*   121
they rest,] L.MS *2nd reading-*; Love rests, L.MS *1st reading*   122] L.MS
2nd reading (. . . w̶[heeling] rolling . . .)-; And, Night delays, until at last L.MS
1st reading   124 strike] L.MS *2nd reading-*; smite L.MS *1st reading*   125
And,] L.MS *2nd reading-*; Who, L.MS *1st reading* life] **Trial-**; lives L.MS   126
Result] L.MS *2nd reading-*; Shall end L.MS *1st reading*   129 Of those]
L.MS *2nd reading-*; The men, L.MS *1st reading*   130 whose] L.MS *2nd
reading-*; their L.MS *1st reading*

Is Earth and Earth's, and in their hand
Is Nature like an open book;

No longer half-akin to brute,
    For all we thought and loved and did,
    And hoped, and suffer'd, is but seed   135
Of what in them is flower and fruit;

Whereof the man, that with me trod
    This planet, was a noble type
    Appearing ere the times were ripe,
That friend of mine who lives in God,   140

That God, which ever lives and loves,
    One God, one law, one element,
    And one far-off divine event,
To which the whole creation moves.

Of the following nine poems, seven are known to have been originally
intended for inclusion in *In Memoriam*. The last two are about Arthur
Hallam and are in the *In Memoriam* stanza. It is likely that these two
were at one time also intended for inclusion in the sequence.

The order in which the poems are printed is according to the
presumed chronology of the manuscripts in which they appear.

(i)

The path by which I walkt alone
    Ere yet thy motion caught mine eye
    Was rich with many a prophecy
In every gale about me blown.

The blackbird warbled, 'Make thee whole   5
    In spirit. Hear how glad I am.'
    The lark on golden vapour swam
And chanted, 'Find a kindred soul.'

131 hand] L.MS *2nd reading-*; hands L.MS *1st reading*   137-8] L.MS *2nd
reading* (whereof . . .), **Trial**-;
                    In them whereof the friend that trod
                    This Earth with me, was once a type
                              L.MS *1st reading*
140 who] L.MS, 1850A-; that **Trial** lives in] L.MS *2nd reading-*; walks with L.MS
1st reading

i] H.Lpr.103 (*a detached leaf from the front of* T.MS), Ricks, 1772-3

And yearning woke and was not still'd.
    I could not find thee here or there.   10
    I cried to all the breezes, 'Where?'
For all my want was unfulfill'd.

But freshly did my feet advance
    For twenty summers all but two
    Till when the time was full I drew   15
To where I met thee as by chance.

(ii)

'The light that shone when Hope was born':
    So whispers my Melpomene,
    'It was the light that lighted thee,
And it shall make me less forlorn.

And where is hope like this', she cries,   5
    'That changes human spites and scorns
    And all a poor man's crown of thorns
To glory when the beggar dies;

Who looks upon his girl and boy:
    How will they live when he is dead?   10
    Where turn to gain a little bread?
Yet − O the wonder − parts in joy;

A hope that spite of tribe and clan

(iii)

Young is the grief I entertain,
    And ever new the tale she tells,
    And ever young the face that dwells
With reason cloister'd in the brain.

Yet grief deserves a nobler name.   5
    She spurs an imitative will.

ii] T.MS, Christopher Ricks, 'The Tennyson Manuscripts', *Times Literary Supplement*, 21 August 1969, 922

iii] T.MS, *in Memoir*, I 306-7 *and Eversley*, III 206, *titled* 'To A.H.H. (originally No.CVIII)'

'Tis shame to fail so far and still
My failing shall be less my shame,

Considering what mine eyes have seen,
   And all the sweetness which thou wast   10
   And thy beginnings in the past
And all the strength thou would'st have been —

A mastermind with masterminds,
   An orb repulsive of all hate,
   A will concentric with all fate,   15
A life foursquare to all the winds.

(iv)

Are these the far-famed Victor Hours
   That ride to death the griefs of men?
   I fear not, if I fear'd them then.
Is this blind flight the winged Powers?

Behold, ye cannot bring but good,   5
   And see ye dare not touch the truth,
   Nor Sorrow beauteous in her youth,
Nor Love that holds a constant mood.

Ye must be wiser than your looks,
   Or wise yourselves, or wisdom-led,   10
   Else this wide whisper round my head
Were idler than a flight of rooks.

Go forward: crumble down a throne,
   Dissolve a world, condense a star,
   Unsocket all the joints of war,   15
And fuse the peoples into one.

---

11 And] T.MS, *Eversley*; In *Memoir*

iv] T.MS, *in Memoir*, I 307 *and Eversley*, III 206-7, *titled* 'The Victor Hours
(originally No.CXXVII)'
   1 these] T.MS; those *Memoir, Eversley*   3 them then.] T.MS; them, then
Memoir; them then; — *Eversley*   4 Powers?] T.MS, *Eversley*; Powers. *Memoir*
11 wide] T.MS, *Eversley*; wild *Memoir*

(v)

I keep no more a lone distress.
    The crowd have come to see thy grave.
    Small thanks or credit shall I have,
But these shall see it not the less.

The happy maiden's tears are free   5
    And she will weep and give them way:
    Yet one unschool'd in want will say,
'The dead are dead and let them be.'

Another whispers, sick with loss,
    'O let the simple slab remain,   10
    The MERCY JESU in the rain,
The MISERERE in the moss!

I love the daisy weeping dew,
    I hate the trim-set plots of Art!'
    My friend, thou speakest from the heart,   15
But look, for these are Nature too.

(vi)

'O Sorrower for the faded leaf',
    A dark and slothful spirit said,
    'Why lingerest thou beside the dead?
Thy songs are fuel to thy grief.

They help not thee, and who will thank   5
    Thy labour? What are these indeed
    But sighings of the wither'd reed?
A little cry from off a plank

Of shipwreck, lost in shoreless seas,
    A print in ever-shifting sands,   10
    A spreading out of feeble hands
To that which hears not?' Ill at ease

v] T.MS, *in Memoir*, I 306 *and Eversley*, III 205, *titled* 'The Grave (originally No.LVII)'
    4 not] T.MS; none *Memoir, Eversley*   10–13 'O . . . moss! / I love] *this edition*; 'O . . . moss / I love T.MS; "O . . . moss!" / "I love *Memoir*; "O . . . moss! / "I love *Eversley*

vi] L.MS (*deleted*), Ricks, 1773

I falter'd in my toil and broke
The moulds that Fancy made; and turn'd
To that fair soul that with me mourn'd   15
About his tomb, and sighing spoke.

(vii)

Let Death and Memory keep the face
Of three and twenty summers, fair.
I see it and no grief is there,
Nor Time can wrong the youthful grace.

I see it and I scarce repine.   5
I hear the voice that held me fast.
The voice is pleasant in the past,
It speaks to me of me and mine.

The face is bright, the lips are bland,
He smiles upon me eye to eye,   10
And in my thoughts with scarce a sigh
I take the pressure of his hand.

(viii)

He was too good and kind and sweet,
Ev'n when I knew him in his hour
Of darkest doubt, and in his power,
To fling his doubts into the street.

Our modern authors young and vain   5
Must print or preach their doubts aloud,
And blurt to every passing crowd
Those indigestions of the brain.

Truth-seeking he and not afraid,
But questions that perplex us now —   10

vii] L.MS, Ricks, 1775

viii] Cambridge University Library MS add. 6346, *Materials*, II 274–5, *Memoir*, I
457, *titled* 'The Philosopher' (1–4, 9–12, 17–20, *but not* 5–8, 13–16), Ricks,
1773–4
     6 print or] MS; point and *Materials*, Ricks

What time (he thought) have loom or plough
To weigh them as they should be weigh'd?

But we that are not kind or just
   We scatter seeds that spring in flame,
   Or bear their fruit in London's shame —   15
The Sabbath journal mixt with lust.

We help the blatant voice abroad
   To preach the freedom of despair,
   And from the heart of all things fair
To pluck the sanction of a God.   20

(ix)

Speak to me from the stormy sky!
   The wind is loud in holt and hill.
   It is not kind to be so still.
Speak to me, dearest, lest I die.

Speak to me: let me hear or see!   5
   Alas, my life is frail and weak.
   Seest thou my faults and wilt not speak?
They are not want of love for thee.

14 in] MS; or   *Materials*, Ricks

ix] H.Lpr.104, *Memoir*, II 517, *Eversley*, III 187

COMMENTARY

Although Tennyson once remarked 'I like those old Variorum Classics — all the Notes make the Text look precious',[1] it is doubtful whether he would have liked a variorum edition of one of his own poems. He was not enthusiastic about writing the notes published in his son's Eversley Edition of the *Works* (1907-13), and he gave in to the request with lugubrious reluctance:

I am told that the public would like notes to my poems. What hope that my prose should be clearer than my verse? Shall I write what dictionaries tell to save some of the idle folk trouble? or am I to try to fix a moral to each poem? or to add an analysis to certain passages? or to give a history of my similes? I do not like the task.[2]

Even less than writing his own notes to his poetry did he like the notes of others: 'The critics won't allow me any imagination. They take a line like "Moanings of the homeless sea" and say: "'Moanings', Horace; 'homeless', Shelley", and so on . . . As if no one else had heard the sea moan except Horace.'[3]

In providing a Commentary to *In Memoriam* we are ignoring Tennyson's wishes. The justification for this is, of course, the poem's greatness and popularity, its 'classic' stature. To know as much as possible about the circumstances of the poem's composition, to understand its meaning as fully as possible, and to appreciate something of its resonance of style and intricacy of structure, are the inevitable and legitimate desires of a readership which persistently finds that *In Memoriam* engages its deepest emotional and intellectual interests.

The Commentary to this edition aims to satisfy these desires by the provision of four kinds of information:

(1) the circumstances and date of composition of the sections, when sufficient evidence to establish these is available from the manuscripts and from other sources;

(2) the bearing of the manuscripts upon the composition of the sections and upon the development of the sequence;

(3) the elucidation of the text by the quotation of remarks of the poet himself concerning it, and of his family and friends, and by a selection of the notes of previous editors and commentators;

[1] *Tennyson and His Friends*, 147. Tennyson was most likely alluding to the Delphin Classics.

[2] A draft of Tennyson's 'Prefatory Notes' eventually printed in the *Eversley* Edition, I 333-4. This is written, in the hand of H.T., on a preliminary page of a copy of the 1884 edition of the *Works* in the TRC.

[3] Cited in W.F. Rawnsley, 'Personal Recollections of Tennyson — II', *The Nineteenth Century*, XCVII (February 1925), 195; *Memoir*, II 385.

(4) parallel passages from other poems written by Tennyson before the publication of *In Memoriam*, and from those writings of his predecessors and contemporaries whose words and ideas are echoed in *In Memoriam*, either consciously or unconsciously.

Quotations

Tennyson's other poems are usually quoted from the 1889 one-volume edition of the *Works*, which has slight corrections and alterations, and many additions made by Tennyson after **1884A**. Early poems which he did not reprint after their first publication in *Poems, by Two Brothers* (Louth, 1827), *Poems, Chiefly Lyrical* (1830), and *Poems* [1832] are quoted from those volumes. Poems first published by Hallam Tennyson (in *Memoir* and in *Eversley*), or by Sir Charles Tennyson (in *The Devil and the Lady* (1930), *Unpublished Early Poems by Alfred Tennyson* (1931), and 'Tennyson's Unpublished Poems', *Nineteenth Century*, CIX (1931), 367-80, 495-508, 625-36) are quoted from these texts. Poems first published by Christopher Ricks are quoted from his edition of the *Poems* (1969).

Information given about other poems of Tennyson (dates of composition, etc.) is usually derived from Ricks. The comments of Tennyson and Hallam Tennyson are quoted from *Eversley*, III 194-265 unless otherwise stated. Tennyson's remarks to Knowles are quoted from Gordon Ray, *Tennyson Reads 'Maud'*, Sedgewick Memorial Lecture (University of British Columbia, Vancouver, 1968), Appendix I, 37-42.

Quotations from Arthur Hallam's poems and prose works are from Motter, except for the poems in *Some Unpublished Poems*, in which case this short-title is specified.

Quotations in Latin and Greek, and the translations, are usually from the Loeb Classical Library. Translations of Dante are by Cary. Translations of Petrarch are from *The Sonnets, Triumphs, and Other Poems of Petrarch, now first completely translated into English verse by various hands* (1859).

A Note on the Stanza

Of the stanzaic and metrical pattern which *In Memoriam* made famous (a quatrain of iambic tetrameters with enclosed rhyme), John Churton Collins alleged (*Cornhill*, 38) that Tennyson had been imitating a 'very rare volume, scarcely known even to professed students of our early poetry', the occasional verses of Lord Herbert of Cherbury (specifically, 'An Ode upon the Question, whether Love should continue for ever'). Tennyson replied, typically, that he believed himself to be the originator of the pattern (*Memoir*, I 305-6). Commentators since Collins have discovered analogues of the *In Memoriam* stanza in the works of several sixteenth-century and seventeenth-century poets (for example, Sidney, Shakespeare, Jonson, George Herbert, Sandys, Carew, Marvell, and Prior). The variety of ways in which the stanza is treated in these poems seems to indicate that it is a not uncommon form which would arise naturally in the minds of poets accustomed to experiment with metre. There seems to be no reason to suppose that Tennyson was influenced by any of his predecessors.

In many of his early poems ('Remorse', 'Persia', 'Time: an Ode', 'Mariana', 'Mariana in the South', 'To − [Clear-headed friend]'), he can be observed 'feeling his way' (as Bradley described it) towards the stanza of *In Memoriam*. He used the form in other poems dating from the early 1830s: 'Hail Briton!', 'You ask me, why', and 'Love thou thy land'.

[Introductory stanzas] *Dating*: The stanzas are dated 1849 from **Trial** onwards. They were thus composed after the sequence had been completed.

T. gave the stanzas no title. Of the early editors, Chapman gives them no title, Gatty calls them 'introductory stanzas', and Jacobs and H.T. refer to them as the 'Introduction'. The title 'Prologue' was first used by Genung and this was adopted by Beeching and Bradley. The term seems unsuitable because it gives a misleading impression of the connection between the stanzas and the poem itself. In **Trial** and all separate editions published during T.'s lifetime, the stanzas are set apart from the poem by being placed before the inscription 'IN MEMORIAM | A.H.H. | OBIIT SEPT. MDCCCXXXIII' and by having the date '1849' after the last line. This suggests that T. intended that the stanzas should be considered separately from the sections which follow. He evidently recognized that the stanzas are not a Prologue in the traditional sense, as is the opening part of *The Princess*.

Strictly, the stanzas seem to be a 'Palinode', 'an ode or song in which the author retracts something said in a former poem'. The unrepresentative nature of the stanzas was first remarked upon by Henry Sedgwick:

> I have always felt that in a certain sense the effect of the introduction does not quite represent the effect of the poem. Faith, in the introduction, is too completely triumphant. I think this is inevitable, because so far as the thought-debate presented by the poem is summed up, it must be summed up on the side of Faith. Faith must give the last word: but the last word is not the whole utterance of the truth: the whole truth is that assurance and doubt must alternate in the moral world in which we at present live, somewhat as night and day alternate in the physical world.   (*Memoir*, I 304)

Some reasons why T. should have added the Introductory stanzas are suggested by Mattes (pp. 91-2). Their 'new, evangelical note' is 'closer to the religious temper of Arthur Hallam than anything in the elegies proper or the Epilogue'. She might have added that the ideas are very like the several themes (God is love; reason alone cannot establish the existence of God; we must love Christ before we can attain the love of God) of Hallam's essay, 'Theodicæa Novissima', which T. had specifically requested Henry Hallam to include in the *Remains*: 'I am inclined to think it does great honour to his originality of thought' (*Eversley*, III 258). Another reason for his adding them may be that they 'would be acceptable to and expected by Henry Hallam, to whom the poem had in a sense been promised'. The strongest reason of all may be that they would reassure Emily Sellwood who (according to H.D. Rawnsley) had refused T.'s proposal of marriage around 1847 because she 'had grown to feel that they two moved in worlds of religious thought so different that the two would not "make one music" as they moved' (*Memories of the Tennysons*, 71). It is probable (as Mattes suggests) that the copy of the 'Elegies' which Emily read towards the end of March 1850 was a copy of **Trial**, which contains the Introductory stanzas, and not (as Willingham Rawnsley states in *Memories of the Tennysons*, 123) a manuscript.

1-12] Collins (*Cornhill*, 39) compares Herbert, 'Love [I] ', 1-4:

> Immortal Love, Author of this great frame,
> Sprung from that beauty that can never fade,
> How hath man parcell'd out Thy glorious name,
> And thrown it on the dust that Thou hast made.

T. wrote 'no' alongside Collins's observation that the Introductory stanzas are 'obviously a transfusion, so to speak, of some verses of ... George Herbert', and 'no – close as it seems' alongside Collins's comparison of lines 9 and 12 with Herbert, 'The Temper', 26-7: 'Whether I fly with angels, fall with dust, / Thy hands made both'; 'The Discharge', 55: 'And God has promised: He is just'.

1 *immortal Love*] T. comments: 'This might be taken in a St. John sense'. H.T. refers to I John 4 and 5.

2-4] Cf. I Peter 1:8: 'Whom having not seen, ye love; in whom, though now ye see him not, yet believing'.

5 *orbs of light and shade*] T. glosses: 'sun and moon'.

7-8 *thy foot / Is on the skull*] 'The characteristic attitude in the ancient epics of a conqueror, the Greek ἐπεμβαίνειν ('to stand upon')', (Collins). Mattes infers an allusion to 'Christ's victory over death, as symbolized in medieval paintings of the Crucifixion in which His feet rest on a skull' (pp. 96-7).

13-16] H.T. comments: 'An old version of this verse was left by my father in MS in a book of prayers written by my mother.' He refers to Prayer Book MS, inside the front board of which is the early version of these lines in T.'s hand. In printing the stanza in *Eversley*, H.T. substituted 'But' for 'Yet' and altered punctuation and capitalization.

15-16] For the importance to T. of the human will and its relation to the divine will, cf. *131* and see the headnote there.

19-20] *broken lights*] Cf.

> this Nature full of hints and mysteries
> Untrackt conclusions, broken lights and shapes.
> ('Song, Who can say', in Trinity College,
> Cambridge MS 0.15.20)

22 *knowledge*] T. recommended the pronunciation 'knōwledge'.

25-6] Cf. *114*, in which lines 26-8 are echoed here. Also cf. 'Love thou thy land', 17-18: 'Make knowledge circle with the winds; / But let her herald, Reverence, fly'.

28 *as before*] T. comments: 'As in the ages of faith'.

35-6] Cf. Psalm 143:2: 'And enter not into judgment with thy servant: for in thy sight shall no man living be justified.'

39 *I trust he lives in thee*] For Hallam as absorbed into the Godhead, cf. *129*.12, *130*.11, Epilogue, 140. H.T. comments: 'Throughout his life [T.] had a constant feeling of the actual Immanence of God in Man and in the Universe, and also that "in God alone all things and all beings exist"' (*Materials*, II 28). Arthur Hallam's statement of belief in the idea is quoted in note to Epilogue, 140.

41-4] Other references to his poems are listed in the headnote to *5*. The influence of the opening sonnet of Petrarch, *In Vita di Madonna Laura*, has been suggested by Turner (p. 119).

41 *wild and wandering cries*] Cf. *16*.1-3; *57*.3-4; Epilogue, 23.

44] Cf. *108*.15-16; *109*.24.

1. This is the genuine introductory poem, for it discusses the two traditional responses to the grief of bereavement: that good will eventually emerge from the experience, and the personality of the mourner will be improved as he is moulded into new sympathies and a better

response to life (lines 5-8); and that Time will eventually conquer the sorrow, however devastating it may be at the moment (lines 13-16).

Although these two ideas are at first rejected by the poet as unacceptable, he continues to explore them throughout *In Memoriam* and eventually, on his own terms, becomes reconciled to them. He does find that he has risen to 'higher things' as a result of the experience of bereavement, and that Time has calmed his sorrow without destroying his love.

1-4] T.MS and L.MS have this stanza alone at the top of a leaf near the front of each notebook. Perhaps T. at one time intended the stanza to be an epigraph for the entire sequence.

him who sings . . . higher things] T. glossed these lines 'it is Goethe's creed' in his copy of Gatty. In 1891 he replied to a correspondent who inquired about the stanza: 'I believe I alluded to Goethe. Among his last words were these: "Von Aenderungen zu hoheren Aenderungen," "from changes to higher changes"' (*Memoir*, II 39). (These words have not been found among all the reported 'last words' of Goethe in the final months of his life, nor in his letters of this time.) T. regarded Goethe as the foremost of modern lyrical poets and thought him 'consummate in so many different styles'.

3-4] This promise is fulfilled in the Epilogue, 19-20.

3 *rise on stepping-stones*] Cf. Byron, 'The Siege of Corinth', 239-41 (suggested by G.G. Loane, *Echoes in Tennyson* (1928), 9):

> Or pave the path with many a corse,
> O'er which the following brave may rise,
> Their stepping-stone — the last who dies!

The image and the idea occur in 'To —' ['Thou mayst remember'], 3-6, 8-11:

> 'From the tomb
> And charnel-place of purpose dead,
> Through spiritual death we come
> Into the light of spiritual life' . . .
>   When from change to change,
> Led silently by power divine,
> Thy thought did scale a purer range
> Of prospect up to self control.

T. wrote to Emily Sellwood in 1839: 'Thou hast proved Time and space very prettily. So mayst thou and I and all of us ascend stepwise to perfection' (letter dated 24 October [1839] in TRC; the similarity was first noticed by C.Y. Lang, *Tennyson in Lincoln*, I xi).

4 *dead selves*] Cf. *The Princess*, III 205: 'We touch on our dead self,

nor shun to do it'. Ricks points out that it occurs in R.C. Trench's poem 'To W.B. Donne' in Heath MS alongside poems by T.

6 This is an important and recurrent idea in *I.M.*; cf. for example, *54*.1-2, *65*.6-7, *66*.5-8; *77*.11; *80*.11-12; *81*.10-12; *108*.15-16; *117*.

7] Cf. *80*.15-16; 'Tiresias', 122-3: 'their example reach a hand / Far thro' all years'; 'Hail Briton', 83-4: 'an example reaching hands / For ever into coming years'.

8] T. comments: 'The good that grows for us out of grief'. The image is common in Shakespeare, for example, *Sonnets*, XXXI 5-7: 'How many a holy and obsequious tear / Hath dear religious love stol'n from mine eye, / As interest of the dead'; *The Rape of Lucrece*, 1796-8, and *Richard III*, IV iv 321-4.

9-16] T. comments: 'Yet it is better to bear the wild misery of extreme grief than that Time should obliterate the sense of loss and deaden the power of love.'

9] Cf. Shelley, 'Adonais', 270: 'And Love taught Grief to fall like music from his tongue'.

10] Cf. *Comus*, 251-2: 'smoothing the Raven doune / Of darknes till it smil'd'.

13 *victor Hours*] Adapted from *Are these the far-famed Victor Hours* (Add. Poem iv), with which lines 13-16 may be compared.

15 *loved and lost*] Anticipates *27*.15-16 and *85*.3-4.

16 *overworn*] Cf. Shakespeare, *Sonnets*, LXIII 1-2: 'Against my love shall be as I am now, / With Time's injurious hand crush'd and o'erworn'.

2. The poet contemplates the constancy and absorption in death of the yew and begins to feel as much a part of the tree as the dead buried beneath it. Section *39*, which was added as a pendant to *2* in **1870**, repeats several images and end-rhymes.

1-4] The lines recall Gray, 'Elegy Written in a Country Churchyard', 13-16:

> Beneath those rugged elms, that yew-tree's shade,
>   Where heaves the turf in many a mould'ring heap,
> Each in his narrow cell for ever laid,
>   The rude forefathers of the hamlet sleep.

3 *the dreamless head*] T. compares *Odyssey*, X 521: Νεκύων ἀμενηνὰ κάρηνα ('the powerless heads of the dead'). Cf. 'The Two Voices', 280: 'if man rot in dreamless ease'.

4] Cf. Job 8:17: 'His roots are wrapped about the heap, and he seeth the place of stones.'

6 *the firstling to the flock*] As in Genesis 4:4: 'And Abel, he also brought of the firstlings of his flock'.

9] This line was understood by Gatty to imply that the yew does not flower, and he suggested that T.'s addition of *39* in **1870** is a confession of error. T. wrote alongside Gatty's discussion of *39*: 'It is impossible that I s^d. not have known that a tree which bears a berry must have a blossom; but Sorrow only saw the winter gloom of the foliage.' In his notes to *Eversley*, T. applied the last clause ('Sorrow only saw . . .') to *2*.

12 *thousand years*] As in Psalm 90:4 (incorporated in the Burial Service): 'For a thousand years in thy sight are but as yesterday when it is past'.

13] The revision from 'the' to 'thee' was suggested by Aubrey de Vere in the copy of **Trial** (Beinecke, Tinker 2065) sent him by T.

stubborn hardihood] Cf. *Comus*, 650: 'dauntless hardihood'.

15 *fail from out*] 'Die away from' (Bradley). Cf. *84.36*.

3. T. comments: 'First realization of blind sorrow'.
This section occasioned *59*, which was added as a pendant to it in **1851A**. It also has affinities to *39*, which was added in **1870** as a pendant to *2*.
A version of *3* was among the first poems to be written on the death of Hallam (see below, lines 5-8) and probably dates from October 1833.

3] Cf. Catullus, LXVIII ('Quod mihi . . .'), 17-18: 'non est dea nescia nostri, / quae dulcem curis miscet amaritiem' ('Not unknown am I to the goddess who mingles with her cares a sweet bitterness').

5-8] Of these lines H.Nbk.17 has an early version (quatrains with alternate rhymes) with two further stanzas:

> *a* A cloud was drawn across the sky
>   The stars their courses blindly run
>   Out of waste places came a cry
> *d*   And murmurs from the dying Sun
>
> *e* In every form the sense receives
>   A something hitherto unmet
>   In every motion of the leaves
> *h*   The shadow of a vain regret
>
> *i* The whole house shaken to it's fall
>   This travelled mind a foreign land

Love mixt with all — love lord of all
l   Thought drifting like the hills of sand

Line *j* was adapted in *10*.6. Cf. 5–8 with 'Hark! the dogs howl!', 10–12:

Lo! the broad Heavens cold and bare,
The stars that know not my distress.
My sighs are wasted in the air.

5–6] Cf. Pope, *An Essay on Man*, I 252: 'Planets and Suns run lawless thro' the sky' (Bradley); 'Adonais', 482: 'Which through the web of being blindly wove' (Ricks); T.'s early poem 'Armageddon', I 36–7: 'Spirits of discord seemed to weave across / His fiery disk a web of bloody haze'.

7–8] T. comments: 'Expresses the feeling that sad things in Nature affect him who mourns'.

7 *waste places*] As in Isaiah 51:3: 'For the Lord shall comfort Zion: he will comfort all her waste places'.

14–15] Ricks compares Shelley, *Queen Mab*, IV 115–20, 125, which has 'blood', 'vile', and 'Stifling with rudest grasp all natural good . . . How withered all the buds of natural good'.

15 *vice of blood*] Cf. *Othello*, I iii 123: 'I do confess the vices of my blood'.

16 *threshold of the mind*] This expression may derive from a famous German psychological term coined in the 1820s, *Schwelle des Bewusstseins* ('threshold of consciousness').

4. This section seems to follow from the deleted stanza at the end of *3*. For other instances of the poet dreaming or imagining, cf. *10, 12–15, 41, 47, 68–71, 80, 84, 85.77–96, 91–5, 98, 103*.

2 *My will*] The importance to T. of free-will is discussed in headnote *131*.

3] Cf. 'Adonais', 489–90: 'my spirit's bark is driven / Far from the shore'.

4] Bradley compares St. Augustine, *Confessions*, IV 4 (Augustine grieves at the death of his best friend): 'I became a great puzzle to myself, and asked my soul why she so exceedingly disquieted me, but she knew not what to answer me.'

11–12] This image may have been suggested by Goethe, *Dichtung und Wahrheit*, XIII. T. would probably have read it in German, but the 1824 English Translation (*Memoirs*, 2 vols., II i 44–5) is similar in diction to these lines:

While my thoughts were thus employed, the death of young Jerusalem took place ... The plan of *Werther* was instantly conceived. The elements of that composition seemed now to amalgamate, to form a whole, just as water, on the point of freezing in a vase, receives from the slightest concussion the form of a compact piece of ice. (See Elaine Jordan, 'Tennyson's *In Memoriam* – An Echo of Goethe', *Notes and Queries*, n.s. XV (November 1968), 414-15).

5. This is the first of the sections 'in which the poet's songs form the subject, pointing backwards and forwards to one another, and showing the change which passes over his mind as time goes on' (Bradley). Other sections which deal wholly or partly with the poet's songs are *8, 16, 19-21, 23, 37, 38, 48, 49, 52, 57, 58, 65, 75-7, 83, 88, 106, 125*, and also the Introductory stanzas and Epilogue.

7-8] Cf. 'Oh! that 'twere possible', 83: 'a dull mechanic ghost'.

8] Cf. Keats, 'Ode to a Nightingale', 1-3:

> a drowsy numbness pains
> My sense, as though of hemlock I had drunk,
> Or emptied some dull opiate to the drains.

9-12] Cf. *Hamlet*, I ii 85-6: 'But I have that within which passeth show; / These but the trappings and the suits of woe.'

9 *weeds*] mourning apparel (widow's weeds).

11-12] There is a similarity in thought and diction to Spenser, *Daphnaida*, 73-4: 'For the huge anguish, which dooth multiplie / My dying paines, no tongue can well vnfold'. Cf. *19*.10; *20*.1,11.

6. *Dating*: This section was composed by Christmas 1841, according to the reminiscences of Edmund Lushington:

> I remember one particular night when we were sitting up together late in his bedroom. He began to recite the poem that stands sixth in 'In Memoriam', 'One writes, that "Other friends remain,"' and I do not know that the deep melodious thunder of his voice with all its overwhelming pathos, often and often as I have heard it, ever imprest me more profoundly. (*Memoir*, I 202)

1-4] Cf. 'To J.S.' (on the death of Spedding's brother in 1832):

> I will not even preach to you,
> 'Weep, weeping dulls the inward pain' ...
>
> I will not say, 'God's ordinance
> Of Death is blown in every wind;'
> For that is not a common chance

> That takes away a noble mind . . .
>
> a tear
> Dropt on the letters as I wrote.
>
> I wrote I know not what. In truth,
>   How *should* I soothe you anyway,
> Who miss the brother of your youth? . . .
>
> it may be
> That only silence suiteth best.
>   (lines 39 ff.)

T. wrote in a letter of condolence in 1871: 'I myself have always felt that letters of condolence, when the grief is yet raw and painful, are like vain voices in the ears of the deaf, not heard or only half heard.' (*Memoir*, II 105).

1 *'Other friends remain'*] But see line 44. Robert Monteith wrote to T. in December 1833: 'all wish, as I do, for still stricter friendship with you, if it might be (which is all but impossible) that together we might help to fill up the gap' (*Materials*, I 202).

2 *'Loss is common to the race'*] Cf. for example, Numbers 16:29: 'If these men die the common death of all men'.

7–8] T. compares Lucretius, II 578–80:

> nec nox ulla diem neque noctem Aurora secuta est
> quae non audierit mixtos vagitibus aegris
> ploratus mortis comites et funeris atri.

(And no night ever followed day, or dawn followed night, but has heard mingled with their sickly wailings the lamentations that attend upon death and black funeral.) Cf. also *The Tempest*, II i 3–6.

9–40] Such scenes were common in classical poetry (as Horace observes in *Odes*, IV ii 21–2). Collins compares the passage in the *Aeneid*, XI 49–52 in which Aeneas laments the death of young Pallas and imagines the father Evander as at that moment pledging his son:

> et nunc ille quidem spe multum captus inani
> fors et vota facit cumulatque altaria donis;
> nos iuvenem exanimum et nil iam caelestibus ullis
> debentem vano maesti comitamur honore.

(And now he, much beguiled by idle hope, perchance is offering vows and heaping the altars high with gifts; we, in sorrow, attend with bootless rites the lifeless son, who no more owes aught to any gods of heaven.)

An editorial note in *Notes and Queries*, X (1963), 449, compares Juvenal, *Satires*, III 261–6:

> domus interea secura patellas
> iam lavat et bucca foculum excitat et sonat unctis
> striglibus et pleno componit lintea guto.
> haec inter pueros varie properantur, at ille
> iam sedet in ripa taetrumque novicius horret
> porthmea.

(At home meanwhile the folk, unwitting, are washing the dishes, blowing up the fire with distended cheek, clattering over the greasy flesh-scrapers, filling the oil-flasks and laying out the towels. And while each of them is thus busy over his own task, their master is already sitting, a new arrival upon the bank and shuddering at the grim ferryman.)

16] An echo of Clarence's dream of drowning in *Richard III*, I iv 39: 'To find the empty, vast, and wand'ring air'.

17-18] H.T. comments: 'My father was writing to Arthur Hallam in the hour that he died'. Turner suggests (p. 115) a reminiscence of Hallam's biographical sketch of Petrarch: 'It is the luxury of grief to connect the memory of the dead with our thoughts, and employments, . . . at the moment of their death' (Motter, 290).

31-2] Emily Tennyson, the betrothed of Arthur Hallam, is described by a friend who saw her after she had been ill with grief for many months:
> We were waiting for her in the drawing-room the first day since her loss that she had been able to meet anyone, and she came at last, dressed in deep mourning, a shadow of her former self, but with one white rose in her black hair as her Arthur loved to see her!

(Memoir, I 108-9)

37, 40 *curse, horse*] This imperfect rhyme is explained by W.F. Rawnsley: 'all his early life Tennyson had heard "horse" in Lincolnshire pronounced "hurse"' ('Personal Recollections of Tennyson – II', *Nineteenth Century*, XCVII (February 1925), 190).

41-4] T. may have had his sister, Emily, in mind. In fact, she did not keep to 'perpetual maidenhood' but married Richard Jesse in 1842.

44] But see *85*, the section dedicated to Edmund Lushington.

7. *Dating*: It is probable that this section and its companion-piece, *119*, were composed between 1848 and 1850, possibly even as late as between **Trial** (March 1850) and **1850A** (May 1850). Likewise *8*, because it has many similarities to *7*, may well belong to the same period. The reasons for this are as follows. No manuscripts survive of *8* and *119* (as well as of six other sections). This may indicate that these sections were composed after 1848, the presumed terminal date of L.MS. One manuscript of *7* survives (H.Lpr.104), but this gives no clue to the date of

composition. It is likely that *7* and *119* were composed together in order to present at the beginning and the end of the sequence the contrasting moods of the poet, and that *8*, a country scene, was composed in order to parallel *7*, a city scene. Valerie Pitt was the first to suggest that *7* and *8* were added to the sequence 'at the very latest stage in its development' (*Tennyson Laureate* (1962), 97).

Sections *7* and *119* (as well as *8*.1-8) are types of a minor genre of classical poetry called *paraclausithyron*, or the song and actions of a lover who is excluded. The lover stands outside the house of his mistress and laments that the door is bolted against him. He addresses the door and holds it responsible for his rejection. Examples of the genre are Catullus, LXVII; Tibullus, I ii 9; Horace, *Odes*, III x; and Propertius, I xvi 17-24:

> 'Ianua vel domina penitus crudelior ipsa,
> quid mihi iam duris clausa taces foribus?
> cur numquam reserata meos admittis amores,
> nescia furtivas reddere mota preces?
> nullane finis erit nostro concessa dolori,
> turpis et in tepido limine somnus erit?
> me mediae noctes, me sidera prona iacentem,
> frigidaque Eoo me dolet aura gelu.

(Door yet more deeply cruel than even my mistress' heart, why are thy grim portals ever closed and mute for me? Why never dost thou unbar and give entrance to my love, thou that knowest not to relent and bear my secret prayers to my mistress? Wilt thou never grant an ending to my woes? And must a doleful sleep be mine on thy chill threshold? For me the midnight and the stars that turn to their setting and the breeze laden with chill frost of dawn grieve as they behold me prostrate.)

This tradition inspired the scene in *Wilhelm Meisters Lehrjahre* in which Wilhelm visits the house of Mariana (Book I xvii). Turner suggests (p. 122) that this scene is a prototype of *7*. Tennyson knew Goethe's novel and seems to have borrowed a detail from the scene (see note 10-12), but he also certainly knew the Latin originals and in most respects *7* and *119* descend directly from these.

It is probable that T. had also read the poem on the death of Arthur Hallam by Richard Monckton Milnes, 'On the Death of —' (in his *Poems of Many Years* (1838), a parallel suggested by Jerome H. Buckley, *Tennyson, the Growth of a Poet* (Cambridge, Mass., 1960), 111).

> I thought, how should I see him first,
> How should our hands first meet,
> Within his room, upon the stair, —
> At the corner of the street?

> I thought, where should I hear him first,
> How catch his greeting tone, —
> And thus I went up to his door,
> And they told me he was gone!
>   (Stanza 5)

Joyce Green ('Tennyson's Development During the "Ten Years' Silence" (1832-1842)', *PMLA*, LXVI (September 1951), 671) compares 7 with 'Oh! that 'twere possible', which has a ghost, noisy streets, the hand of the loved one, the sense of guilt, and the dawning of a hopeless day.

1 *Dark house*] T. comments, '67 Wimpole Street', the home of Henry Hallam. Cf. *8*.7,12. The house in Wimpole Street was, incidentally, an ill-fated house for the Hallam family. Two young children, Arthur (aged twenty-two), a daughter (aged twenty), and, in 1846, the mother, Julia, all died during the family's residence there. T. may have visited Wimpole Street less than a fortnight after receiving word of Hallam's death. Henry Hallam wrote to T. on 10 October 1833: 'We cannot express in letters what we would say to each other — therefore I must expect you to meet me in Wimpole Street on Thursday next [17 October] at one' (letter in TRC). It is not known if T. accepted the invitation.

2] The unusual length of Wimpole Street is enhanced by the perspective of an almost unbroken line of flat Georgian housefronts, particularly along the west side, where is number 67. Georgian domestic architecture in London streets was often regarded with disdain by the Victorians. Cf. for example, Disraeli, *Tancred; or the New Crusade*:

> It is Parliament to whom we are indebted for your Gloucester Places, and Baker Streets, and Harley Streets, and Wimpole Streets, and all those flat, dull, spiritless streets, resembling each other like a large family of plain children.   (Bk. II x)

4] The H.Lpr.104 reading is too reminiscent of *6*.30: 'In expectation of a guest'. The revisions in this line and in 5 are the first of several which obscure specific references to Hallam.

4-5 *a hand, / A hand that can be clasp'd no more-*] Other instances of the recurrent image of hands are *10*.19; *13*.7; *14*.11; *40*.29; *69*.17; *80*.16; *84*.7,43; *95*.34; *119*.12. The image occurs in several early poems associated with Hallam: 'My life is full of weary days', 6-8; 'If I were loved, as I desire to be', 9; 'Hark! the dogs howl', 7-8; 'Oh! that 'twere possible', 24-5; 'Break, break, break', 11. 'Tiresias' and 'Hail Briton' were also composed around the time of Hallam's death and have hints of T.'s responses to the event. In 'Tiresias', the examples of dead warriors 'reach a hand / Far through all years' (122). In 'Hail Briton', the British wrought 'an example reaching hands / For ever into coming years' (83). Also cf. 'The Two Voices' (noting the context), 244-5: 'Will he obey when one commands? / Or answer should one press his hands?'

7-8] Cf. *Hamlet*, I i 148-9: 'And then it started like a guilty thing / Upon a fearful summons', which is echoed by Wordsworth in 'Ode: Intimations of Immortality . . .', stanza ix: 'our mortal Nature / Did tremble like a guilty thing surprised'. Cf. also 'Oh! that 'twere possible', 47-8, 61:

> And on my heavy eyelids
> My anguish hangs like shame . . .
>
> Always I long to creep . . .

9 *He is not here*] J.D. Rosenberg suggests (*Journal of English and Germanic Philology*, LVIII (1959), 230) an allusion to Luke 24:6 where the angel announces that the sepulchre is empty: 'He is not here, but is risen'.

10-12] Turner suggests (p. 122) a comparison with *Wilhelm Meisters Lehrjahre* (Bk. I xvii), in which Wilhelm finally gives up the vigil in front of Mariana's house: 'he heeded not the clear gray of the morning, and the crowing of the cocks; till the early trades began to stir, and drove him home' (translated by Carlyle).

10] T. commented to Knowles: 'say in Oxford St.'

8. *Dating*: See headnote 7.

1-8] This scene may derive from Crabbe, 'The Lover's Journey'. The synopsis of the poem by Jeffrey (in T.'s set of Crabbe, 8 vols., 1834; TRC) expresses the relevance of the poem to this section:
> A lover takes a long ride to see his mistress; and, passing in full hope and joy through a barren and fenny country, finds beauty in everything. Being put out of humour, however, by missing the lady at the end of this stage, he proceeds through a lovely landscape, and finds every thing ugly and disagreeable.

3 *'lights*] A reviewer of *I.M.* in *The Times* (28 November 1851) misunderstood 'lights' in the sense of 'lantern'. In the next edition (**1855**), T. added an apostrophe before the word. T.'s manuscript revision of ''lights' is in a copy of **1850B** in the Beinecke Library (Tinker 2066).

5 *magic light*] Cf. Coleridge, 'France: an Ode', 35: 'And flung a magic light o'er all her hills and groves'.

8 *emptied of delight*] Cf. Keats, *Lamia*, II 307: 'And Lycius' arms were empty of delight' (Bradley).

11] Cf. 'O! that 'twere possible', 72: 'In the chamber or the street.'

12] Cf. Hallam, 'To Two Sisters', i 42-4: 'sick and lone / Roaming the weary desert of my doom / Where thou art not' (Bradley).

15] Cf. Wordsworth, 'The Small Celandine', 12: 'buffeted at will by rain and storm.'

21] Hallam acted as T.'s literary adviser, and published a very favourable review of *Poems, Chiefly Lyrical* in the *Englishman's Magazine* (August 1831).

22] Hallam was in fact buried in the vault of the Elton family in the south transept of Clevedon parish church (see headnote *18*), but elsewhere in *I.M.* are other allusions to a churchyard grave: *10*.13; *18*.1-2; *21*.3; Add. Poem v.

9-18. In T.Nbk. sections *9*, *17*, and *18* appear on adjacent leaves and are numbered sequentially (*17* is headed 'II' and *18* is headed 'III'). Sections *17* and *18* are companion-pieces to *9*, which was the first section to be written; they develop the subject of *9* and have the same number of stanzas (five). In *9*, the voyage of the ship which brings the body home is imagined; in *17*, the safe arrival of the ship; and in *18*, the burial of the body.

T. later composed seven more sections (*10-16*), each having five stanzas, on the same subject. Like *9*, several of the new sections incorporate elements of the classical rhetorical genre, the *propemptikon*, or farewell to the departing traveller. A long example of this genre is Statius, *Silvae*, III 2, which is addressed to the soldier, Celer, on his sailing to join his legion. Some earlier examples of *propemptika* which feature ships include Euripides, *Helen*, 1451 ff.; Theocritus, *Idylls*, VII 52 ff.; Tibullus, I 3; Horace, *Odes*, I 3; *Epodes*, I. Section *9* is modelled on a primary element of the *propemptikon*, the invocation for a safe journey. Section *14* (as well as *17*) illustrates a genre sometimes included in a *propemptikon* (as in *Silvae*, III 2), the *prosphonetikon*, or speech of welcome to a traveller who has just arrived. Sections *15* and *16* are modelled on another element, the expression of anxiety for the safety of the traveller or vessel during the journey.

As well as constituting, with *9*, a traditional *propemptikon*, the new sections suggest the passage of time between the departure of the ship from Italy and its arrival in England. This is emphasized by the references to the changing seasons: in *11* it is autumn and in *15*, winter.

9. *Dating*: In Heath MS *9* is dated October 6 1833. T. learnt of the death of Hallam in a letter (quoted on p. 8) which Hallam's uncle,

Henry Elton, wrote and posted on 1 October. T. would have received the letter within the next day or two. In 1870-1 he told James Knowles that *9* was 'the first written' section, and H.Lpr.98 is inscribed by H.T.: 'The first section of *In Memoriam* that was written down 1833'.

The subject was suggested by a phrase in Henry Elton's letter: 'I believe his remains come by sea from Trieste'. The section is a prayer addressed to the ship ('Fair ship'), the heavens ('Sleep, gentle heavens'), the winds ('Sleep, gentle winds'), and Arthur Hallam ('My Arthur'). This prayer is alluded to in *17*. 2-4: 'my prayer / Was as the whisper of an air / To breathe thee over lonely seas'. Sections *10*, *14*, and *17* also directly address the ship.

2, 7] Cf. Shelley, *Queen Mab*, VIII 65: 'Ruffle the placid ocean-deep' (Ricks). With 'placid ocean-plains', Mustard compares *Aeneid*, X 103: 'eo dicente . . . placida aequora pontus' (as he speaks . . . Ocean stills his waters into rest).

3 *Arthur's*] The first mention of the deceased by name. It appears twice in this section and twice more in the poem: *80*.2; *89*.6.

5-6] With the image cf. Gray, 'Ode on a Distant Prospect of Eton College', 85-7:

> This racks the joints, this fires the veins,
> That every labouring sinew strains,
> Those in the deeper vitals rage.

Cf. 'Friendship', 14-15, 'whene'er the heart is rack'd and riven / By the hot shafts of baleful calumny'.

10-12] Bradley suggests an unconscious reminiscence of Pope, 'Epistle to Dr Arbuthnot', 309-10: 'Yet let me flap this bug with gilded wings, / This painted child of dirt, that stinks and stings'.

10 *Phosphor*] 'Light-bringer'. T. comments: 'star of dawn'; Venus when it appears before sunrise.

13 *lights*] A common classical image for 'stars', as in Catullus, LXVI 59: 'lumine caeli'. See also Genesis 1:14: 'And God said, Let there be lights in the firmament of the heaven'.

16, 20] An echo of Proverbs 18:24: 'there is a friend that sticketh closer than a brother'. Hallam wrote of their friendship: 'I felt as of two brothers I were one, / And he of all men nearest to my soul' (*Meditative Fragments* vi, 102-3).

18] This line is repeated in *17*.20. The poet frequently depicts himself as the spouse, widow, or lover of his friend: *13*; *40*.1; *41*.20; *60*; *85*.113; *93*.13 (first reading): 'Stoop soul and touch me: wed me': *97*.5-20. The

line 'Long married souls, dear friend, are we' appears above a draft of
97 in H.Nbk.19.

19-20] In T.Nbk., where *9* immediately precedes *17, 17* ends with the
lines:

> Dear as a brother is to me
> Dear as the mother to the son.

10.

5-8] These lines give a complete picture of a ship's purpose: the crew,
the passengers, the mail, and the cargo.

6] Adapted from the line 'This travelled mind a foreign land' in the
stanzas in H.Nbk.17 associated with *3.5-8*.

11 *home-bred fancies*] H.T. comments: 'the wish to rest in the church-
yard or in the chancel'.

12-20] Cf. Ovid, *Tristia*, I ii 52 ff.:

> demite naufragium, mors mihi munus erit.
> est aliquid, fatove suo ferrove cadentem
> in solida moriens ponere corpus humo . . .
>   et sperare sepulcrum
> et non aequoreis piscibus esse cibum.

(Save me from shipwreck and death will be a boon. 'Tis something
worth if falling by fate or by the steel one rests in death upon the solid
ground . . . and looks forward to a tomb − not to be the food of fishes
in the sea.); Cf. also *The Tempest*, I i 62-5, and 'Lycidas', 152-8.

11-14] Cf. Collins, 'Ode, Written in the beginning of the year 1746', 1-6:

> How sleep the Brave, who sink to Rest,
> By all their Country's Wishes blest!
> When Spring, with dewy Fingers cold,
> Returns to deck their hallow'd Mold,
> She there shall dress a sweeter Sod,
> Than Fancy's Feet have ever trod.

17 *wells*] 'Whirlpools'. The term is specifically applied to certain
whirlpools in the Orkneys. T. may have known this, but it is likelier
that he borrowed the word from Scott, *The Pirate*, XXXVIII: '"even
as the wells of Tuftiloe can wheel the stoutest vessel round and round,
in despite of either sail or steerage"' (see *OED* sb.[1] 2.e).

19] Cf. *The Princess*, VI 168: 'in hands so lately claspt with yours'.

20 *tangle*] T. glosses 'tangle' as 'oar-weed', a general term for the larger

seaweeds. He refers to 'polyps and sea-tangle' in a letter from Aberystwyth in 1839 (*Memoir*, I 173).

11. The five stanzas form a single sentence (as in *14, 64, 86, 129, 131*) in which the word *calm* occurs eleven times. According to Willingham Rawnsley, this is the view T. would see 'on his way east from Spilsby and Partney to Miles-cross-hill, where he would have the panorama before him' (*Tennyson and His Friends*, 12). That *11* (along with *100*) is in the tradition of the 'prospect poem' has been noticed by C.N. Deane (*Aspects of Eighteenth-Century Nature Poetry* (1935), 109).

4 *chestnut*] The first reading, 'chesnut', was the predominant form until about 1820.

5 *high wold*] T. comments: 'A Lincolnshire wold or upland from which the whole range of marsh to the sea is visible'.

6, 14] The revisions increased the number of demonstratives (in 5, 6, 9, 13, 14) which prepare for the distant demonstrative in 19.

7–8] Adapted from 'The Ruined Kiln', 1–2: 'A million gossamers in field and fold / Were twinkling into green and gold'.

8] Ruskin quotes this line as an example of 'landscapes whose best character is sparkling, and there is a possibility of repose in the midst of brilliancy, or embracing it, – as on the fields of summer sea, or summer land' (*The Stones of Venice*, XXIX, in Cook and Wedderburn, IX 404).

12 *bounding*] 'Limiting'; cf. *17*.6; *89*.30.

20] Ricks compares Byron, 'The Bride of Abydos', II 26: 'As shaken on his restless pillow, / His head heaves with the heaving billow'. Also cf. 'Adonais', 311: 'The heavy heart heaving without a moan.'

12. This section follows on from the end of *11* in an extended metaphor of the poet's impatience to be with the body on board ship. The metaphor conflates the ancient notion (usually associated with the moment of death) that the soul can escape and fly away from the body, and an incident in the story of Noah in Genesis 8:8–9:

Also he sent forth a dove from him, to see if the waters were abated from off the face of the ground; But the dove found no rest for the sole of her foot, and she returned unto him into the ark, for the waters were on the face of the whole earth.

4] Cf. 'Locksley Hall', 109: 'Make me feel the wild pulsation that I felt before the strife'.

6] T. comments: 'My spirit flies from out my material self'. T.'s experience of this state is discussed in headnote to 95. Cf. 'Hark! the dogs howl!', 3: 'I leave the dreaming world below'; 'The Two Voices', 389: 'Who sought'st to wreck my mortal ark'.

9] This line was incorporated (Ricks observes) from an early draft of 'The Voyage' in Trinity College, Cambridge MS 0.15.21: 'On that smooth Ocean rounded large'. H.T. comments, 'The circles of water which bound the horizon as seen below in the flight', and compares the description of the homeward voyage of the ship in 'Enoch Arden', 538: 'Thro' many a fair sea-circle, day by day'.

14, 16] Cf. Kent's cry when Lear enters carrying the dead Cordelia: 'Is this the promised end?' (*King Lear*, V iii 264).

13. Of the seven sections (*10-16*) composed to link *9* (the departure of the ship) and *17* (the arrival), only *13* appears in T.MS; the other intervening sections first appear in L.MS. This suggests that *13* was composed before them. Moreover, T.MS has only *13*.1-16, which contain no allusion to the ship. The section was made part of the ship sequence by the addition in L.MS of a further stanza (17-20).

The spouse who attempts to embrace in bed the dead partner is a recurrent subject in classical and English literature. A well-known example (compared by Mustard) is Ovid, *Heroides*, X 9-12:

> incertum vigilans a somno languida movi
> Thesea prensuras semisupina manus —
> nullus erat! referoque manus iterumque retempto,
> perque torum moveo bracchia — nullus erat!

(Half waking only, languid from sleep, I turned upon my side and put forth hands to clasp my Theseus — he was not there! I drew back my hands, a second time I made essay, and o'er the whole couch moved my arms — he was not there!)

It is the subject of Milton, *Sonnet* XIX ('Methought I saw my late espoused saint') and occurs, as Bradley notes, in Pope, 'Eloisa to Abelard', 233-40. In 1862 the Duke of Argyll wrote to T. from Osborne to tell him of the solace which Queen Victoria found in *I.M.* after the death of Prince Albert: 'It will touch you, I think, to know that she had substituted in pencil "widow" for "widower" and "her" for "his" in the lines "Tears of the Widower".' (Letter, 23 February 1862, TRC.)

12] References to Hallam's voice are frequent in *I.M.* and elsewhere in T.: *56*.26; *69*.15,19; *80*.10; *82*.15-16; *85*.83-4; *113*.11; *116*.11-12; *130*.1,15; *Let Death and Memory keep the face* (Add. Poem vii), 6-8; *Speak to me from the stormy sky!* (Add. Poem ix); 'Hark! the dogs howl', 7: 'I seek the voice I loved'.

Spirit, breathing] The Latin *spiritus* means 'breath'. For other examples of this word-play, cf. *40*.2; *56*.7; *105*.20; *125*.10.

15] The revision seems to have been initiated by criticism from Spedding, who placed a question mark against this line in T.MS.

18-19] Cf. 'Locksley Hall', 121-2 (MS first reading): 'unimagined sails, / Merchants in a rosy sunset, dropping down with costly bales' (Ricks).

14. This section, like *17*, is a type of *prosphonetikon*, or speech of welcome to a traveller who has just arrived. Here the speech is addressed to the ship, but the subject is Arthur Hallam. The section illustrates several of the conventions of the genre: the formal announcement of the arrival (1-4); expressions and demonstrations of affection (10-11); the traveller or the friend receiving him gives an account of what has occurred during the traveller's absence (12-14). Cf. for example, Statius, *Silvae*, III 2, in which the poet imagines how he shall receive his friend when he returns from the war:

> at nos hoc iterum stantes in litore vastos
> cernemus fluctus aliasque rogabimus auras.
> o tum quantus ego aut quanta votiva movebo
> plectra lyra! cum me magna cervice ligatum
> attolles umeris atque in mea pectora primum
> incumbes e puppe novus servataque reddes
> colloquia inque vicem medios narrabimus annos.
> (129-35)

(I standing again upon this shore shall view the mighty waves and pray for other breezes. How proud then shall I be! How bravely shall I sound my votive lyre! when you lift me to your shoulders and I cling about your stalwart neck, and you, fresh from the ship, fall first upon my breast, and give me all your stored-up converse, and in turn we tell the story of the years between.)

Other examples of the genre include: Theocritus, *Idylls*, XII; Catullus, IX; Horace, *Odes*, I 36; Ovid, *Amores*, II 11 37-56.

The poet's imaginary reunion with Hallam is like the heavenly reunion depicted in 'In deep and solemn dreams', 13-20:

> All adown the busy ways
> Come sunny faces of lost days,
> Long to mouldering dust consigned,
> Forms which live but in the mind.
>
> Then methinks they stop and stand,
> And I take each by the hand,

And we speak as we have spoken
Ere our love by death was broken.

Jacobs (pp. 68-9) draws attention to the distance between the apodosis
(line 1) and the protasis (line 20). The section forms a single sentence
(like *11, 64, 86, 129, 131*) which is loosely co-ordinative (*And* is used
eleven times as the first word in a line), presumably to intensify the
effect of reverie.

2 *thou*] The ship.

2, 3 *to-day . . . quay*] The modern pronunciation of 'quay' as rhyming
with 'free' was standard in the nineteenth century. T. obviously intended
the older pronunication (to rhyme with 'day', as in Dryden and Swift)
to be retained here.

10] H.T. comments: 'My father said, "He was as near perfection as
mortal man could be."' Hallam is elsewhere likened to Christ or God:
51.14; *64*.2; *87*.36; *111*.20; *129*.5; *130*.4h; *130*.11.

15. Ricks finds verbal similarities with the early poem, 'On Sublimity';
for example: 'pore', 'labouring', 'dote', 'wild', 'roar', 'whirl'd'.

3] Cf. Coleridge, 'Christabel', I 48: 'There is not wind enough to twirl /
The one red leaf, the last of its clan' (Bradley).

9-16] If it were not for his fancied image of the ship on a calm sea,
he could not tolerate the storm around him. On the other hand, his
fears that his picture of the ship may be incorrect prevent him from an
indulgent identification with wild nature. H.T. comments of 14-16:
'The stormy night, except it were for my fear for the "sacred bark",
would be in sympathy with me.'

11] T. wrote 'only the plane of molten glass here is the sea' alongside
Gatty's comparison of this line with Job 37:18: 'Hast thou with him
spread out the sky, which is strong, and as a molten looking glass?'
Bradley compares Revelation 15:2: 'And I saw as it were a sea of glass
mingled with fire'.

14 *it is not so*] T. glossed this 'all is not peace with thee' (University
of London Library, *Works*, 1884), (Ricks).

15-20] Cf. Hallam, 'The Garden Trees', 10-11: 'The wild gray light
that fronts yon massive cloud, / Or the half bow, rising like pillared fire'
(Ricks); 'Hark! the dogs howl', 18: 'The vapour labours up the sky'.

18] Bradley compares 'L'Allegro', 73-4: 'Mountains on whose barren
brest / The labouring clouds do often rest'.

16.

12-14] Bradley compares Herbert, 'Miserie', 76-8:

> A sick toss'd vessel, dashing on each thing;
> Nay, his own shelf:
> My God, I mean my self.

12 *unhappy bark*] Cf. *17*.14: 'Sacred bark'; 'Lycidas', 100: 'that fatal and perfidious bark'.

18 *fuses*] A scientific word which began to be used figuratively in the early nineteenth century; for example, Coleridge, *Biographia Literaria*, 149: 'He diffuses a tone and spirit of unity that blends, and (as it were) fuses, each into each'; Hallam, 'On Some of the Characteristics of Modern Poetry, and on the Lyrical Poems of Alfred Tennyson': 'his vivid, picturesque delineation of objects, and the peculiar skill with which he holds all of them *fused*, to borrow a metaphor from science, in a medium of strong emotion'.

17-18. These sections were occasioned by letters which Henry Hallam wrote to T. on 9 and 30 December 1833. In both letters Henry Hallam gave details about the ship and the burial:

> I have been informed that you have expressed a wish to attend our dear Arthur's funeral. If that is the case, I have a place for you in my carriage; it is to be at Clevedon in Somersetshire.
>
> I have yet no tidings that the ship has sailed from Trieste, [part of page torn off] probably that is the case before [part of page torn off] time — There is little reason to suppose that she can arrive before the 2nd week in January.   (9 December 1833, TRC)

> It may remove some anxiety from the minds of yourself & others to know that the mortal part of our dearest Arthur will be interred at Clevedon on Friday — I leave town to-morrow — My first thought was not to write you till all was over. But you may have been apprehensive for the safety of the vessel — I did not expect her arrival so soon.   (30 December 1833, TRC; *Memoir*, I 106)

The earliest surviving drafts of both sections are in a notebook (H.Nbk.17) having other poems known to have been composed in 1833.

17. See head note to *14*.

1-7] Written in T.'s hand in Heath MS.

14] With the H.Nbk.17 reading. cf. *103*.40: 'A great ship lift her shining sides'.

15-16] The image alludes to the legendary origin of the Milky Way

as being formed from the milk expressed from the breasts of Juno.
The subject is depicted in a painting by Tintoretto (National Gallery,
London; exhibited in 1828 at the British Institute) and in one by
Rubens (Prado).

19-20] The early version echoed the final lines of 9 which in T.Nbk.
immediately precedes 17. The published reading retains a verbal link
with 9 in repeating 9.18: 'Till all my widow'd race be run'.

18. The original version of this section (H.Nbk.10) consisted of seven
stanzas of which 1-4 was the last. H.Nbk.10 has three stanzas which are
numbered sequentially: 13-16 is headed 'V'; 17-20 is headed 'VI';
and 1-4 is headed 'VII'. This and other evidence (see p. 308) indicate
that there were originally four preceding stanzas which were presumably
5-8 and 9-12, plus two further stanzas of which nothing survives.

The funeral took place on 3 January 1834 at the parish church of
St. Andrew, Clevedon, near Clevedon Court, the family home of Henry
Hallam's wife. T. did not attend, although Henry Hallam had understood
that he wished to and had offered him a place in the Hallam carriage
(Letter, 9 December 1833, quoted on p. 179. The events surrounding
the burial are described by Gatty (1900):

> The corpse was landed at Dover, and was brought by sixteen
> black horses all the way to Clevedon — so says Augustus James, who,
> when a boy, witnessed the interment. Sir A.H. Elton, the late Baronet,
> kindly corroborated this statement. Besides the coffin, there was a
> square iron box, deposited in the vault, which may have contained
> 'The darken'd heart that beat no more'. It is certain that the Poet
> always thought that the ship put in at Bristol. [See note 19.1.]

> Hallam's family resided in London, which accounts for the
> mourners coming from so great a distance. Augustus James told me,
> that the funeral procession consisted of a hearse and three mourning
> coaches, each of which was drawn by four horses . . .

> The tenant farmers on the Clevedon estate were the bearers. The
> Revd William Newland Pedder, who was Vicar of Clevedon for forty
> years, and died in 1871, read the burial service.

2] See note 8.22.

3-4] T. compares *Hamlet*, V i 232-4:

> Lay her i' th' earth,
> And from her fair and unpolluted flesh
> May violets spring!

Collins describes these lines as 'a graceful and pathetic application of
Hallam's own blessing on his friend', an allusion to Hallam's review of

T.'s early poems in *Englishman's Magazine*: 'When this Poet dies, will not the Graces and the Loves mourn over him, "fortunataque favilla nascentur violae"?' The reference is to Persius, *Satires*, I 39-40. (These lines from Persius are quoted by T. as 'a chance parallel' in connection with 'Aylmer's Field', 845 (*Eversley*, II 360).

6 *quiet bones*] A classical commonplace; for example, Ovid, *Amores*, III ix 67: 'ossa quieta, precor, tuta requiescite in urna' (O bones, rest quiet in protecting urn, I pray).

7] Henry Hallam recorded that Arthur was brought home 'to rest among his kindred and in his own country' (*Memoir*, I 107). For the traditional idea that this is to be desired, cf. Catullus on the death of his brother, LXVIII ('Non possum . . .'), 57-60:

> quem nunc tam longe non inter nota sepulcra
> nec prope cognatos compositum cineres,
> sed Troia obscena, Troia infelice sepultum
> detinet extremo terra aliena solo.

(Thee now far, far away, not among familiar graves, nor laid to rest near the ashes of thy kinsfolk, but buried in hateful Troy, ill-omened Troy, a foreign land in a distant soil.)

14-16] Cf. *13*.6; *97*.9-10 (H.Nbk.19). Ricks compares 2 Kings 4.34, Elisha's miracle: 'And he went up, and lay upon the child, and put his mouth upon his mouth . . . and the flesh of the child waxed warm.'

15 *Would*] The revision in Heath MS is in T.'s hand.

19. *Dating*: May 1839. T. comments that the description of the motion of the river was 'taken from my own observation — the rapids of the Wye are stilled by the incoming sea'. H.T. adds that *19* was 'written at Tintern Abbey'. T. visited Wales in May 1839 (letter from Charles Tennyson Turner to Emily Tennyson, 31 May 1839; TRC).

T. remarked to Knowles: 'After the burial these thoughts come.'

1] T. comments: 'He died at Vienna and was brought to Clevedon to be buried'. The body is represented as landing at Bristol, whereas it actually landed at Dover (see headnote *18*). The fact was first published by Edward Malan, 'Hallam's Grave', *Notes and Queries*, VIII, Sixth Series (September 1883), 221-3. Malan sent T. a copy of the article and T. replied on 14 November: 'It is news to me that the remains of A.H.H. were landed at Dover. I had always believed that the ship which brought them put in at Bristol' (*Memoir*, I 305).

3-4] Henry Hallam records that Clevedon church was selected for the place of burial 'not only from the connexion of kindred, but on account of its still and sequestered situation, on a lone hill that overhangs the Bristol channel' (*Remains*, xxxv).

3 *pleasant shore*] Cf. Keats, 'Hyperion', II 262: 'I stood upon a shore, a pleasant shore'.

8] Cf. Wordsworth's description of the Wye in 'Tintern Abbey', 3-4: 'These waters, rolling from their mountain-springs / With a soft inland murmur'.

21. Above this section in Hn.Nbk. are the words 'This yearning', cancelled. In H.Nbk.17 (following 9) is a stanza which was not published by T.:

> Time is not merely lapse of hours.
> This yearning is not idly given.
> The hearts of angels ache for ours.
> Earth's laws are recognized in Heaven.

5-6] Cf. *I keep no more a lone distress* (Add. Poem v), 1-4.

5 *traveller*] 'Such a one as is addressed by the "Siste, viator" inscribed on tombs' (Percival).

8c-d] Ricks compares *The Princess*, VI 321 (1847-8 text): 'To find low motives unto noble deeds'.

15-16] This anxiety about the future of the social order recurs in *127* and *128*. Also cf. *Are these the far-famed Victor Hours* (Add. Poem iv), 13.

18-20] The image alludes to the telescope which was capable of sophisticated stellar observations by the 1820s. There is probably not an allusion to the spectroscope, as seems to be implied in *Memoir*, II 336. T. may have drawn the image from a book in his possession by J.P. Nichol, *Views of the Architecture of the Heavens* ... (1838), second edition: 'Instruments exist . . . through which a quarter of a mile in the moon is appreciable, and in which one of the mountains of that enigmatical luminary may be distinctly seen' (p. 30). In 1834, the Revd T.J. Hussey of Hayes, Kent, suggested that an unknown planet might be pulling Uranus from its position as predicted in the almanacs. This suggestion initiated theoretical work leading to the discovery of Neptune in 1846. As Bradley remarks, the image is beautifully appropriate to the process by which the existence of Neptune was guessed at from irregularities in the motion of Uranus.

21] A reminiscence of Matthew 12:36: 'But I say unto you, that every idle word that men shall speak, they shall give account thereof in the day of judgement'.

24 *linnets*] Cf. the harper's song in Goethe, *Wilhelm Meisters Lehrjahre* (Bk II ii) 'I sing but as the linnet sings' (translated by Carlyle).

25, 27] T. revised these lines for **1855** in response to a comment by Francis T. Palgrave. In his copy of **1850A** (TRC), Palgrave wrote alongside them, 'The sound of "unto" seems always slightly feeble. Here it comes *twice.*' T. revised the lines in Palgrave's copy. Palgrave made many other criticisms of *I.M.* but this seems to be the only instance where T. responded directly to his annotations. See John O. Waller, 'Francis Turner Palgrave's Criticisms of Tennyson's *In Memoriam*,' *Victorian Newsletter*, 52 (Fall 1977), 13–17.

27–8] Watkin Watkins compares (*The Birds of Tennyson* (1903), 42) Virgil, *Georgics*, IV 511–15:

> qualis populea mœrens philomela sub umbra
> amissos queritur foetus, quos durus arator
> observans nido implumes detraxit; at illa
> flet noctem, ramoque sedens miserabile carmen
> integrat, et mœstis late loca questibus implet.

(As mourning Philomel under a poplar shade bemoans her lost young, which the hard-hearted clown observing in the nest, has stole unfledged. But she weeps through the night, and perched upon a bough, renews her doleful song, and fills the places all around with piteous wailings.)

22–26. These sections are linked by the traditional image of the path of life, along which the two friends travel, and then the poet alone. The likelihood that the T.MS sequence was originally intended to open with *The path by which I walkt alone* (Add. Poem i), *22, 23, 24,* and *25* is discussed on p. 13.

22. Above this section in H.Lpr.103 (a detached leaf from T.MS) appears *The path by which I walkt alone* (Add. Poem i) which has the images of the path, the springtime journey, and the figure waiting at the end of the journey. The poem was intended to lead into *22,* for it depicts the poet's life up to the time he met Hallam, and *22* depicts their life together.

With *22* Collins compares Petrarch, and Shepherd (pp. 68-9) compares Shakespeare:

> Tutta la mia fiorita e verde etade
> Passava; e 'ntepidir sentia già 'l foco
> Ch'arse 'l mio cor; ed era giunto al loco
> Ove scende la vita, ch'alfin cade . . .
>
> Morte ebbe invidia al mio felice stato,
> Anzi alla speme; e feglisi all'incontra
> A mezza via, come nemico armato.
>   (*In Morte di Madonna Laura,*
>   XLVII 1–4, 12–14)

(Now of my life each gay and greener year
Pass'd by, and cooler grew each hour the flame
With which I burn'd: and to that point we came
Which life descends, as to its end more near . . .

Death envied me the joys of such a state;
Nay, e'en the hopes I form'd: and on them fell
E'en in midway, like some arm'd foe in wait.)

Three winters cold
Have from the forests shook three summers' pride,
Three beauteous springs to yellow autumn turn'd
In process of the seasons have I seen,
Three April perfumes in three hot Junes burn'd,
Since first I saw you fresh, which yet are green.

(*Sonnets*, CIV 3–8)

1–8] The period described here is recalled in *95*.22: 'that glad year which once had been'. With the imagery, cf. the description by Catullus of the time before the death of his brother, LXVIII 16: 'iucundum cum aetas florida ver ageret' (when my youth in its flower was keeping jocund spring time).

3, 10] T.H. Vail Motter understands these lines to mean: 'Our friendship, beginning in April, 1829, proceeded smoothly for four years; but as the fifth autumn, i.e., the autumn of 1833, arrived, Death came on September 15, 1833. I therefore look back upon the five years, 1829–33, as the richest of my life.' ('When Did Tennyson Meet Hallam', *Modern Language Notes*, LVII (March 1942), 209–10). H.T. glosses 'four sweet years': '1828–32', but Motter offers several probable reasons for T. and Hallam meeting in April 1829, not before. Moreover, 1833, which is not included by H.T., was a 'sweet year' until the autumn. The MS readings *three* and *fourth* can only be explained as miscalculations. In 1861 T. revisited the Pyrenees (where he had been with Hallam in 1830) and composed 'In the Valley of Cauteretz' in which he refers to 'The two and thirty years were a mist that rolls away'. Strictly, he should have written 'The one and thirty years . . .', but he allowed the inaccuracy to stand.

4 a–d] This stanza is deleted from *22* in H.Lpr.103 but is the concluding stanza in *23*. If *22* was composed after *23*, as the manuscript evidence suggests, then it would seem that T. considered transferring the final stanza of *23* to *22*. If, as seems less likely, *22* was composed before *23*, then the stanza deleted in *22* was merely salvaged for use in *23*.

10] The MS reading is a syllable short. Hallam died on 15 September 1833, the fifth autumn after meeting T. Cf. *46*.12: 'And those five years its richest field'.

10, 19] The journey down the slope and towards the waste has been compared to Dante's arrival at the 'piaggia diserta' (desert slope) in *Inferno*, I 29 (Gordon D. Hirsch, 'Tennyson's *Commedia*,' *Victorian Poetry*, VIII (1970), 100).

12, 20] With 12, cf. lines in an early version of 'Tithon' (Trinity College, Cambridge MS 0.15.20): 'Thou knowest not the uncertain shadow feared / Of Gods and men'. With 'Shadow' cf. *23*.4; *26*.15; Psalm 23:4: 'the valley of the shadow of death.'

17-18] Cf. Henry King, 'An Exequy', 89-94:

> Stay for mee there: I will not faile
> To meet Thee in that hollow Vale.
> And think not much of my delay;
> I am already on the way,
> And follow Thee with all the speed
> Desire can make, or Sorrowes breed.

23. In T.MS this section follows *38*, with which it shares the idea of the wandering poet and the contrast between the past and present.

1 *Now*] The T.MS reading, 'And', was a syntactical link with *38*.

3 *Alone, alone*] For the depersonalization of this revision, and for similar revisions, see p. 25. In T.MS 'I' was accidentally not cancelled. With the pathetic effect of the repetition, Bradley compares *18*.13: 'Ah yet, ev'n yet, if this might be'; and Shakespeare, *The Rape of Lucrece*, 795: 'where I alone alone must sit and pine'.

5] T. comments: 'After death we shall learn the truth of all beliefs'. Collins (*Cornhill*, 42) remarks of *51*.11: 'Milton has described Death as the "keeper of the keys of all creeds"'. T. has glossed this: 'Not known to me'. (Collins's parallel cannot be found in Milton's poetry.)

9 *How changed*] Cf. Virgil, *Aeneid*, II 275: 'quantum mutatus ab illo' (how changed from him) which became a well-known tag.

15-16] Cf. Pope, 'Eloisa to Abelard', 95: 'Ev'n thought meets thought ere from the lips it part' (Bradley).

17-20] Cf. 'The Gardener's Daughter' (unadopted passage in T.Nbk.17), in which the narrator and his friend, who is based on Hallam, journey forth in spring:

> My heart was filled with sunshine without shade,
> For I was vain, and young, and felt my blood
> How pure it swept the veins, and how my heart
> Beat in my bosom, like a Life in Life.

17] '... great [and] good, καλὸς κἀγαθός as the Athenians said of their best' (T. in a letter quoted in *Memoir*, II 270-1).

19-20] T. comments: 'Re-awakening of life'. Cf. 'Early Spring', 13-14: 'My leaping blood obeys / The season's lure!'

21-2] A reminiscence of *Comus*, 476: 'How charming is divine Philosophy!'. Cf. *53*.14: 'divine Philosophy'.

22 *Argive*] In Virgil *Argivus* is a usual word for 'Greek'.

24.

1-8] The idea is: 'The past could not actually have been as ideal as I have made it out to be: even the sun has its dark spots (1-4); if everything had indeed been perfect, it would have been so for the first time since the Creation of man' (5-8).

3 *The very source and fount*] Cf. *Macbeth*, II iii 96-7: 'The spring, the head, the fountain of your blood, / Is stopp'd; the very source of it is stopp'd.'

4 *wandering isles of night*] T. comments: 'sun-spots'. Ricks compares Shelley, *Hellas*, Prologue, 18: 'The fairest of those wandering isles that gem / The sapphire space of interstellar air'.

6 *Paradise*] T. wrote in a letter in 1863: 'Cauteretz, which I had visited with my friend before I was twenty, had always lived in my recollection as a sort of Paradise' (*Memoir*, I 491-2).

8, 10] T. revised these lines apparently in response to criticism by Aubrey de Vere, who made marginal marks against them in the copy of **Trial** (Beinecke, Tinker 2065) sent him by T.

8] With the first reading cf. 'The Day Dream', L'Envoi, 41: 'For since the time when Adam first / Embraced his Eve in happy hour'.

10] For the depersonalization of this revision (and the one in 11) see pp. 25-6.

13-14] Collins compares Campbell, *Pleasures of Hope* I 3-8; in particular, cf. 7-8:

> 'Tis distance lends enchantment to the view,
> And robes the mountain in its azure hue.

13-14] T. describes his 'Passion of the Past' in 'The Ancient Sage', 216-28. Spedding referred to T.'s 'almost personal dislike of the present, whatever it may be' (Charles Tennyson, 155).

15-16] H.T. compares 'Locksley Hall Sixty Years After', 187-8:

'Hesper — Venus — were we native to that splendour or in Mars, / We should see the Globe we groan in, fairest of their evening stars'.

15] Cf. 'Eleänore', 89–93:

> As though a star, in inmost heaven set,
> Even while we gaze on it,
> Should slowly round his orb, and slowly grow
> To a full face, there like a sun remain
> Fixed —

This image refers to 'the old theory of variability, namely that the variation in the light is caused by the star being a flattened disc, or having one side more luminous than the other' (Norman Lockyer and Winifred L. Lockyer, *Tennyson As a Student and Poet of Nature* (1910), 31–2). *OED* cites this line as the earliest example of 'orb' used as a verb to mean 'to form itself into an orb' (v.2.b.).

25. Collins compares Schiller, 'Die Ideale', which has the figure of a youth on a journey. His load is lightened and his journey is encouraged by his love for his companion; especially cf.

> Wie leicht ward er dahin getragen,
> Was war dem Glüctlichen zu schwer! . . .
> Des lebens Burden liebend theilest.
> (49–50, 79)

> (Though laden with delight, how lightly
> The wanderer heavenward still could soar . . .
> Thy task, the load more light to render.)

1 *Life*] T. comments: 'checquered, but the burden was shared'.

2 *with equal feet*] Cf. *Aeneid*, II 724: 'non passibus aequis' (Bradley).

4] Cf. Galatians 6:2: 'Bear ye one another's burdens, and so fulfil the law of Christ'.

10–12] Cf. the early poem probably addressed to Hallam, 'If I were loved, as I desire to be', 5–6: 'All the inner, all the outer world of pain / Clear Love would pierce and cleave, if thou wert mine'.

12] Recalls the description in 'The Gardener's Daughter' of T.'s friendship with Hallam: 'a friendship so complete / Portioned in halves between us' (4–5).

26.

2–4] Cf. *1*. 13–16.

3 *canker Love*] A common image in Shakespeare; for example, *Venus and Adonis*, 656: 'This canker that eats up Love's tender spring'.

5-6 *that eye which watches guilt / And goodness*] T. comments: 'The Eternal Now. I AM'.

12] H.T. explains: 'And that the present love will end in future indifference'.

13-14] H.T. compares *Comus*, 139: 'The nice morn, on the Indian steep'.

13] The revision from 'So' to 'Then' was suggested by Aubrey de Vere in the copy of **Trial** (Beinecke, Tinker 2065) sent him by T.

15-16] T. changed 'cloak' to 'shroud' probably in response to criticism of these lines in a review of *I.M.* in *The Times*, 28 November 1851: 'That a Shadow should hold keys at all, is a noticeable circumstance; but that it should wait with a cloak ready to be thrown over a gentleman in difficulties, is absolutely amazing' (Shannon, 157, 162).

16 *my proper scorn*] T. comments: 'scorn of myself'.

27. Love involves responsibility, effort, and suffering. The poet does not envy the conditions in life which do not demand these commitments. The challenges of travellers (*21*), his retrospect (*22-5*), and his own doubts about the decay of love (*26*) have brought him to this attitude.

2-3] Cf. Gray, 'Ode on a Distant Prospect of Eton College', 27: 'The captive linnet which enthrall'; 'Elegy Written in a Country Churchyard', 51: 'Chill Penury repress'd their noble rage'.

5-8] Cf. Keats, 'Hyperion', II 66-7: 'once tame and mild / As grazing ox unworried in the meads'. Cf. also T.'s letter of 1839 to Emily Sellwood (noticed by Bradley):

> God might have made me a beast; but He thought good to give me power, to set Good and Evil before me that I might shape my own path. The happiness, resulting from this power well exercised, must in the end exceed the mere physical happiness of breathing, eating, and sleeping like an ox.   (*Memoir*, I 170)

T. elsewhere associates sexual licence, the absence of a spiritual nature, and pleasure in the present moment; cf. *35*.21-4, and also:

> The vast leviathan, which takes
> His pastime in the sounding floods.
> ('Love' ('Almighty Love'), 27-8)

> Where wert thou when thy father played
> In his free field, and pastime made.
> ('The Two Voices', 319-20)

> Why took ye not your pastime? To that man
> My work shall answer, since I knew the right
> And did it.
> ('Love and Duty', 28-30)

11] A reminiscence of *Hamlet*, I v 32-4:

> And duller shouldst thou be than the fat weed
> That roots itself in ease on Lethe wharf,
> Wouldst thou not stir in this.

Cf. 'Sonnet' 'Conrad!', 14: 'This sloth-sprung weed' (Ricks); Hallam, 'A Farewell to the South', 631-3:

> I will never drift
> Before the varying gale in aimless sloth
> Of purpose, like a battered wreck.

12 *want-begotten rest*] In page-proofs of the *Eversley* notes in TRC, this is glossed 'desired', but H.T. deleted this and substituted 'any repose that comes from want of thought'. The published note reads: 'rest — the result of some deficiency or narrowness'.

13-16] Bradley comments: 'With this conviction the poem comes to a break, as though a definite stage of advance were reached'. He suggests that 'I hold it true' and 'loved and lost' are intended to recall *1*.1: 'I held it truth' and *1*.15: 'Behold the man that loved and lost'. The stanza is echoed in *85*.1-4, which was, in fact, composed before *27*.

15-16] There are many analogues to this maxim. Cf. Seneca, 'Consolation to Marcia', XII 3: 'si ponatur electio, utrum satius sit non diu felicem esse an numquam, melius est descessura nobis bona quam nulla contingere' (For if we should be given the choice — whether it is better to be happy for a short time only or never at all — it is better for us to have blessings that will flee than none at all.) Collins compares Congreve, *The Way of the World*, II 2: ''Tis better to have been left than never to have been loved.' Bradley compares Campbell, 'The Jilted Nymph', 19-20: 'Better be courted and jilted / Than never be courted at all'.

28-30. These sections refer to the Christmas following Hallam's death. The second Christmas after his death is described in *78*, and the third Christmas and New Year's Eve in *104-6*. T. stated in 1883 that the divisions of *I.M.* were marked by these three Christmases (*Memoir*, I 305). Sections *28-30* thus begin the second part of the poem, a part in which the 'idea of the continued life of the beloved dead now emerges, and in various forms becomes the principal subject' (Bradley).

Sections *28* and *29* describe in the present tense the outdoor and indoor scenes of Christmas Eve. Section *30* looks back on them from the dawn of Christmas Day; as Bradley observes, 'The Christmas eve which had been anticipated and had begun in sadness, ends in cheerfulness and hope'.

28. *Dating*: probably 1834; it is in T.Nbk. (see Appendix A.1).

The section is a companion-piece to *104* which describes the third Christmas, the Christmas in the Tennyson family's new home.

2–4] Cf. Coleridge, 'Christabel', II 360–1: 'The air is still! through mist and cloud / That merry peal comes ringing loud.'

3 *Christmas bells*] T. comments: 'They always used to ring on Xmas Eve'.

from hill to hill] Somersby and its environs are described by Willingham Rawnsley as 'a tiny village surrounded by low green hills; and close at hand, here nestling in a leafy hollow, and there standing boldly on the "ridged wold", are some half a dozen churches' (*Tennyson and His Friends*, 9).

5] The churches of the four hamlets were identified by Gatty as probably Somersby, Wood Enderby, Bag Enderby, and Mavis Enderby. T. deleted Wood Enderby and Mavis Enderby and wrote three names alongside. He subsequently crossed out these names, and now only two – Hagworthingham and Tetford – are legible. The revised note in Gatty's edition of 1900 reads: 'The churches are not to be identified. Those in the neighbourhood of Somersby have too small belfries to allow of change ringing. The sounds may have been only in the Poet's mind.' H.D. Rawnsley asked the Rector of Bag Enderby which nearby churches had peals of bells which could be heard at Somersby. The Rector replied that

> there were many, and that he was often asked the question, but could not particularise. An American had written him, and, as Mr. Horatio Tennyson was in the neighbourhood, he appealed to him; he, in turn, wrote to his brother the Laureate, but, as was natural enough, the Laureate's reply was that he had forgotten.
>
> (*Memories of the Tennysons*, 11–12)

13] As Bradley observes, 'This year' at first suggests that this is the second Christmas after Hallam's death. But *30*.15–16 make clear that it is the first: 'A merry song we sang with him / Last year'. The meaning is slightly ambiguous; either during the year both his sleeping and waking were painful or, one night he slept and woke in the morning to the painful news of Hallam's death.

29.

1–4] The false start in T.MS is a version of 1–4. 'My sister' refers to T.'s sister, Emily, the betrothed of Arthur Hallam. Their forthcoming marriage is referred to in *84*.10–12. Ten months after Hallam's death Emily wrote to T. from Somersby:

> You will be sorry to hear that I have been considerably worse in

health since your departure . . . And once or twice indeed I thought that the chilly hand of death was upon me: however I still exist, tho' reduced again to a great state of weakness . . . I can no longer continue in this deepening grave of tears . . . What is life to me! if I die (which the Tennysons never do) the effort [to visit Henry Hallam and his family] shall be made.   (*Memoir*, I 135)
The T.MS reading of 1–4 is printed with minor variants in *Eversley* and is described as 'Original reading of third verse'.

2 *household peace*] Cf. *Paradise Lost*, X 107–8: 'Which infinite calamity shall cause / To human life, and household peace confound'.

5–6] Cf. *6*.29–30. Hallam had spent the previous Christmas Eve (1832) at Somersby. He described the arrangements for his forthcoming visit in two letters (TRC) to Emily Tennyson. On 12 December he wrote: 'Tell me — you do not surely leave Somersby before Xmas? I purpose being with you *the twenty third*; Sunday I believe.' A week later (20 December) he wrote:

I have secured my place in the Mail for Saturday night . . . Be visible — that's a good girl — when I arrive. Every hour of you will be precious, since I cannot stay longer than I did last time . . . you must try to pluck up a bit, & make me properly merry for the Eve. If you set up a 'reg'lar good cry' because it is your *last* Eve at Somersby, how shall I remember it is my *first*?

(The Tennysons feared that they would have to leave Somersby after the death of Dr Tennyson in 1831. They did not leave, however, until 1837.)

6] Cf. 'The Voyage', 18: 'burn the threshold of the night'.

8 a–d] A reply to 4. The stanza is printed with minor variants in *Eversley*.

11 *Use and Wont*] (the 'Old sisters' and 'Gray nurses' of 13 and 14) an old-fashioned legality much used by Scott; Gatty quotes the motto to *The Pirate*, XIV.

30. *Dating*: probably 1834; it is in T.Nbk. (see Appendix A.1.). The numerous verbal variants in Heath MS (see minor variants, lines 9, 17, 19, 22, 26, 27) suggest that Heath transcribed the section from memory and afterwards corrected the transcript by reference to an original.
The section is titled 'Christmas Eve.1833' in Heath MS. It was occasioned by an actual gathering of family and friends at Christmas 1833. R.J. Tennant wrote to T. on 8 June 1834 and recalled 'the glorious three days of my Christmas sojourn at Somersby' (MS *Materials*, I 206). In October he wrote of the coming Christmas holidays: 'I shall think of the merry Christmas sports, and the New Year revels, that I fancy Somersby will see. I am glad John [Heath] will be with you, &

Douglas [Heath] too (if he does come): I confess I wish I was there too' (MS *Materials*, I 230).

In Hn.Nbk. *30* is followed by *78*, a companion-piece modelled on *30* to commemorate the second Christmas following the death of Hallam. Of the sections which commemorate the third Christmas (*104-6*), *105* is a companion-piece to *30* and *78*.

5 *the hall*] An allusion to the dining room at Somersby (in Gothic style, with a lofty groined ceiling and stained glass windows) which Dr Tennyson designed and built in 1819.

7-8] *an awful sense / Of one mute Shadow watching all*] Cf. Epilogue, 85-8. The 'one mute Shadow' is the dead friend ('umbra'), as distinct from the 'Shadow' (of death) in *22*, *23*, and *26*. Cf. *38*.9-10 and note.

18-19] Cf. the Burial Service: 'blessed are the dead which die in the Lord . . . for they rest from their labours' (Revelation 14:13); Proverbs 3:24: 'Yea, thou shalt lie down, and thy sleep shall be sweet'.

22-32] In **1850A** the song (distinguished by inverted commas) extends to the end of the section ('They . . . born.'). **1850B** reverts to the reading of **Trial** which is the final reading. This makes the last stanza the direct speech of the poet rather than the reported words of the song. It is improbable that the **1850A** reading results from typographical errors.

23] Cf. *85*.87-8. With idea and diction, cf. Gray, 'Ode for Music', 19-20: 'Yet hither oft a glance from high / They send of tender sympathy'. The importance Hallam attached to sympathy, which he defined as 'assumed similarity' between one person and another, resulting in understanding and compassion, is expressed in his essay 'On Sympathy'.

25-8] The notion of successive stages of life after death was one of the principles of T.'s philosophy: 'I can hardly understand how any great, imaginative man, who has deeply lived, suffered, thought and wrought, can doubt of the Soul's continuous progress in the after-life' (*Memoir*, I 321). Of the countless discussions of this ancient theological idea the observations of two eighteenth-century writers, whose works were at Somersby, may be compared with these lines:

> Our posthumous life, whatever there may be in it additional to our present, yet may not be entirely beginning anew, but going on. Death may, in some sort, and in some respects, answer to our birth, which is not a suspension of the faculties which we had before it, or a total change of the state of life in which we existed when in the womb, but a continuation of both, with such and such great alterations.   (Joseph Butler, *The Analogy of Religion*, I i 2)

How can it enter into the thoughts of man, that the soul, which is
capable of such immense perfections, and of receiving new improve-
ments to all eternity, shall fall away into nothing almost as soon as it
is created? Are such abilities made for no purpose? . . . Were a
human soul thus at a stand in her accomplishments, were her faculites
to be full blown, and incapable of farther enlargements, I could
imagine it might fall away insensibly, and drop at once into a state
of annihilation. But can we believe a thinking being that is in a
perpetual progress of improvements, and travelling on from perfection
to perfection, after having just looked abroad into the works of its
Creator, and made a few discoveries of his infinite goodness, wisdom
and power, must perish at her first setting out, and in the very
beginning of her enquiries?   (Joseph Addison, *Spectator*, No. 111)

27-8] Cf. 24 (T.Nbk.). Ricks compares Shelley, 'The Revolt of Islam',
XII 5: 'Pierce like reposing flames the tremulous atmosphere'; 'Adonais',
493-5:

> Whilst burning through the inmost veil of Heaven,
> The soul of Adonais, like a star,
> Beacons from the abode where the Eternal are.

27] The subject and verb are inverted. In T.Nbk. a space was left for
the initial word, and 'Pierces' was inserted after the rest of the stanza had
been written.

28] Cf. 'Œnone', 163 (MS reading): 'Circled through all experience,
narrowing up / From orb to orb' (Ricks). Here 'veil' represents a stage of
the afterlife. For 'veil' as an image of life hiding the future, cf. *56*.28.

29 *happy morn*] Cf. Milton, 'On the Morning of Christ's Nativity', 1:
'This is the month, and this the happy morn'.

30 *cheerful day*] A traditional phrase, as in Gray, 'Elegy . . .', 87: 'the
warm precincts of the cheerful day'.

32] This line is repeated as the opening of an uncompleted poem (Add.
Poem ii) which appears in T.MS on the verso of the leaf having *30*.

shone] T. recommended the pronunciation 'shōne'.

31-36. The connection of these sections is explained by Bradley:
The poet finds 'revealed' in the story of Lazarus the fact of a life
beyond death, but only the fact (XXXI). He thinks that in the mind
of Lazarus' sister curiosity as to the state beyond death was absorbed
in love and adoration; and in this attitude he finds a blessedness less
securely attained by minds whose faith in immortality rests solely on
inward evidence (XXXII, XXXIII). It is true that such a faith is not

only possible but seems forced on us by the inward evidence (XXXIV, XXXV); but he is thankful for the sanction given to it by the revelation of Christ's life and teaching (XXXVI).

31. *Dating*: probably 1834; it is in T.Nbk. (see Appendix A.1).

Sections *31* and *32* were originally one section of which there are two drafts (a, b) in T.Nbk (see Plate I). T.Nbk.a has five stanzas in the following order: *31*.1-4, *31*.5-8, *32*.5-8, *32*.9-12, *32*.13-16. This draft is deleted and a revised version, T.Nbk.b, is written on the opposite leaf. T.Nbk.b has five stanzas in the following order: *31*.1-4, *31*.5-8, *32*.1-4, *32*.5-8, *32*.9-12. T.Nbk.b adds *32*.1-4 and omits *32*.13-16. Lines *31*.1-3, 5-8 are significantly revised.

T. greatly admired the painting *The Raising of Lazarus* by Sebastiano del Piombo, in the National Gallery, London (formerly in the Angerstein Collection) (*Memoir*, I 371, II 235). He may have recalled the remarks of Charles Lamb on the painting in *The Last Essays of Elia*, 'Barrenness of the Imaginative Faculty in the Productions of Modern Art':

The world has nothing to show of the preternatural in painting, transcending the figure of Lazarus bursting his grave-clothes, in the great picture at Angerstein's. It seems a thing between two beings. A ghastly horror at itself struggles with newly-apprehending gratitude at second life bestowed. It cannot forget that it was a ghost. It has hardly felt that it is a body. It has to tell of the world of spirits.

A fine print of the painting hung over the fireplace in the drawing room at Farringford (MS catalogue of pictures, sculpture, etc., at Farringford; Beinecke).

Bradley compares with this section and the next Sir Thomas Browne, *Religio Medici*, I 21: 'I can read . . . that Lazarus was raised from the dead, yet not demand where, in the interim, his soul awaited'. Ricks compares (but could not quote) a deleted stanza from 'Thou mayst remember' (Trinity College, Cambridge MS 0.15.23):

Not Mary felt ~~more~~ ∧ such ∧ full delight
When having heard her brother's name
[*illegible word*] with come forth and waiting
Forth in the open sunshine came
The languid corpse bound hand and foot
Winking his eyelids at the light.

With the idea, cf. 'Oh! that 'twere possible', 13-16:

Ah God! that it were possible
For one short hour to see
The souls we loved, that they might tell us
What and where they be.

1] With this section T. quotes John 11:31: 'She goeth unto the grave to weep there.'

9-12] T. interpolates this scene into the biblical account. It is apparently suggested by the references (John 11:19, 31, 33, 42, 45) to the friends who comfort Mary and Martha and who accompany them to the tomb.

10] Cf. Psalm 89:15: 'Blessed is the people that know the joyful sound.'

11-12] The Mount of Olives, the scene of the Ascension.

14-16] Bradley compares Pope, 'Eloisa to Abelard', 9-10: 'rest ever unreveal'd, / Nor pass these lips in holy silence seal'd.

32. See headnote *31*.

1 *are*] The version of *31* and *32* in T.Nbk. is in the past tense.

3-4, 11-12] See John 12:2-3: 'There they made him a supper; and Martha served; but Lazarus was one of them that sat at the table with him. Then Mary therefore took a pound of ointment of spikenard, very costly, and anointed his feet with her hair.'

7-8] T. wrote to Emily Sellwood in 1839: 'Who knows whether revelation be not itself a veil to hide the glory of that Love which we could not look upon without marring our sight, and our onward progress?' (*Memoir*, I 170).

13-16] This kind of piety is described in 'Supposed Confessions of a Second-rate Sensitive Mind', 68-76, in which T. had in mind his own mother:

> Would that my gloomèd fancy were
> As thine, my mother, when with brows
> Propt on thy knees, my hands upheld
> In thine, I listened to thy vows,
> For me outpoured in holiest prayer —
> For me unworthy! — and beheld
> Thy mild deep eyes upraised, that knew
> The beauty and repose of faith,
> And the clear spirit shining through.

Similar sentiments occur in the poems of Arthur Hallam, for example:

> wherefore do I err
> In that I stoop to rise, and deem the lore,
> Which profiteth to strength, may best from her
> Be learnt, who draws each breath in purity —
> That inmost valour, that bright character
> Of Godhead, stamped on woman's soul — that we,
> Whose paths are in the perilous mist, may take
> Its impress, and be safe?
> ('A Farewell to the South', 597-604)

33. The section recalls a passage in Cowper's poem, 'Truth':

> She, for her humble sphere by nature fit,
> Has little understanding and no wit . . .
> Just knows, and knows no more, her Bible true –
> A truth the brilliant Frenchman never knew;
> And in that charter reads with sparkling eyes
> Her title to a treasure in the skies.
>
> (323–4, 327–30)

Arthur Hallam, writing to Emily Tennyson (22 January 1832), expressed the traditional notion that the innocence and ignorance of women in matters of religion should not be corrupted by philosophical inquiry or scepticism:

> I was half inclined to be sorry that you looked into that Theodicaea of mine. I must have perplexed rather than cleared your sight of those high matters. I do not think women ought to trouble themselves much with theology: we, who are more liable to the subtle objections of the Understanding, have more need to handle the weapons that lay them prostrate. But where there is greater innocence, there are larger materials for a singlehearted faith. It is by the heart, not by the head, that we must all be convinced of the two great fundamental truths, the reality of Love, & the reality of Evil. Do not, my beloved Emily, let any cloudy mistrusts & perplexities bewilder your perception of these, & of the great corresponding fact, I mean the Redemption.   (Motter, 199)

1–2] Cf. the beginning of Dante's 'Purgatorio', where the poet describes his delight on ascending from hell:

> aer puro infino al primo giro,
> agli occhi miei ricominciò diletto,
>   tosto ch' i' uscii fuor dell' aura morta,
>   che m' avea contristati gli occi e il petto.
>
> (15–18)

(air pure even to the first circle, to mine eyes restored delight, soon as I issued forth from the dead air which had afflicted eyes and heart.)

1 thou] A type of religious intellectual whose abstract theism is contrasted with the anthropomorphic faith of the 'sister' who sees in Christ an embodiment of divine truth.

3–4] H.T. observes of his father's religious beliefs:

> He thought, with Arthur Hallam, that 'the essential feelings of religion subsist in the utmost diversity of forms,' that 'different language does not always imply different opinions, nor different opinions any difference in real faith.' 'It is impossible,' he said, 'to imagine that the Almighty will ask you, when you come before Him in the next life what your particular form of creed was.'
>
> (Memoir, I 309)

T. comments on 'form' in line 4: 'I dread the losing hold of forms. I have expressed this in my "Akbar". [See 'Akbar's Dream', 122-6.] There must be forms, but I hate the need for so many sects and separate shrines.' Cf. *127*.1-2.

5-8] T. is reported to have been 'full of compunction at once having shown a poor man what he thought an inconsistency in the Gospel, lest he should have weakened his faith in the Bible' (*Memoir*, II 169). In old age, T. remarked to his doctor: ' "Beware of breaking up the soil of any Faith, when you have no better seed to sow" ' (*Memoir*, II 350).

6 *early Heaven*] The heaven she learnt of in childhood, that is, a definable place. The idea is expressed in the first reading, 'local Heaven', an image which occurs in *The Devil and the Lady*, I v 21-23.

> Dost thou think that Heaven is local, and not rather
> The omnipresence of the glorified
> And liberated Spirit . . .?

8] T. compares Statius, *Silvae*, I iii 22-3: 'ceu placidi veritus turbare Vopisci / Pieriosque dies et habentes carmina somnos' (as if afraid to disturb the Pierian days and music-haunted slumbers of tranquil Vopiscus).

13-16] The Bishop of Ripon recorded of T.: 'He warned the man proud of his emancipation from formal faith, that in a world of so many confusions he might meet with ruin "Even for want of such a type"' (*Memoir*, I 309). Cf. *53*.13-16.

34. T.'s belief in the immortality of the soul is a subject in many of his poems (notably 'Vastness') and of many of his remarks. His son records that he 'more than once said':

> Hast Thou made all this for naught? Is all this trouble of life worth undergoing if we only end in our own corpse-coffins at last? If you allow a God, and God allows this strong instinct and universal yearning for another life, surely that is in a measure a presumption of its truth. We cannot give up the mighty hopes that make us men.

H.T. adds: 'I have heard him even say that he "would rather know that he was to be lost eternally than not know that the whole human race was to live eternally"' (*Eversley*, III 219).

1 *dim life*] Cf. Pope, 'Elegy to the Memory of an Unfortunate Lady', 19-20: 'Dim lights of life, that burn a length of years / Useless, unseen, as lamps in sepulchres'.

3] With this idea cf. Carlyle, 'Characteristics': 'Under all [Nature's] works, chiefly under her noblest work, Life, lies a basis of Darkness which she benignantly conceals.' T. read Carlyle's *Miscellanies* (which includes 'Characteristics') in November 1839 when he stayed with FitzGerald (Barton, p. 12).

6–8] Perhaps T. had in mind a passage from Henry Taylor, *Philip van Artevelde*, which he read closely on its publication in 1834 (*Memoir*, I 141):

> 'Mr. Shelley and his disciples, however, — the followers (if I may so call them) of the PHANTASTIC SCHOOL . . . would transfer the domicile of poetry to regions where reason, far from having any supremacy or rule, is all but confusion, an alien and an outcast; the seats of anarchy and abstraction, where imagination exercises the shadow of an authority, over a people of phantasms, in a land of dreams.' (Preface)

14–16] The idea and the diction are reminiscent of a passage (quoted at length in note *30*.25–8) from the *Spectator*, No. 111: 'Were a human soul . . . annihilation'. T. may have read of the charming of birds in his copy of *Hundred Wonders of the World*:

> The snake creeps to the foot of a tree, and by shaking his rattle, awakens the little creatures which are lodged in it. They are so frightened at the sight of their enemy, who fixes his lively piercing eyes upon one or other of them, that they have not the power to get away, but leap about from bough to bough, till they are quite tired, and at last falling to the ground, are snapped into his mouth. This is, by the people of the country, called the charming of squirrels and birds. (p. 479)

Cf. also 'The Lovers' Tale', II 184–6, 200–5:

> the eye
> Was riveted and charm-bound, gazing like
> The Indian on a still-eyed snake . . .
> and over my dim eyes,
> And parted lips . . . down-hung
> The jaws of Death . . .
> and I
> Down welter'd thro' the dark ever and ever.

35.

9–12] T. commented to Knowles: 'The vastness of the future — the enormity of the ages to come after your little life would act against that love'.

9] T. wrote 'Nonsense' alongside the suggestion by Collins (*Cornhill*, 41) that this line was partly inspired by Horace, *Odes*, II xx 14: 'gementis litora Bosphori' (the shores of the moaning Bosphorus). He is recorded as having remarked:

The critics won't allow me any imagination. They take a line like 'Moanings of the homeless sea' and say: '"Moanings", Horace; "homeless", Shelley' and so on . . . As if no one else had heard the sea moan except Horace.

(W.F. Rawnsley, 'Personal Recollections of Tennyson − II', *Nineteenth Century*, XCVII (February 1925), 195; *Memoir*, II 385) Ricks compares Shelley's translation of Euripides's *The Cyclops*, 702: 'wandering long over the homeless sea'. Cf. also *Alastor*, 566: 'The thunder and the hiss of homeless streams' (Jacobs).

10-12] This description may have been suggested by two chapters in Charles Lyell, *Principles of Geology* (I x, xi) on the power of the torrents and rivers which descend at various speeds from mountainous regions to transport large quantities of gravel, sand and mud. T. read Lyell in 1837 (*Memoir*, I 162).

11 *Æonian hills*] T. comments: 'the everlasting hills'. 'Æonian' seems to have been coined by Abraham Tucker ('Edward Search'), *The Light of Nature Pursued*, 4 vols. (1768), I 650: 'I might insist that the term translated "everlasting" ought to be preserved untranslated, as a kind of technical term, and called "aionian"'. Cf. *The Princess*, VI 40 (H.Nbk.25 − 1848 edition): 'With music in the Æonian breeze of Time'.

13-16] In T.MS this stanza is written on the leaf opposite for insertion between lines 12 and 17. The stanza may be an afterthought. It seems likelier, however, that in transcribing the section into T.MS from an earlier draft, T. merely left out the stanza from its proper place by accident.

14 *that forgetful shore*] T. comments: 'The land where all things are forgotten', the shore of the river Lethe in Hades. Collins compares *Paradise Lost*, II 74: 'that forgetful lake'.

23] Cf. *Comus*, 46-7: 'Bacchus that first from out the purple Grape, / Crusht the sweet poison of mis-used Wine' (Ricks); 'Sonnet' ['Alas! how weary'] 9-10: 'laughing cheerily / Bruise his gold grain upon his threshing-floor'.

24] Cf. *Hamlet*, III iv 66-7: 'Could you on this fair mountain leave to feed, / And batten on this moor?'.

36. This section returns to the subject of *32* and *33*, the truths which Christ embodies for mankind. In the intervening sections the poet has reaffirmed to himself the reality of the foremost of these − eternal life. H.T. applies to this section a remark of his father: 'When questions were written to him about Christ, he would say to me: "Answer for me that I have given my belief in *In Memoriam*"' (*Eversley*, III 222).

1-4] Natural religion (1-2) is contrasted with revealed religion (3-4).

1 *truths*] H.T. wrote of his father:

> He consistently emphasized his own belief in what he called the
> Eternal Truths; in an Omnipotent, Omnipresent and All-loving God,
> Who has revealed Himself through the human attribute of the
> highest self-sacrificing love; in the freedom of the human will; and in
> the immortality of the soul.   (*Memoir*, I 311)

darkly] Cf. 1 Corinthians 13:12: 'For now we see through a glass
darkly; but then face to face'.

5-8] T. comments: 'For divine Wisdom had to deal with the limited
powers of humanity, to which truth logically argued out would be
ineffectual, whereas truth coming in the story of the Gospel can influ-
ence the poorest.' H.T. records that his father

> hoped that the Bible would be more and more studied by all ranks
> of people, and expounded simply by their teachers; for he maintained
> that the religion of a people could never be founded on mere moral
> philosophy: and that it could only come home to them in the
> simple, noble thoughts and facts of a Scripture like ours.

(*Memoir*, I 308)

8] Cf. John 10:9: 'I am the door: by me if any man enter in, he shall
be saved'.

9] An allusion to John 1:14: 'And so the Word became flesh, and
dwelt among us'. T. explained that 'the Word' is '"The Word" as used
by St. John, the Revelation of the Eternal Thought of the Universe'
(*Memoir*, I 312).

13-14] In his 'Essay on the Philosophical Writings of Cicero', Hallam
described Christianity as a 'mighty revolution which brought the poor
and unlearned into the possession of a pure code of moral opinion,
that before had existed only for the wise' (Motter, 163).

15-16] T. comments: 'By this is intended the Pacific Islanders, "wild"
having a sense of "barbarian" in it'. T. may have remembered an
account of the Islanders' sports by William Ellis, *Polynesian Researches
. . . in the South Sea Islands*, 2 vols. (1829):

> One of their most favourite sports, is . . . swimming in the surf, when
> the waves are high, and the billows break in foam and spray among
> the reefs . . . They usually selected the openings of the reefs . . .
> where the long heavy billows of the ocean rolled in unbroken majesty
> upon the reef . . . They used a small board . . . swam from the beach
> to a considerable distance . . . watched the swell of the wave . . . and,
> amid the foam and spray, rode on the crest of the wave to the shore.

(I xi 304-5)

T.'s copy of this work is in TRC.

37. The section is modelled upon the elegy of Propertius (III 3) in which the poet is rebuked by Apollo for presuming to treat of a subject which is beyond his ability. The poet is adopted by the Muse Calliope who encourages him to sing of human love.

This section may be compared with *48* and *49* which reinforce Melpomene's argument that her songs are not a serious discussion of the issues but merely 'Short swallow-flights of song'.

In T.MS (f. 15ᵛ) this section appears to have been squeezed in between two sections, *36* and *40*, already on the page: lines 1-16 are written very near to the outer margin and lines 17-24 are written lengthwise parallel to the inner margin.

1 *Urania*] The muse of astronomy, but here of heavenly poetry, as in *Paradise Lost*, VII 1: 'Descend from Heaven Urania'. Presumably she is the 'high Muse' of *58.9*.

5-8] Cf. the poet's address to Urania in *Paradise Lost*, VII 12-16:

> Up led by thee
> Into the Heaven of Heavens I have presum'd,
> An earthly guest . . .
> Return me to my native element.

9 *Melpomene*] The Muse of tragedy who is invoked by Horace in *Odes*, IV 3: 'Quem tu, Melpomene . . .', and I 24: 'praecipe lugubres / Cantus Melpomene' (2-3) (teach me to compose mournful song, O Melpomene). Melpomene speaks to the poet in *'The light that shone when Hope was born'* (Add. Poem ii).

12 *prevailing*] 'Probably in the sense of the Latin *praevalens*, "very strong", since there is no reason why Urania should prevail over Melpomene' (Ricks).

13] Cf. *57.1-2*.

17] This seems to have been adapted from *59.8* c-d: 'And broodings on the change that lies / Shut in the second birth of death'.

18] Hallam's religious views are most fully expressed in the 'Theodicæa Novissima' which he read to the Apostles in 1831 and which T. specifically requested Henry Hallam to include in the *Remains* (*Eversley*, III 258). Hallam deals with religious subjects in his essays 'On Sympathy', 'On the Philosophical Writings of Cicero', and 'Remarks on Professor Rossetti's "Disquisizioni Sullo Spirito Antipapale"'.

19 *sacred wine*] Suggests the 'vinum divinum' of poetry. In his copy of Gatty, T. underlined 'sacramental wine' (the first reading, which Gatty

quotes in commenting on the substitution) and wrote alongside: 'sounds too commonplace'. This comment suggests that he may not have altered the line in response to criticism in *The Times*, 28 November 1851, as has been proposed (Shannon, 161). Shannon's explanation for T.'s revision, 'By the alteration he emphasized the purely personal application intended', is the very explanation given by Gatty which prompted T.'s comment.

23 *master's field*] T. comments: 'the province of Christianity'. He glossed this 'God's acre' in a copy of the *Works* (1884, University of London Library) (Ricks).

38. In T.MS this section precedes *23*, with which it has in common the idea of the wandering poet and the contrast between the past and present.

This section describes the first of three springs which occur in the poem (*86* and *88* describe the second spring, and *115* and *116* describe the third spring). Such indications of the seasonal chronology of *I.M.* are listed by Bradley (p. 22) who observes that in spite of occasional deviations from the chronology, the fact that 'these passages are so few is a proof of the care taken by the author to preserve the clearness and consistency of the scheme'.

5-6] T. glosses 'blowing season' as 'the blossoming season'.

6] Shepherd compares Shakespeare, *Sonnets*, I 10: 'only herald to the gaudy spring'.

9-12] H.T. compares *Aeneid*, IV 34, 'id cinerem aut manis credis curare sepultos?' (Thinkest thou that dust or buried shades give heed to that?). Ricks compares Catullus, XCVI 1-2: 'Si quicquam mutis gratum acceptumve sepulcris / accidere a nostro, Calve, dolore potest'. (If the silent grave can receive any pleasure, or sweetness at all from our grief, Calvus.) and points out that the theme is that of 'My life is full'.

9-10] Whether the dead take an interest in life on earth is an ancient theological question. It is amply discussed in St. Thomas Aquinas, *Summa Theologiae*, I, q.89, a.8: 'utrum animae separatae cognoscant ea quae hic aguntur' (Do separated souls know what is happening here?). T. raises the question again in the group *60-5* and in *85*.81-94.

39. *Dating*: The section was composed in April 1868 (*Memoir*, II 53). It was not published until 1870 because the draft of it had slipped into the back of a writing desk and so had become lost or forgotten (note by Sir Charles Tennyson in volume 8 of his notebooks (TRC) in preparation for *Alfred Tennyson*).

Section *39* was added as a pendant to *2* and repeats several images and end-rhymes. The emphasis on the flowering of the yew was understood by Gatty to be T.'s confession of error in having implied in *2* that the yew does not flower. T. wrote alongside this remark: 'It is impossible that I sd. not have known that a tree which bears a berry must have a blossom; but Sorrow only saw the winter gloom of the foliage.'

2-3] T. comments: 'The yew, when flowering, in a wind or if struck sends up its pollen like smoke.' In the month this section was composed Emily Tennyson recorded in her diary: 'There has been a great deal of smoke in the yew-trees this year. One day there was such a cloud that it seemed to be a fire in the shrubbery' (*Memoir*, II 53). During the same month, according to H.T. (*Memoir*, II 53), T. composed the speech of Ambrosius in 'The Holy Grail'; see lines 12-16, 18-19. Ricks compares Lyell, *Principles of Geology* (4th ed., 1835), III 8:

How often, during the heat of a summer's day, do we see the males of dioecious plants, such as the yew-tree, standing separate from the females, and sending off into the air, upon the slightest breath of wind, clouds of buoyant pollen.

8-10] Cf. *3*.2-4 (addressed to Sorrow).

11-12] Cf. Shelley, 'Triumph of Life', 309-11: 'In the April prime, / When all the forest tips began to burn / With kindling green' (Ricks). Whether these lines refer to the shoots or to the flowers has been much argued. T.'s own gloss is not specific: 'In Section II, as in the last two lines of this section, Sorrow only saw the winter gloom of the foliage'. In a letter in 1838 he described 'the tops of the elms on the lawn at Somersby beginning to kindle into green' (*Memoir*, I 167). Chapman glosses the lines 'tender green shoots', but Bradley supports Gatty's view that the reference is to the flowers because 'the point which Sorrow has to meet concerns the flower' and because he believes that the new shoots are not conspicuous while the yew is in bloom. In fact, the young spring shoots are a brighter green than the rest of the tree. For Collins, the distinction is 'surely not worth considering. The sole point is that reviving hope is beginning to read itself into the object which before (see II) was at once the symbol and incarnation of deepest gloom.'

40-47. This group of sections discusses the state of the soul after death, a subject suggested by *31-7*, and the possibility of the poet's eventual reunion with Hallam.

40. The T.MS draft suggests that this section originally ended with 20 a-d and that 21-32 were substituted for this stanza when it was deleted.

1-4] T. commented to Knowles: 'See Poem 97 where the writer is compared to the female — *here* the spirit becomes the female in the parable'.

5-12] These are commonplace sentiments, no doubt, but for Victorian readers the classic expression of them was given in *The Pickwick Papers*, XXXVI:

> Mixed up with the pleasure and joy of the occasion, are the many regrets at quitting home, the tears of parting between parent and child, the consciouness of leaving the dearest and kindest friends of the happiest portion of human life, to encounter its cares and troubles with others still untried and little known.

8] Cf. *Antony and Cleopatra*, III ii 43 (of Octavia departing from Rome with Antony): 'The April's in her eyes: it is love's spring'.

18-20] A recurrent idea in *I.M.* is the traditional notion that the dead enter upon a larger and more active life in which they will be able to utilize their earthly virtues and capabilities. Cf. *82*.11-12: 'I know transplanted human worth / Will bloom to profit, otherwhere'; also, *30*.26; *42*.7; *63*.10-12; *65*.12; *73*.15; *75*.19-20; *118*.5-7.

19] Of the sibilation in the original line T. commented to Knowles: 'I hate that. I should not write so now. I'd almost rather sacrifice a meaning than let two s's come together'.

29] Cf. *3 Henry VI*, I iv 102-3: 'you should not be king / Till our King Henry had shook hands with death'. See Arthur Palmer Hudson, 'To Shake Hands with Death', *Modern Language Notes*, LIII (1938), 510-13). Cf. also 'My life is full of weary days' (addressed to Hallam), 6-8:

> And now shake hands across the brink
> Of that deep grave to which I go:
> Shake hands once more.

31-2] In his copy of Gatty T. glossed 'the fields I know', 'this earth', and 'undiscover'd lands', 'the other world'.

32] Cf. *Hamlet*, III i 79-80: 'The undiscovered country, from whose bourn / No traveller returns'. Ricks compares Shelley, 'Alastor', 77: 'To seek strange truths in undiscovered lands'.

41. A cancelled stanza in *41* (8 a-d) which is known only from Hn.Nbk. was published in a review of an exhibition of Tennyson material at the Fine Art Society, New Bond Street, in 1909: 'Tennyson Exhibition', *Daily Graphic*, 6 July 1909, 3. (The exhibition catalogue, however, does not mention either Hn.Nbk. or any autograph MS book.) The newspaper reference may indicate that the MS book had been disbound by 1909.

H.T. comments: 'This section alludes to the doctrine which from first to last, and in so many ways and images, my father proclaimed — "the upward and onward progress of life".'

3] Cf. Judges 13:20: 'For it came to pass, when the flame went up toward heaven from off the altar, that the angel of the Lord ascended in the flame of the altar'.

4-8] T. commented to Knowles: 'Love fears to be lost in the advance of the dead beyond the Survivor'.

5-8] Turner compares (p. 115) Crabbe, 'The Parting Hour':

> Minutely trace man's life; year after year,
> Through all his days let all his deeds appear,
> And then, though some may in that life be strange,
> Yet there appears no vast nor sudden change:
> The links that bind those various deeds are seen,
> And no mysterious void is left between.
>
> But let these binding links be all destroy'd,
> All that through years he suffer'd or enjoy'd:
> Let that vast gap be made, and then behold —
> This was the youth, and he is thus when old.

5] Cf. *The Tempest*, I ii 405: 'something rich and strange'. The form of Hallam's being in the afterlife is elsewhere described in terms similarly imprecise: *47*.6-7; *61*.1; *85*.35; *91*.15-16; *129*.5-12; *130*.

6-8] Turner notes (p. 115) a parallel with Hallam, 'Essay on the Philosophical Writings of Cicero':

How little, in fact, does one creature know of another, even if he lives with him, sees him constantly, and, in popular language, knows all about him! Of that immense chain of mental successions, which extends from the cradle to the death bed, how few links, comparatively speaking, are visible to any other person!   (Motter, 143)

8 c] This was adapted in *83*.6.

10-12] This wish is fulfilled in *95*.35-6: 'And all at once it seem'd at last / The living soul was flash'd on mine'. For the idea, cf. Isaac Taylor, *Physical Theory of Another Life* (1836):

The second supposition . . . in relation to the future communion of minds, is this, namely, that . . . the mind should be endowed with a power of communication by a direct conveyance of its own state, at any moment, to other minds; as if the veil of personal consciousness might, at pleasure, be drawn aside, and the entire intellectual being could spread itself out to view . . . we are now supposing, namely, an instantaneous and real unfolding of the thought and feeling of one mind, by an act of its own, to other minds.   (Ch. VIII)

16] T. comments: 'The eternal miseries of the Inferno'. H.T. suggests that T. had in mind *Inferno*, III 25-51, a passage which he 'often quoted as giving terribly the horror of it all':

> Quivi sospiri, pianti, ed alti guai
> Risonavan per l'aere senza stelle . . .
> Diverse lingue, orribili favelle,
> Parole di dolore, accenti d'ira,
> Voci alte e fioche.
>
> (22-3, 25-7)
>
> (Here sighs with lamentations and loud moans,
> Resounded through the air pierced by no star . . .
> Various tongues,
> Horrible languages, outcries of woe,
> Accents of anger, voices deep and hoarse.)

See also *Measure for Measure*, III i 27-9 and Deuteronomy 32:10: 'He found him in a desert land, and in the waste howling wilderness'.

23] T. comments: 'aeons of the future'. The allusion is to the *saecula* into which the Cumaean Sibyl divided time. Cf. *76*.6: 'The secular abyss to come'.

42.

2] 'He was always ahead of me.'

5-8] T. commented to Knowles: 'Sympathy of the teacher & taught'.

8] T. explained his belief that man's free-will can be utilized and developed:

> 'Man's Free-will is but a bird in a cage; he can stop at the lower perch, or he can mount to a higher. Then that which is and knows will enlarge his cage, give him a higher and a higher perch, and at last break off the top of his cage, and let him out to be one with the Free-will of the Universe.' (*Memoir*, I 318-19)

the] This objectification is similar to *24*.11: 'the present state' (revised from 'my present state'); *92*.3: 'the brain' (revised from 'my brain'). For similar revisions, see pp. 25-6.

43. The drafts in T.MS and L.MS show *43* to have been originally three stanzas: 1-4, 5-8, and a version of 13-16. In L.MS, the version of 13-16 is deleted, lines 9-12 are added, and below them the version of 13-16 is written a second time.

T. explains the idea:

> If the immediate life after death be only sleep, and the spirit between this life and the next should be folded like a flower in a night

slumber, then the remembrance of the past might remain, as the smell and colour do in the sleeping flower; and in that case the memory of our love would last as true, and would live pure and whole within the spirit of my friend until it was unfolded at the breaking of the morn, when the sleep was over.   (*Memoir*, II 421)

The section presents an alternative to the idea in *42* that the soul is conscious and progresses to higher accomplishments. Here the idea is that the sleep of the soul following death is a transitional stage, an intermediate period of blessedness while the soul awaits the final consummation with the body on the Day of Judgement. (The traditional alternatives to this notion are the doctrine of purgatory, and the belief that at death the virtuous soul instantaneously enjoys a vision of God.) Isaac Taylor (*Physical Theory of Another Life*, 1836) explains the probable nature of this stage in the progress of the soul:

We are also taught to think of the state of souls, as a state, not of unconsciousness indeed, but of comparative inaction, or of suspended energy . . . The chrysalis period of the soul may be marked by the destitution of all the instruments of active life, corporeal and mental. And this state of inaction may probably be also a state of seclusion, involving, not improbably, an unconsciousness of the passage of time.

(Ch. XVII)

1] Cf. *68*.2, 3 and note.

3 *intervital gloom*] T. comments: 'In the passage between this life and the next'. T. apparently coined 'intervital'.

5-8] T. commented to Knowles: 'Sympathy of equal learning in the new life'.

5-6] Cf. Marvell, 'The Garden', 49-52:

> Here at the Fountain's sliding foot,
> Or at some fruit-trees mossy root,
> Casting the Bodies Vest aside,
> His Soul into the boughs does glide.

7-8] T. discusses the possibility of the dead retaining memories of life on earth in his note to *44* (see headnote).

9-12] This stanza may have been added in response to criticism by Spedding. His comments in T.MS indicate that he found this section obscure, especially 6-8.

11-12] The image is similar to a passage in a book owned by T., J.P. Nichol, *Views of the Architecture of the Heavens* (1838), second edition (a description of the process of change in the progressive development of the universe): 'probably all is passing, in a silence next to motionless

— quietly as the leaf grows, towards some unknown consummation (p. 196).

11 *figured leaf enrolls*] T. commented to Knowles: 'painted with the past life'.

15 *spiritual prime*] T. comments: 'Dawn of the spiritual life hereafter'; *prime* suggests both 'the first canonical hour of the Divine Office', and 'the period or state of greatest perfection or vigour'.

44. The idea is an alternative to that in *43*: perhaps at death the soul does not sleep but enters upon a new conscious life in which it retains no memory of its life on earth. T.'s gloss to line 4 explains the thought of the section:

> The dead after this life may have no remembrance of life, like the living babe who forgets the time before the sutures of the skull are closed, yet the living babe grows in knowledge, and though the remembrance of his earliest days has vanished, yet with his increasing knowledge there comes a dreamy vision of what has been; it may be so with the dead; if so, resolve my doubts, etc.

1-8] Many commentators (for example, Gatty, Beeching, Mustard, Genung) have understood these stanzas to refer to pre-existence (a subject T. deals with elsewhere, notably in 'The Two Voices') and they compare Wordsworth, 'Ode: Intimations of Immortality', V. But as T.'s gloss makes clear, *44* refers not to pre-existence but to infancy. Other arguments against a reference to pre-existence are given by Bradley. There is an analogy, however, between the Wordsworthian–Platonic idea that in childhood there are glimpses of the glories of a previous existence and T.'s idea that the adult may have obscure intimations of his experience between birth and age one.

1] That the dead are happy is a commonplace in classical and Christian poetry, for example, Statius, *Silvae*, II 220: 'quem gemimus, felix' (he whom we mourn is happy). John Sparrow ('Tennyson and Thomson's Shorter Poems', *London Mercury*, XXI (1930), 429) compares Thomson, 'Song', 1-4:

> Tell me, thou soul of her I love,
>   Ah! tell me, whither art thou fled;
> To what delightful world above,
>   Appointed for the happy dead?

Cf. also 'Tithonus', 70-1: 'Of happy men that have the power to die, / And grassy barrows of the happier dead'.

4] T. comments: 'Closing of the skull after babyhood'. The line is adapted from 'Hail Briton', 175-6: 'ere yet / God shut the doors within his head'. T. revised the reading in T.MS apparently in response to criticism by Spedding, who queried the meaning of 'within' and thought 1-4 obscure. With the idea, cf. 'The Two Voices', 368-9: 'For is not our first year forgot? / The haunts of memory echo not'.

5-8] T. remarked on a Christmas tree to his daughter-in-law and her baby: 'Perhaps your babe will remember all these lights and this splendour in future days as if it were a memory of another life' (*Memoir*, II 382).

6 *the hoarding sense*] T. commented to Knowles: 'the memory'.

10] T. commented to Knowles: 'in the same way as the infancy is forgot'.

12 *thy peers*] Cf. *91*.6 (of Hallam on earth). The idea that Hallam has joined the assembly of noble dead is discussed in note *61*.3-4.

13-16] T. commented to Knowles: 'if you *have* forgot all earthly things − yet as a man has faint memories, even so in the new life a sort of vague memory of the Past would come. This is fortified by considering that the use of flesh & blood were lost if they do not establish an identity.'

14 *the doubt*] Refers to 'Surprise thee' (12).

45. Arthur Hallam's essay, 'On Sympathy', supplied the model for the description of the process by which the individual perceives itself as distinct from other human beings and the material world. He is concerned to show how the principle of association operates in the production of sympathy, and by reference to an infant and its mother he explains how the soul becomes aware of the existence of another soul:

Let us take the soul at that precise moment in which she becomes assured that another soul exists . . . capable of thoughts and feelings like her own. How does this discovery affect her? . . . The person thus recognised by the soul will probably have been occupied in acts of kindness towards it, by which indeed its attention was first attracted and the recognition rendered possible. Before that recognition, therefore, pleasure has been associated with that person as a mere object. The infant cannot separate the sensations of nourishment from the form of his nurse or mother.   (Motter, 133-4)

(The similarity between the last sentence and *45* was first noticed by Turner (p. 115).) Hallam then discusses the manner in which the subjective consciousness perceives itself as a separate identity:

It is an ultimate fact of consciousness, that the soul exists as one subject in various successive states . . . Far back as memory can carry us . . . are forms of self. With the first dawn of feeling began the conception of existence . . . Material objects were indeed perceived as external. But how? As unknown limits of the soul's activity, they were not a part of subjective consciousness, they defined, restrained, and regulated it. Still the soul attributed itself to every consciousness, past or future. At length the discovery of another being is made. Another being, another subject, conscious, having a world of feelings like the soul's own world! How, how can the soul imagine feeling which is not its own? I repeat, she realizes this conception only by considering the other being as a separate part of self, a state of her own consciousness existing apart from the present.

13 *blood and breath*] Bradley compares *King John*, IV ii 246: 'This kingdom, this confine of blood and breath'.

16] Adapted from *59*.8 d: 'Shut in the second-birth of death'.

46. The early commentators vary widely in their interpretations of *46*. The most probable interpretation seems that of Bradley:
 The poet in XLV has persuaded himself that the dead remember. Now the thought seems to occur to him that here on earth, though we remember the past, our memory is very imperfect, and that accordingly the memory of the dead also may be imperfect; from which it would follow that his friend after all may not remember him. To this he answers that there is a good reason why memory on earth should be dim and broken, and that this reason does not hold in the next life.

He suggests that the final two stanzas, in addition to 'shall' in 7, show that the poet is thinking of some future time in another life when he and Hallam will look back on the earthly life and the five years of friendship. According to this interpretation,
 The first three stanzas say, 'we shall remember'; the last adds, 'we shall love one another too.' If this interpretation is correct, I should suppose the poet was thinking both of himself and of his friend. It connects the section well with its successor, and it also leads back to the idea of XLII, last stanza, and XLIII, last stanza — an idea from which the poet was diverted by his question, 'But do the dead remember the earthly life?'

2] Cf. Hallam, 'On My Sister's Birth-Day', VI: 'thy career / Is all before thee, thorn and flower'.

3 *growing hour*] Cf. 'Love thou thy land', 61: 'The warders of the growing hour'.

4] T. substituted 'Life' for 'this' in response to a query by Spedding in T.MS. T. explained to Knowles: 'If there were a perfect memory of all sorrows and sins we should not be able to bear it'. Perhaps there is a reference to the story of Lot's wife in Genesis 19:26.

5-8] In *44*.5-8 the poet suggested that the dead might retain only 'A little flash, a mystic hint' of their earthly life. Here he seems to have become assured that the dead retain a distinct and unbroken memory of the past.

5 *So be it*] T. revised the first reading in response to criticism by Spedding, who queried the meaning of 'Yet'.

9 *tract of time*] Cf. *Paradise Lost*, V 498: 'Improved by tract of time' (Bradley). The expression recurs in *77*.4.

12 *those five years*] T. commented to Knowles: 'only 5 years!' (of his friendship with Hallam). The actual period of time of the friendship, and T.'s occasional uncertainty on this point are discussed in note *22*.3, 10.

13-14] Cf. 'The Lover's Tale', I 427-8: 'Spirit of Love! that little hour was bound / Shut in from Time, and dedicate to thee'.

13] T. explained the meaning to Knowles as '"O Love, thy province were then 'not large'"'.

15] T. commented to Knowles: 'As if Lord of the whole life', H.T. adds (*Eversley*): 'not merely of those five years of friendship'. The *brooding star* is Venus, the planet closest to the earth. As the morning and evening star, Venus appears on both horizons.

47. T. explains the idea: 'The individuality lasts after death, and we are not utterly absorbed into the Godhead. If we are to be finally merged in the Universal Soul, Love asks to have at least one more parting before we lose ourselves.' He expressed on another occasion a slightly different notion about the fate of the personal consciousness after death: 'If the absorption into the divine in the after-life be the creed of some, let them at all events allow us many existences of individuality before this absorption; since this short-lived individuality seems to be but too short a preparation for so mighty a union' (*Memoir*, I 319). The treatment here of this ancient theological question is prepared for in *45* which is concerned to show that the purpose of mortal life is to establish individual identity.

1-4] T. commented to Knowles: 'Love protests against the loss of identity in the theory of absorption.' The stanza was criticized for its obscurity in a review of *I.M.* in *The Times*, 28 November 1851 (Shannon, 157).

4 *Remerging*] Apparently coined by T.

6-12] This hope, as Mattes observes (p. 44), is expressed by Hallam in 'To One Early Loved, Now in India':

> Oh tell me not, ye sages, that our end
> Shall merge us in the godhead; I am made
> To seek with kindred souls my soul to blend . . .
> . . . I will confide, thou cherish'd of my youth,
> That we shall be of one delight possessed,
> And each embracing what the other doth,
> Live an harmonious life of energetic truth.
> (VII, VIII)

8] Perhaps a reminiscence of Hallam, 'A Meeting and a Farewell' (*Meditative Fragments* I), 30, 38-40:

> There is another world . . .
> Oh, may we recognize each other there,
> My bosom friend! May we cleave to each other
> And love once more together!

11 *vaster*] T. explained the meaning to Knowles as 'less defined'.

13-15] Cf. 'Timbuctoo', 194-6:

> And step by step to scale that mighty stair
> Whose landing-place is wrapt about the clouds
> Of glory of Heaven.

Ricks suggests that T.'s use of 'landing-place' 'may owe something to Coleridge's prominent use of it in *The Friend*'.

13] T. explained this image as representing the last of the 'many existences of individuality' (*Memoir*, I 319).

14-16] T. commented to Knowles: 'into the Universal Spirit — but at least one last parting! and always would want it again — of course'.

48-49. These sections disclaim the poet's desire or authority to speak conclusively on the issues raised in *40-7*. He will allow the lighter moods of his sorrow to issue in song but he cannot express its deeper promptings. This is the theme of *19* and *20*; it is touched on in *5* and *37*.

48.

5 *part*] Cf. 'The Two Voices', 134: 'To put together, part, and prove'.

8] Cf. Shakespeare, *Sonnets*, XXVI 1-2: 'Lord of my love, to whom in vassalage / Thy merit hath my duty strongly knit' (Shepherd).

15-16] These lines are adapted, as Ricks observes, from lines in a poem ('Dear friend . . .' printed in Ricks, 1786) composed around 1831:

> By thy placid scorns that play
> Round the surfaces of things
> And like swallows dip their wings
> Evermore, and skim away.

With the idea, cf. *52*.3-4.

49.

5-8] T. told Knowles that these lines refer to the previous stanzas (that is, the previous sections, *40-7*).

5] Cf. 'The Lover's Tale', 533-4: 'the waters answering lisped / To kisses of the wind'.

9] T. told Knowles that this is addressed to 'the reader'.

11] Ricks compares 'The wanton ripples chased themselves', a line not published by T. from 'The Miller's Daughter', in his revised copy of *Poems*, 1832 (TRC).

50-56. Bradley characterizes this group as follows:
They start from, and return to, the poet's desire for *present* communion with his friend, a desire which has scarcely appeared up to this point. The main subject, however, is not this present communion, but the pain, defect, and evil in the world, and the doubts which they cast upon the faith that Love is 'Creation's final law' and that man is not made to die. The problem is first suggested by the poet's consciousness of his own defect, is then rapidly generalized [*54*], and finally concentrates itself again on the question of immortality [*55-6*].

50. In T.MS *49* is followed by *51*. L.MS, the earliest extant draft of *50*, has *50* between *49* and *51*. This suggests that *50* was composed in order to prepare for *51*.
T. wrote to Queen Victoria in 1888:
Yet, if the dead, as I have often felt, tho' silent, be more living than the living and linger about the planet in which their earth life was passed — then *they*, while we are lamenting that they are not at our side, may still be with us.   (Charles Tennyson, 498)

1-4] A reminiscence, Collins observes, of Shelley, *The Cenci*, IV i 163-5:

> My blood is running up and down my veins,
> A fearful pleasure makes it prick and tingle;
> I feel a giddy sickness.

T. may also have had in mind a poem by Hallam:

> But when our feelings coil upon themselves
> At time's rude pressure; when the heart grows dry,
> And burning with immedicable thirst
> As though a plague-spot seared it, while the brain
> Fevers with cogitations void of love.
>
> (*Meditative Fragments* VI, 128–32)

1] 'Be near me' anticipates *51*.2: 'be near us at our side'; 13: 'Be near us when we climb or fall'. Cf. *122*.10: 'be with me now'.

2–3] In 1843, T. wrote to FitzGerald: 'The perpetual panic and horror of the last two years had steeped my nerves in poison' (Charles Tennyson, 201).

4] Cf. Shelley, *Queen Mab*, IX 151–2: 'urge / The restless wheels of Being on their way' (noticed by J.D. Jump, 'Shelley and Tennyson', *Notes and Queries*, CXCVI (8 December 1951), 541).

51. *Dating*: The account by Edmund Lushington (written in 1893 on his death-bed) of the composition of this section might suggest that it was composed around Christmas 1841: 'On one other occasion he came and showed me a poem he had just composed, saying he liked it better than most he had done lately, this was (*51*)' (*Memoir*, I 202–3). What is not clear is whether 'On one other occasion' actually refers to Christmas 1841; it may mean 'on one other occasion during Christmas 1841', or 'on one occasion other than Christmas 1841'. That *51* is in H.Lpr.101 (conjecturally dated 1837–40 for reasons given on p. 11) suggests that the section was composed earlier than Christmas 1841.

3 *baseness*] Cf. 'The Two Voices', 301: 'He knows a baseness in his blood'.

5–8] Shepherd compares Shakespeare, *Sonnets*, LXI 5–7:

> Is it thy spirit that thou send'st from thee
> So far from home into my deeds to pry,
> To find out shames and idle hours in me.

7–8] Cf. *Speak to me from the stormy sky!* (Add. Poem ix), 7.

13–16] H.T. comments: 'The Queen quoted this verse to my father about the Prince Consort, just after his death, and told him that it had brought her great comfort.' Rawnsley (*Nineteenth Century and After*, 194) recorded that T. said: 'I thought that was very pretty of the Queen to answer me out of my own writing'.

52.

1-4] T. explained the idea to Knowles: 'There is so much evil in me that I don't really reflect you and all my talk is only *words*'.

4] T. wrote 'Nonsense' alongside the comparison by Collins (*Cornhill*, 42) of Persius, *Satires*, I 104-5: 'summa delumbe saliva / hoc natat in labris' (nerveless stuff — it floats in the mouth on the top of the spittle).

5-8] T. commented to Knowles: 'Then the Spirit of true love replies — all life fails in some measure'.

11-12] 'Tennysonese for Christ, or, the life of Christ' (Collins).

15 *Abide*:] T. explains: 'wait without wearying'.

53. T. explains the idea: 'There is a passionate heat of nature in a rake sometimes. The nature that yields emotionally may turn out straighter than a prig's. Yet we must not be making excuses, but we must set before us a rule of good for young as for old.' This in part recalls *Measure for Measure*, IV i 444-6:

> They say, best men are moulded out of faults,
> And, for the most, become much more the better
> For being a little bad.

Bradley compares 'Love and Duty', 4-9:

> Shall Error in the round of Time
> Still father Truth? O shall the braggart shout
> For some blind glimpse of freedom work itself
> Thro' madness, hated by the wise, to law
> Systems and empire? Sin itself be found
> The cloudy porch oft opening on the Sun?

5, 7 *fancy, scarce had*] T. wrote to his publisher in June 1850 to ask him to make these substitutions 'if there is time in the 3rd edition' (letter in Pierpont Morgan Library, quoted in H.G. Merriam, *Edward Moxon, Publisher of Poets* (New York, 1939), 177).

9 *Or, if*] T. made this substitution in pencil in a copy of the *Works* (1881) which he used as a proof (TRC).

13-16] T. remarked to Knowles: 'There's need of rule to men also — tho' no particular one that I know of — it may be arbitrary'. Cf. *33*.13-16.

13] A reminiscence of I Thessalonians 5:21: 'Prove all things; hold fast that which is good'.

14 *divine Philosophy*] Cf. *Comus*, 476: 'How charming is divine Philosophy'; Ricks compares Colossians 2:8: 'Beware lest any man spoil you through philosophy and vain deceit, after the tradition of men, after the rudiments of the world, and not after Christ.'

54.

9-12] T. remarked in 1863: ' "What do we know of the feeling of insects? nothing. They may feel more pain than we." ' On another occasion he commented on boys catching butterflies: ' "Why cut short their lives?—What are we? We are the merest moths . . . Let the moths have their little lives" ' (Allingham's *Diary*, 88, 118).

15] Cf. Epilogue, 143-4.

18-20] 'infant' = 'infans', unable to speak. Cf. Jeremiah 1:6: 'Then said I, Ah, Lord God! behold, I cannot speak: for I am a child'; *58*.8b: 'A speechless child can move the heart'; *124*.17-20. T. commented on the diction of these lines in 1892:

> He spoke of the great richness of the English language due to its double origin, the Norman and Saxon words. How hard it would be for a foreigner to feel the difference in the line 'An infant crying for the light' had the word *baby* been substituted, which would at once have made it ridiculous.   (*Tennyson and His Friends*, 218)

55 and 56. *Dating*: H.T. states that the sections about evolution had been read by T.'s friends 'some years' before the publication of Robert Chambers's *Vestiges of the Natural History of Creation* in 1844 (*Memoir*, I 223). On reading a review of the book soon after its publication, T. asked Moxon to send him a copy and added: 'It seems to contain many speculations with which I have been familiar for years' (*Memoir*, I 222-3).

The doubt and anxiety expressed in these sections reflect the feelings of many thoughtful persons in the first half of the nineteenth century when they confronted the new theories in comparative anatomy, geology, and natural history which appeared to contradict the scriptural account of the Creation and the notion of a benificent Creator. T. seems to have read most of the conventional scientific sources of these theories. As a child he had read Buffon's *Natural History* (*Memoir*, I 16). For several months in 1837 he was 'deeply immersed' in Charles Lyell's *Principles of Geology* (3 vols., 1830-3) (*Memoir*, I 162). In 1844 he read *Vestiges*. He surely read Charles Babbage's *Ninth Bridgewater Treatise* (1837) and Lyell's *Elements of Geology* (1838), for he owned copies of both works (TRC). He must also have read one of the most famous works on natural history, Cuvier's great *Recherches sur les ossemens fossiles de quadrupèdes* (Paris, 1812), published in English in 1813 under the title *Essay on the Theory of the Earth.*

55. The idea of this section (as Potter explains, 333-4) concerns two traditional biological concepts which contemporary scientific research made specially interesting to the early nineteenth century: the prodigality of nature and the struggle for survival.

1-8] T. exclaimed in 1892:
> 'Yet God *is* love, transcendent, all-pervading! We do not get *this* faith from Nature or the world. If we look at Nature alone, full of perfection and imperfection, she tells us that God is disease, murder and rapine. We get this faith from ourselves, from what is highest within us, which recognizes that there is not one fruitless pang, just as there is not one lost good.'   (*Eversley*, III 214)

Cf. *34*.1-2; *124*.13-16 and note.

4] T. comments: 'The inner consciousness – the divine in man'.

5-8] T. explained the idea to Joseph Joachim in 1877 or 1878:
> 'In that verse, I did not make an assertion; I asked a question – the great question of the ages – why is there so much evil in this world of ours? There have been innumerable attempts to answer it; the entire book of Job is one of them. To me it is plain that nature is God's handmaiden, and that she operates with the human race generically; nature, evidently, is not concerned with the needs of the individual but with mankind as a whole. The laws of nature, established by the Creator, are immutable, and when they are violated, the consequences are terrible. Man himself is largely to blame, however, for most of the sickness, sorrow and misery we find in the world because he has transgressed those laws. Man is a free moral agent, and can do as he pleases, but he must pay the penalty for his sins against nature.'
> (Arthur M. Abell, *Conversations with Great Composers*
> (Spiritualist Press, London, 1955), 30-1)

7-8] Bradley compares Buffon: 'La nature s'embarrasse peu des individus, elle ne s'occupe que de l'espèce.' Cf. also Chambers, *Vestiges of . . . Creation*, final chapter:
> It is clear, moreover, from the whole scope of the natural laws, that the individual, as far as the present sphere of being is concerned, is to the Author of Nature a consideration of inferior moment. Everywhere we see the arrangements for the species perfect; the individual is left, as it were, to take his chance amidst the *mêlée* of the various laws affecting him.

7 *type*] The use of this term to mean a specific group or division of animals, plants, etc., having a common structure was introduced in the 1830s and is common in Lyell.

11-12]
> [T.] was occasionally much troubled with the intellectual problem of the apparent profusion and waste of life . . . No doubt in such moments he might possibly have been heard to say what I myself have heard him say . . . 'The lavish profusion too in the natural world appals me, from the growths of the tropical forest to the capacity of man to multiply, the torrent of babies'.
> (*Memoir*, I 313-14)

11 *fifty*] T. underlined this in his copy of Gatty and wrote '*myriad* seeds would be truer'.

14-16] Collins compares Young, *Night Thoughts*, 'Night', IX: 'Teach me by this stupendous scaffolding, / Creation's golden steps, to climb to thee'.

20] H.T. explains: 'he means by *the larger hope* that the whole human race would through, perhaps, ages of suffering, be at length purified and saved' (*Memoir*, I 321-2), and he associates this line with 'The Vision of Sin':
> At last I heard a voice upon the slope
> Cry to the summit, 'Is there any hope?'
> To which an answer pealed from that high land,
> But in a tongue no man could understand;
> And on the glimmering limit far withdrawn
> God made Himself an awful rose of dawn.
> (219-24)

56. T. compared *56* to *55* in his comment to Knowles on this section: 'There's a deeper tone about these [stanzas] than the last lot'. The position and handwriting of *56* in L.MS suggest it was a late addition to the group.

The exact form of evolution referred to here and in *118, 120, 123*, and elsewhere in T. has been much discussed (for example, by Potter; Harrison; Graham Hough, 'The Natural Theology of *In Memoriam*', *Review of English Studies*, XXIII (1947), 244-56; John Killham, *Tennyson and 'The Princess': Reflections of an Age* (1958), 230-66). Some of T.'s allusions seem to refer to a genuinely organic, 'uniformitarian' form of evolution, and others seem to refer to 'catastrophic' or successive and progressive acts of special creation (see note *118*.8-12). The writers on the subject conclude, in general, that T. seems not to have been concerned to be either specific or consistent in his references to geology and evolution:

In all probability, for years following the appearance of Lyell's *Principles* Tennyson did not feel himself enough of an expert to avow publicly a belief in either Lyell's ideas or those of his opponents. The facts of geology – its proof that long ages stretch back of historic time, and that species of life now are not the same as those which used to inhabit the earth – he accepted and used. But he very possibly did not try to decide among the geologists' special theories.

(Potter, 332)

He concerned himself with books and articles on scientific topics in no dispassionate manner as becomes the scientist. As scientific evidence of one sort and another came to his notice he dwelt not on its implications for the further development of science, but on the hints it afforded concerning man's nature and his place in a mysterious universe. (Killham, 241)

2-4] The serious study of fossils had begun in the mid-eighteenth century. By the early nineteenth century geology had become a subject of public interest and argument, and it soon became the most popular science of the century. It became fashionable to go on expeditions in search of fossils. In *The Princess*, for example, Sir Walter Vivian displays in his house 'Huge Ammonites, and the first bones of Time' (Prologue, 15), and Princess Ida and her students journey to a place where

> stuck out
> The bones of some vast bulk that lived and roar'd
> Before man was. She gazed awhile and said,
>   'As these rude bones to us, are we to her
> That will be.'
> (III 276-80)

2 *scarpèd*] 'Cut away vertically'. Of a walk with T., a friend records: 'When I was walking with him toward the Needles and looking at the magnificent chalk cliffs below the downs . . . he said, "The most wonderful thing about that cliff is to think it was all once alive"' (*Tennyson and His Friends*, 137).

3] The idea of the extinction of species originated with Georges Cuvier (1769-1832), who proved by the new methods of comparative anatomy that recently discovered fossils derived from species distinct from any of those known now to be alive.

5-8] Added to L.MS in margin.

8-20] Ricks compares Thomson, *The Seasons*, 'Spring':

> But man, whom nature form'd of milder clay,

> With ev'ry kind emotion in his heart,
> And taught alone to weep . . .
> shall he, fair form!
> Who wears sweet smiles, and looks erect on heav'n,
> E'er stoop to mingle with the prowling herd,
> And dip his tongue in gore? The beast of prey,
> Blood-stain'd, deserves to bleed.
>   (349–57)

Other examples of this idea include the passage from the *Spectator* quoted in note *30*.25–8, and a passage in a book T. received at Christmas 1838, Perceval B. Lord, *Popular Physiology* (1834):

> And shall it be said that the mind of man . . , which elevates us from earth, and forms the link that binds us to ethereal beings is alone mortal; that it goes down 'to the vile dust from whence we sprung;' that it perishes with the disorganization of the brain, and that all our advances in science, our progression in knowledge, our extension of intellect, every effort of reason or education towards improvement and perfection, must at last terminate in annihilation?   (p. 355)

9] The line was revised on the addition of 5–8. With the idea and diction, cf. *118*.12: 'Till at the last arose the man'; Browning, *Paracelsus*, V 681–711:

> Thus he dwells in all,
> From life's minute beginnings, up at last
> To man . . .
> Hints and previsions . . .
> Are strewn confusedly everywhere about
> The inferior natures, and all lead up higher . . .
> And man appears at last.

11] Ricks compares T.'s childhood translation of Horace, (TRC): 'roll away / Along yon wintry skies'.

12 *fruitless prayer*] Cf. 'The Death of Œnone', 40–1: 'The Gods / Avenge on stony hearts a fruitless prayer'.

19] In *Principles of Geology*, II xiv 240–1, Lyell discussed the imbedding of human and other remains in the blown sand of the deserts of North Africa (Turner, 124). T. may also have read in his copy of *Hundred Wonders of the World* the account of the 'Sands of the Desert' (pp. 252–7) which describes how the sands, called by the natives 'the dust of the desert', are continually swept about in sandstorms which often engulf travellers and caravans. Cf. 'The Two Voices', 32: '"Tho' thou wert scatter'd to the wind'.

20] Cf. *The Princess*, V 140: 'Rusting on his iron hills'.

22–3] T. comments: 'The geological monsters of the early ages'. The fossils of dinosaurs had begun to be discovered and identified only recently (from 1811). Cf. an unadopted stanza in 'The Two Voices' (following line 267, Trinity College, Cambridge MS 0.15.15):

> When Mammoth, in the primal woods,
> Wore, trampling to the fountain-floods
> Broad roads thro' blooming solitudes –

The Princess, II 104, 106:

> The planets: then the monster, then the man . . .
> Raw from the prime, and crushing down his mate.

Byron, *Cain*, II ii 97–8: 'Reptiles engendered out of the subsiding / Slime of a mighty universe'.

26] For the idea, cf. *Speak to me from the stormy sky!* (Add. Poem ix).

28] The 'veil' is a traditional image perhaps deriving from the passages in Hebrews (for example, Hebrews 6:19) which refer to the temple where the Holy of Holies was guarded by a veil through which the high priest alone entered. The image of life as a veil hiding the future is common in Shelley, for example, 'Sonnet', 1–2: 'Lift not the painted veil which those who live / Call life'. T. associated the image and the idea of this stanza in a letter to Emily Sellwood (24 October 1839, TRC):

> Who knows whether revelation be not itself a veil to hide the glory of that love which we could not look upon without marring our [eye] sight and our onward progress. If it were proclaimed as a truth 'no man shall perish: all shall live after a certain time have gone by in his bliss with God' such a truth might tell well with one or two lofty spirits but would be the hindrance of the world. I dare say my own progress is impeded by holding this hope however dimly.

> Bradley suggests that T. refers to the myth of the veiled statue of Truth at the temple at Sais. This is the subject of a poem by R.C. Trench in Heath MS (p. 145), 'The veiled Statue of Isis'. The story is told, as Motter observes (p. 83), by Schiller, 'Das verschleierte Bild zu Sais'. Arthur Hallam refers to it in 'After first meeting Emily Tennyson':

> > Art thou not She
> > Who in my Sais-temple wast a light
> > Behind all veils of thought, and fantasy.

and in his 'Essay on the Philosophical Writings of Cicero':

> He did not come *alone*; he brought with him a thousand worldly prepossessions, which were to him as the veil of the temple at Sais, hiding impenetrably, 'that which was, and had been, and was to be.'
>
> (Motter, 154)

T. seems to allude to the legend, Mattes notices (p. 63, *n*. 14), in his essay, 'Ghosts': 'He who has the power of speaking of the spiritual

world . . . speaks of life and death, and the things after death. He lifts
the veil, but the form behind it is shrouded in deeper obscurity' (*Memoir*,
I 497). In *30*.28 'veil' is used as an image of successive stages of life after
death: 'From orb to orb, from veil to veil'.

57. The section seems to have been originally intended to close the
T.MS version of *I.M.* (see pp. 13–14). It comes at the end of T.MS, and T.
remarked to Knowles of the final stanza: 'I thought this was too sad
for an ending'. Early commentators, who were, of course, unaware of
the manuscript evidence, noticed that *57* gives the impression of being
at the end of the sequence. The idea was first suggested by Jacobs
(p. 92): 'From comparison of LVIII, it would seem that *In Memoriam*
was originally intended to cease with LVII'. This suggestion was not
(apparently) known to Beeching, who later drew the same conclusion:

> Here the poem, as at first designed, seems to have ended. The 5[8]th
> elegy represents the Muse as urging the poet to a new beginning; and
> the 5[9]th was added in the fourth edition, as though to account for
> the difference in tone between the earlier and later elegies.   (p. x)

Bradley does not agree with the idea partly because he cannot believe
that T. 'ever thought of ending his poem in tones of despair'. But he
does admit that there is a 'marked break' at *57*, and that it would be a
'tempting proposal'

> to consider section LVII as marking the centre of *In Memoriam*. In
> these verses the most troubled and passionate part of the poem
> reaches the acme of a climax, while after them there is, on the whole,
> a steady advance towards acquiescence.

The section replaces *I keep no more a lone distress* (Add. Poem v)
which was 'originally No LVII'. In T.MS the poem comes two leaves
before *57*. In L.MS *57* is preceded by *'O Sorrower for the faded leaf'*
(Add. Poem vi). This poem takes up the reference in *I keep no more a
lone distress* to the 'happy maiden' and describes her as 'that fair soul
that with me mourn'd' (15). This description prepares for *57*. For the
relationship between *57* and *123*, see headnote *123*.

1 *Peace; come away*] This address follows on from the last stanza of
'O Sorrower for the faded leaf':

> I . . .
> > > turn'd
> To that fair soul that with me mourn'd
> About his tomb, and sighing spoke.

The identity of the addressee, the female mourner referred to in *I keep
no more a lone distress* and *'O Sorrower . . .'* was obscured with the
deletion in L.MS of the latter poem. She may be considered to be T.'s
sister Emily.

2] Cf. *37*.13.

5 *your cheeks*] T. told Knowles that this refers to the cheeks of the auditor, that is, the female mourner.

6 *half my life*] An adaptation of a Latin commonplace; as in, for example, Horace, *Odes*, I 3 8: 'animae dimidium meae' (the half of my own life). Cf. *59*.3 (of Sorrow).

7-8] To Knowles in 1870-1 T. explained 'richly shrined' as 'in half a life!', that is: 'Hallam's life on earth, although so curtailed, is a rich monument to him'. In 1883 T. gave a different interpretation when he wrote alongside these lines in his copy of Gatty: 'The author speaks of these poems – methinks I have built a rich shrine for my friend, but it will not last'.

8 a-d] T. deleted this stanza at the suggestion of Spedding, who thought it unnecessary.

9-12] Bradley compares *2 Henry IV*, I i 101-3: 'his tongue / Sounds ever after as a sullen bell, / Remember'd tolling a departing friend.'

14-16] T. compares 'these terribly pathetic lines' in the elegy of Catullus on his brother's death, CI 9-10: 'accipe fraterno multum manantia fletu, / Atque in perpetuum, frater, ave atque vale' (Take them, wet with many tears of a brother, / And forever, O my brother, hail and farewell). Of these lines T. wrote to Gladstone in 1879: 'Nor can any modern elegy, so long as men retain the least hope in the after-life of those whom they loved, equal in pathos the desolation of that everlasting farewell' (*Memoir*, II 239). Cf. T.'s poem occasioned by his brother's death in 1879, 'Frater Ave Atque Vale'.

15-16] Cf. *123*.11-12.

58. The composition of *58* seems to have been occasioned by the substantive revision of *123*, the section originally intended to follow *57*.

3] Cf. 'The Lover's Tale', 564-6: 'While her words, syllable by syllable, / Like water, drop by drop, upon my ear / Fell' (Bradley).

8 a-h] Adapted in 9-12. Lines a, f, g answer the poet's urgings in *57*.1-4 to 'come away' and 'let us go'.

8 b] Cf. *54*.18-20 and note.

9 *the high Muse*] Urania, who appears in *37*.1.

11-12] T. comments on the entire section: '*Ulysses* was written soon after Arthur Hallam's death, and gave my feelings about the need of going forward and braving the struggle of life perhaps more simply than anything in *In Memoriam*'.

59. The section was first published in **1851A**. T. later remarked of it to Knowles: 'Added afterwards but one of the old poems nevertheless'. That lines 8 c, d, h were adapted in sections which appear in T.MS indicates that *59* antedates at least three (and perhaps more) T.MS sections.

The section was added as a pendant to *3*, and the imagery is associated with the idea there of the poet's 'fellowship' with sorrow which is now regularized into a steady relationship into which hope and cheerfulness can be admitted.

7] T. commented to Knowles: 'A time has now elapsed and he treats sorrow in a more familiar and less dreading way'. Cf. *48*.6 (of Sorrow).

8 a] Cf. 'When thy best friend draws sobbing breath', an unadopted line from 'The Two Voices', in Trinity College, Cambridge MS 0.15.15.

8 c–d] This seems to have been adapted in *37*.17.

8 d] Adapted in *45*.16.

8 e] Cf. *Hamlet*, IV v 177–8: 'there's rue for you . . . you must wear your rue with a difference'.

8 h] T. must have intended to substitute *dipt in*. Ricks reads the manuscript line as 'Not ~~dasht~~ ∧ dipt ∧ with tears . . .' (p. 914). This was adapted in *83*.11: 'Deep tulips dash'd with fiery dew'.

60–65. This group of sections is connected by the idea of the poet's present relationship with Hallam and his hope that Hallam will think of him. The argument gently draws towards the concluding 'happy thought' of *65*, that 'thine effect so lives in me, / A part of mine may live in thee'.

60. The metaphor of a simple girl in love with a worldly and intellectual man is repeated in *97* and is hinted at in *62*.5–8. Other examples of the poet depicting himself as the spouse, widow, or lover of Hallam are given in note *9*.18.

2] Cf. *61*.11; *103*.14.

16] Cf. 'Locksley Hall', 148: 'I am shamed thro' all my nature to have loved so slight a thing'.

61.

1] Hallam's 'second state' is in contrast to his 'first form' (10). The notion of successive stages of life after death is discussed in note *30*.25–8. Ricks observes that the expression 'state sublime' occurs in a passage in Gray, 'Ode for Music', in which the famous dead look down from heaven:

> Rapt in celestial transport they;
> Yet hither oft a glance from high
> They send of tender sympathy
> To bless the place, where on their opening soul
> First the genuine ardour stole . . .
> Meek Newton's self bends from his state sublime.
>
> (18-22, 25)

3-4] The assembly of the great spirits of all ages in the afterlife is a traditional notion. In the *Odyssey*, XI, for example, Odysseus visits Hades and converses with the ghosts of deceased heroes. The idea is fully developed by Virgil in the *Aeneid*, VI. In the *Inferno*, IV 79-147, Dante and Virgil visit the first circle of hell and meet the great poets of the past. Hallam describes such a scene in 'To One Early Loved, Now in India' XIII in which he imagines himself in heaven keeping company with his favourite poets:

> Brave spirits are, whom I will have to friend . . .
> Men, who have lived for man, and made an end
> In righteous joy; to whom th' approach is free
> Of unbarred Heaven, and the full mystery
> Unfolded to the penetrative mind.
> Such is the mighty Florentine, and He
> Who saw the solar angel, nor was blind;
> Such the deep, simple Shakspeare, greatest of mankind.

The alexandrine seems to have suggested line 12.

11-12] T.'s gloss to the entire section is particularly relevant here: 'In power of love not even the greatest dead can surpass the poet.' Of these lines, however, he remarked to Knowles: 'perhaps he might — if he were a greater soul'. Hallam's love of Shakespeare is referred to by his father: 'It was in Shakspeare alone that he found the fulness of soul which seemed to slake the thirst of his own rapidly expanding genius for an inexhaustible fountain of thought and emotion. He knew Shakspeare thoroughly' (*Remains*, vii). See note 3-4.

12 *Shakspeare*] This spelling was promoted by Malone. The spelling 'Shakspere' (cf. L.MS *Shakespere*) was promoted by the editor Charles Knight.

62.

1-2] The possibility that Hallam's love for the poet might prevent his advancement in heaven is discounted in *63*.1-4, in which the poet denies the same possibility in regard to himself.

5 *declined*] As in *Hamlet*, I 47-52:

> O Hamlet, what a falling-off was there!
> From me . . .
>   . . . to decline
> Upon a wretch, whose natural gifts were poor
> To those of mine!

Cf. 'Locksley Hall', 43–4: 'Having known me – to decline / On a range of lower feelings and a narrower heart than mine'.

6] Hallam was eighteen when he met T. (see note *22*.3, 10).

63.

1–4] T. explained the idea to Knowles: 'Man can love below as well as above himself; So surely it cannot be a weight upon the Spirit to remember the writer –'.

10–12] Mattes compares (p. 43) a coincidence of expression in Isaac Taylor, *Physical Theory of Another Life* (1836):
> If each sun be a place of assembly, and a home of immortality to the rational planetary tribes of its system, the vast world around which all suns are supposed to be revolving, may be the home of a still higher order of life, and the theatre of a still more comprehensive convocation of the intellectual community . . . Let every one then . . . read, in the visible heavens, a dim, and yet not fallacious presage of the vastness, and depth, and height, of that unseen economy, with which he shall find his destinies involved.   (pp. 234, 324–5)

64. H.T. comments that T. composed *64* 'when he was walking up and down the Strand and Fleet Street'. The metaphor simultaneously represents Hallam's attainment of heaven and what he would have achieved had he lived.

The section has been much admired: Bradley says, '*In Memoriam* contains greater poems, but none perhpas more exquisitely imagined and written'; Collins comments, 'Nothing could be more perfect than this poem, so pathetic, so subtle in its analogue'.

1 *Dost thou*] The section forms a single sentence (like *11, 14, 86, 129, 131*), but as Bradley observes, a question mark is required at the end in addition to the one within the inverted commas.

3 *low estate*] Cf., for example, Psalm 136:23: 'Who remembered us in our low estate'.

10 *golden keys*] H.T. comments: 'keys of office of State'. The image recalls *Comus*, 12–14:

> Yet some there be, that by due steps aspire

> To lay their just hands on that golden key,
> That opes the palace of Eternity.

65. T. commented to Knowles: 'Another higher thought now comes — a great lift-up — part of mine will live in thee'. Bradley observes that *65* is 'perhaps the first section of *In Memoriam* that can be described as cheerful or happy'.

4] Cf. Amos 9:9: 'Like as corn is sifted in a sieve, yet shall not the least grain fall upon the earth'. The grain image (for the poet's love) also occurs in *81* and *82*.

5] Cf. *38*.7–8. See also *5*.5–8 and note.

66.

1] T. told Knowles that 'You' refers to 'the auditor'.

3–4] T. commented on these lines to Knowles: 'my old blind grandmother'. She was Mary Turner Tennyson (who died in 1825 when T. was sixteen), the wife of George Tennyson.

5–8] T. commented to Knowles: 'The very sense of loss makes me social'.

13 *he plays with threads*] 'He makes cats-cradles to amuse them' (Percival).

15] T. explained to Knowles: 'The remembrance of the day' (when Hallam was alive).

67–71. These sections are linked in their descriptions of the poet's sleep and dreams. In *67* and *68* the poet sleeps and wakes fitfully. Sections *69, 70*, and *71* describe the poet dreaming, and they might even be considered as descriptions of progressive stages in the same dream. In *69* he has a painful dream which ends with a vision of an 'angel of the night'. In *70*, this vision melts into a faint picture of Hallam, but this is mixed with nightmare-like images. Gradually the picture of Hallam becomes clear and stills the nightmare scenes. In *71*, having attained a clear picture of his friend, the poet dreams peacefully of their happy past.

67. T. commented to Knowles: 'One I like very much. The visions of the night.'

3] T. commented to Knowles: 'The Bristol channel'. Clevedon parish church stands on a cliff overlooking the Bristol channel.

5 *Thy marble*] The 'tablet' (16) is located in the south transept.

bright in dark] Cf. Shakespeare, *Sonnets*, XLIII 4: 'And, darkly bright, are bright in dark directed' (Bradley).

7-8] The epitaph was composed by Henry Hallam (*Memoir*, I 296).

11] Cf. 'The Lover's Tale', II 121: 'the low-dropt eaves of sleep'.

15 *dark church*] T. comments:
I myself did not see Clevedon till years after the burial of A.H.H. (Jan. 3rd, 1834), and then in later editions of *In Memoriam* I altered the word 'chancel,' which was the word used by Mr. Hallam in his Memoir, to 'dark church.'

T. refers to the statement by Henry Hallam in *Remains*, xxxv: 'The remains of Arthur were . . . interred . . . in the chancel of Clevedon church.' In fact, the vaults of the Hallam and Elton families are not in the chancel but in the south end of the south transept. T. went to Clevedon with his wife on their honeymoon in June 1850. He wrote from Weston-super-Mare to John Forster on 22 June: 'I have just been to see A.H's tomb at Clevedon. The tablet is not (as I supposed) in the chancel but in a transept' (letter in TRC). T. could have corrected the line in time for **1850C**, but the revision did not appear until **1855**. (It is possible that T. visited Clevedon church before 1850. He could have done so when he stayed with Henry Hallam at Clevedon Court in the autumn of 1845 (see *Materials*, I 298, 303).)

15-16 *like a ghost / Thy tablet glimmers*] Cf. *The Princess*, VII 165-6: 'Now droops the milkwhite peacock like a ghost, / And like a ghost she glimmers on to me'.

68. T. commented to Knowles: 'The visions of the night'.

2, 3 *Sleep, Death's twin-brother*] T. compares *Aeneid*, VI 278: 'Consanguineus Leti Sopor' (Sleep, that is akin to Death), an image which derives from *Iliad*, XIV 231: "Ὕπνῳ . . . κασιγνήτῳ Θανάτοιο' (Sleep, the brother of Death).

5-8] In this stanza added in T.MSb, the images of nature and of the path recall *22-6* and the 'four sweet years' of friendship described there.

5] Cf. 'Mariana', 30: 'In sleep she seem'd to walk forlorn' (Bradley).

10-16] In a comment to Knowles, T. associated line 10 with *71.7*. With the poet's vagueness as to the exact source of his sorrow, cf. also *4.8-16*.

69. In L.MS *69* (f. 42ᵛ) comes between *66* (f. 42ᵛ) and *67* (f. 43ʳ). The section was omitted from **Trial** but was reinstated in the sequence in **1850A**.

T. commented to Knowles: 'I tried to make my grief into a crown of these poems — but it is not to be taken too closely — To write verses about sorrow grief and death is to wear a crown of thorns which ought to be put by — as people say'.

2 *Nature's ancient power*] Ricks compares 'The Two Voices', 160-2: 'If Nature put not forth her power / About the opening of the flower, / Who is it that could live an hour?' In *56*.6 Nature says 'I bring to life, I bring to death'.

5] Ricks compares 'The Gardener's Daughter' (MS version): 'Tired of the noisy town I wandered there' (Ricks, 517).

12] Cf. John 19:5: 'Then came Jesus forth, wearing the crown of thorns'.

14-20] T. explained to Knowles: 'the divine thing in the gloom'. In *Eversley* T. commented: 'But the Divine Thing in the gloom brought comfort'.

16-18] Cf. *'The light that shone when Hope was born'* (Add. Poem ii), 5-8.

17] Cf. *84*.42-3.

19-20] For the difficulty which the living have in comprehending the messages of spirits, cf. *85*.89-90, and also:

> A second voice was at mine ear,
> A little whisper . . .
> A notice faintly understood.
> ('The Two Voices', 427-8, 431)

> 'At last I heard a voice upon the slope
> Cry . . .
> But in a tongue no man could understand.
> ('The Vision of Sin', 219-20, 222)

70. This is the only section of this group (*67-71*) which is not in T.MS. L.MS contains two drafts (L.MSa, L.MSb). The later draft (L.MSb) has a stanza added between lines 8 and 9, but this was not published by T. The published text also reverts to the earlier draft (L.MSa) in the readings of lines 5 and 16.

1-3] Cf. Hallam ['Three Sonnets to Emily Tennyson'], I:

> Still am I free to close my happy eyes,
> And paint upon the gloom thy mimic form.

There are similarities with 'Ah! yes, the Lip may faintly smile':

> That glance, that smile of passing light,
> Are as the rainbow of the night;
> But seldom seen, it dares to bloom
> Upon the bosom of the gloom.
>
> Its tints are sad and coldly pale.
> (5-9)

5-12] The imagery recalls the passage in the *Aeneid*, VI in which Aeneas visits Hades and sees the ghosts of souls waiting to cross the Acheron:

> Turbidus hic cāeno, vastaque voragine gurges
> Aestuat, atque omnem Cocyto eructat arenam . . .
> Huc omnis turba ad ripas effusa ruebat . . .
> Haec omnis, quam cernis, inops, inhumataque turba est;
> . . . hi, quos vehit unda, sepulti.
> Nec ripas datur horrendas, nec rauca fluenta
> Transportare prius, quam sedibus ossa quierunt.
> Centum errant annos, volitantque haec litora circum.
> (296-7, 305, 325-9)

(Here a gulf, turbid and impure, boils up with mire and vast whirlpools, and disgorges all its sand into Cocytus . . . Hither the whole tribe of ghosts in swarms came pouring to the banks . . . All that crowd, which you see, is naked and unburied . . . these whom the stream carries are interred. Nor is it permitted to transport them over the horrid banks, and hoarse resounding waves, till their bones are quietly lodged in urns. They wander an hundred years, and flutter about the shores.)

Ricks compares these stanzas to Carlyle, *The French Revolution*, III v 3 — the taking of Fort L'Eguillette. See also, in the same chapter, the description of the abolition of Lyons.

Also cf. 'The Coach of Death', 7-8: 'A land of thin faces and shadowy forms, / Of vapours, and mist, and night'.

8] T. wrote 'Nonsense' alongside Collins's comparison (*Cornhill*, 42) of Sophocles, *Oedipus Tyrannus*, 67: πολλὰς δ' ὁδοὺς ἐλθόντα φροντίδος πλάνοις ((know that I have) gone many ways in wanderings of thought), and of Mary Shelley's note to *Prometheus Unbound* which prints Shelley's extended analysis of this famous line.

8 c *dreary margin*] Adapted from 9 in L.MSa: 'dreary moors'.

71.

4, 13-16] In the summer of 1830 T. and Hallam visited the Pyrenees, carrying money for the Spanish insurgents under General Torrijos (*Memoir*, I 51). The visit is recalled in 'In the Valley of Cauteretz'.

5-8] The idea is slightly obscure; the poet seems to be saying to Sleep: 'Did you really have such powers to divert the mind from the present to the past? If so, complete your enchantment so that no intimation of sorrow may spoil my visions of the past'.

7] In a comment to Knowles, T. associated this line with *68*.10: 'I find a trouble in thine eye'.

72. The section refers to the first anniversary of Hallam's death, 15 September 1834. It is paired with *99*, which commemorates the second anniversary and repeats the opening line of *72*.

8] The deleted reading, 'suck'd', recalls *The Tempest*, II ii 1: 'All the infections that the sun sucks up'. Cf. *The Princess*, VII 24: 'And suck the blinding splendour from the sand'.

16 *yet look'd*] 'Yet wouldst have looked' (H.T.).

19-20] Cf. *Macbeth*, III ii 46-50:

> Come, seeling night . . .
> And with thy bloody and invisible hand
> Cancel and tear to pieces that great bond
> Which keeps me pale!

A related image occurs in *85*.20: 'God's finger touch'd him, and he slept'.

27] T. comments: 'the dull sunset'.

28] Ricks compares Shakespeare, *Sonnets*, XXXI, 7-8 (on the sun): 'And from the forlorn world his visage hide, / Stealing unseen to west with his disgrace'.

73-77. This group concerns two related ideas. In *73-5* the poet laments the fame which Hallam has lost by his early death, but he is consoled by the knowledge that Hallam's virtues will be useful and appreciated in the afterlife. In *75, 76, 77* he realizes that his own songs are short-lived and that it is therefore foolish for him to write them in the hope of immortalizing Hallam. His reason for continuing to sing Hallam's praises is because his songs relieve his grief.

73.

7] With this acceptance of death, cf. *80*.2-3; *81*.9; *82*.1.

8] T. compares Zoroaster: 'Nought errs from law'.

11-12] Perhaps a reminiscence, as Bradley suggests, of 'Lycidas':

> Fame is no plant that grows on mortal soil . . .
> But lives and spreds aloft by those pure eyes,
> And perfet witnes of all judging Jove;
> As he pronounces lastly on each deed,
> Of so much fame in Heav'n expect thy meed.
>
> (78, 81–4)

74.

1–4] This experience (which is referred to as though it were a common one) is described by Sir Thomas Browne, 'Letter to a Friend' (of someone near death): 'He lost his own face, and looked like one of his near relations; for he maintained not his proper countenance but looked like his uncle' (noticed by Gatty, 1900).

5] The revisions in T.MS revert to the earlier reading.

dearest] T. commented to Knowles: 'If any body thinks I ever called him "dearest" in his life they are much mistaken, for I never even called him "dear".' This comment was apparently elicited by the review of *I.M.* in *The Times* (28 November 1851) which criticized the poem for its 'tone of . . . amatory tenderness' and cited *74*.5-12 as an example (see Shannon, 156-7, 200 n. 45). The epithet is used again in *Speak to me from the stormy sky*! (Add. Poem ix), 4, and it is applied to the poet himself in *110*.13 (first reading); also cf. *90*.21: 'Ah dear, but come thou back to me'.

12] Collins compares Petrarch, *In Morte di Madonna Laura*, LXXX: 'Non può far morte il dolce viso amaro; / Ma 'l dolce viso, dolce può far Morte' (Death cannot make that beauteous face less fair, / But that sweet face may lend to death a grace). Bradley compares *Romeo and Juliet*, V iii 85-6: 'For here lies Juliet, and her beauty makes / This vault a feasting presence full of light'.

75.

13–16] Hn.Nbk. has this stanza transposed with 17-20, but 17-20 is deleted and written again below 13-16.

13] T. comments: 'At twenty-three.'

20] Cf. 'The Dying Swan', 33: 'the tumult of their acclaim'. Ricks compares a poem by T. and Hallam, 'To Poesy', 8: 'Accompanied with tumult of acclaim' (Motter, 46).

76-77. The idea in these sections is an inversion of the ancient notion that poetry lasts for ever and so has the power to immortalize the poet and his subject.

These sections have been prepared for in 57.1-2, 8: 'the song of woe / Is after all an earthly song'; 'But I shall pass; my work will fail'; and the idea recurs in Epilogue, 13-14: 'No longer caring to embalm / In dying songs a dead regret'.

76.

1-6] Bradley compares 'Adonais', 417-21:

> Clasp with thy panting soul the pendulous Earth;
> As from a centre, dart thy spirit's light
> Beyond all worlds, until its spacious might
> Satiate the void circumference: then shrink
> Even to a point within our day and night.

1-4] T. comments: 'So distant in void of space that all our firmament would appear to be a needlepoint thence' (see note 3-4).

1] T. wrote '!!! nonsense' alongside the comparison by Collins (*Cornhill*, 42) of Petrarch, *In Morte di Madonna Laura*, LXXXII: 'Volo con l'ali de pensieri al Cielo' (I fly with wings of thought to heaven).

2 *set thy face*] Cf. for example, Ezekiel 6:2: 'Son of man, set thy face toward the mountains of Israel'.

3-4] A reminiscence of *Cymbeline*, I iii 18-19: 'Till the diminution / Of space had pointed him sharp as my needle'.

5 *lighten*] Cf. 'The Lover's Tale', I 49: 'Flash upon flash they lighten thro' me'.

6] T. comments: 'The ages upon ages to be'.

9 *matin songs*] T. comments: 'The great early poets'. Chaucer is called 'the morning star of song . . . the first warbler' in 'A Dream of Fair Women', 3, 5.

14 *With fifty*] The first reading, 'A hundred', seems to refer to the familiar idea, expressed, for example, by Dr Johnson, of outliving one's century, 'the term commonly fixed as the test of literary merit' (Preface to his edition of Shakespeare, 1765).

77.

1] Cf. Shakespeare, *Sonnets*, LXXXIII 8: 'How far a modern quill doth come too short'.

2] Cf. Campbell, *The Pleasures of Hope*, I 3: 'Why to yon mountain turns the musing eye'.

4] Cf. Marvell, 'First Anniversary', 139: 'Foreshortened Time its useless course would stay'; *Paradise Lost*, V 498: 'Improved by tract of time' (Bradley).

15-16] Cf. Petrarch, *In Morte di Madonna Laura*, XXV:

> E certo ogni mio studio in quel temp'era
> Pur di sfogare il doloroso core
> In qualche modo, non d'acquistar fama.
> Pianger cercai, non già del pianto onore.

> (And certes, my sole study and desire
> Was but − I knew not how − in those long years
> To unburthen my sad heart, not fame acquire.
> I wept, but wish'd no honour in my tears.)

78. The section commemorates the second Christmas following the death of Hallam. The first Christmas is described in *28-30* and the third Christmas and New Year's eve in *104-6*. Sections *78* and *105* are companion-pieces to *30*. In Hn.Nbk. *78* follows *30* (see Appendix A.1).

The importance of *78* in the structure of the poem is commented on by Bradley:

> If a turning-point in the general feeling of *In Memoriam* is to be sought at all, it must certainly be found . . . in the second Christmas poem . . . It seems true that, in spite of gradual change, the tone of the poem so far is, on the whole, melancholy, while after LXXVIII the predominant tone can scarcely be called even sad; it is rather the feeling of spring emerging slowly and with difficulty from the gloom of winter . . . [Nevertheless] it would seem to be a mistake to regard *In Memoriam* as a poem which, like 'Adonais', shows a dividing line clearly separating one part of the whole from the other. Its main movement is really one of advance almost from the first, though the advance is for a long time very slow.

5 *clog*] A dialect word for 'log'. The expression 'yule-clog' is used by Charles Lamb (whose father was a Lincolnshire man) in 'A Few Words on Christmas' (*The London Magazine*, 1822): 'And *this* night is CHRISTMAS EVE . . . Our forefathers observed it . . . with placing the *yule clog* on the fire, and roaring themselves thirsty till morning'.

10-12] The Christmas holidays at Somersby in 1834 (the second Christmas after the death of Hallam) were celebrated with friends. R.J. Tennant wrote to T. in October 1834: 'I shall think of the merry Christmas sports, and the New Year revels, that I fancy Somersby will see. I am glad John [Heath] will be with you, & Douglas [Heath] too (if he does come): I confess I wish I was there too' (MS *Materials*, I 230).

11] T. comments: 'Tableaux vivants'.

12 *hoodman-blind*] T. compares *Hamlet*, III iv 76-7: 'What devil was't / That thus hath cozened you at hoodman-blind?'.

14 *mark of pain*] The expression is used by Hallam in 'On Sympathy': Pleasure, therefore, will be the surest sign of life to the soul. Hence there is the strongest possible inducement to be pleased with those marks of pleasure in another, which justify, as it were, the assumed similarity of that other to its own nature. Marks of pain, in a less degree, will also be proofs.   (Motter, 135)

16 *be changed to*] T. revised the first reading in response to criticism by Spedding, who questioned the grammatical accuracy of 'become the less'.

17] Cf. Epilogue, 17: 'Regret is dead'.

79-89. Of these eleven sections Bradley observes that many are occasional poems, having little connection with one another beyond a certain unity of tone. The 'calmness' which is the note of LXXVIII is maintained. There is much of quiet retrospection, and, in some poems, of thoughts of what might have been: in three sections (LXXXIII, LXXXVI, LXXXVIII) there is the sense of new life and joy, and the last poem is quite happy. The idea of immortality and the hope of reunion appear but rarely, the centre of interest being shifted to the present life of the poet enriched by love for the dead.

79. T. comments: 'The section is addressed to my brother Charles (Tennyson Turner)'. Charles (1808-79) was T.'s favourite brother, and T. considered him 'almost the most lovable human being I have ever met' (*Eversley*, III 246). He was a co-author of *Poems by Two Brothers* (1827). See T.'s tribute to his brother in 'Prefatory Poem to My Brother's Sonnets' published in 1880 with Charles Tennyson Turner's *Collected Sonnets*.

1] Repeats *9*.20.

5-12] The lines recall 'Lycidas', 23-4, and *passim*:

> For we were nurs'd upon the self-same hill,
> Fed the same flock by fountain, shade, and rill.

6] Cf. Shakespeare, *A Midsummer Night's Dream*, III iii 211: 'Two lovely berries moulded on one stem'.

9] Cf. Crabbe, 'Delay Has Danger', 707: 'And the cold stream curl'd onward' (Bradley). This is the brook at Somersby so often referred to in T. and mentioned elsewhere in *I.M.*: *89*.43-5; *95*.7; *99*.6-8; *100*.14-16, *101*.9-10, 13-16.

11] Ricks compares 'Argosies that roam the twilight', an early version of 'Locksley Hall', 122 (quoted in Ricks, 695).

80. The poet imagines the effect on his friend of his own death. Hallam would have turned his loss into gain, and the poet resolves to imitate his response and so resemble him more closely. The idea of gain arising from loss is continued in *81* and *82*.

2 *Arthur*] See note *9*.3.

12] See notes *1*.6 and 8.

13] 'That with which I credit him shall serve as an example to release me from the burden of my loss'.

13-17] Cf. 'The Lover's Tale', I 227-36:

> She was my foster-sister: on one arm
> The flaxen ringlets of our infancies
> Wandered, the while we rested: one soft lap
> Pillowed us both: a common light of eyes
> Was on us as we lay: our baby lips,
> Kissing one bosom, ever drew from thence
> The stream of life, one stream, one life, one blood,
> One sustenance, which, still as thought grew large,
> Still larger moulding all the house of thought,
> Made all our tastes and fancies like.

15-16] Adapted from 'Hail Briton', 83-4: 'an example reach hands / For ever into coming years'. Cf. Tiresias', 122-3: 'Their examples reach a hand / Far through all years'.

18-20] The idea is reminiscent of Shakespeare, *Sonnets*, XXV, XXIX, XXXVII, in which the poet declares that the perfections of his friend compensate him for his own deficiencies; especially cf. XXXVII 3-4, 11-12:

> So I, made lame by fortune's dearest spite,
> Take all my comfort of thy worth and truth.
> . . . I in thy abundance am sufficed
> And by a part of all thy glory live.

81.

1-5] Spedding suggested that the section would be better without the first stanza, but T., although usually responsive to Spedding's criticism, left the stanza in. The meaning of this stanza and of line 5 is obscure and has puzzled commentators. The most likely interpretation, in view of T.'s own gloss on line 1 (see below), is as follows:

I wish I had been able to say, while he was alive, that my love for him had reached completion and maturity. Then I should have known that, on his death, a richer harvest of love would have been available for me to garner for the future than would be possible from an unripe love.

1 *Could I have said*] T. explains: 'Would that I could have said'.

3-4] Adapted from an early reading of 'The Gardener's Daughter', 234-9: 'Beyond a mellower growth mature in ear?' (Ricks).

4 *ear.*'] H.T. comments: 'he told me, as far as I remember, that a note of exclamation had been omitted by accident after "ear" (thus, "ear!").' But in T.MS, L.MS, and **Trial**, 'ear' is followed by a full stop, as in the published reading.

82.

5-8] The idea that the dead progress through stages of lives is discussed in note *30*.25-8.

6] With the idea and diction, cf. Thomson, *The Seasons*, 'Winter', 605-8:

With earnest eye anticipate those scenes
Of happiness and wonder, where the mind,
In endless growth and infinite ascent,
Rises from state to state, and world to world.

Cf. 'The Two Voices', 351: 'The slipping through from state to state'.

8] Cf. 'St. Simeon Stylites', 153-4: 'This dull chrysalis / Cracks into shining wings'.

14] Cf. *Othello*, IV ii 57: 'But there where I have garner'd up my heart'.

83. This section prepares for the arrival of the second spring celebrated in the poem, the spring which is the subject of *86*. It may be compared with the first spring, in *38*, which gave the poet 'No joy', and with the third spring, in *115* and *116*, which encourages him to look forward to the future. The likelihood that in L.MS *83* was intended to precede *107* is discussed in headnote to *107*.

2,4 *delaying long . . . Delaying long*] Cf. Shelley, *Prometheus Unbound*, II i 15: 'Too long desired, too long delaying, come' (Ricks).

6] Adapted from *41*.8 c (Hn.Nbk.): 'The sweetness of thy proper smile'.

10 *darling blue*] A reminiscence of Shakespeare, *Sonnets*, XVIII 3: 'the darling buds of May'.

11] Adapted from *59*.8 g-h (H.Lpr.99): 'And sweeter blooms which thou shalt have / Not dipt [in] tears but dasht with dew'.

11, 15] Cf. Shelley, 'Epipsychidion', 110-11: 'Beyond the sense, like fiery dews that melt / Into the bosom of a frozen bud' (Ricks).

12] T. explained the image to Mrs G.F. Watts in 1889: 'Once under a laburnum he asked me if I thought "dropping wells of fire" was not a true description. Some critic had written that it was not fire at all; "not coal fire certainly," he said, "but little golden flames of fire, or so at least it seems to me"' (M.S. Watts, *George Frederic Watts: The Annals of an Artist's Life*, 3 vols. (1912), II 162).

84. T. remarked on this section to Knowles: 'I like that one'.

4] Cf. 'Adonais', 241-2: 'Or hadst thou waited the full cycle, when / Thy spirit should have filled the crescent sphere'.

10-12] T. comments: 'The projected marriage of A.H.H. with Emily Tennyson'.

15] With the idea Bradley compares *Romeo and Juliet*, IV v 89: 'Our bridal flowers serve for a buried corse'; and Jeremy Taylor, *The Rule and Exercises of Holy Dying*, I 1: 'changes his laurel into cypress, his triumphal chariot to a hearse'.

19-20] These lines recall, as Bradley observes, Lamb, 'Dream Children; A Reverie':

> while I stood gazing, both the children gradually grew fainter to my view, receding, and still receding, till nothing at last but two mournful features were seen in the uttermost distance, which, without speech, strangely impressed upon me the effects of speech: 'We are not of Alice, nor of thee, nor are we children at all. The children of Alice call Bartrum father. We are nothing; less than nothing, and dreams. We are only what might have been, and must wait upon the tedious shores of Lethe millions of ages before we have existence, and a name' — and immediately awaking, I found myself quietly seated in my bachelor armchair, where I had fallen asleep.

23-4] James Spedding remarked of Hallam: 'No man tempered wit and wisdom so gracefully' (*Remains*, xxv). Cf. *87*.29-34 and note.

25-6] Cf. 'Hail Briton', 139-40 (MS reading): 'An evil scorn / Has filled the lips of men with lies' (Ricks).

39-40] This is reminiscent of the description of the ghosts of souls waiting to cross the Acheron in the *Aeneid*, VI 305-29 (quoted in note *70*.5-12).

41] T. compares *Paradise Lost*, II 409: 'ere he arrive / The happy isle'.

45] A reminiscence of Isaiah 36:6: 'Behold, thou trustest in the staff of this broken reed, on Egypt, whereon if a man lean, it will go into his hand, and pierce it'.

85. *Dating*: The ten stanzas which constitute the early version can be dated 1833-4 because they are in T.Nbk. (see Appendix A.1). The addition of twenty stanzas probably took place in 1841, the period of most intimate friendship between T. and Lushington (Mary Joan Ellmann, 'Tennyson: Revision of *In Memoriam*, Section 85', *Modern Language Notes*, 65 (1950), 22-30).

The identity of the addressee has been much discussed. Gatty suggested that throughout the section the poet is conversing with his 'once affianced sister', and that 113-16 refer to 'the lady who became Mrs Tennyson'. T. wrote alongside the first comment, 'no — a friend. apparently the one to whom the epithalamion is addressed'. He also crossed out 'Mrs Tennyson' and wrote 'no' alongside. H.T. in *Eversley* states that the section is 'Addressed to Edmund Lushington'. He omitted this note, as Ricks observes, in the 1913 Eversley edition, but he added a note to 115-16: 'refers to his "bride to be", Emily Sellwood'. This statement is refuted by T.'s marginal note in Gatty; moreover, the entire section is clearly addressed to another man ('I crave your pardon, O my friend'; 'I, clasping brother-hands'), and the poet is making a plea for friendship, not conjugal love. Mary Joan Ellmann suggests that although Lushington is the addressee of the section in its revised form, he is perhaps not the addressee of the early version (pp. 27-8). It seems probable that the early version was occasioned not by a friendship with a particular person but rather by a desire for such a friendship. Three months after learning of Hallam's death, T. visited for three days a friend and neighbour, the Revd John Rashdall, curate of Orby. Rashdall noted in his diary on 14 January 1834: 'A.T. improves greatly, has evidently a mind yearning for fellowship; for the joys of friendship and love. Hallam seems to have left his heart a widowed one' (quoted by Ralph Wilson Rader, 'Tennyson in the Year of Hallam's Death', *PMLA*, LXXVII (September 1962), 421). For the similarity of the diary entry to *85*.113-16, see note.

The section seems to be modelled on Hallam's poem, 'To A.T.' (in which the earlier friend is identified by Motter as most likely Gladstone):

> Oh, last in time, but worthy to be first
> Of friends in rank, had not the father of good
> On my early spring one perfect gem bestowed,
> A friend, with whom to share the best and worst.
> Him will I shut close to my heart for aye.
> There's not a fibre quivers there, but is
> His own, his heritage for woe, or bliss.
> Thou would'st not have me such a charge betray.
> Surely, if I be knit in brotherhood
> So tender to that chief of all my love,
> With thee I shall not loyalty eschew.
> And well I ween not time with ill or good
> Shall thine affection e'er from mine remove,
> Thou yearner for all fair things, and all true.

1-92] Some of (if not all) these stanzas were probably originally in T.MS for the following reasons: there is one stub in the spine-fold between f. 34 (having *83* on recto) and f. 35 (having *85*.93-120 on recto); moreover, T.MS f. 35ʳ has *85*.93-120 and L.MS f. 55ʳ also has *85*.93-120.

1-4] This echoes *27*.13-16.

5-6] Edmund Lushington is addressed, as he is in the Epilogue, of which the opening, 'O true and tried, so well and long, / Demand not thou . . .', is an echo of these lines.

12 *capabilities*] The word had only recently been elevated from being a vulgarism (Byron apologizes for using it).

18-20] This seems to be an allusion to the description given by Hallam's uncle in his letter (1 October 1833) informing T. of Hallam's death:
> It has pleased God, to remove him from this his first scene of Exist-
> ence, to that better World, for which he was Created —
> He died at Vienna on his return from Buda, by Apoplexy . . . He
> suddenly became insensible, and his Spirit departed without Pain.
> (TRC; printed in *Memoir*, I 105)

20] J.H. Buckley (*Tennyson: The Growth of a Poet* (1960), 114) observes that this is 'an image reversing Michelangelo's view of Creation'. It also recalls Job 19:21: 'Have pity upon me . . . for the hand of God hath touched me'. Cf. 'On a Mourner', 11: 'And on thy heart a finger lays'.

21-8] T. compares 'Lycidas', 178-81:

> There entertain him all the saints above,
> In solemn troops, and sweet societies,
> That sing, and, singing, in their glory move,
> And wipe the tears for ever from his eyes.

These stanzas imitate the conventional description in classical literature of the reception of the dead into heaven by the great spirits of all ages. One of the great spirits takes charge of the new arrival and shows him grand vistas in which the workings of the universe, of Nature, and of the future are revealed. For examples of such descriptions, cf. Cicero, 'Somnium Scipionus'; and Seneca, 'Consolation to Marcia', 25, 26.

21-4] Cf. an unadopted passage, noticed by Ricks, in 'The Two Voices':

> And those Intelligences fair,
> That range above thy state, declare
> If thou can'st fathom what they are.

21] Cf. Dante, *Il Convito*, II 5: 'Intelligenze, le quali la volgare gente chiama Angeli' (Intelligences, whom the vulgar call angels) (Bradley); Spenser, *The Tears of the Muses*, 509-10: 'The Spirites and Intelligences fayre, / And Angels waighting on th' Almighties chayre' (Ricks).

25] A reminiscence of *Paradise Lost*, XI 707-8: 'to walk with God / High in salvation and the climes of bliss'.

26] Cf. Revelation 22:1: 'And he showed me a pure river of water of life, clear as crystal.'

30] Cf. 'The Two Voices', 331: 'A life of nothings, nothing-worth'.

33] Cf. an unadopted passage from 'The Gardener's Daughter', in T.Nbk.17:

> . . . a friendship so complete
> Portioned in perfect halves between us both
> That us two souls have ever counterweighed
> Each other, justlier poised.

35] See *41*.5 and note.

37-40] T. explains the idea: 'Yet I know that the knowledge that we have free will demands from us action.'

40] Bradley compares Pope, *Essay on Man*, IV 4: 'For which we bear to live, or dare to die'.

41-4] In Heath MS this stanza comes at the end of the poem with an indication ('X Stanza Second') that it is to be inserted after 1-4.

48] James Spedding observed of Hallam: 'His chief pleasure and strength lay certainly in metaphysical analysis. He would read any metaphysical book under any circumstances with avidity . . . I have met with no man his superior in metaphysical subtlety' (*Remains*, xxii, xxiv).

53] H.T. explains 'imaginative woe' as 'imaginative and speculative sorrow'.

61-4] In T.Nbk. and Heath MS this stanza is repeated (with variants) as the final stanza of the poem (see the textual note to these lines).

69-84] T. placed a question mark alongside the comparison by Collins (*Cornhill*, 42) of Petrarch, *In Morte di Madonna Laura*, XI, but the parallel is close:

> Se lamentar augelli, o verdi fronde
>> Mover soavemente a l'aura estiva,
>> O roco mormorar di lucid'onde
>> S'ode d'una fiorita e fresca riva,
> Là 'v'io seggia d'amor pensoso, e scriva;
>> Lei che 'l Ciel ne mostrò, terra n'asconde,
>> Veggio ed odo ed intendo, ch'ancor viva
>> Di si lontano a'sospir miei risponde.
> Deh perchè innanzi tempo ti consume?
>> Mi dice con pietate: a che pur versi
>> Degli occhi tristi un doloroso fiume?
> Di me non pianger tu; ch'e' miei di fersi,
>> Morendo, eterni; e nell'eterno lume,
>> Quando mostrai di chiuder, gli occhi apersi.

> (If the lorn bird complain, or rustling sweep
> Soft summer airs o'er foliage waving slow,
> Or the hoarse brook come murmuring down the steep,
> Where on the enamell'd bank I sit below
> With thoughts of love that bid my numbers flow;
> 'Tis then I see her, though in earth she sleep!
> Her, form'd in heaven! I see, and hear, and know!
> Responsive sighing, weeping as I weep:
> 'Alas,' she pitying says, 'ere yet the hour,
> Why hurry life away with swifter flight?
> Why from thy eyes this flood of sorrow pour?
> No longer mourn my fate! through death my days
> Become eternal! to eternal light
> These eyes, which seem'd in darkness closed, I raise!')

93-6] H.T. records: 'He said that there might be a more ultimate communion than we could dream of between the living and the dead, at all events for a time' (*Memoir*, I 320).

113-16] Rader observes that if we did not know that this stanza was probably not composed until much later, we might suppose that T. had read Rashdall the early version of *85* (p. 421).

86. *Dating*: T. comments that *86* was written at Barmouth. (Knowles recorded him as saying 'Bournemouth', but he must have misunderstood.)

T. visited Barmouth, apparently for the first time, in 1839 (*Memoir*, I 173), and again in July 1844 (postmarked letter to G.S. Venables, Dept. of Special Collections, Spencer Library, University of Kansas).

T. told Knowles: 'This is one I like too'. H.T. comments that *86* 'gives pre-eminently his sense of the joyous peace in Nature, and he would quote it in this context along with his Spring and Bird songs' (*Memoir*, I 313). The section has been prepared for by *83*. With *88* it describes the second of the three springs which occur in the poem. Section *38* describes the first spring and *115* and *116* the third spring.

The section forms a single sentence (like *11, 14, 64, 129, 131*). On hearing Allingham recite the poem T. commented (of the first five lines, up to 'The round of space'): 'It all goes together' (*Allingham's Diary*, 328). The implication is that these lines should be read in one breath. Revisions in the punctuation of lines 3, 4, 5, 8 in L.MS and **Trial** indicate T.'s desire to increase the steady, sweeping movement of the verse. The experience described here, Bradley suggests, is 'perhaps more "mystic" than we at first imagine'; indeed, it may even be the experience recalled in *122* (for which see headnote *122*). The high proportion of poetical diction is remarked upon by Alan Sinfield, *The Language of Tennyson's 'In Memoriam'* (Oxford, 1971), 63. The section is reminiscent of Dante, *Purgatorio*, XXVIII:

> Su per lo suol che d'ogni parte oliva.
>   Un'aura dolce, senza mutamento
> Avere in sè, mi fería per la fronte
> Non di più colpo che soave vento.
>   (6-9)

> (Delicious odour breathed. A pleasant air,
> That intermitted never, never veer'd,
> Smote on my temples, gently, as a wind
> Of softest influence.)

1-4, 9] Cf. Coleridge, 'The Destiny of Nations, A Vision', 384-6:

>   sweet,
> As after showers the perfumed gale of eve,
> That flings the cool drops on a feverous cheek.

1] T. comments: 'It was a west wind'.

3 *brake*] T. glossed 'brakes' (*107*.9) 'bushes', in his Gatty.

6] Cf. *The Princess*, I 93: 'dewy-tassell'd trees'.

7] Cf. *The Princess*, V 526-7: 'And shadowing down the champaign till it strikes / On a wood'.

horned flood] T. comments: 'Between two promontories'. This adapts the Latin commonplace 'corniger Hesperidum fluvius', as in (for example) *Aeneid*, VIII 77. Cf. *Paradise Lost*, XI 831: 'push'd by the horned flood'.

9–11] Cf. Coleridge, 'Fears in Solitude', 20–1: 'from the breezy air, / Sweet influences trembled o'er his frame';

> Come, beat a little quicker now,
> When all things own my quickening breath.
> ('On a Mourner', T.MS, following 15)

12 *the fancy*] T. commented to Knowles: 'Imagination – *The* Fancy – no particular fancy'.

13–16] T. commented to Knowles: 'The west wind rolling to the Eastern Seas till it meets the evening Star'.

13] Barmouth is famed for the sunsets over its estuary (Bradley).

15–16] According to the theory of the plurality of worlds (in which T. believed; see *Memoir*, I 379), other planets may be inhabited by forms of rational life. These lines also suggest the belief that the spirits of the dead inhabit the stars.

15 *yonder orient star*] T. commented: 'Any rising star is here intended'. In spite of his statement, the reader would naturally associate this star with Venus, so often referred to in *I.M.*

87.

1–2] T. went up to Trinity College, Cambridge, in October 1827. He came down without taking a degree in 1831.

5–8] The lines recall the description of King's College Chapel in 'Il Penseroso', 159–66:

> And storied Windows richly dight,
> Casting a dimm religious light.
> There let the pealing Organ blow,
> To the full voic'd Quire below,
> In Service high, and Anthems cleer,
> As may with sweetnes, through mine ear,
> Dissolve me into extasies,
> And bring all Heav'n before mine eyes.

6–7] Cf. 'Lines on Cambridge of 1830', 8–9:

> your solemn organ-pipes that blow
> Melodious thunders thro' your vacant courts;

The Princess, II 450-2:

> While the great organ almost burst his pipes,
> Groaning for power, and rolling through the court
> A long melodious thunder.

8] Perhaps a particular reference to the famous windows of King's College Chapel, each of which has two prophets. T. cancelled the 's' in 'prophets' (probably to lessen sibilation) in his copy of Gatty which he corrected in May 1883.

10] Cf. 'The Gardener's Daughter', 41: 'stirred with languid pulses of the oar'.

15] The limes at Trinity; cf. 'To the Rev W.H. Brookfield', 6: 'How oft with him we paced that walk of limes' (referring to Hallam).

16] Hallam had rooms in New Court. He entered into residence in October 1828 and left Cambridge on taking his degree in January 1832.

18-33] Cf. Cowley, 'On the Death of Mr William Hervey', 34-40:

> How oft unweary'd have we spent the nights . . .
> We spent them not in toys; in lusts, or wine;
> But search of deep Philosophy,
> Wit, Eloquence, and Poetry,
> Arts which I lov'd, for they, my friend, were thine.

21-4] T. remarked to Knowles: 'The "water club" because there was no wine — They used to make speeches — I never did.'

25-30] As Ricks remarks, this metaphor is used in another poem to Arthur Hallam, 'If I were loved', 5-6:

> All the inner, all the outer world of pain
> Clear Love would pierce and cleave, if thou wert mine.

29-34] Hallam was a celebrated speaker and conversationalist. James Spedding, for example, recalled Hallam's 'natural skill in the dazzling fence of rhetoric' (*Remains*, xxiii). John Kemble liked to arrange meetings between T. and Hallam so that their friends might listen to what Kemble called their 'magnificent conversations' (Charles Tennyson, 75).

36-40] Fanny Kemble recalled Hallam's appearance:
There was a gentleness and purity almost virginal in his voice, manner, and countenance; and the upper part of his face, his forehead and eyes . . . wore the angelic radiance that they still must wear in heaven. Some time or other, at some rare moments of the divine spirit's supremacy in our souls, we all put on the heavenly face that will

be ours hereafter, and for a brief lightning space our friends behold us as we shall look when this mortal has put on immortality. On Arthur Hallam's brow and eyes this heavenly light, so fugitive on other human faces, rested habitually, as if he was thinking and seeing in heaven.   (*Record of a Girlhood*, 3 vols. (1878), II 3) (It is possible, of course, that she was influenced by *I.M.*)

39 *ethereal eyes*] With the first reading, 'seraphic', cf. *30*.27: 'seraphic flame'; *109*.5: 'Seraphic intellect and force'.

40] T. comments: 'The broad bar of frontal bone over the eyes of Michael Angelo . . . These lines I wrote from what Arthur Hallam said after reading of the prominent ridge of bone over the eyes of Michael Angelo: "Alfred, look over my eyes; surely, I have the bar of Michael Angelo!"' (*Eversley*, III 249; *Memoir*, I 38). The book read by Hallam may have been Condivi's biography of the artist containing the observation that the forehead of Michelangelo was square, and when seen in profile it projected almost beyond his nose ('quasi avanza il naso'). For the significance of such a bar, Ricks compares Coleridge: 'A few whose eyes were bright, and either piercing or steady, and whose ample foreheads, with the weighty bar, ridge-like, above the eyebrows, bespoke observation followed by meditative thought' (*A Lay Sermon*, 'Allegoric Vision'). Cf. also 'The Ante-Chamber', 10–14 (a portrait of Hallam):

> And look you what an arch the brain has built
> Above the ear! and what a settled mind,
> Mature, harboured from change, comtemplative,
> Tempers the peaceful light of hazel eyes
> Observing all things.

88. In T.MS *88* has alongside it the 'X' which T. used to indicate sections which he intended to omit. The section does not appear in L.MS, but it was reinstated in the sequence in **Trial**.

1 *Wild bird*] T. comments: 'To the Nightingale'. Cf. Shakespeare, *Sonnets*, CII 11 (of the nightingale): 'that wild music burthens every bough'.

2 *Eden*] T. wrote 'a paradisal song' in a copy of the *Works* (**1884A**) now in University of London Library (Ricks).

5 *fierce extremes*] Ricks compares *King John*, V vii 13–14, and *Paradise Lost*, II 598–9: 'the bitter change / Of fierce extremes'.

7–8] Cf. 'The Gardener's Daughter', 248–51:

> like the whispers of the leaves
> That tremble round a nightingale − in sighs

Which perfect Joy, perplex'd for utterance,
Stole from her sister Sorrow.

11 *the sum of things*] For a discussion of this common Latinism
(*summa rerum*) see H.A. Mason, 'The Sum of Things', *Notes and
Queries*, n.s. 22 (July 1975), 309–10.

89. *Dating*: The section was probably written after the autumn of
1838. During this time T. composed 'Audley Court' (*Memoir*, I 165)
which has many similarities to *89*; for example, Francis arrives from a
sea journey (Arthur from town); the friends picnic in the orchard, talk
of various subjects, and sing songs; their homeward journey is a counter-
part to that in *89*. A comparison of the poems suggests that *89* was
probably written later.

1–4] T. commented in May 1883: 'The 'towering sycamore' is cut down,
and the four poplars are gone, and the lawn is no longer flat.' H.T.
describes the Rectory garden as it was when the Tennysons lived there:
The lawn at Somersby was overshadowed on one side by the wych-
elms, and on the other by larch and sycamore trees . . . Beyond the
path, bounding the greensward to the south, ran in the old days a
deep border of lilies and roses, backed by hollyhocks and sunflowers.
Beyond that was

a garden bower'd close
With plaited alleys

sloping in a gradual descent to the parson's field, at the foot of
which flows . . . the swift steep-banked brook. (*Eversley*, I 342)

1–2] The image is heraldic: two tinctures on a field are reversed ('counter-
changed') with a chequered effect. T. uses the image in 'Recollections
of the Arabian Nights', 84–6 and in 'Ode: O Bosky Brook', 58–9:
'counterchanged embroidery / Of light and darkness'.

5–8] The joy of leaving the city for the country is a familiar theme in
Roman and English poetry. The classic example is Horace, *Odes*, III
xxix; cf. especially 12: 'fumum et opes strepitumque Romae' (the
smoke, the riches, and the din of wealthy Rome). Hallam wrote to
Emily Tennyson in May 1833 (?): 'To be sure London in dogdays is
very hot. The kind Nature who sent us these warm hours did not intend
them to be wasted on white pavements & dusty streets of a metropolitan
city' (TRC).

5–6] Hallam paid several visits to Somersby, primarily to see Emily
Tennyson. His first meeting with her was probably on his visit to

Somersby in December 1829.

On 29 May (1832?) he wrote to her from Cambridge: 'All except you and Somersby seems so blank to me . . . Oh for a short while at Somersby this summer!' On 5 December 1832 he wrote: 'Is it necessary for me to assure you that every hour of time I can give to Somersby shall be given? Were I the master, oh how gladly would I abandon every place & every thing to be beside you for ever.' Later that month (12 December) he wrote again, alluding to the Tennysons' expectation that they would have to vacate the Rectory soon afterwards:

I too love Somersby. How dearly! But I love it *principally* for your sake. I trust I am not too late to see it once more, to take a farewell of it with you — a last farewell of the objects & places eternally engraven on my heart, because connected with a passion that has made the destiny of my life.   (all letters in TRC)

In fact, Hallam's last visit to Somersby was in July 1833, when T. was not present. He wrote to T. on 31 July: 'I missed you much at Somersby, not for want of additional excitement, I was very happy. I had never been at Somersby before without you' (*Memoir*, I 103).

6 *Arthur*] See note 9.3.

10] For example, during Hallam's visits to Somersby there were 'dances on the lawn by twilight' (MS *Materials*, I 109).

11-12] In 1833 Hallam was working in the office of a conveyancer in Lincoln's Inn Fields.

11 *brawling*] 'Litigious', but cf. 'Ode to Memory', V 111-12: 'Whither in after life retired / From brawling storms'.

19-20] Adapted from lines in an unadopted passage of 'The Gardener's Daughter' in Heath MS following line 216: 'The wind was fitful: every musky gust / Tumbled the mellow pear' (Charles Tennyson, 'Tennyson Papers II, J.M. Heath's "Commonplace Book"', *Cornhill Magazine*, CLIII (1936), 441).

21-4] Cf. Coleridge, 'Monody on the Death of Chatterton', 152-3: 'And we, at sober eve, would round thee throng. / Would hang, enraptured, on thy stately song'.

23-4] Dante and Petrarch were, in the words of Henry Hallam, 'Arthur's beloved masters'. Hallam 'greatly admired' Petrarch, and published a brief memoir of the poet, but Dante became 'the master mover of his spirit', the poet who was most 'congenial to the character of his own reflective mind'. Hallam spoke Italian fluently and eloquently, composed sonnets in Italian, and translated most of the sonnets of the *Vita Nuova* (*Remains*, vi, x, xii, xxxii, xxxiii). According to Willingham Rawnsley,

Hallam taught Emily Tennyson Italian,

> and, as the family were never without books in their hands and had the admirable custom of reading the best authors aloud, Shakespeare, Milton, Chaucer, Spenser and Campbell gave place when Arthur Hallam was with them to Dante, Petrarch, Tasso and Ariosto.
>
> (*Tennyson 1809-1909: A Lecture* (Ambleside, 1909), 16)

26-28] Cf. Hallam's lines on Emily Tennyson's harp-playing:

> Sometimes I dream thee leaning o'er
> The harp I used to love so well.
>
> ('To the Loved One', 25-6)
>
> the harp I used to hear
> When the look of love was on thy face, and blessed I was near.
>
> 'A Plaint' (in *Some Unpublished Poems*, 13)

31-2] Cf. Horace, *Odes*, II vii 6-7: 'cum quo morantem saepe diem mero / Fregi' (with whom I often broke the tedious day with wine) (Mustard).

36] Henry Hallam remarks that Arthur's mind was 'deeply imbued with the higher philosophy, especially that of Plato, with which he was very conversant'. He describes the 'Platonic spirit' of his son's literary creed, and how he occupied his leisure when not studying law: 'His time was however principally devoted . . . to metaphysical researches, and to the history of philosophical opinions' (*Remains*, xviii, xxxii-xxxiii). T. probably substituted 'Socratic' because 'Platonic' was sometimes understood to mean 'homosexual' (*OED* a.A.2.).

47-8] T. explains: 'Before Venus, the evening star, had dipt into the sunset. The planets, according to Laplace, were evolved from the sun.'

49] Cf. Keats, *Hyperion*, III 35: 'Full ankle-deep in lilies of the vale'.

90-95. The subject of this group of sections is the communion of the dead with the living. Sections *90-4* express the desire for a communion and thus prepare for *95* in which the communion takes place.

With this group may be compared *Speak to me from the stormy sky!* (Add. Poem ix), and an unadopted passage from 'The Two Voices' (Trinity College MS 0.15.15) in which the poet urges his dying friend to pledge himself to return after death:

> When thy best friend draws sobbing breath
> Plight thou a compact ere his death
> And comprehend the words he saith
>
> Urge him to swear, distinct & plain
> That out of bliss or out of pain
> He will draw nigh thee once again

Is that his footstep on the floor
Is this his whisper at the door
Surely he comes. He comes no more.

90.

5-20] The idea is the subject of 'Enoch Arden', and occurs elsewhere in
T: 'The Coach of Death', 65-8; 'The Lotus Eaters', 114-9:

Dear is the memory of our wedded lives
And dear the last embraces of our wives
And their warm tears: but all hath suffered change:
For surely now our household hearths are cold:
Our sons inherit us: our looks are strange:
And we should come like ghosts to trouble joy.

19] Adapted from 'The Lotos-Eaters', 128: 'There *is* confusion worse
than death'.

21-4] This stanza was substituted for the deleted 20 a-d.

91. This section was probably originally in L.MS. On f. 60^v appears
90. The top third of the opposite leaf, f. 61, has been cut out. On the
remaining part of f. 61^r are *92* and *93*. An autograph MS of *91* was
'inserted by the poet' in a copy of **1850A** owned by Miss Gwenllian F.
Palgrave and exhibited (item 213) in the Tennyson Centenary Exhibition
at the Fine Art Society, New Bond Street, July 1909. The manuscript,
which may well be from L.MS, cannot be traced.

3-4] T. explained the phrase in a letter in 1864:
As to 'sea-blue birds' &c. defendant states that he was walking one
day in March by a deep-banked brook, and under the leafless bushes
he saw the kingfisher flitting or fleeting underneath him, and there
came into his head a fragment of an old Greek lyric poet [Alcman,
fr. 26], 'ἀλιπόρφυρος εἴαρος ὄρνις,' 'The sea-purple or sea-shining
bird of Spring,' spoken of as the halcyon. Defendant cannot say
whether the Greek halcyon be the same as the British kingfisher,
but as he never saw the kingfisher on this particular brook before
March, he concludes that in that country at least, they go down to
the sea during the hard weather and come up again with the Spring.
(*Memoir*, II 4)
In 1890, however, when he was asked to identify 'the sea-blue bird', he
answered: 'I don't know, but I suppose it's the kingfisher.' When the
blue tit was suggested as a likelier bird, he replied: 'Well, make it a tit;
I daresay it was a tit, but I have quite forgotten, and I know I have told
other folk it was a kingfisher' (*Memories of the Tennysons*, 109-10).

7-8] Ricks suggests an allusion to the nimbus of Iulus in *Aeneid*, II 682-4:

> ecce levis summo de vertice visus Iuli
> fundere lumen apex, tactuque innoxia mollis
> lambere flamma comas et circum tempora pasci

(lo! from above the head of Julus a light tongue of flame seemed to shed a gleam and, harmless in its touch, lick his soft locks and pasture round his temples.)

92. This section and *93* reject the idea of the visible return of the dead, or of communication with them through the senses, as either the results of a diseased imagination or as utterly impossible.

3] Cf. 'Oh! that 'twere possible', 69: "Tis the blot upon the brain'.

4, 9] The diction and idea are reminiscent of *Hamlet*, I i.

13-16] A reminiscence, as Gatty has noticed, of Coleridge's translation of Schiller, *The Death of Wallenstein*, V i 98-102:

> As the sun
> Ere it is risen, sometimes paints its image
> In the atmosphere, so often do the spirits
> Of great events stride on before the events,
> And in to-day already walks to-morrow;

Bradley notes Coleridge's discussion of the idea elsewhere in *The Statesman's Manual*, Appendix C, and *Table Talk*, May 1 1823. Also cf. Campbell, 'Lochiel's Warning', 56: 'coming events cast their shadows before'.

15 *refraction*] T. comments: 'The heavenly bodies are seen above the horizon, by refraction, before they actually rise'.

93. T.'s belief that the spirits of the dead do not make themselves manifest but rather communicate directly with the spirit of the living is expressed in his opinions on spiritualism, as given by H.T.:

Frederick has grown more of a spiritualist than ever, and believes in visions of visions of his dead friends and of interwoven angels on back-grounds of celestial azure. My father respected these visions of a poet, whose temperament was highly strung and overwrought, but though he took much interest in spiritualism he could not abide the thought of the souls of dead men manifesting themselves by table-rappings. He would speak after this fashion: 'God and the ghosts of men would speak to the heart of men through the medium of the spirit not of table legs'.

(marginal note by H.T. in a copy of *Materials*, IV 171 in TRC)

H.T. elaborates this idea: 'In certain states of high strung consciousness he thought it *possible* that soul might touch soul' (*Materials*, II 29), and he compares 'Aylmer's Field':

> Star to star vibrates light: may soul to soul
> Strike thro' a finer element of her own?
> So, − from afar, − touch us at once?
>   (578-80)

1-4] Beeching compares Wordsworth, 'The Affliction of Margaret', 57-60:

> I look for ghosts; but none will force
> Their way to me: 'tis falsely said
> That there was ever intercourse
> Between the living and the dead.

5-6] Cf. Hallam, 'Sonnets written after my return from Somersby', I (to Emily Tennyson):

> Come to me in my sleep and comfort me;
>   But let the dream that wafts upon my sense . . .
>   With no false tone perplex the holy trance
> Oh let him bring thyself, a perfect thee! . . .
> No shadowy form, no fleeting countenance.
>   (in *Some Unpublished Poems*)

9 *sightless*] 'invisible'. Cf. *Macbeth*: 'sightless substances', 'the sightless couriers of the air' (I v 50, I vii 23).

10] H.T. compares *Comus*, 11: 'Among the enthroned gods on sainted seats'. Other references to Hallam as joining the assembly of noble spirits in the afterlife are given in note *61*.3-4.

12 *tenfold-complicated*] Cf. *98*.13 (L.MS): 'In tenfold frequence'. H.T. refers 'tenfold' to 'the ten heavens of Dante', *Paradiso*, XXVIII 15 ff.

94. The idea of the section alludes to the old notion that by spiritual purification and pacification one can attain to communion with the spirit world. T. wrote 'Not known to me' alongside Collins's remark in *Cornhill* (p. 43): 'The whole of this piece is little else than a translation of the noble passage about the mood in which man is fitted for communion with his God in Jeremy Taylor's Fifth Golden Grove Sermon.'

3-4] Cf. *The Duchess of Malfi*, IV ii 20-1: 'O that it were possible we might / But hold some two days' conference with the dead' (G.G. Loane, *Notes and Queries*, CLXXIX (1940), 275). Cf. 'On Sublimity' 67: 'For thou dost hold communion with the dead'; Hallam, 'Who has not dreamt', 3-4: 'spirits that but seem / To hold communion with the dead' (Ricks).

5 *thou*] The reader.

9-12] T. remarked to Knowles: 'I figure myself in this rather'. In *Eversley* he comments: 'This was what I felt'.

11-12] Ruskin described these lines as 'The image of the state of a perfect Human Spirit' (*The Harbours of England*, Ch. XII, in *Cook and Wedderburn*, XIII 76).

13-16] With this metaphor cf. Herbert, 'The Family', I 13: 'What doth this noise of thoughts within my heart', 'Humble Obedience neare the doore doth stand'; Cowper, 'The House of Prayer', 1-4, 13-16:

> Thy mansion is the Christian's heart
> O Lord, thy dwelling place secure!
> Bid the unruly throng depart
> And leave the consecrated door . . .
>
> I know them all and hate their din;
> Am weary of the bustling crowd;
> But while their voice is heard within
> I cannot serve them as I would.

16] Cf. *Paradise Lost*, X 108: 'household peace confound'.

95. *Dating*: The section was possibly composed in 1841-2, for T. described to friends in August 1841 (or 1842) the same scene depicted in *95*. Dean Stanley recorded his memories of the occasion:

I was greatly struck by his describing to us on one singularly still starlit evening, how he and his friends had once sat out far into the night having tea at a table on the lawn beneath the stars, and that the candles had burned with steady upright flame, disturbed from time to time by the inrush of a moth or cockchafer, as tho' in a closed room. I do not know whether he had already written, or was perhaps even then shaping, the lines in *In Memoriam*, which so many years afterwards brought back to me the incident.

(Memoir, I 205)

T. described his experience of trances:

A kind of waking trance I have frequently had, quite up from boyhood, when I have been all alone. This has generally come upon me thro' repeating my own name two or three times to myself silently, till all at once, as it were out of the intensity of the consciousness of individuality, the individuality itself seemed to dissolve and fade away into boundless being, and this not a confused state, but the clearest of the clearest, the surest of the surest, the wierdest of the wierdest, utterly beyond words, where death was an almost laughable impossibility, the loss of personality (if so it were) seeming no extinction but the only true life. This might . . . be the state which St Paul describes, 'Whether in the body I cannot tell, or whether out of the body I cannot tell.'   (*Eversley*, III 217) See also *Memoir*, II 473-4. Trance experiences are described in several early poems: 'Armageddon', 'Timbuctoo', 'The Mystic', 'The Poet', 'The Two Voices', 'To − [As when with downcast eyes]', and also in 'The Ancient Sage'.

1] T. commented to Knowles: 'This happened in my native place.' The scene is Somersby, as in *89* when Hallam was present.

7] T. comments: 'It was a marvellously still night, and I asked my brother Charles to listen to the brook, which he had never heard so far off before.'

9-12] Ricks compares Shelley, *Unfinished Drama*, 236-8:

> And on it little quaint and filmy shapes,
> With dizzy motion, wheel and rise and fall,
> Like clouds of gnats with perfect lineaments.

Also cf. Charles Tennyson, *Sonnets and Fugitive Pieces* (Cambridge, 1830), Sonnet XI:

> The bat is circling softly by my door,
> And silent as the snow-flake leaves his lair,
> In the dank twilight flitting here and there,
> Wheeling the self-same circuit o'er and o'er.

11-12] Gatty applied these lines to the bats. T. deleted 'bats' and wrote alongside: 'moths. The moth I mean has a white cape. I don't know the name of it. How can bats have *ermine* capes?' T. notes in *Eversley*: 'the ermine or the puss-moth'.

15-20] The lines recall Gray, 'Elegy Written in a Country Churchyard', 1-6.

22 *that glad year*] The whole period of their friendship; cf. *22*.8: 'glad at heart from May to May'.

24] Most of Hallam's letters to T. were destroyed by H.T.

25-8] Shepherd compares Shakespeare, *Sonnets*, CXXIII (note 'change', 'strange', 'defy'):

> No, Time, thou shalt not boast that I do change:
> Thy pyramids built up with newer might
> To me are nothing novel, nothing strange . . .
> Thy registers and thee I both defy.
> (1-3, 9)

29-32] This is very like the remarks of James Spedding on Hallam (*Remains*, xxii):

His chief pleasure and strength lay certainly in metaphysical analysis ... And I never knew him decline a metaphysical discussion. He would always pursue the argument eagerly to the end, and follow his antagonist into the most difficult places.

31-2] Ricks compares Gray's translation of Tasso, *Gerusalemme Liberata*, XIV 32:

down the steep he led ...
Through subterraneous passages they went,
Earth's inmost cells, and caves of deep descent.

and also Shelley, *The Cenci*, V ii 163: 'the heart's inmost cell'; 'Epipsychidion', 568-9: 'the wells / Which boil under our being's inmost cells'.

33] A reminiscence of Isaiah 28:13: 'But the word of the Lord was unto them precept upon precept, precept upon precept; line upon line, line upon line' (Ricks).

36-7 *The living soul ... mine in this*] T. commented to Knowles: '*The Living Soul*, perchance the Deity — the first reading was His living Soul was flash'd on mine — but my conscience was troubled by 'his'. I've often had a strange feeling of being wound and wrapped in the Great Soul.' H.T. adds: 'With reference to the later reading, my father would say: "Of course the greater Soul may include the less." He preferred, however, for fear of giving a wrong impression, the vaguer and more abstract later reading.' For other revisions which depersonalize, see pp. 25-6.

39 *that which is*] An expression in Greek philosophy for the supreme Truth of things: τι τῶν ὄντων. T. used the expression in writing of free-will:

Man's Free-will is but a bird in a cage; he can stop at the lower perch, or he can mount to a higher. Then that which is and knows will enlarge his cage, give him a higher and higher perch, and at last break off the top of his cage, and let him out to be one with the Free-will of the Universe.   (*Memoir*, I 318-19)

Hallam used the expression in 'Sonnets written after my return from Somersby', VIII 8:

glimpses of a law
Which IS in that it IS, dim seen on earth
Because to few revealed thro' sight or sound.
(in *Some Unpublished Poems*)

T. referred to the idea in a comment in 1869: 'Yes, it is true that there are moments when the flesh is nothing to me, when I feel and know the flesh to be the vision, God and the Spiritual the only real and true. Depend upon it, the Spiritual *is* the real' (*Memoir*, II 90).

40] Incorporated, as Ricks observes, from 'An Idle Rhyme', 39-40:

> I cool my face in flowers, and hear
> The deep pulsations of the world.

Also cf. 'Armageddon', IV 29-31:

> An indefinable pulsation
> Inaudible to outward sense, but felt
> Thro' the deep heart of every living thing.

41-2] Cf. *The Princess*, VI 40 (H.Nbk.25): 'With music in the Aonian breeze of time'.

42-3] Cf. Milton, 'On Time', 22: 'Triumphing over Death, and Chance, and thee O Time' (Bradley).

43-4] T. comments: 'The trance came to an end in a moment of critical doubt, but the doubt was dispelled by the glory of the dawn of the *boundless day*.'

45-8] This seems to be, as Collins suggests, a reminiscence of Dante, *Paradiso*:

> Nel ciel . . .
> Fu' io, e vidi cose che ridire
> Nè sa nè può qual di là su discende:
> Perchè appressando sè al suo disire,
> Nostro intelletto si profonda tanto,
> Che retro la memoria non può ire.
> (I 4-9)

> (In heaven . . .
> was I,
> Witness of things, which, to relate again,
> Surpasseth power of him who comes from thence;
> For that, so near approaching its desire,
> Our intellect is to such depth absorb'd,
> That memory cannot follow.)

> Da quinci innanzi il mio veder fu maggio
> Che 'l parlar nostro, ch'a tal vista cede,
> E cede la memoria a tanto oltraggio.
> (XXXIII 55-7)

> (Thenceforward, what I saw,
> Was not for words to speak, nor memory's self
> To stand against such outrage on her skill.)

Cf. also 'The Two Voices', 379–84:

> 'Moreover, something is or seems,
> That touches me with mystic gleams,
> Like glimpses of forgotten dreams –
>
> 'Of something felt, like something here;
> Of something done, I know not where;
> Such as no language may declare.'

54–5] Adapted from 'In deep and solemn dreams' 47–8: 'And the sweet winds tremble o'er / The large leaves of the sycamore' (noticed by Charles Tennyson, *Nineteenth Century*, CIX (1931), 279).

63 *dim lights*] Cf. Pope, 'Elegy to the Memory of an Unfortunate Lady', 19: 'Dim lights of life'.

96. *Dating*: This section precedes *97* in H.Nbk.19. That neither section is in T.MS, L.MS, or **Trial** may indicate that they were composed after 1848 (the terminal date of L.MS), and perhaps as late as between March and May 1850.

The spiritual crisis which Hallam experienced is described by James Spedding:

> Perhaps I ought to mention that when I first knew him he was subject to occasional fits of mental depression, which gradually grew fewer and fainter, and had at length I thought disappeared, or merged in a peaceful Christian faith. I have witnessed the same in other ardent and adventurous minds, and have always looked upon them as the symptom indeed of an imperfect moral state, but one to which the finest spirits, during the process of their purification, are most subject.
>
> (*Remains*, xxv)

T. refers to it in *He was too good* . . . (Add. Poem viii) 1–4.

Hallam's spiritual crisis and the depression which resulted are recurrent subjects in his own poems and in his letters; for example:

> When barren doubt like a late coming snow
> Made an unkind December of my spring . . .
> Then the remembrance of thy gentle faith,
> Mother beloved, would steal upon my heart;
> Fond feeling saved me from that utter scathe . . .
> ('To My Mother', 1–2, 5–7)

> He had left us to murmur on awhile
> And question still most fruitlessly this pile
> Of natural shews: What life is? Why man weeps?
> Why sins? – and whither when the awful veil
> Floats on to him he sinks from earthly sight?

> Some are who never grow a whit more pale
> For thinking on the general mystery,
> Ground of all being; yet may I rather be
> Of those who know and feel that it is Night.
>> ('Then what is Life?', 6-14)

> the cloudy mass
> That long had dwarfed my soul — thoughts without aim,
> Yet morbidly alive — hopes, fears, that pass
> No right ordeal of reason —
>> ('A Farewell to the South', 113-16)

Other examples include: 'Lines Written in Great Depression of Mind'; 'A Meeting and a Farewell'; and ['A Melancholy Thought']. Hallam wrote to T. (July 1831) of how he had found comfort in religion: 'I have derived lately much consolation and hope from religious feelings. Struggle as we may Christianity draws us all within its magic circle at last'. (TRC)

1-4] This recalls the contrast between the simple faith of women and the scepticism of educated men which is the subject of *33*. The stanza may be understood to refer to Emily Sellwood.

11] This is apparently a reminiscence of Bailey, *Festus*:

> *Festus.* Thus must I doubt — perpetually doubt.
> *Lucifer.* Who never doubted never half believed.
>> Where doubt there truth is — 'tis her shadow.

This passage, as Ricks observes, was marked by T. in his copy of *Festus* (2nd edition, 1845; 63).

18-19] Motter compares Hallam's poem 'Then what is Life?' (quoted in headnote) 13-14.

21-4] T. compares Exodus 19:16:
> And it came to pass on the third day, in the morning, that there were thunders and lightenings, and a thick cloud upon the mount, and the voice of the trumpet exceeding loud.

97. *Dating*: 1848-50? for the reasons given in headnote *96*.

T. remarked to Knowles: 'A running comment on life. The soul left behind is only acquainted with the narrow circle of the old house — thus resembling a wife married to a mighty man of Science.' T. wrote in his copy of Gatty, 'The relation of one on earth to one in the other and higher world. Not my relation to him *here*. He looked up to *me* as I looked up to him.'

The metaphor recalls *60* and *62*.5-8. See also *9*.18 and note.

1-4] The notion of pantheistical survival is elaborated in *129* and *130*.

1] Cf. Wordsworth, 'A slumber did my spirit seal', 7-8: 'Roll'd round in earth's diurnal course / With rocks and stones and trees.'

2-3] T. comments: 'Like the spectre of the Brocken'. The phenomenon is alluded to by Coleridge in 'Constancy to an Ideal Object', 26-32:

> The woodman winding westward up the glen
> At wintry dawn, where o'er the sheep-track's maze
> The viewless snow-mist weaves a glist'ning haze,
> Sees full before him, gliding without tread,
> An image with a glory round its head;
> The enamoured rustic worships its fair hues,
> Nor knows he makes the shadow he pursues!

One of the places in which T. might have read about the spectre is in his copy of *Hundred Wonders of the World* (pp. 434-7), and he surely would have remembered the detailed description of the phenomenon given in Scott, *The Antiquary*, XVIII. T. refers to the spectre in the early poem, 'On Sublimity', 94: 'The shadowy Colossus of the mountain'.

5] Cf. the isolated line in H.Nbk.a: 'Long-married souls, dear friend, are we'.

29-32] T. remarked to Knowles: 'Just as the poor gift of Poesy is exercised because he loved it.'

31-2] T. commented to Knowles: 'of earth' (31), 'of Heaven' (32).

33] The final reading reverts to H.Nbk.b.

34] Cf. Pope, *Essay on Man*, II 4: 'A being darkly wise, and rudely great' (Ricks).

98. This section refers to the wedding tour of Charles and Louisa Tennyson, who were married 24 May 1836. T. was present at the wedding and escorted into church the bride's sister, Emily Sellwood (*Memoir*, I 148).

1] T. comments: '"You" is imaginary.' This is contradicted, of course, by *Memoir*, I 148.

2-4] T. and Hallam toured the Rhine in July 1832. Hallam described the journey in a letter to Emily Tennyson (*Memoir*, I 87-8).

6 *That City*] H.T. writes: 'To *that* city my father would never go, and he gave me a most emphatic "no" when I once proposed a tour there with him' (*Memoir*, I 149). See 11-12.

17 *Gnarr*] 'Snarl' (T.). Bradley compares *The Faerie Queene*, I v 34 (of Cerberus): 'felly gnarre'.

20-32] Hallam wrote to T. and his sister, Emily, from Vienna on 6 September 1833:

> The squares & streets here are wide & well built. Everything wears an appearance of gaiety & liveliness. Altogether I should say Vienna resembles Paris but is more uniformly handsome . . . We have seen the Imperial Palace which is not worth much . . . There is a collection of curiosities at Schonbrunn, the Imperial country house . . . This is the dull time of the year; the Prater, the great public drive, is perfectly empty, and I never saw a more insipid place, worse even that the Corso at Milan or the Cascine at Florence, which I used to think the most stupid drives possible. The pictures of course are the great thing at Vienna . . .
>
> (Letter in TRC; excerpts are quoted in *Memoir*, I 104)

24-5] *under brown / Of lustier leaves*] Cf. the usage in Milton; for example, 'Il Penseroso', 133-4: 'arched walks of twilight groves, / And shadows brown'.

26] With the L.MS reading, 'Sits on the foreheads', cf. *114.5*.

32] In L.MS the final stanza, 29-32, is followed by a short dash, T.'s customary way of concluding a section or of setting off one section from the next. But the dash was deleted and another stanza added.

32 b-d] Ricks observes that Hallam refers to 'the mighty Florentine' at the close of his 'Oration on the Influence of Italian Works of Imagination on the Same Class of Compositions in England'. The quotation alludes to *Purgatorio*, XI 91: 'O vana gloria dell' umane posse!' (O empty glory of human powers!).

99. L.MS has two drafts. The first (L.MSa) comes between *85* and *86* but is deleted. The second (L.MSb) comes between *98* and *100*. This suggests that T. originally deleted the section from the sequence but decided to reinstate it upon inserting, in L.MSb, an additional stanza (5-8), and revising 9-10.

1] The second anniversary of the death of Hallam. The line repeats the opening of *72*, which commemorates the first anniversary.

5-10] The stanza added in L.MSb and the revisions in 9-10 add a description of features of the Somersby landscape which were associated with Hallam in *89* and *95*. This prepares for *100-2*.

8] For the contrasting idea, cf. *104*.12 (of High Beech): 'But all is new unhallow'd ground'.

10 *the coming care*] H.T. comments: 'the hardship of winter'. The image is suggested by L.MSa: 'a world of care'.

13 *balmy breath*] Cf. *Othello*, V 2 16-17: 'Ah, balmy breath, that dost almost persuade / Justice to break her sword!'.

18] Cf. Marlowe, *Dr Faustus*, I i: 'All things that move between the quiet poles' (Bradley). T. comments: 'The ends of the axis of the earth, which move so slowly that they seem not to move, but slumber.'

100-103. This group is written as if composed while the Tennysons were living at Somersby. They moved into their new home at High Beech, Epping Forest in October 1837 (letter from Cecilia Tennyson to Susan Haddelsey in TRC). Perhaps *100* and *101*, which are not in T.MS, were composed in order to prepare for *102*.

Departure from Somersby is the theme of two other poems, 'Home' (composed 1828), presumably occasioned by T.'s leaving Somersby for Cambridge, and 'A Farewell' (published 1842) on the family's departure in 1837.

100. The section is in the tradition of the 'prospect poem', an earlier example of which is *11*.

1-4] Cf. Hallam, 'On My Sister's Birth-Day', IX:

> Here fortune, fancifully kind,
> Has led me to a lovely spot,
> Where not a tree or rock I find,
> My sister, that recalls thee not!

5 *gray old grange*] The house adjacent to Somersby Rectory known as 'Baumber's Farm', a picturesque manor house with castellated brick walls which is believed to have been designed by Vanbrugh. H.T. records that the house was called by some the 'Moated Grange' (the property does in fact have a moat with an island), but T. denied that Baumber's Farm was the original for the home of Mariana (*Memoir*, I 4).

13 *the rock*] T. comments: 'The rock in Holywell, which is a wooded ravine, commonly called there "The Glen".'

101.

11 *the lesser wain*] The constellation of *ursa minor* of which the pole-star appears as the axis.
.H.T. comments:
My father would often spend his nights wandering about the wolds, gazing at the stars. Edward FitzGerald writes: 'Like Wordsworth on the mountains, Alfred too, when a lad abroad on the wold, sometimes of a night with the shepherd, watched not only the flock on the greensward, but also "the fleecy star that bears / Andromeda far off Atlantic seas"'.

21-2] Cf. 'Tithon', 3: 'Man comes and tills the earth and lies beneath'.

23-4] With the idea, cf. Job 7:10: 'He shall return no more to his house, neither shall his place know him any more', a passage which is alluded to in 'The Two Voices', 264: 'The place he knew forgetteth him'.

102. *Dating*: 1839? T. described the sentiments here to Emily Sellwood in a letter in 1839:

Dim mystic sympathies with tree and hill reaching far back into childhood. A known landskip is to me an old friend, that continually talks to me of my own youth and half-forgotten things, and indeed does more for me than many an old friend that I know.

(*Memoir*, I 172)

This might suggest that he composed *102* at this time.

4] The Tennysons' move was caused by the desire of the patron of the living and the incumbent to take over the Rectory where the Tennysons had been allowed to remain after the death of Dr Tennyson in 1831.

7-8] Gatty identified the spirits as 'Dr Tennyson and Arthur Hallam'. T. crossed out 'Dr Tennyson' and wrote alongside: 'no. the first is the love of the native place "pure and simple". the 2nd the same love enhanced by the memory of the friend' (a version of this comment appears in later editions of Gatty and in *Eversley*). Cf. Shakespeare, *Sonnets*, CXLIV 1-2: 'Two loves I have of comfort and despair, / Which like two spirits do suggest me still'.

12] Cf. *The Princess*, I 93: 'dewy-tassell'd trees'.

19] Bradley compares Shelley, *Queen Mab*, III 172-3: 'mutual foes, for ever play / A losing game into each other's hands'.

21-2] These lines recall Virgil, *Eclogues*, I 3: 'Nos patriae fines, et dulcia linguimus arva' (We are leaving our country's bounds and sweet fields), (Bradley); and *Paradise Lost*, IX 448: 'the pleasant Villages and Farms' (Ricks).

23 *They*] the two spirits.

103. The draft of this section in L.MS appears to have been added later than *100-2*.

6 *maidens*] T. remarked to Knowles: 'All the human powers and talents that do not pass with life but go along with it'. His note in *Eversley* reads: 'They are the Muses, poetry, arts — all that made life beautiful here, which we hope will pass with us beyond the grave'. Corrected proofs of the notes (TRC) show that H.T. deleted 'human powers, talents, and hopes' and substituted for these 'poetry'.

7 *hidden summits*] T. remarked to Knowles: 'The high — the divine — the origin of life'.

8] Cf. Virgil, *Georgics*, II 157: 'fluminaque antiquos subterlabentia muros' (and the streams that glide beneath those ancient walls), (Bradley).

river] 'Life' (T.)

14-15] Cf. *60*.2; *61*.11.

16] T. glossed 'the sea' 'eternity'.

17-40] Cf. the final stanza of 'Adonais':

> my spirit's bark is driven
> Far from the shore, far from the trembling throng
> Whose sails were never to the tempest given;
> The massy earth and sphered skies are riven!
> I am borne darkly, fearfully, afar;
> Whilst burning through the inmost veil of Heaven,
> The soul of Adonais, like a star,
> Beacons from the abode where the Eternal are.

19-20] Such little boats are common (and symbolic) in Shelley. Cf. for example, 'Alastor', 299: 'A little shallop floating near the shore'.

25-8] T. explained to Knowles: 'The great progress of the age as well as the opening of another world'.

27] Cf. *131*.9 (H.Nbk.18, first reading): 'With ever growing strength and grace'.

31] Cf. Deuteronomy 2:10: 'a people great, and many, and tall, as the Anakim'; 'A Fragment', 20: 'the strong and sunborn Anakim'; *The Princess*, VII 266: 'Nor lose the wrestling thews that throw the world'.

33-6] T. explained to Knowles: 'All the great hopes of Science and men'. The stanza introduces an idea which is of great importance in the rest of the sequence.

40] Cf. *17*.14 (Hn.Nbk.): 'Thee moving swift thy burnisht sides'.

41-3] That the ghosts of the dead are larger than mortals is an ancient idea; for example, cf. Ovid, *Fasti*, II 503-4:

> pulcher et humano maior trabeaque decorus
> Romulus in media visus adesse via.

(It seemed to him that Romulus, fair of aspect, in stature more than human, and clad in a goodly robe, stood there in the middle of the road.)
Cf. 'Hark! the dogs howl!', 20-1:

> Larger than human passes by
> The shadow of the man I loved.

T. alluded to the idea in his unfinished essay on Ghosts: 'Forth issue from the inmost gloom the colossal Presences of the Past majores humano, some as they lived, seemingly pale with exhaustion and faintly smiling; some as they died in a still agony.' (From the fragment in Houghton Library, Harvard University MS Eng 952 (7), as noticed by Jerome Hamilton Buckley, *Tennyson, the Growth of a Poet* (Cambridge, Mass., 1960), 33.)

43-4] Cf. the poet's imaginary reunion as Hallam embarks from a ship in *14*.

44] Cf. for example, Genesis 33:4: 'Esau fell on his neck and kissed him'; 45:14: 'Joseph fell on Benjamin's neck and wept'.

45-8] T. remarked to Knowles: 'He was wrong to drop his earthly hopes and powers — they will be still of use to him'.

104-106. These sections describe the third Christmas referred to in *I.M.* The first Christmas is described in *28-30* and the second in *78*. *104* and *105* were presumably not written before late 1837 in that they refer to Christmas 1837, the first Christmas the Tennysons spent in their new home at High Beech, Epping Forest, and the fifth after Hallam's death.

104.

3-5] T. comments: 'Waltham Abbey church'.

12] T. comments: 'High Beech, Epping Forest (where we were living)'.

105.

1-2] T.'s gloss in his copy of Gatty supplies the reason for the revision in **1863**. Gatty quoted the **Trial-1862** reading in a footnote. T. underlined 'eave' in 'cottage-eave' and wrote alongside: 'There is no such word as "eave" in the language. EFES is the Anglo Saxon word.' ('Eave' is a back-formation from 'eaves', treated as plural.) In the copy of **Trial** (Beinecke, Tinker 2065) sent him by T., de Vere had pointed out the repetition of '-eave' (1) and 'eve' (4).

5-6] Dr Tennyson is buried in the churchyard at Somersby.

23-5] T. comments: 'the scintillating motion of the stars that rise'.

26] Cf. Epilogue, 135-6; 'The Progress of Spring', 113-14: 'Thy warmth from bud to bud / Accomplish that blind model in the seed'.

106. *Dating*: November 1846 or later, for the following reason: The section is based on a passage in P.J. Bailey's *Festus* (1839) (as noticed by Hoxie N. Fairchild, '"Wild Bells" in Bailey's *Festus* ?', *Modern Language*

Notes, LXIV (1949), 256-8). T. wrote to his publisher on 5 November 1846 to ask for a copy of the new edition (much revised and enlarged): 'and get "Festus" from Pickering for me: I want to read it' (*Materials*, I 319). Moxon apparently sent the copy of the second edition (1845) which is now in TRC. T. wrote to FitzGerald on 12 November: 'I have just got *Festus*; order it and read. You will most likely find it a great bore, but there are really *very grand* things in Festus' (*Memoir*, I 234).

The passage from *Festus* on which *106* is modelled is quoted here from the second edition, pp. 75-82 (line numbers added).

> The bells of time are ringing changes fast.
> Grant, Lord! that each fresh peal may usher in
> An era of advancement, that each change
> Prove an effectual, lasting, happy gain.
> And we beseech Thee, overrule, oh God!   5
> All civil contests to the good of all;
> All party and religious difference
> To honourable ends . . .
>   and let all strife, political
> Or social, spring from conscientious aims,   10
> And have a generous self-ennobling end,
> Man's good and Thine own glory in view always! . . .
>   We entreat Thee
> In Thy great mercy to decrease our wants,
> And add autumnal increase to the comforts   15
> Which tend to keep men innocent . . .
>   that the mass,
> The millions in all nations may be trained,
> From their youth upwards, in a nobler mode,
> To loftier and more liberal ends . . .   20
>   Oh that the Son
> Might come again! There should be no more war,
> No more want, no more sickness; with a touch,
> He should cure all disease, and with a word,
> All sin . . .   25
> May peace and industry and commerce weld
> Into one land all nations of the world . . .
> Oh! may all help each other in good things,
> Mentally, morally, and bodily! . . .
>   But we pray   30
> That all mankind may make one brotherhood,
> And love and serve each other; that all wars
> And feuds die out of nations . . .
>   the great world shall be at last,
> The mercy-seat of God, the heritage   35
> Of Christ, and the possession of the Spirit . . .
> Its ruler God, its practice righteousness,
> Its life peace!

T. explained one of the meanings of the section by reference to 'Akbar's Dream' (*Memoir*, I 326): 'when Christianity without bigotry will triumph, when the controversies of creeds shall have vanished, and

> Shall bear false witness, each of each, no more,
> But find their limits by that larger light,
> And overstep them, moving easily
> Thro' after-ages in the Love of Truth,
> The truth of Love.'
>
> (93–7)

18] H.T. explains the idea: 'My father expressed his conviction that "Christianity with its divine Morality but without the central figure of Christ, the Son of Man, would become cold, and that it is fatal for religion to lose its warmth' (*Memoir*, I 325–6).

19 *mournful rhymes*] One of the possible interpretations of ἐλεγεία (see p. 26).

32] T. comments: 'The broader Christianity of the future'. On another occasion he remarked that 'the forms of Christian religion would alter; but . . . the spirit of Christ would still grow from more to more "in the roll of the ages"' (*Memoir*, I 326).

107. In L.MS *107* comes between *83* and *84*. This suggests that it was once intended to form part of another group of sections. With *83*, it has in common the time of year and a preoccupation with the season. The anticipation of the blossoming of flowers in *83* prepares for the reference to the absence of flowers in *107*. With *84*, it has in common diction ('crescent', 'iron'), imagery ('A central warmth', 'a solid core of heat'), and a domestic interior scene. That *107* may have been originally intended to come earlier in the sequence would account for the impression that the setting is Somersby. In its location in the published sequence, *107* ought strictly to be set in Epping Forest. The present location of the section does accord, however, with the internal chronology of the sequence in respect to the season: it is set in February and so follows from *106*.

The section is a type of *genethliakon*, or birthday ode. A characteristic of the genre is that the celebrations described are appropriate to the person being honoured. The celebrations described in lines 19–24 are appropriate to Hallam's character.

The section is modelled, Bradley observes, on Horace, *Odes*, I ix, and on Alcaeus *fr.* 135 on which the ode is based:

> κάββαλλε τὸν χείμων', ἐπὶ μὲν τίθεις
> πῦρ, ἐν δὲ πίρναις οἶνον ἀφειδέως
> μέλιχρον.

(Beat down the cold, placing fire upon the hearth, and mixing honey-sweet wine with unsparing hand.)

> Vides ut alta stet nive candidum
> Soracte, nec iam sustineant onus
> silvae laborantes, geluque
> flumina constiterint acuto?
>
> dissolve frigus ligna super foco
> large reponens atque benignius
> deprome quadrimum Sabina,
> o Thaliarche, merum diota.
>
> permitte divis cetera, qui simul
> stravere ventos aequore fervido
> deproeliantes, nec cupressi
> nec veteres agitantur orni.
> (I ix 1-12)

(Seest thou how Soracte stands glistening in its mantle of snow, and how the straining woods no longer uphold their burden, and the streams are frozen with the biting cold? Dispel the chill by piling high the wood upon the hearth, and right-generously bring forth in Sabine jar the wine four winters old, O Thaliarchus! Leave to the gods all else; for so soon as they have stilled the winds battling on the seething deep, the cypresses and ancient ash-trees are no longer shaken.)

1] 1 February 1811, in Bedford Place, London.

9 *brakes*] T. glossed this 'bushes' in his copy of Gatty.

11 *grides*] 'Grates' (T.). The world originally meant 'pierce'. Now the usual meaning is 'to scrape or graze with a grating sound', as in T.'s early poem 'Chorus', 13: 'The heavy thunder's griding might'. Bradley suggests the influence of Shelley, *Prometheus Unbound*, III i 47-8: 'Hear ye the thunder of the fiery wheels / Griding the wind?'. Ricks comments: 'The word "iron" suggests Wordsworth, 'Guilt and Sorrow' 492-3, where however the sense follows that in Milton, "piercing": "Through his brain / At once the griding iron passage found".'

13 *drifts*] Gatty explains: 'drifts of snow which falling into water immediately blacken before they dissolve'. This is the source of H.T.'s note in *Eversley*.

23 *whate'er he be*] See note *41.5*.

108. The section originally intended to prepare for *109-14* was *Young is the grief I entertain* (Add. Poem iii), which *Memoir* and *Eversley* describe as 'originally No. CVIII'.

T. explains:

Grief shall not make me a hermit, and I will not indulge in vacant yearnings and barren aspirations; it is useless trying to find him in the other worlds — I find nothing but the reflections of myself; I had better learn the lesson that sorrow teaches.

1] Cf. *85*.57–120, in which the poet seeks another friendship and is encouraged to do so by the voice of Hallam.

3] Mustard compares *Iliad*, VI 203, *Aeneid*, XII 801, and Horace, *Epistles*, I 2 239. Ricks compares *Faerie Queene*, I ii 6, where the Red Cross Knight 'could not rest, but did his stout heart eat'.

5–8] A reminiscence, as Ricks notes, of Romans 10:6–7: 'But the righteousness which is of faith speaketh on this wise, Say not in thine heart, Who shall ascend into heaven? (that is, to bring Christ down from above:) Or, Who, shall descend into the deep? (that is, to bring up Christ again from the dead.)'

7] Cf. 'Œnone' (following 131 in 1832 text): 'The highest height and topmost strength of power' (Ricks).

11–12] Bradley compares Shelley, *Alastor*, 469–74:

> Hither the poet came. His eyes beheld
> Their own wan light through the reflected lines
> Of his thin hair, distinct in the dark depth
> Of that still fountain; as the human heart,
> Gazing in dreams over the gloomy grave,
> Sees its own treacherous likeness there.

16] This prepares for the poet's preoccupation with 'wisdom' in *109–14*.

109.

1–4] The list of Hallam's virtues carries on from *Young is the grief I entertain*.

2 *household fountains*] 'Springing from within', 'original' (Bradley).

3] Spedding wrote of Hallam: 'I have met with . . . no man his equal as a philosophical critic on works of taste', and Gladstone recorded: 'As a critic there was no one upon whose taste and judgment I had so great a reliance. I never was sure that I thoroughly understood or appreciated any poem till I had discussed it with him'. Hallam gave advice to T. on his recently composed poems (for example, cf. Hallam's comments in *Memoir*, I 88–90) and was considered T.'s literary adviser. On his death his place was taken by Spedding (*Materials*, I 117).

11–12] Hallam fell in love with Anna Wintour in Italy in 1827 when he was sixteen. She was the subject of his early love poems, notably 'To One Early Loved, Now in India'. At Christmas 1829, he met and fell in love with Tennyson's sister Emily, to whom he later became betrothed.

15-16] Cf. 'Hail Briton', 19: 'that unstable Celtic blood'. T.'s prejudice is several times recorded by Allingham, for example: 'T. rages against the Fenians — "Kelts are all mad furious fools!"' (*Diary*, 167).

17] This is a recurrent idea in T.; for example:

> Yet in the long years liker must they grow;
> The man be more of woman, she of man.
> He gain in sweetness and in moral height,
> Nor lose the wrestling thews that throw the world.
> (*The Princess*, VII 263-6)

T. spoke of '"the man-woman" in Christ, the union of tenderness and strength' (*Memoir*, I 326). Hallam's 'graceful and manly form' are remarked upon by his father (*Remains*, xxxv).

24 Nor] T. comments: 'If I do not . . .'.

110.

13] Cf. *103*.29: 'And I myself, who sat apart'. On the application of 'dearest' to Hallam, see note *74*.5.

20] Adapted from *Young is the grief I entertain* (Add. Poem iii), 6: 'She spurs an imitative will'.

111.

3] T. revised this line apparently in response to criticism by Aubrey de Vere, who made a marginal mark against it in the copy of **Trial**(Beinecke, Tinker 2065) sent him by T.

19 *Drew in*] 'Contracted, narrowed' (H.T.).

21-4] That T. should allude to a popular song title which had become a cliché led a contemporary critic (T.'s brother-in-law, Franklin Lushington) to condemn this stanza in an anonymous review in *Tait's Edinburgh Magazine*, August 1850:

> There are one or two of the poems from which we should like to cut off the final stanza. The 'grand old name of gentleman' . . . has not only been 'defamed by every charlatan', and 'soiled with all ignoble use' of theatrical and other parodies of the original 'good old song', but has even crossed the seas, and naturalised itself in Paris as *un vrai gentleman*, till, we fear, nothing can be done to retrieve its character.

22 *charlatan*] T. comments: 'From Ital. *ciarlatano*, a mountebank;

hence the accent on the last syllable'.

112. The idea of the section, particularly 1–8, would seem to be obscure but for T.'s glosses and the summary provided by H.T. Generally the early commentators either evaded interpreting the section (for example, Beeching, Genung, Robertson), or misinterpreted it (Bradley, Collins). The only interpretation which is in accord with the notes of T. and H.T. is the one given by Miss Chapman. She observes that the poet is chided by 'High wisdom'

> for a seeming blindness to any lesser merit than the surpassing merit of [his friend]. But all his field of vision is occupied by his image. It was so while he lived. To watch the development of such a character, so rich and fertile, yet so well governed, was a task all absorbing, excluding every other.

1–4] H.T. comments: '*High wisdom* is ironical. "High wisdom" has been twitting the poet that although he gazes with calm and indulgent eyes on unaccomplished greatness, yet he makes light of narrower natures more perfect in their own small way.' For T. as the source of the remark about irony, see note 5–8.

3 *glorious insufficiencies*] T. explains: 'Unaccomplished greatness such as Arthur Hallam's'.

4] Cf. Hallam, 'Timbuctoo', 117–18: 'In the Eternal Reason's perfectness, / To our deject and most imbased eye' (Ricks).

5–8] T. revised the first reading in T.MS in response to criticism by Spedding who noted below the draft that he did not understand which 'wisdom' was speaking in the original stanza: he supposed it was 'High wisdom'. Above this last comment T. wrote: 'in an ironic sense'. Spedding's comment on 'the lesser' has been cut out by H.T.

5] H.Lpr.101 verbally echoes Marlowe, *The Jew of Malta*, I i 37: 'Infinite riches in a little room'.

8] T. explains: 'Those that have free-will, but less intellect'.

9 *novel power*] Ricks compares Hallam, 'Sonnet', 7: 'What novel power is mine that makes me bold?' (*Some Unpublished Poems*, 9).

14] Ricks compares Hallam, who described himself as one who had 'faced / Himself the tempest, and can prize the calm', in 'Lines for Ellen Hallam', 11–12.

113. The idea is: 'I may grow wise as a result of my sorrow, but you had wisdom in such abundance that it would have benefitted not only myself, but also the entire nation in its coming troubles.'

1-2] Cf. *108*.15-16. Line 2 incorporates *108*.16 (T.MS first reading).

11] Cf. *Paradise Lost*, VII 100: 'Held by thy voice, thy potent voice'.

13-20] Incorporated from two stanzas of 'Hail Briton' in Houghton Library, Harvard University MS Eng 952 (11). The stanzas are inserted in pencil after line 96:

> And licensed boldness gathers force
> Becoming when the time has birth
> A lever to uplift the earth
> And roll in it another course
>
> With many shocks that come and go,
> With agonies with energies
> With overthrowings and with cries
> And undulations to and fro

15-16] An allusion to the famous remark of Archimedes, δός ποῦ στῶ καὶ κόσμον κινήσω (Give me where I may stand and I will move the world) which T. acknowledged as the source of *The Princess*, III 245-7:

> Tho' she perhaps might reap the applause of Great,
> Who learns the one POU STO whence after-hands
> May move the world.

17] An echo of *Hamlet*, III i 62-3: 'The thousand natural shocks / That flesh is heir to'.

18] In L.MS this line appears to have been added to the stanza after 17, 19, and 20 had been written. Cf. 'Youth', 59: 'An energy, an agony'; 'St. Simeon Stylites', 23-4 (MS): 'All agonies, / All energies'; Hallam, 'Timbuctoo', 74-6: 'the energies / Of Guilt, and desolate the poor man's sleep. / Yet not alone for torturing agonies' (Ricks).

114. The philosophical distinction between 'wisdom' and 'knowledge' is drawn by Plato (*Republic*, VI) and by Coleridge (*Aids to Reflection*, Commentary on Aphorism, viii), as is explained by Collins:

> In Plato νοῦς or νόησις is the faculty by which we apprehend the highest objects of knowledge, *real* existence, it is spiritual insight, so is 'reason' in Coleridge. It is the faculty which we derive directly from God ... and this is Tennyson's 'Wisdom'. But διάνοια or 'understanding', is the faculty whereby we apprehend not abstract but physical and sensuous truth; it is concerned with the world of matter, the Platonic ὁρατὸς τόπος, as opposed to the world of essence, νοητὸς τόπος: and this is Tennyson's 'knowledge'.

With the idea, cf. 'Locksley Hall', 141, 143: 'Knowledge comes, but wisdom lingers'; 'Love and Duty', 23-5:

> Wait, and Love himself will bring
> The drooping flower of knowledge changed to fruit
> Of wisdom.

1-4] Incorporated from 'Hail Briton', 133-6. The earliest surviving draft of the poem is in Heath MS, where the stanza is an afterthought written in the margin by T. That passages from 'Hail Briton' were incorporated in *I.M.* was first noticed by Sir Charles Tennyson, *Unpublished Early Poems by Alfred Tennyson* (1931), 74.

3-4 *Who shall fix / Her pillars?*] T. compares Proverbs 9:1: 'Wisdom hath builded her house, she hath hewn out her seven pillars'.

5] Cf. *98*.26 (L.MS reading): 'Sits on the foreheads of the crowd'; *King John*, V ii 176-7: 'in his forehead sits / A bare-ribb'd death'.

12] Pallas sprang from the brain of Zeus.

13 *of Demons?*] In the placement of the mark of interrogation here rather than after 'power' (the position preferred by Bradley), the exclamatory force of the sentence is anticipated. For this kind of stopping as characteristic of Shelley, see *The Complete Poetical Works of Percy Bysshe Shelley*, edited by Neville Rogers (1971-), I xl.

17-20] Cf. *The Princess*, Conclusion 77-9:

> This fine old world of ours is but a child
> Yet in the go-cart. Patience! Give it time
> To learn its limbs: there is a hand that guides.

27-8] Cf. 'Love thou thy land', 17-20:

> Make knowledge circle with the winds;
> But let her herald, Reverence, fly
> Before her to whatever sky
> Bear seed of men and growth of minds.

27 *by year and hour*] Perhaps this was revised in order to avoid repetition with *112*.12: 'In watching thee from hour to hour'.

115-116. These sections describe the last of the three springs which are celebrated in the poem. Section *38* describes the first spring and sections *86* and *88* describe the second spring.

116.

Dating: The fact that no manuscript of *116* survives may be an indication that it was composed after 1848, the presumed terminal date of L.MS.

The section may have been composed after T. had decided to omit *Let Death and Memory keep the face* (Add. Poem vii), which comes

between *117* and *122* in L.MS. Section *116* (like *119*, which seems to
have been composed at the same time) incorporates diction, imagery,
and ideas from the omitted poem. In composing *116* for insertion
between *115* and *117* (L.MS has *115* followed by *117*), T. took care to
relate it in imagery and in thought to both sections. In several lines
(1-2, 4, 5) it refers back to *115*, and the final lines of *116* prepare for
the thought of *117*.

4 *crescent prime*] 'Growing spring' (T.).

117. T.MS shows that *117* was originally part of a group of three
sections on the triumph of Time: f.43ʳ has *Are these the far-famed
Victor Hours* (Add. Poem iv); *128*.9–24, which begins 'Wild Hours that
fly with Hope and Fear'; and *117*. In L.MS *117* is preceded by *118* and
115, respectively. This order is changed in the published sequence so
that *117*, a short, intimate poem about the effects of time on the poet's
personal relationship, serves as an introduction and contrast to *118*, a long
intellectual poem about the effect of time on the earth and mankind.

The idea elaborates the proverb 'Absence sharpens love'. The section
is reminiscent of two Sonnets of Shakespeare:

> O absence, what a torment wouldst thou prove,
> Were it not thy sour leisure gave sweet leave
> To entertain the time with thoughts of love.
> (XXXIX 9–11)

> Let this sad int'rim like the ocean be
> Which parts the shore where two contracted new
> Come daily to the banks, that, when they see
> Return of love, more blest may be the view.
> (LVI 9–12)

1 *O days and hours*] Cf. *123*.4a: 'Like days and hours the cycles fleet'.

10] 'The sun-dial' (T.); Bradley compares Shakespeare, *Sonnets*,
LXXVII 7: 'thy dial's shady stealth'.

11] 'The clock' (T.).

12] Cf. Shakespeare, *Sonnets*, LIX 6: 'five hundred courses of the sun'.

118. The section may be one of those referred to in the statement by
H.T. that the sections of *In Memoriam* about evolution had been read
by T.'s friends 'some years' before the publication of Robert Chambers's
Vestiges of the Natural History of Creation in 1844 (*Memoir*, I 223).
This is not necessarily true, however, of all the sections about evolution.

Here the poet views the progress of the past as an analogue and an
assurance of progress in the future. Collins compares the section with
Browning, *Paracelsus*, V 679-777:

> savage creatures seek
> Their loves in wood and plain – and God renews
> His ancient rapture. Thus he dwells in all,
> From life's minute beginnings, up at last
> To man – the consummation of this scheme
> Of being, the completion of this sphere
> Of life . . .
> Hints and previsions . . .
> Are strewn confusedly everywhere about
> The inferior natures, and all lead up higher,
> All shape out dimly the superior race,
> The heir of hopes too fair to turn out false,
> And man appears at last. So far the seal
> Is put on life; one stage of being complete,
> One scheme wound up . . .
> With apprehension of his passing worth,
> Desire to work his proper nature out,
> And ascertain his rank and final place,
> For these things tend still upward, progress is
> The law of life, man is not Man as yet . . .
> But in completed man begins anew
> A tendency to God. Prognostics told
> Man's near approach; so in man's self arise
> August anticipations, symbols, types
> Of a dim splendour ever on before
> In that eternal circle life pursues.

The passage immediately preceding this one is similar to *115*, which in L.MS follows *118*.

1-4] The idea is: 'Cast your mind back to the origins of the earth, when Time was a youth; but do not imagine that man's spiritual nature is composed of the same transient material which makes up the earth.'

2] Cf. lines deleted in MS from 'The Palace of Art' (quoted in Ricks, 413):

> How the strong Ages had their will,
> A range of Giants breaking down the shore
> And heaving up the hill.

4 *earth and lime*] Alluding to the materialistic analysis of living matter into chemicals and simple compounds (Milton Millhauser, '"Magnetic Mockeries": The Background of a Phrase', *English Language Notes*, V (December 1967), 111).

6 *ampler day*] With this traditional idea of the atmosphere in the spiritual world, Bradley compares *Aeneid*, VI 640: 'Largior hic campos aether' ('Here the air they breathe is freer and more enlarged'), and Wordsworth, 'Laodamia', 105: 'An ampler ether, a diviner air'.

7 *They*] Astronomers and geologists, such as Laplace, Cuvier, and Lyell. That 'They say' might imply T.'s circumspection in dealing with scientific theories is suggested by Potter (pp. 332-3):

> Even the nebular theory, so widely held by astronomers, is described by Princess Ida with a cautious 'If that hypothesis of theirs be sound'.

Tennyson did not consider himself an astronomer, a geologist, or a biologist, but a layman looking on those sciences from the outside and attempting to assimilate their significance.

8-12] These images of the origin and development of the earth conflate the Nebular Hypothesis (8-10) with the theory of catastrophism (11) propounded by the comparative anatomist, Georges Cuvier (1769-1832). Cuvier theorized that whole faunas had disappeared from the earth owing to sudden changes or 'revolutions' on different parts of the earth's surface. These revolutions caused irruptions and retreats of the sea, between long periods of generally tranquil conditions. Though an entire terrestrial fauna might be made extinct by a sudden revolution, a new species could be created by migration of animals from other continents, which had remained undisturbed. Cuvier's work was translated into English by Robert Kerr and edited by Robert Jameson under the title *Essay on the Theory of the Earth* (Edinburgh, 1813). Among the readers of Cuvier was Byron, who refers to the theory of revolutions in *Cain*, II.2 and *Don Juan*, IX. The reference to 'cyclic storms' does not necessarily imply that T. believed in catastrophism. The opposing theory, uniformitarianism, is alluded to in *123*.

9-10] Cf. 'Supposed Confessions of a Second-rate Sensitive Mind', 146-50:
>   as from the storm
> Of running fires and fluid range
> Of lawless airs, at last stood out
> This excellence and solid form
> Of constant beauty.

'The Palace of Art' (a stanza describing 'the results of astronomical experiment' printed in a footnote by T. in the 1832 text):

> Regions of lucid matter taking forms,
>   Brushes of fire, hazy gleams,
> Clusters and beds of worlds, & bee-like swarms
>   Of suns, and starry streams.

The Princess, II 101-4:

> 'This world was once a fluid haze of light,
> Till towards the centre set the starry tides,
> And eddied into suns, that wheeling cast
> The planets; then the monster, then the man.

(T. notes: 'The nebular theory as formulated by Laplace'.)

13 *branch'd*] 'Divided into different races' (Potter). Ricks compares *Vestiges of the Natural History of Creation*: 'It may have only been when a varied climate arose, that the originally few species branched off into the present extensive variety' ('Macleay System of Animated Nature'). The idea also occurs in Lyell, *Principles of Geology*, II 5 (a summary of Lamarck on the mutability of species):

> In proportion as the individuals of one of our species change their situation, climate and manner of living, they change also, by little and little, the consistence and proportions of their parts, their form, their faculties, and even their organization, in such a manner that everything in them comes at last to participate in the mutations to which they have been exposed.

Potter maintains that there is no allusion to mutability in species in 7-17, but in the light of Lamarck's beliefs, line 13 could be understood as such an allusion. Doubtless T. did not intend a specific reference to either the idea of an evolutionary Nature or to the theory of mutability.

clime] 'climate', as used by Chambers and Lamarck.

14] H.T. comments (*Eversley*, III 220-1):

> He was inclined to think that the theory of Evolution caused the world to regard more clearly the 'Life of Nature as a lower stage in the manifestation of a principle which is more fully manifested in the spiritual life of man, with the idea that in this process of Evolution the lower is to be regarded as a means to the higher.'

16-25] Beeching comments: 'To some self-cultivation is possible; others who are at the mercy of circumstances, may yet transfigure their woes into glories, and forge their character out of calamity.' (H.T. seems to have adapted this interpretation as the basis of his own note in *Eversley*.)

16-17] Cf. *Paracelsus*, V: 'so in man's self arise / August anticipations, symbols, types'.

16 *type*] 'Parallel', 'reproduce'. Cf. the slightly different use, meaning 'provide a pattern for', in *The Princess*, VIII 281-2: 'Dear, but let us type them now / In our own lives'.

17 *from more to more*] 'With progressive improvement', as in *44*.2: 'For here the man is more and more'.

18 *Or*] The change from 'And' creates a distinction between the human development described in 13-17 and that described in 18-28. It may be, as Bradley suggests, that when T. wrote the passage he had no such

distinction in mind. What seems likelier is that the distinction was intended from the beginning and that T. sharpened the meaning by the substitution of 'Or'.

22-3] Ricks compares the chorus from *The Devil and the Lady*, quoted by Charles Tennyson, Tennyson Papers II, 'J.M. Heath's "Commonplace Book"', *Cornhill Magazine*, CLIII (1936), 444:

> And our frequent tears
> Hiss into drought on the burning cheek.

'Sense and Conscience', 119-22:

> Which would not fall because his burning eyes
> Did hiss them into drought. Aloud he wept,
> Long did he weep, for now the iron had come
> Into his soul.

25-8] The ancient notion that man's nature is composed of the natures of all beasts, and that he must strive to subdue his tendencies towards beastly passions such as violence, lust, etc. The idea is common in T. Cf. Charles Wesley, 'Jesus, the Sinner's Friend' (*Works*, i 83), 7-8:

> Tread down Thy foes, with power control
> The beast and devil in my soul.

See also *27.5-8* and note.

26 *sensual feast*] Ricks compares Shakespeare, *Sonnets*, CXLI 7-8:

> to be invited
> To any sensual feast with thee alone.

28] Lyell (*Principles of Geology*, II 15) summarizes Lamarck's theory of the transformation of the orang-outang into the human species, 'the last grand step in the progressive scheme, whereby the orang-outang ... is made slowly to attain the attributes and dignity of man'.

119. *Dating*: 1848-50?, for the reasons given in headnote 7.

7] T. commented to Knowles: '4 o'clock on a Summer morning'.

120-121. *Dating*: No manuscripts survive for these sections, nor are they in **Trial**. This suggests that they were composed after 1848, the presumed terminal date of L.MS, and possibly even between March (**Trial**) and June 1850 (**1850A**).

120. The section has been understood as a reaction against the 'rather dreary world-view, half-way between deism and outright materialism' of

Vestiges (Milton Millhauser, ' "Magnetic Mockeries": The Background of a Phrase', *English Language Notes*, V (December 1967), 111). Millhauser summarizes the idea:

> If it can be established that there is no soul, but merely a complex electrical 'mockery' of free will and our other higher faculties, then Science has reduced man to . . . a web of subtle material contrivances uninformed by spirit . . . the evolutionist may appropriately consider himself no more than 'the greater ape' and develop a morality to suit this vision (p. 112).

3 *Magnetic mockeries*] Cf. *125*.15-16. Electricity and magnetism were closely associated phenomena in the 1830s and so were treated together in popular manuals and by reputable authorities. T. doubtless read a number of works on the subject, for his programme of studies in the 1830s included, on Thursdays, 'Electricity' (*Memoir*, I 124). He would certainly have encountered descriptions of the famous experiments (by Galvani and his followers) which used electricity to cause convulsive motions in dead bodies, motions which seemed to duplicate the behaviour of living bodies. It was generally believed by physiologists that there is an analogy between Galvanism and the vital principle and that the phenomena of life have an electric origin (Millhauser, 109-10). This belief was maintained in *Vestiges of . . . Creation* which, in the section entitled 'Mental Constitution of Animals', suggests that electricity is the agent of thought:

> There are many facts which tend to prove that the action of [the brain] is of an electric nature, a modification of that surprising agent, which takes magnetism, heat, and light, as other subordinate forms, and of whose general scope in this great system of things we are only beginning to have a right conception.   (pp. 333-4)

John Killham (*Tennyson and 'The Princess'; Reflections of an Age* (1958), 252) suggests the above passage as a possible source for *120*.1-4. Millhauser thinks the influence 'difficult to determine', but 'whether one accepts [its influence] or not, it seems probable that *Vestiges* reinforced the impression produced by Tennyson's earlier studies, and very probable that it reawakened a dormant line of thought (p. 111 n. 6).

4] T. compares I Corinthians 15:32 (incorporated into the Burial Service): 'If after the manner of men I have fought with beasts at Ephesus, what advantageth it me, if the dead rise not? let us eat and drink; for tomorrow we die.'

8 *I would not stay*] Cf. Bacon, 'Essay on Truth': 'What is truth? said jesting Pilate, and would not stay for an answer.'

9-12] T. comments: 'Spoken ironically against mere materialism, not against evolution'.

121. Willingham Rawnsley (b. 1845) records of T.:
My earliest remembrance of him is of his visiting my parents at Shiplake, before 1850, when I was turned out of my little room in order that he might have a place of his own to smoke in. He was then still working on 'In Memoriam,' and it was in this room of mine that he wrote the 'Hesper Phosphor' canto.
(Memories of the Tennysons, 121)
The idea may derive, as Israel Gollancz suggests (*In Memoriam*, The Temple Classics, 1899), from an epigram attributed to Plato which Shelley used as the motto for 'Adonais' and translated as 'To Stella':

> Thou wert the morning star among the living,
> Ere thy fair light had fled; —
> Now, having died, thou art as Hesperus, giving
> New splendour to the dead.

With the image, cf. 'Lycidas', 168-71:

> So sinks the day-star in the Ocean bed,
> And yet anon repairs his dropping head,
> And tricks his beams, and with new spangled Ore,
> Flames in the forehead of the morning sky.

1-4] T. remarked to Knowles: 'The grief over the end of things'. For Hesper as a consoler, cf. 'Mariana in the South' (1832 text), last stanza:

> far on, alone
> In the East, large Hesper overshone
> The mourning gulf, and on her soul
> Poured divine solace.

5-8] Cf. Sappho, *Fr.* 146:

> Ἔσπερε πάντα φέρων ὅσα φαίνολις ἐσκέδασ' αὔως,
> φέρεις ὄιν, φέρεις αἴγα, φέρεις ἄπυ μάτερι παῖδα.

> (Thou, Hesper, bringest homeward all
> That radiant dawn sped far and wide,
> The sheep to fold, the goat to stall,
> The children to their mother's side.)

5] A classical commonplace for 'the end of the day'; cf. for example, *Iliad*, XVI 779 and *Odyssey*, IX 58: βουλυτόνδε (the unyoking of oxen).

8] T. remarked to Knowles: 'sleep, image of death'.

9-12] T. remarked to Knowles: 'The progress of mankind is the under-meaning which he has before referred to, alluding — all the previous poems — to the greater thing which is to come.'

11 *wakeful bird*] Cf. *Paradise Lost*, III 38-9: 'the wakeful bird / Sings darkling'.

12] Cf. Genesis 1:16: 'The greater light to rule the day'.

17-20] Gatty understood these lines to mean: 'Hallam has only been removed: he is not altered into something else'. T. wrote alongside: 'the writer is rather referrring to himself'. In *Eversley* T. comments: 'death and sorrow brighten into death and hope'. This stanza anticipates the paradoxes in *129*, a section which may well have been composed at the same time as *121*.

18] Cf. Revelation 1:11: 'Alpha and Omega, the first and the last'.

122. Two 'perplexing and probably unanswerable questions' which the section raises are discussed at length by Bradley, the only commentator to study the section in detail and to present alternative interpretations.

The questions are (I): What is the former occasion on which the poet was visited by the soul of Hallam? (II): What is the still earlier occasion (alluded to in 'again', 4, 'once more', 5)? Bradley comments:

It is easy and convenient to answer that these two occasions have not been mentioned in the poem: and of course this may be true. But it is surely unlikely that the first of them, at any rate, would be spoken of as it is in this section, unless the reader had heard of it before.

It is conceivable, again, that the reference is not to any particular occasions, but (1) to the unhappy time after Hallam's death, and (2) to the poet's youth before the calamity. But the language in lines 1, 2, 9, 10, 15, seems to convey almost irresistibly the impression that, at any rate, one specific occasion is in the poet's mind.

Bradley's discussion centres on the relationship of *122*, *95*, and *86*. He came to believe, from his second edition (1902) onwards, that the answer to question (I) lies in *95* and *86* in which the experiences described 'are nearer akin than appears at first sight' and describe the experience alluded to in lines 1, 2, 9, 10, 15 of *122*. In answer to the second question, 'What is the still earlier occasion (alluded to in 'again', 4, 'once more', 5)?', Bradley's final opinion is that the poet refers to the time before Hallam's death and to 'two distinct moods' of that time: an intellectual one (4-8) 'in which he saw the unclouded Heavens of law and order', and an emotional one (9-20) in which he felt 'the joy of life and sense, and of the play of fancy'. The poet says to his friend, '"As you were with me in my effort to regain the first, so be with me in the return of the second, and hallow it too."'

1 *dearest*] Cf. *74*.5 and note.

3] 'Of grief' (T.'s comment to Knowles).

9 *If thou wert with me*] 'at all helping me — then' (T. to Knowles).

10] The image is a commonplace, but Ricks compares Hallam, 'To One

Early Loved, Now in India', 2: 'Th' innumerable waves divide us now'.

18] T. comments: 'Every dew-drop turns into a miniature rainbow'.

20] A reminiscence of Meleager's proverbial words about Sappho: Σαπφοῦς βαιὰ μέν, ἀλλὰ ῥόδα (her poems were few, but roses), (*Anthologia Palatina*, IV 1 6). This was a familiar Greek metaphor; for example, Aristophanes, *Clouds*, 910: ῥόδα μ᾽ εἴρηκας (you have spoken roses of me).

123. *Dating*: This may be one of the sections referred to in H.T.'s statement that the sections of *In Memoriam* about evolution had been read by T.'s friends 'some years' before the publication of Chambers's *Vestiges of the Natural History of Creation* in 1844 (*Memoir*, I 223). Although this is not necessarily true of all the sections about evolution, *123* was probably composed at least by 1842, as its appearance at the end of T.MS suggests.

123 is the last section in T.MS. It is preceded by *57* and 'On a Mourner', and has echoes of the diction and thought of *57*. The role of *123* in the growth of the sequence is discussed on pp. 13-14. With its position at the end of T.MS, cf. Francis T. Palgrave's selection from *I.M.* in *The Lyrical Poems of Alfred Lord Tennyson* (London, 1885), where *123* concludes the first half of the selection. Palgrave recorded (*Memoir*, II 503) that the sections from *I.M.* 'follow a list which he gave me'.

In L.MS the section comes before *130*. The likelihood that it was at one time intended to precede *130* in the published sequence is discussed in headnote *130*.

The images of geological change are doubtless intended as allusions to the theories of such geologists as James Hutton and Charles Lyell. A parallel with passages in Lyell's *Principles of Geology* has been noticed by Mattes (p. 61):

How constant an interchange of sea and land is taking place on the face of our globe. In the Mediterranean alone, many flourishing inland towns, and a still greater number of ports, now stand where the sea rolled its waves since the era when civilized nations first grew up in Europe.   (I xv 255)

A somewhat earlier description of geological change occurs in another scientific book which T. read, *Hundred Wonders of the World*:

Demonstrative proofs exist in Great Britain, and in various parts of the world, that great changes have taken place in the relative positions of the present continents with the ocean, which, in former ages, rolled its waves over the summits of our present elevated mountains.

('Geological Changes of the Earth', 211)

There was also a literary tradition of such descriptions. An early example is Ovid, *Metamorphoses*, XV 259 ff.:

> nil equidem durare diu sub imagine eadem
> crediderim . . .
> vidi ego, quod fuerat quondam solidissima tellus,
> esse fretum, vidi factas ex aequore terras;
> et procul a pelago conchae iacuere marinae,
> et vetus inventa est in montibus ancora summis;
> quodque fuit campus, vallem decursus aquarum
> fecit, et eluvie mons est deductus in aequor.

(Nothing, I feel sure, lasts long under the same appearance . . . I have myself seen what once was solid land changed into sea; and again I have seen land made from the sea. Sea-shells have been seen lying far from the ocean, and an ancient anchor has been found on a mountain top. What once was a level plain, down flowing waters have made into a valley; and hills by the force of floods have been washed into the sea.)

3-6] Cf. 'The New Timon, and the Poets' [Part II], 29-31 (in Ricks, p. 739):

> This London once was middle sea,
>   Those hills were plains within the past,
> They will be plains again – . . .

4] T. comments: 'Balloonists say that even in a storm the middle sea is noiseless'.

4 a-d] This stanza, Ricks has noticed, is in H.T.'s hand in a copy of the Works (1884B) in TRC. It is titled 'Unpublished verse (your epitaph)'. In the second line T. has substituted 'pass' for 'roll' (perhaps a mistranscription by H.T.).

4 a] In a letter to Emily Sellwood (*c.* 1839), T. wrote of 'the immortality of man to which the cycles and the aeons are as hours and as days' (*Memoir*, I 169).

5-7] Cf. Isaiah 64:1, 3: 'The mountains flowed down at thy presence'; Judges 5:5: 'The mountains melted from before the Lord'. T. quotes the lines from Isaiah and Judges in a note to 'Babylon', 31: 'And the mountains shall flow at my presence'.

5, 8 *and they flow . . . go*] Reversion to the first reading.

8] Cf. Wordsworth, 'The White Doe of Rylstone', 969-70: 'A thousand, thousand rings of light / That shape themselves and disappear' (Ricks).

8 a-d Turner compares (p. 117) Horace, *Odes*, III iii:

Iustum et tenacem propositi virum
non civium ardor prava iubentium . . .

si fractus inlabatur orbis,
impavidum ferient ruinae.
(1-2, 7-8)

(The man tenacious of his purpose in a righteous cause is not shaken
from his firm resolve by the frenzy of his fellow citizens bidding what is
wrong . . . Were the vault of heaven to break and fall upon him, its ruins
would smite him undismayed.) Cf. also Isaiah 2:12-22.

H.T. originally planned to print this stanza in his notes to *Eversley*
(1905) with the explanation: 'Before the last verse was thus: —', but
he deleted the note in the proofs (TRC).

9 *But*] 'In spite of these geological changes'; substituted for 'And' with
the omission of 8 a.

11-12] Cf. *57*.15-16: 'And "Ave, Ave, Ave," said, / "Adieu, adieu"
for evermore'.

124. *Dating*: For 9-16, 21-4: 1845-8? for reasons given on p. 8. For 1-8,
17-20: 1850, because the text of the earlier written stanzas in H.Lpr.
102 comes between **Trial** (March 1850) and **1850A** (June).

In the L.MS version the poet declares that if doubt were to trouble
him in a weak moment and attack his reason, his heart would affirm
to him the existence of God and his mysterious workmanship. As
Mattes remarks (p. 102), the three stanzas added later amplify and
modify this affirmation.

5-8] Cf. 'The Two Voices', 292-3: 'That type of Perfect in his mind /
In Nature can he nowhere find'. The poet rejects the classic evidences
(most comprehensively put forth by William Paley, *Natural Theology,
or Evidences of the Existence and Attributes of the Deity*, 1802) for
the existence of God based on design in the natural world. At Cambridge
T. had voted 'No' to a question discussed by the Apostles, 'Is an
intelligible First Cause deducible from the phenomena of the Universe?'
(*Memoir*, I 44). He remarked in 1892:

> Yet God *is* love, transcendent, all-pervading! We do not get *this*
> faith from Nature or the world. If we look at Nature alone, full of
> perfection and imperfection, she tells us that God is disease, murder
> and rapine. We get this faith from ourselves, from what is highest
> within us, which recognizes that there is not one fruitless pang, just
> as there is not one lost good.   (*Memoir*, I 314).

H.T. commented that his father 'never allowed that the higher imagin-
ation might bow down before the dogmatic despotism which claims

supremacy for the mere reasoning intellect and places Science before
God, and Art' (deleted interlineation in *Materials*, II 22; TRC).

Hallam had written on the subject in his 'Theodicæa Novissima':
'Can man by searching find out God? I believe not. I believe that the
unassisted efforts of man's reason have not established the existence
and attributes of Deity on so sure a basis as the Deist imagines.'

13-16] Cf. Carlyle, *Sartor Resartus*, Ch. VII, 'The Everlasting No',
in which Carlyle describes his conversion from doubt to faith: 'then
was it that my whole ME stood up, in God-created majesty, and with
emphasis rendered its Protest'. He then describes the indignation and
defiance he felt on having been a victim of despair and the Devil.

A letter from Hallam to T. implies that T. had asked Hallam's opinion
on the subject. Hallam replied: 'With respect to prayer, how am I to dis-
tinguish the operations of God in me "from motions in my own heart"?
Why should you distinguish them? or how do you know there is any
distinction?' (Quoted from MS *Materials*, I 62, which has inverted commas
enclosing 'from . . . heart', implying that Hallam is quoting T. The
passage is printed in *Memoir*, I 44 with the inverted commas omitted.)

That the stanza might allude to a mystical experience has been
suggested by Graham Hough ('The Natural Theology of *In Memoriam*',
Review of English Studies, XXIII (1947), 255-6) who compares the
account by John Tyndall (*Memoir*, II 478) of his discovery that 'The
Ancient Sage' (229-39) was based on a mystical experience T. had told
him of years before.

13-14] Cf. 'The Two Voices', 283-5; 422-3:

> 'Who forged that other influence,
> That heat of inward evidence,
> By which he doubts against the sense? . . .
>
> My frozen heart began to beat,
> Remembering its ancient heat.

17-20] Cf. *54*.17-20; *58*.8 b. Gatty compares Herbert, 'The Collar',

> But as I raved and grew more fierce and wild
>   At every word,
> Methought I heard one calling, 'Child':
> And I replied, 'My Lord.'

Henry Sidgwick remarked of this section:

> If the stanzas had stopped here [at 16], we should have shaken
> our heads and said, 'Feeling must not usurp the function of Reason.
> Feeling is not knowing. It is the duty of a rational being to follow
> truth wherever it leads.'
> But the poet's instinct knows this; he knows that this usurpation
> by Feeling of the function of Reason is too bold and confident;

accordingly in the next stanza he gives the turn to humility in the
protest of Feeling which is required (I think) to win the assent of the
"man in men" at this stage of human thought.   (*Memoir*, I 303)

18 *blind clamour*] H.T. (on his father's authority?) refers this to 10-12.

125. In T.MS *125* and *126* have alongside them the 'X' which T. used
to indicate sections which he intended to omit. They do not appear in
L.MS, but they were reinstated in the sequence in **Trial**.

2] Bradley suggests that the first five lines form one sentence of which
line 5 is the principal clause. 'In that case line 2 may be a parenthesis
explaining line 1, or it may possibly be an ungrammatical way of saying,
"Whatever bitter notes my harp might give," "which" being understood
after "notes".'
5-8] This stanza may have been inspired by *Are these the far-famed
Victor Hours* (Add. Poem iv), 1-8. In T.MS the poem appears on the
leaf (f.43^r) preceding the one having *125* (f.44^v).

7 *gracious lies*] Beeching's suggestion that 'gracious' means 'graceful'
is confirmed by the first reading.

11 *sweet and strong*] Alluding to Samson's riddle in Judges 14:14:
'And out of the strong came forth sweetness'. Perhaps this is an echo
of the earlier allusion to the riddle: 'all the sweetness which thou wast
/ . . . And all the strength thou would'st have been' in *Young is the grief
I entertain* (Add. Poem iii), the poem which in T.MS comes two leaves
before *125*.

12] This image may have been suggested by the metaphor of Love as
King in *126*, for in T.MS *126* precedes *125*.

15-16] Alludes to the contemporary physiological theory that electricity
is associated with the phenomena of life. Cf. *120*.3 and note.

126-128. The composition of these sections is closely associated with
Are these the far-famed Victor Hours (Add. Poem iv) ('originally No.
CXXVII') which T. omitted from the published sequence. In T.MS
f.43^r has three sections on the triumph of Time: *Are these the far-
famed* . . . ; *128*.9-24, which begins 'Wild Hours that fly with Hope and
Fear'; and *117*. The verso has *126* which seems to have been originally
intended to precede *Are these the far-famed* . . . rather than to precede
127 T. omitted the poem on the advice of Spedding (see p. 14) and
substituted *127*, the opening phrase of which repeats the last words
of *126*. Whereas *Are these the far-famed* . . . was related to *128*.9-24
in diction and thought, the substitute section, *127*, did not relate.
Perhaps this is the reason why T. decided to omit *128*.9-24 also, for

this section is not in L.MS or **Trial**. However, it reappears in **1850A** with two stanzas added (1-8) which connect it to *127*. The conjectured order of composition of all these sections can be thus summarized: the composition of *Are these the far-famed* . . . was followed by *128*.9-24, *117*, *126*, *127*, and *128*.1-8, respectively.

With this group may be compared a stanza in H.Nbk.17 (following *9*) which was not published by T. It is quoted in headnote *21*.

126. For T.'s intention to omit this section from the sequence, see headnote to *125*.

Although *126* is not in L.MS, f.84ᵛ does have the words 'Love is my' isolated at the top of an otherwise blank page. This might be a false start for a revised version of *126* which T. decided not to carry on with.

The section is reminiscent of Shakespeare, *Sonnets*, LVII 1-4:

> Being your slave, what should I do but tend
> Upon the hours and times of your desire?
> I have no precious time at all to spend,
> Nor services to do, till you require.

2-4] Cf. Herbert, 'The Holy Communion', 23-4: 'While those to spirits refin'd, at door attend / Dispatches from their friends'.

4 a-d] The germ of 5-8. *Eversley* quotes the stanza incorrectly.

9-12] Cf. *Are these the far-famed Victor Hours* (Add. Poem iv), 11, and see note.

127. *Dating*: 1845-8?, for reasons given on p. 8. T. wrote in his copy of Gatty that this section was 'written long before, I believe' the French Revolution of 1848. This may well be true, but T.'s memory in later years was often imperfect (for example, see his remarks in 1890 quoted in note *91*.3-4).

The section is a substitute for *Are these the far-famed Victor Hours* (Add. Poem iv) which was 'originally No. CXXVII'. The apocalyptic vision of *127* elaborates the images of social upheaval and chaos depicted in the last stanza of *Are these the far-famed* . . . In **Trial**, *127* is followed by *130*. For the connection of these sections, see headnote *130*.

In 1831 T. and Hallam 'interchanged thoughts on the political state of the world' (*Memoir*, I 82). In 1832 he wrote to his Aunt Russell (*Memoir*, I 98-9):

> What think you of the state of affairs in Europe? Burking and cholera have ceased to create much alarm. They are our least evils, but reform and St Simonism are, and will continue to be, subjects

of the highest interest. The future is so dark in the prospect . . .
  Reform (not the measure, but the instigating spirit of reform,
which is likely to subsist among the people long after the measure
has past into a law) will bring on the confiscation of Church property,
and maybe the downfall of the Church altogether: but the existence
of the sect of St Simonists is at once a proof of the immense mass
of evil that is extant in the nineteenth century, and a focus which
gathers all its rays.
Hallam wrote to T. in 1832:
  I am indeed disposed to take dark & apprehensive views of things.
  I believe that times are coming on Europe, perhaps on the entire
  earth, in which the utter weakness of all ordinary habits & feelings
  to resist the pressure of appalling calamities will be made apparent.
                                                (Letter in TRC)

4] Ricks compares Revelation 16:17-18:
  And the seventh angel poured out his vial into the air; and there
  came a great voice out of the temple of heaven, from the throne,
  saying, It is done. And there were voices, and thunders, and lightnings,
  and there was a great earthquake, such as was not since men were
  upon the earth, so mighty an earthquake, and so great.

6 *thrice*] Perhaps revised so as to allude to the latest revolution in
France, that of 1848.

7-8] For other allusions in T. to revolutions in France, cf. 'Come
hither, canst thou tell me if this skull' (in Ricks, 152); 'Hands All Round'
[1852]; 'Beautiful City' (in Ricks, 1423); *The Princess*, Conclusion
59-65. T. wrote in his copy of Gatty (which finds an allusion to the
French revolution of 1848): 'written long before, I believe'.

7] With the first reading, cf. 'The Vision of Sin', 141-2: 'And I think
we know the hue / Of that cap upon her brows'. Red cloth caps were
worn by the Jacobins.

8] Ricks compares 'Switzerland', 28-9: 'And bid the Seine / Be chok'd
with slain'.

9-20] Cf. *Are these the far-famed Victor Hours* (Add. Poem iv), 13-16;
The Princess, IV 52-6:

> While down the streams that float us each and all
> To the issue, goes, like glittering bergs of ice,
> Throne after throne, and molten on the waste
> Becomes a cloud: for all things serve their time
> Toward that great year of equal mights and rights.

9] Cf. *2 Henry IV*, III.i 31: 'Uneasy lies the head that wears a crown'.

11-17] The analogy between politics and geology has similarities, noticed by Ricks, to passages in Lyell, *Principles of Geology* (4th ed., 1835, II 290-1, 403):

> the general tendency of subterranean movements, when their effects are considered for a sufficient lapse of ages, is eminently beneficial, and that they constitute an essential part of that mechanism by which the integrity of the habitable surface is preserved, and the very existence and perpetuation of dry land secured. Why the working of this same machinery should be attended with so much evil, is a mystery far beyond the reach of our philosophy, and must probably remain so until we are permitted to investigate, not our planet alone and its inhabitants, but other parts of the moral and material universe with which they may be connected . . .
>
> Causes acting in the interior of the earth; which, although so often a source of death and terror to the inhabitants of the globe — visiting, in succession, every zone, and filling the earth with monuments of ruin and disorder — are, nevertheless, the agents of a conservative principle above all others essential to the stability of the system.

11-14] Cf. 'This Earth is wondrous, change on change' (in Ricks, 499), 22-4:

> Set round with many a toppling spire
> And monstrous rocks from craggy snouts
> Disploding globes of roaring fire.

12-20] Ricks compares Hallam, 'A Farewell to the South', 679-83:

> as when mountains fling
> Their central fire aloft, strugglings and rout,
> Which uproar all our being's harmony,
> And yoke our very consciousness to doubt.
> Who smiles on such a scene? Yes, poesy!

Also cf. *Prometheus Unbound*, II iii 28-42:

> And far on high the keen sky-cleaving mountains
> From icy spires of sun-like radiance fling
> The dawn . . .
>   a howl . . .
> Of cataracts . . .
>   Hark! the rushing snow!
> The sun-awakened avalanche! . . .
>   till some great truth
> Is loosened, and the nations echo round,
> Shaken to their roots, as do the mountains now.

15] T. commented to Knowles: 'The back stroke of lightning — The people rise.'

brute earth] A reminiscence of *Comus*, 797-9:

> And the brute earth would lend her nerves, and shake,
> Till all thy magic structures rear'd so high,
> Were shatter'd into heaps.

The image derives from Horace, *Odes*, I xxxiv 9: 'bruta tellus'.

128. The composition of the section is discussed in detail in the introductory headnote to *126-128*. Lines 1-8, which are added in order to connect the section with *127*, have some allusions and verbal similarities to *127*. The images and ideas in the added stanzas were incorporated from the omitted section, *Are these the far-famed Victor Hours* (Add. Poem iv).

11] Ricks compares 'The constant spirit of the world exults' (in Ricks, 292), 4: 'Old principles still working new results'.

14 *glorious lies*] Bradley compares Horace, *Odes*, III xi 35: 'splendide mendax'. Collins compares Crashaw, 'To Mistress M.R.': 'gilded dunghills, glorious lies'. T. wrote '!!' alongside Collins's suggestion (*Cornhill*, 43) that this is probably a mistranslation of Plato, θ εῖα ψευδή.

22 *you and yours*] The 'Wild Hours' and 'Hope and Fear' (9).

I see in part] A reminiscence of I Corinthians 13:12: 'For now we see through a glass, darkly: but then face to face: now I know in part, but then shall I know even as also I am known.'

129. In **Trial**, *129* is transposed with *130*, which follows *127*, so that the order is *127, 130, 129*. **1850A** introduces *128* and has the four sections in their final order. The section forms a single sentence (like *11, 14, 64, 86, 131*).

1 *Dear friend*] Cf. 7, 9. **Trial** had additional reiteration: 'Sweet friend' (2), 'Dear friend' (3), 'My friend' (8). Also cf. the isolated line above *97* in H.Nbk.19a: 'Long married souls, dear friend, are we'.

2] Cf. the other paradoxes in 5, 9, 10.

6] Cf. Shakespeare, *Sonnets*, CVI 5-6: 'in the blazon of sweet beauty's best, / Of hand, of foot, of lip, of eye, of brow' (Shepherd). Also cf. 'In deep and solemn dreams I view', 57: 'Dear lips, loved eyes, ye fade, ye fly'; 'Oh! that 'twere possible', 25: 'the hand, the lips, the eyes'.

11-12] Ricks suggests that the revision of these lines results from T.'s concern to 'retreat from a possibly offensive notion', namely, 'that for Tennyson what counted supremely was not his faith in good but his love for Arthur Hallam' (*Tennyson's Methods of Composition*, Chatterton Lecture on an English Poet, British Academy, 1966, 213). The revision more likely results from the reversal of the original order of *129* and *130* in **Trial**. The revised final line of *129* prepares for the images of *130* and anticipates in particular 11: 'Tho' mix'd with God and Nature thou'. Moreover, in *I.M.* 'faith in good' and 'love for thee' are not antithetical but synonymous. Hallam is elsewhere identified with good, for example *84*.4: 'I see thee sitting crown'd with good', and *109*.9: 'High nature amorous of the good'. With the equation of 'faith' and 'love', cf. *128*.1, 3: 'The love that rose on stronger wings / ... Is comrade to the lesser faith'.

130. *Dating*: 1845-8?, for reasons given on p. 8.

L.MS shows that the original section was three stanzas (1-4, 4 a-h). They are followed by T.'s customary short dash which he used to set off one section from the next, so they were clearly intended to be the completed section. In revising the section, he deleted 4 a-h, crossed out the short dash, and added three stanzas (5-16) below. This draft appears opposite *123* (f.87ᵛ). It is likely that *130*, particularly in its revised form, was originally intended to follow *123* in the final sequence, as it does in L.MS. *123* would logically lead into *130*, and there are also several verbal similarities between the two sections.

In **Trial**, *130* is transposed with *129* and follows *127*, so that the order is *127*, *130*, *129*. Sections *127* and *130* are connected in that the final stanza of *127* prepares for *130*, and *130* has verbal echoes of *127*.

With the notion of pantheistical survival, cf. 'Adonais', 370-1, 373-6, 379-82, 386-7.

3] A reminiscence, as Ricks observes, of Revelation 19:17: 'And I saw an angel standing in the sun; and he cried with a loud voice'. Hallam had alluded to this passage in 'To One Early Loved . . .' quoted in note *61*.3-4.

Also cf. *Paradise Lost*, III 622-6 (of Uriel):

> Saw within kenn a glorious Angel stand,
> The same whom John saw also in the Sun:
> His back was turnd, but not his brightness hid;
> Of beaming sunnie Raies, a golden tiar
> Circl'd his Head.

8] Perhaps cf. Shakespeare, *Sonnets*, CII 2: 'I love not less, though less the show appear' (Shepherd).

131. *Dating*: 1848? for reasons given by Joseph Sendry in '*In Memoriam*: The Minor Manuscripts', *Harvard Library Bulletin*, XXVII (January 1979), 57): In H.Nbk.18 a draft of the section (showing an extremely early stage of composition) appears opposite a page which has notes mentioning the River Shannon and Valencia. In the spring of 1848 T.

journeyed to Ireland to stay with de Vere at Curragh Chase and went on to Valencia to visit the Knight of Kerry (see Charles Tennyson, 225-6). This suggests to Sendry that T. must have used the notebook during the visit and so may well have composed *131* at this time. For the likelihood that *131* was at least composed after 1848, see p. 17.

In L.MS *131* comes after *127*. This order may have been intentional. The thought of *127* prepares for the image of *131*.1-2, and both drafts of *131* (H.Nbk.18 and L.MS) have echoes of *127*.

The interpretation of this section depends upon the meaning of 'living will'. This would be understood as a reference to the divine will were it not for T.'s statements to the contrary. He wrote in a notebook (TRC): '"O living Will" was taken to mean the Divine Will — but I meant it for the human Will, the strongest part of the Individuality.' Gatty understood 'living will' to refer to 'the Deity', but T. corrected this: 'free will in man'. Elsewhere he explained the term as

that which we know as Free-will, the higher and enduring part of man. He held that there was an intimate connexion between the human and the divine, and that each individual will had a spiritual and eternal significance with relation to other individual wills as well as to the Supreme and Eternal Will.   (*Memoir*, I 319)

H.T. records that

Free-will and its relation to the meaning of human life and to circumstance was latterly one of his most common subjects of conversation. Free-will was undoubtedly, he said, the 'main miracle, apparently an act of self-limitation by the Infinite, and yet a revelation by Himself of Himself.' 'Take away the sense of individual responsibility and men sink into pessimism and madness.'
(*Memoir*, I 316-17)

The section forms a single sentence (like *14*, *64*, *86*, *129*).

2] This recalls the descriptions of geologic and social upheaval in *123* and *127*, but it also refers to the mortal body.

all that seems] The opposite of 'that which is' (*95*.39).

3 *spiritual rock*] A reminiscence of I Corinthians 10:4: 'they drank of that spiritual Rock that followed them: and that Rock was Christ'. This section is remarkable for a high proportion of biblical allusions (see 5-6, 8, 11-12).

5-6] Cf. Isaiah 29:4:

And thou shalt be brought down, and shalt speak out of the ground, and thy speech shall be low out of the dust, and thy voice shall be as of one that hath a familiar spirit, out of the ground, and thy speech shall whisper out of the dust.

7 *A cry above the conquer'd years*] This answers the fear expressed in

1.13-14: 'that the victor Hours should scorn / The long result of love'.

8] Cf. Mark 16:20: 'And they went forth, and preached everywhere, the Lord working with them'.

11-12] With H.Nbk.18 reading, cf. Genesis 32:30: 'I have seen God face to face'; I Corinthians 13:12: 'For now we see through a glass, darkly: but then face to face: now I know in part, but then shall I know even as also I am known'. Also cf. Hallam, 'To Two Sisters' [I], 40: 'Till our souls see each other face to face'.

[Epilogue]. This edition follows Genung (and later, Bradley) in referring to this as the 'Epilogue', although T. did not title it. *Eversley*, III 265 refers to it as the 'Conclusion'.

Dating: The Epilogue describes the marriage of T.'s sister, Cecilia, to his friend, Edmund Lushington, on 10 October 1842. Internal evidence suggests that part of the Epilogue was composed in 1842 (see lines 9-10 and note 15-16). Most of the Epilogue, however, was apparently not composed until two years or two and a half years after the wedding. Lushington records that in the summer of 1845 T. said to him: '"I have brought in your marriage at the end of 'In Memoriam',"' and then showed me those poems of "In Memoriam", which were finished and which were a perfectly novel surprise to me' (*Memoir*, I 203).

The probable period of composition is further limited by Mattes (p. 124):

Since Tennyson had spent August and September of 1844 at the Lushingtons' home, Park House (*Letters and Literary Remains of Edward Fitzgerald*, I 140), he would hardly have failed to show Lushington the Epilogue, or at least to mention it, if it were already written at that time. So one may date it between October, 1844, and the summer of 1845 on this evidence.

Moreover, Mattes identifies in the Epilogue a number of verbal echoes of Chambers's *Vestiges of . . . Creation*, of which T. asked Moxon to send him a copy in November 1844 (*Memoir*, I 222-3). She remarks that this 'further narrows [the dating] to sometime between December, 1844, and the summer of 1845'. (H.T. states that the sections of *I.M.* about evolution had been read by T.'s friends 'some years' before the publication of Chambers's *Vestiges of . . . Creation* in 1844. This is not necessarily true, however, of all the sections about evolution.) The late 1844-Summer 1845 dating is further supported by L.MS, which has the Epilogue on the last leaves (ff.85-7). This draft appears to have been initially a fair-copy which was then revised.

The Epilogue is modelled upon classical *epithalamia* (as is hinted in line 2), the primary model for which is Catullus, LXI, the main influence on the Renaissance epithalamic tradition.

T.'s *epithalamion* contains almost all the commonplaces of the genre. The poem (strictly, a 'song', 4) refers to a specific day and assumes that the occasion is at hand (3-4). The structure of the poem is based on the events of the day: there is a procession (41, 71) leading to the religious ritual (49-60) and the banqueting (75-84, 101-5); then comes the retirement of the couple (117-21) and the consummation (121-2). Allusion to the offspring of the marriage (123-8) conventionally occasions thoughts of the future, and a universal significance is attached to the union (127-44). The poet himself plays an important role in the activities (5-7, 29, 42-4, 68, 70) and acts as a master of ceremonies who directs the proceedings (41, 57, 65 (first reading), 69 (first reading), 109), and who urges no delay (25-6, 41, 89-91). In contrast to his associating himself with the other wedding guests (81-4, 93-104), he sometimes maintains his own individuality (5-24, 45-8, 73, 77-80, 85-8, 102). The arrival of the bride is announced (27) and her beauty is described in images of flowers and light (25, 27-8, 31-6). Her virtue (36) and modesty (43-4) are admired. The worthiness of the bridegroom is praised (37-40). There are maidens in attendance (67-8). The guests are joyful and they express wishes for the happiness of the couple (65-7, 82-4, 97-105). There is music and dancing (4, 61-4, 101, 105). There is a cessation of activities when it is time to retire (105-6). The moon is a witness to the consummation of the marriage (108-20).

T. commented on *I.M.* to Knowles: 'It begins with a funeral and ends with a marriage — begins with death and ends in promise of a new life — a sort of divine comedy — cheerful at the close'.

1-2 *O true and tried . . . Demand*] An address to Edmund Lushington which echoes the address to him in *85*.5-6: 'O true in word, and tried in deed, / Demanding . . .'.

7 *A daughter of our house*] Emily Tennyson, who was six years older than Cecilia, thus the first reading: 'Her' [Cecilia's] 'elder sister'.

9-10] Hallam died in September 1833. These lines suggest that at least part of the Epilogue was composed soon after the wedding in 1842. It is possible, of course, that all of it was composed between 1844 and 1845 (see headnote) and that T. exercised poetic licence in saying 'nine' years instead of 'eleven'.

11] The traditional idea that all the physical elements of the body are periodically renewed is explained in a book which T. was given at Christmas, 1838, Perceval B. Lord, *Popular Physiology* (1834), 353:

> Physiology teaches us that the particles of all living bodies are in a constant state of change . . . But the man does not change, though his body does; he is *conscious* he is the same individual now as he was ten years since [but we can prove that his mind has been] built

up several times within that period.

15-16] The image is similar to a passage in the first issue of the *Illustrated London News*, which appeared on 14 May 1842 and which carried a lengthy review of the sculptures in the Royal Academy. The sculptures (according to the review)

> gathered a calmness from the solemn simplicity of those images that seem to have started instinct with an enhanced vitality, bearing to time's latest date the figured type of high ennobled virtue.

The similarity in diction perhaps supports the evidence of 9-10 in suggesting that parts of the Epilogue were composed in 1842. In 1839 T. wrote to Emily Sellwood: 'Sculpture is particularly good for the mind: there is a height and divine stillness about it which preaches peace to our stormy passions' (*Memoir*, I 172).

19-20] This fulfils the promise of *1*.3-4: 'men may rise on stepping-stones / Of their dead selves to higher things'.

21-4] Cf. this stanza and the deleted stanza with Introductory stanzas, 41-4.

26] Cf. 41: 'the noon is near'. During most of the nineteenth century, marriages in church without a special licence could be celebrated only between the hours of eight o'clock a.m. and twelve o'clock noon.

33-6] Cecilia (b. 1817) was eleven years old when Hallam ('He too foretold') first visited Somersby in 1828. Lushington did not meet Cecilia until the summer of 1840 (*Memoir*, I 201-3).

37-40] Lushington was Professor of Greek at Glasgow from 1838 to 1875. He had met T. at Cambridge and was a member of the Apostles. The virtues for which he is praised are those which the poet admired in Hallam.

42] Dr Tennyson (T. and Cecilia's father) had died in 1831.

49] The marriage service was performed by the elder brother of T. and Cecilia, the Revd Charles Tennyson Turner (the addressee of *98*).

59] Cf. Shakespeare, *Sonnets*, LXXXI 10: 'Which eyes not yet created shall o'er-read' (Shepherd).

64 *the dead leaf*] The only indication in the Epilogue that the season is autumn. Cf. 96 a-d.

65] The first reading, 'Come out', parallels 41: 'But now set out', and also 69, first reading: 'Return with him'.

71-3] These lines recall (Bradley notes) Wordsworth, *The Excursion*, V 532-51 particularly 540-5:

Look, from the quarter whence the lord of light,
Of life, of love, and gladness doth dispense
His beams; which, unexcluded in their fall,
Upon the southern side of every grave
Have gently exercised a melting power;
Then will a vernal prospect greet your eye . . .

76] Adapted from 88 d.

77, 79 *genial spirits . . . drooping memory*] Cf. *Samson Agonistes*, 594: 'So much I feel my genial spirits droop' (Bradley).

88 c] Used instead in 89.

88 d] Used instead in 76.

96] Park House, the Lushington family home near Boxley, Maidstone. It stood on a wooded ridge looking south across the valley through which runs the railway line from London to Maidstone. At the end of 1841 the Tennyson family moved to a house in Boxley in order to be near the Lushingtons. The grounds of Park House inspired the description of Vivian-place, in the Prologue to *The Princess*. The Prologue mentions 'broad lawns', 'the park', 'the sloping pasture', 'the lake', 'the knolls', 'the dusky groves', 'The broad ambrosial aisles of lofty lime'.

96 a–d] The stanza was adapted (as Ricks observes in *Tennyson's Methods of Composition*, Chatterton Lecture on an English Poet, British Academy, 1966, 225) in *The Princess*, VII 335–7:

all the rich to-come
Reels, as the golden Autumn woodland reels
Athwart the smoke of burning weeds.

107, 108, 111 *the streaming cloud . . . a rising fire . . . the shining vapour*] The Aurora Borealis.

115 *the*] In L.MS the word is written on top of *with*, which has been rubbed out.

118 *tender gloom*] Cf. Thomson, *The Castle of Indolence*, I 56: 'a certain tender gloom o'erspread'. With the first reading Ricks compares 'The Progress of Spring', 58: 'And scatters on her throat the sparks of dew'.

119 *the splendour fall*] Cf. *The Princess*, Song between III and IV: 'The splendour falls on castle walls'.

121–4] For the idea of the bride conceiving on her wedding night, cf. Spenser, 'Epithalamion', 404: 'Send us the timely fruit of this same night'; Donne, 'Epithalamion on the Lady Elizabeth and Count Palatine', VIII: 'And by this act of these two Phenixes / Nature againe restored is'.

122] With the first reading, cf. Shelley, *The Daemon of the World*, I 163: 'Innumerable systems widely rolled'; 'God and the Universe', 3: 'Rush of Suns, and roll of systems'.

122-6] T. elsewhere associates cosmic and biological (and social) evolution:

> 'From change to change four times within the womb
>   The brain is moulded,' she began,
> 'So thro' all phases of all thought I come
>   Into the perfect man.
>
> All nature widens upward: evermore
>   The simpler essence lower lies.
> More complex is more perfect, owning more
>   Discourse, more widely wise.
>   ('The Palace of Art', 1832 text,
>   following line 128)

(For a discussion of T.'s associating these different kinds of development, see James Harrison, 'Tennyson and Embryology', *Bulletin de L'Association Canadienne des Humanités*, 23 (1972), 28-32.)

123-4] The idea is that the individual soul emerges at conception from a general soul. In *47*.1-4, T. considers, but rejects, the idea that after death the soul re-merges with the general soul. Perhaps there is also a suggestion in 122-4 of the ancient idea that souls stand by waiting to adopt a body at the moment of conception (Turner, 122).

125] The early evolutionists (von Baer, Tiedemann) theorized that the brain of the human foetus resembles at progressive stages of development the brains of other vertebrates (fishes, reptiles, birds), before it acquires its final form. In a discussion at Cambridge T. had proposed the theory that the 'evolution of man might possibly be traced thro' the Radiated, Vermicular, Moluscous, and Vertebrate Organisms' (MS *Materials*, I 63; printed in *Materials*, I 55; a version is in *Memoir*, I 44). This theory is alluded to in 'The Palace of Art' (passage quoted in note 122-6 above). That T. first encountered the theory in two articles on the nervous system which appeared in *Westminster Review* for January and April 1828 has been suggested by John Killham, *Tennyson and 'The Princess': Reflections of an Age* (1958), 237-40. The theory is discussed by Lyell in *Principles of Geology*, II 65-6; by Whewell in *History of the Inductive Sciences*, 3 vols. (1837), III 452-5 (T.'s copy is in TRC); and by Chambers in *Vestiges of . . . Creation*, 198-235. The application of this theory to lines 125 ff. is discussed by Harrison, 28-32; Potter, 339; and Rutland, 21-2.

126-8] Of babies T. would say: 'There is something gigantic about them. The wide-eyed wonder of a babe has a grandeur in it which as children they lose. They seem to me to be prophets of a mightier race' (*Memoir*, I 369).

128 *crowning race*] Cf. *The Princess*, VII 279: 'Then springs the crowning race of humankind'. A parallel with *Vestiges of . . . Creation* has been noted by Rutland (p. 23):

Is our race but the initial of the grand crowning type? Are there yet to be species superior to us in organization, purer in feeling, more powerful in device and act, and who shall take a rule over us! . . . There may then be occasion for a nobler type of humanity, which shall complete the zoological circle on this planet, and realize some of the dreams of the purest spirits of the present race.   (p. 276)

140] Cf. Hallam's statement of belief in the idea in his 'Theodicæa Novissima':

The tendency of love is towards a union so intimate, as virtually to amount to identification; when then by affection towards Christ we have become blended with his being, the beams of Eternal Love falling, as ever, on the one beloved object will include us in him . . . and so shall we be one with Christ and through Christ with God.

who] In two copies of **Trial** (TRC, Beinecke), T. has deleted 'that' and substituted 'who'.

141 *lives and loves*] Cf. *Sartor Resartus*, 'The Everlasting Yea': 'O Heavens, is it, in very deed, HE, then, that ever speaks through thee; that lives and loves in thee, that lives and loves in me?' (Mattes, 85-6).

143-4] A reminiscence, as noticed by Mattes (pp. 85-6), of Hallam, 'On the Picture of the Three Fates': 'the Love / Toward which all being solemnly doth move.

Additional Poems i–ix

Of the following nine poems, seven are known to have been originally intended for inclusion in *In Memoriam*. The last two are about Arthur Hallam and are in the *In Memoriam* stanza. It is likely that these two were at one time also intended for inclusion in the sequence.

They are ordered according to the presumed chronology of the manuscripts in which they appear.

(i) *The path by which I walkt alone.* This poem is written above *22* in H.Lpr.103 (a detached leaf from the front of T.MS). The connection is discussed in the headnote to *22*. In structure and theme the poem resembles 'Youth', in which Youth is led onwards through various natural scenes towards 'the realms of Love' until he finally meets 'figures as of Gods'.

(ii) *'The light that shone when Hope was born'*. T.MS has these thirteen lines on the verso of the leaf having *30*. Alongside them is the 'X' which T. used to indicate sections to be omitted from the sequence. The section was printed (with added punctuation) by Christopher Ricks in 'The Tennyson Manuscripts', *Times Literary Supplement* (21 August 1969), 922).

The section elaborates the idea introduced in the last stanza of *30*: belief in eternal life is available to all men, even to those whose lot in life is most unfortunate.

In the reference to Melpomene, the section is linked to *37*. In both sections Melpomene offers consolation by referring to stories of 'truth reveal'd' (*37*.22).

6-8] The allusion is to Christ's parable of the rich man and the beggar Lazarus (Luke 16:19-31):

> There was a certain rich man . . . And there was a certain beggar named Lazarus, which was laid at his gate, full of sores. And desiring to be fed with the crumbs which fell from the rich man's table: moreover the dogs came and licked his sores. And it came to pass, that the beggar died, and was carried by the angels into Abraham's bosom: the rich man also died, and was buried; And in hell he lift up his eyes, being in torments, and seeth Abraham afar off, and Lazarus in his bosom.   (19-23)

7-8] Cf. the image in *69*.17-18 of the crown of thorns which buds into leaf at Hallam's touch.

12 *parts*] Departs.

(iii, iv, v). T. explained that he omitted from *In Memoriam* three sections, *Young is the grief I entertain*, *Are these the far-famed Victor Hours*, and *I keep no more a lone distress*, 'because I thought them redundant' (*Memoir*, I 306, *Eversley*, III 205). In fact, the original version of this statement reads: '(because Spedding and I thought them redundant)' (*Materials*, II 15). A copy of *Materials*, II in TRC shows H.T.'s deletion of 'Spedding and'.

The three sections are in T.MS which T. gave Spedding to read. Spedding wrote his comments on many sections in the manuscript itself. Some of these have been cut out or erased, doubtless by H.T. The notes which remain are not permitted to be quoted.

All the sections come towards the end of T.MS: f.42^r has *Young is the grief I entertain*; f.43ʳ has *Are these the far-famed Victor Hours*; and f.44ʳ has *I keep no more a lone distress*. Statements in *Memoir* and *Eversley* indicate that T. had got as far as positioning each of the sections within the sequence before it was decided to omit them all: *Young is the grief I entertain* was 'originally No. CVIII'; *Are these the far-famed Victor Hours* was 'originally No. CXXVII'; and *I keep no more a lone distress* was 'originally No. LVII'.

(iii) *Young is the grief I entertain. Memoir* and *Eversley* give this section the title 'To A.H.H.' and state that it was 'originally No. CVIII'. In this position it would have prepared for the group of sections (*109–114*) which describes the character of Hallam. In T.MS the section (f.42ʳ) is preceded by *108* (f.40ʳ), *112* (f.41ʳ), and *111*.21-4 (f.41ᵛ).

Spedding put question marks after lines 5 and 7 and he apparently wrote comments below, for the lower part of the leaf has been cut out (by H.T.). Beneath the final stanza H.T. has written: 'Omitted because the thought did not seem coherent enough'. This probably summarizes Spedding's criticism.

6] Adapted in *110*.20: 'That spurs an imitative will'.

10-12] An allusion to Samson's riddle in Judges 14:14: 'Out of the strong came forth sweetness'.

13] Here begins the list of Hallam's virtues which is continued in *109*.1-20.

15] Cf. 'On a Mourner', 19-20: 'Till all thy life one way incline / With one wide Will that closes thine' (these lines are a revision of 'Till all my soul concentric shine / With that wide will that closes mine', in Heath MS, H.Nbk.16).

16] This line inspired 'Ode on the Death of the Duke of Wellington', 39-40: 'That tower of strength / Which stood foursquare to all the winds that blew'. With this T. compares Simonides, τετράγωνος (foursquare), 'Though I did not think of this parallel when I wrote it.' Cf. also *The Princess*, V 221-2: 'we four may build some plan / Four-square to opposition'.

(iv) *Are these the far-famed Victor Hours. Memoir* and *Eversley* give this section the title 'The Victor Hours' and state that it was 'originally No. CXXVII'. The images of social upheaval and chaos in the last stanza are elaborated in *127*. In T.MS the section comes between Add. Poem iii and *128*.9-24. The relationship of this section to *126-8* is discussed in the introductory headnote to those sections.

1-2] Cf. *1*.13-14: 'Than that the victor Hours should scorn / The long result of love, and boast'.

3 *then*] The time immediately following Hallam's death.

11] This may refer to the 'flight' of the 'winged Powers' in which case the idea of the stanza is: 'If there is not a good reason behind all the terrible effects of Time, then the passage of time (that is, life itself, 'this wide whisper round my head') is in vain'. On the other hand, if this section was originally intended to be preceded by *126*, as seems likely, these lines might be understood to refer to *126*.11-12: 'And whispers to the worlds of space, / In the deep night, that all is well'. In this case the idea would be: 'If there is not a good reason behind all the terrible effects of Time, then my intimation that all will be well is misleading me and does not mean anything at all'.

11 *wide whisper*] T. wrote neatly in T.MS 'wide'. H.T. emended this to 'wild' in *Memoir*, but reverted to the T.MS reading in *Eversley*. (Ricks prints 'wild'.)

14] Alluding to the nebular hypothesis.

(v) *I keep no more a lone distress.* *Memoir* and *Eversley* give this section the title 'The Grave' and state that it was 'originally No. LVII'. In T.MS the section (f.44^r) comes two leaves before *57* (f.46^r).

4 *these*] The three visitors: the 'happy maiden'(5), 'one'(7), 'Another'(9).

5, 7 *happy maiden . . . unschool'd*] Cf. *The Merchant of Venice*, III ii 160-4: 'an unlesson'd girl, unschool'd, unpractis'd; / Happy in this . . . happier than this . . . Happiest of all'. Also cf. *Hamlet*, I ii 97: 'An understanding simple and unschool'd'. The 'maiden' is the 'fair soul' in *'O Sorrower for the faded leaf'*, and thus the figure to whom the poet speaks in *57* (see note *57*.1).

8] Cf. Matthew 8:22: 'Follow me, and let the dead bury their dead'.

11] T. comments: 'As seen by me in Tintern Abbey'.

12] 'Miserere mei Deus' (Have mercy upon me, O God) is Psalm 51, one of the penitential psalms. Cf. unadopted lines from *The Princess*, VII (H.Nbk.23): 'He plucked a flower that like a moral grew / From MISERERE on the broken tomb'.

16 *these*] His poems.

(vi) *'O Sorrower for the faded leaf'.* In L.MS the section comes between *56* and *57*. It serves as an introduction to *57*, which was substituted for *I keep no more a lone distress* (Add. Poem v). It takes up the reference in this section to the happy maiden and describes her as 'that fair soul

that with me mourn'd'. She is the figure whom the poet addresses in
57, but when 'O Sorrower . . .' was deleted in L.MS, the identity of
the addressee was obscured.

8-9] Cf. Propertius, III vii 52-6:

> et miser invisam traxit hiatus aquam;
> hunc parvo ferri vidit nox improba ligno . . .
> flens tamen extremis dedit haec mandata querelis,
> cum moribunda niger clauderet ora liquor.

(His gasping throat gulped down the waters: yet him did the wild night
see borne on a slender plank . . . Natheless with his last lamentations he
gave this charge and wept, when the dark wave was closing his dying lips.)
Prometheus Unbound, I 718-22:

> I alit
> On a great ship lightning-split
> And speeded hither on the sigh
> Of one who gave an enemy
> His plank, then plunged aside to die.

9 *shoreless seas*] Cf. *Prometheus Unbound*, III i 74-6:

> Even as a vulture and a snake outspent
> Drop . . .
> Into a shoreless sea.

Also cf. *Laon and Cythna*, III xxiii 9.

10] Cf. *The Tempest*, V i 34-5: 'And ye that on the sands with printless
foot / Do chase the ebbing Neptune'.

11-12] Cf. 55.17: 'I stretch lame hands of faith, and grope'.

15] The 'happy maiden' described in *I keep no more a lone distress*.

16 *spoke*] It is the poet who speaks ('I falter'd in my toil . . . and
spoke'). The words he speaks are given in 57 ('Peace; come away . . .').

(vii) *Let Death and Memory keep the face.* In L.MS the section comes
between 117 and 122. Sections 116 and 119 incorporate diction,
imagery, and ideas from this section.

9-12] This stanza was adapted in 119.9-12.

(viii) *He was too good and kind and sweet.* Dating: 1848?, for reasons
given on p. 305. H.T. attributes it to 1859.
The second and fourth stanzas may have offended H.T., for he
omitted them when he printed the others in *Materials* and *Memoir*
under the title, 'The Philosopher'.

The idea is that Hallam was too benign and responsible to publicize his doubts, unlike the generality of modern writers who perplex and inflame the 'passing crowd' by their intemperate journalism. T. elaborated his attitude towards the moral responsibility of the Press in a poem published in 1852 in *The Examiner*, 'Suggested by Reading an Article in a Newspaper' (Ricks, 1004–7).

2–3] Hallam's spiritual crisis is the subject of *96*.

19–20] Cf. *Hamlet*, III ii 357: 'you would pluck out the heart of my mystery'.

(ix) *Speak to me from the stormy sky!* The stanzas appear opposite *7* in H.Lpr.104. This might suggest that they were composed about the same time (1848–50). H.T. comments: 'I do not know when these stanzas were written', but he associates them with the first written sections (*Eversley*, III 187). In *Memoir* (II 517) he titles them 'Epilogue'.

The desire of the living for communion with the dead is the subject of *90–5*.

2 *holt*] A wood or copse.

4 *dearest*] See note *74.5*.

APPENDICES

APPENDIX A

1. Descriptions of the Manuscripts

The manuscripts described are autographs unless it is otherwise stated. The descriptions of the Harvard University manuscripts have been compiled partly with the help of the 'Revised Index and Calendar' to the Tennyson Papers, a typescript list of these manuscripts in the Houghton Library.

Cambridge University Library MS add. 6346

Description:

A notebook of which 36 ff. survive, with numerous stubs; 19 cm X 12 cm. The wove paper is watermarked 'Webster'. Inside the front board is a label reading 'W. Webster / Successor to / G. Fell / Stationer &c. / 60, Piccadilly'.

Contents:

On f.140^V is *He was too good and kind and sweet*, Add. Poem viii.

Notes:

A fair copy. Of the five stanzas, three (1-4, 9-12, 17-20) are printed in *Materials*, II 274-5 and *Memoir*, I 457, where they are titled 'The Philosopher'.

The poem is included in this edition because it is in the *In Memoriam* stanza and because it clearly refers to Arthur Hallam. It was probably intended at one time for inclusion in the sequence.

On the adjacent leaves are notes on King Arthur and Tintagel which may well have been made in 1848 when Tennyson toured Cornwall and the West Country and gathered material for an Arthurian epic. *He was too good and kind and sweet* may have been composed at this time. At the other end of the notebook (which has been inverted) are songs from *The Princess* which were composed in 1849. For this reason Ricks (p. 1773) dates the poem 1849, but it is likelier that it belongs to 1848.

[H.Lpr.98] Houghton Library, Harvard University bMS Eng 952.1 (98)

Description:

1 f . (2 pp.) 18.5 cm X 15.5 cm. The laid paper is watermarked 'Munn & Co.'.

Contents:
    9.

Notes:
    A fair copy transcribed from H.Nbk.16. From it is copied 9 in
T.Nbk. Hallam Tennyson has written at the top of p. 1: 'The first
section of *In Memoriam* that was written down 1833'.

[H.Lpr.99] Houghton Library, Harvard University bMS Eng 952.1 (99)

Description:
    1 f. (1 p.) 22 cm × 18.5 cm. The wove paper has no watermark.

Contents:
    59, including three stanzas (4 a–d, 8 a–h) which are omitted in the
later Sparrow MS (59).

[H.Lpr.100] Houghton Library, Harvard University bMS Eng 952.1 (100)

Description:
    2 ff. (2 pp.) 10 cm × 9 cm and 11 cm × 9 cm. The wove paper has
no watermark. The leaves are pasted down on to the recto and verso of
a sheet of blank paper 21 cm × 14 cm.

Contents:
    On the recto of the sheet is 3, having a deleted stanza (16 a–d). It
comes between the early version in H.Nbk.17 and L.MS.
    On the verso of the sheet is 9. A fair copy which comes between
T.Nbk. and H.Lpr.101.

Notes:
    These leaves, along with H.Lpr.103, were originally part of T.MS,
where they doubtless came towards the front of the notebook.

[H.Lpr.101] Houghton Library, Harvard University bMS Eng 952.1 (101)

Description:
    10 ff. (19 pp.) 18.5 cm × 11.5 cm folded into a gathering which was
originally sewn. The wove paper is watermarked 'R. Turner / Chafford
Mills / 1833'. The hand is Emily Sellwood's.

Contents:
    9, 1.1–4, 31, 32, 60, 73, 112, 91, 105, 51, 33, 34, 36, 44, 46, 48, 30.

Notes:
    The earliest known MS of 1.1–4, 33, 34, 36, 46, 48, 51, 60, 73, 91,

105, 112. The draft of *9* comes between T.Nbk. and H.Lpr.100. The draft of *30* comes between Hn.MS and T.MS. The draft of *31* comes between Heath MS and T.MS. The draft of *32* comes between T.Nbk.b and T.MS. However, H.Lpr.101 does not descend from any other known MS. It dates almost certainly from 1837–40, when Emily was engaged to Tennyson.

[H.Lpr.102] Houghton Library, Harvard University bMS Eng 952.1 (102)

Description:
2 ff. (4 pp.) 18 cm × 11 cm. The bluish wove paper has no watermark.

Contents:
One leaf contains *124*, adding three stanzas (1–8, 17–20) to the version in L.MS and **Trial**.

Notes:
A fair copy. It comes between **Trial** and **1850A** and therefore can be dated 1850.

Contents:
The other contains *128*, adding one stanza (5–8) to the version in T.MS.

Notes:
A fair copy. Most likely, it, too, dates from 1850. Hallam Tennyson has numbered it 'CXVII', the section which in T.MS comes below *128* and with which *128* is closely associated.

[H.Lpr.103] Houghton Library, Harvard University bMS Eng 952.1 (103)

Description:
1 f. (2 pp.) 30 cm × 9 cm. The wove paper is watermarked '[ ] ton Mill', which is doubtless 'Downton Mill 1834', the watermark on the leaves of T.MS.

Contents:
The path by which I walkt alone (Add. Poem i), a fair copy; *22*, having a deleted stanza (4 a–d); *21*, having a deleted stanza (8 a–d).

Notes:
Like H.Lpr.100, this leaf was originally part of T.MS and must have come from towards the front of the notebook. *21* descends, through a now lost intermediary, from Hn.Nbk. *22* antedates L.MS.

[H.Lpr.104] **Houghton Library, Harvard University bMS Eng 952.1 (104)**

Description:

1 f. (2 pp.) 22 cm X 18 cm. The laid paper is watermarked with a post-horn.

Contents:

7, *Speak to me from the stormy sky!* (Add. Poem ix).

Notes:

Speak to me . . . , a fair copy, is marked by Hallam Tennyson with the 'X' which Tennyson gave to sections omitted from the published sequence.

[H.Nbk.10] **Houghton Library, Harvard University MS Eng 952 (10)**

Description:

20 ff. survive, with numerous stubs; 18 cm X 11 cm. The wove paper is watermarked 'Hagar & Son / 1826'. Inscribed on the front flyleaf is 'J.M. Heath. Septr. 1834'.

Contents:

On f.19^v (which has been inverted) are three stanzas of *18*: 13–16 (headed 'V'), 17–20 (headed 'VI'), 1–4 (headed 'VII'). On the stub preceding f.19 (i.e. the stub between f.20 and f.19) are initial letters of three lines. This, and the headings 'V', 'VI', 'VII', indicate that four stanzas of *18* were originally on the leaf preceding f.19.

Notes:

A fair copy. This early version of *18* had seven stanzas. Presumably these were 5–8 and 9–12, plus two further stanzas of which nothing survives. It comes between H.Nbk.17 and T.Nbk.

H.Nbk.10 has only one other poem, 'Milton's Mulberry' (composed about 1827–31).

[H.Nbk.16] **Houghton Library, Harvard University MS Eng 952 (16)**

Description:

26 ff. survive, with numerous stubs; 12.5 cm X 9.5 cm. The white, yellow, and pink wove paper is watermarked 'J. Whatman / Turkey Mill / 1833'. 'Alfred Tennyson' is inscribed inside the front cover.

Contents:

9 is on f.19 (2 pp).

Notes:

The earliest surviving MS of *9*. H.Nbk.17 and H.Lpr.98 have been transcribed from it.

Of the other poems in H.Nbk.16, most are known to have been composed in 1833, and some in 1834.

[H.Nbk.17] Houghton Library, Harvard University MS Eng 952 (17)

Description:
   55 ff. survive, with some stubs; 12.5 cm X 10 cm. The white, yellow, and pink wove paper is watermarked [J. Gre]en & Son / [18]32.

Contents:
   9.1-7 is on f.1^r; an early version of *3* (three quatrains with alternate rhymes), a fair copy, is on f.10^v; *17* is on f.13 (2 pp.); *18*.1-4, a fair copy, is on f.14^r.

Notes:
   9 was apparently intended to be a fair copy of H.Nbk.16, but Tennyson stopped writing after 'Ruffle' (7). The ends of the lines are missing because the right side of the leaf has been torn away.
   H.Nbk.17 is the earliest surviving MS of *17* and of *18*.1-4. It contains other poems composed *c.* 1833.

[H.Nbk.18] Houghton Library, Harvard University MS Eng 952 (18)

Description:
   4 ff. survive, with numerous stubs; 18 cm X 10.5 cm. The wove paper is watermarked 'Webster'.

Contents:
   131 is on f.3^v (which has been inverted).

Notes:
   Of the MSS of *In Memoriam* this alone shows what is clearly an early stage of composition: there are lacunae in lines 2 and 8.
   Opposite f.3^v, on f.4 (which has been inverted) are lines mentioning the River Shannon and Valencia. It has been suggested that Tennyson used H.Nbk.18 when he visited Ireland in 1848, and so *131* may have been composed at this time (see headnote to *131*).
   At the other end of H.Nbk.18 (not inverted) is 'The Doctor's Daughter', which, although composed in 1830, Tennyson may have copied out again (in 1848?) because he intended to insert it in *The Princess* in 1850.

[H.Nbk.19] Houghton Library, Harvard University MS Eng 952 (19)

Description:
   5 ff. survive, with numerous stubs; 18 cm X 12 cm. The laid paper has no watermark.

Contents:
  96 is on f.1 (2 pp.).
  On ff.2^v-4^v are two versions (a, b) of *97*: H.Nbk.19a contains 9-12,
33, 18-20, 13-16, 21-4, 29, 31, 30, 32, 25-8, 33-6; H.Nbk.19b lacks
1-4 but has the other lines in the published order.
  Above the early version of *97* is the isolated line (a false start?):
'Long married souls, dear friend, are we'.

Notes:
  96 and *97* are the only items in H.Nbk.19.

**[Heath MS] Fitzwilliam Museum, Cambridge University, John M. Heath
Commonplace Book**

Description:
  vii + 280 paged ff. 20 cm X 12.5 cm. The wove paper is watermarked
'C. Wilmot 1827'. Inscribed inside the front board is 'J.M. Heath / 24th
Sept. 1832'. The greater part is in the hand of John Heath, but a few
transcripts are by an unidentified hand. Tennyson has made numerous
revisions and additions.

Contents:
  9 (pp. 72-3); *17* (p. 252); *18* (p. 253); *85*.1-4, 41-4, 49-52, 57-76,
97-108, in which (except for also having 41-4) it agrees with T.Nbk.
(pp. 254-6); *30*, titled 'Christmas eve. 1833' (pp. 257-8); *31* (p. 259);
19 (p. 278).

Notes:
  Tennyson has written *17*.1-7 and has made revisions in *17*.1-4,
9.5, and *9*.18 (a correction of an error in transcription).
  Heath MS has all but one (*28*) of the sections in T.Nbk., in addition
to *19*. The draft of *9* antedates that in T.Nbk., but in respect of the
other five sections which the MSS have in common, T.Nbk. antedates
Heath MS. None of the sections in Heath MS is copied from T.Nbk.
  Of the other poems in Heath MS, most are by Tennyson, but there
are also poems by his brothers Frederick, Charles, Edward, and
Septimus, and by Arthur Hallam, W.B. Donne, and R.C. Trench. For
most of the poems, a date between 1829 and 1833 is attached.
  There are four transcripts which descend directly or indirectly from
Heath MS and which are of no authority, and which, therefore, are not
included in the textual apparatus:

*Beinecke Rare Book and Manuscript Library, Yale University MS
Tinker 2041*
In this commonplace book belonging to the sister of John Heath is
Heath's transcript from his own commonplace book of *9* (ff.4^v-5^r).

This is dated 'Oct. 6. 1833'. Inscribed on f.1 is 'J[ulia] H[eath] from Alfred Tennyson Oct. 29. 1833'.

Houghton Library, Harvard University bMS Eng 952.1 (106) and bMS Eng 952.1 (274)

bMS Eng 952.1 (106) contains *30*, *31*, and *85* transcribed from Heath MS by an unidentified hand. Sections *30* (17–32 only) and *85* in (106) were in turn transcribed by another unidentified hand in bMS Eng 952.1 (274). The paper of this MS is watermarked 'J. Whatman / 1846'.

Houghton Library, Harvard University MS Eng 952 (21)

This notebook contains transcripts by James Spedding of *9* (ff.25^v–26^r) and *31* (f.37^v). Both sections obviously descend from Heath MS, but the numerous verbal variants (especially in *31*) suggest that they are memorial reconstructions. The paper is watermarked 'J. Green & Son / 1836'.

[Hn.Nbk.] Henry E. Huntington Library MS HM 1321, and MS in the possession of Richard L. Purdy, New Haven, Connecticut

Description:

2 ff. (4 pp.) 31 cm X 20 cm. The laid paper is watermarked with a Britannia figure.

Contents:

One leaf (HM 1321) contains eleven sections: recto, left column has *41*, *42*, *68*; right column has *66*, *61*, *75*; verso, left column has *30*, *78*; right column has *44*, *45*, *74*.

The other (owned by Richard L. Purdy) contains four sections: recto has *9*; verso, left column has *17*, *18*; right column has *21*.

Notes:

Of the total of fifteen sections, eleven are fair copies. *18* descends from Sparrow MS(*18*). In respect of *21*, H.Lpr.103 descends from Hn.Nbk., although between them is a revised draft which no longer survives.

Hn.Nbk. is probably the next stage after T.Nbk. in which Tennyson assembled a number of sections and arranged some of them with respect to each other. Of the fifteen, ten are arranged in pairs: *17* and *18* (which are, of course, linked in earlier MSS: T.Nbk. and Heath MS); *41* and *42*; *44* and *45*; *30* and *78* (poems on Christmas); and *18* and *21* (poems set at the graveside).

Hn.Nbk. contains the earliest surviving drafts of eleven sections: *21*, *41*, *42*, *44*, *45*, *61*, *66*, *68*, *74*, *75*, *78*.

These leaves are from a MS book which has become dispersed. Sixteen further leaves from the book are in a collection of twenty-two leaves (HM 1320) owned by the Huntington Library. Most of the sixteen measure 31 cm × 20 cm, but a few have been cut down or torn. They are laid paper and have as a watermark either 'Snelgrove 1835' or the Snelgrove device, a Britannia figure. The leaves contain poems which were published in 1842 and which are known to have been composed 1833-8. This suggests that the eleven sections which appear for the first time in Hn.Nbk. were composed 1834-8.

A cancelled stanza in *41* (8 a–d) which is known only from Hn.Nbk. was published in a review of an exhibition of Tennyson material at the Fine Art Society, New Bond Street, in 1909: 'Tennyson Exhibition', *Daily Graphic*, 6 July 1909, 3. (Curiously, however, the *Tennyson Centenary Exhibition Catalogue* (July 1909) does not mention either Hn.Nbk. or any autograph MS book.) The newspaper reference may indicate that the MS book had been disbound by 1909.

[L.MS] Tennyson Research Centre, Lincoln Central Library

Description:

89 ff.[1] (103 pp.) 36.5 cm × 15 cm. The laid paper has the watermark 'Golding & Snelgrove 1814' on ff.2-43 and a shield enclosing a post horn on ff.44-88 (f.1 and f.89 are end papers, f.1^r and f.89^v being marbled). On f.1^v is a drawing of a church, inside of which is inscribed:

$$\text{November } 3\text{.th.}$$
$$* \quad 4$$
$$.$$
$$5$$
$$.$$
$$3 \text{ n.m.}$$
$$1842 \quad \text{N.M.5}$$
$$.W.$$

An inscription in T.MS (f.6^v) has 'VIII / 1842 / Novaitu / Nov', so both T.MS and L.MS are inscribed with the same date. As T.MS antedates L.MS, however, November 1842 must be the *terminus ad quem* for T.MS and the *terminus a quo* for L.MS. Beneath the drawing in L.MS is 'N.8' and then a man's face in profile. Farther below is a complicated problem in long division checked by multiplication. On f.2^v is the inscription 'Hallam & Lionel Tennyson', by Emily Tennyson.

Contents:

The 114 sections and the Epilogue published in *In Memoriam*, and two sections originally intended for inclusion in the sequence but not published by Tennyson, in the following order:

[1] f.56 has become detached and is now pasted down along the left edge to f.57^r. The conjugate leaf is missing.

f.2^r: *1*.1-4.
f.2^v: 'Hallam & Lionel Tennyson'
f.3^r: *3*
f.3^v: blank
f.4^r: *4*
f.4^v: *2*
f.5^r: *5*
f.5^v: *6*
f.6: blank
f.7^r: *9*
f.7^v: blank
f.8^r: *10*
f.8^v: blank
f.9^r: *11*
f.9^v: blank
f.10^r: *12*
f.10^v: blank
f.11^r: *13*
f.11^v: *14,15*
f.12^r: blank
f.12^v: *16*
f.13^r: *17*
f.13^v: blank
f.14^r: *18*
ff.14^v-15^v: blank
f.16^r: *19,20*
f.16^v: blank
f.17^r: *21*
ff.17^v-18^v: blank
f.19^r: *22*
f.19^v: blank
f.20^r: *23*
f.20^v: blank
f.21^r: *24,25*
f.21^v: *26,27*
f.22: blank
f.23^r: *28*
f.23^v: *29*
f.24^r: *30*
f.24^v: blank
f.25^r: *31*
f.25^v: blank
f.26^r: *32*

f.26^v: *33*
f.27^r: *34*
f.27^v: *35*
f.28^r: blank
f.28^v: *36*
f.29^r: blank
f.29^v: *37*
f.30^r: *38*
f.30^v: blank
f.31^r: *40*
f.31^v: *41,42*
f.32^r: blank
f.32^v: *43*, having 13-16 deleted
    from between 8 and 9 and
    then added after 12
f.33^r: *44*
f.33^v: *45*
f.34^r: blank
f.34^v: *46,47*
f.35: blank
f.36^r: *48*
f.36^v: *49*
f.37^r: *50*
f.37^v: *51*
f.38^r: *52*
f.38^v: *53,54*
f.39^r: *55,56*.1-24
f.39^v: *56*.25-8
f.40^r: *'O Sorrower for the faded
    leaf'* (Add. Poem vi), deleted;
    57; 58, having 8 a-h deleted
    and 9-12 inserted in margin
f.40^v: *60*
f.41^r: *61,62*
f.41^v: *63,64,65*
f.42^r: blank
f.42^v: *66,69*
f.43^r: *67,68*
f.43^v: *70*, two drafts
f.44^r: *71,72*
f.44^v: *73*
f.45^r: *74*
f.45^v: *75*

f.46^r: *76*
f.46^v: blank
f.47^r: *77*
f.47^v: blank
f.48^r: *78*
f.48^v: *79*
f.49: blank
f.50^r: *80*
f.50^v: blank
f.51^r: *81, 82*
f.51^v: *83*
f.52^r: *107*
f.52^v: *84*
f.53^r: blank
f.53^v: *85*.1-44, adding 5-40 to
  T.MS
f.54^r: blank
f.54^v: *85*.45-92, adding 45-8,
  53-6, 77-92 to T.MS
f.55^r: *85*.93-120
f.55^v: *99*, lacking 5-8; deleted
  here but revised on f.66^v
f.56^r: *86*
f.56^v: blank
f.57^r: *87*
ff.57^v-58^r: blank
f.58^v: *89*
ff.59-60^r: blank
f.60^v: *90*, having 20 a-d deleted
f.61^r (top third cut out): *92, 93*
f.61^v: *94*
f.62^r: blank
f.62^v: *95*.1-52
f.63^r: *95*.53-64
ff.63^v-64^r: blank
f.64^v: *98*
ff.65^r-66^r: blank

f.66^v: *99*, revised from version
  on f.55^v
f.67^r: *100*
f.67^v: blank
f.68^r: *101*
f.68^v: blank
f.69^r: *102*
f.69^v: *103*
f.70^r: *104*
f.70^v: *105*
ff.71-3: blank
f.74^r: *108*
f.74^v: *109*
f.75^r: *110*
f.75^v: *112, 113*
f.76^r: blank
f.76^v: *111*
f.77^r: *118*
f.77^v: *115, 117*
f.78^r: *Let Death and Memory
  keep the face* (Add. Poem vii)
f.78^v: *122*
ff.79-84^r: blank
f.84^v: 'Love is my' (these words
  only)
f.85^r: [Epilogue] 1-56
f.85^v: blank
f.86^r: [Epilogue] 57-108
f.86^v: blank
f.87^r: [Epilogue] 109-44
f.87^v: *123*
f.88^r: *130*, having 4 a-h deleted
  and 5-16 substituted
f.88^v: *124*.9-16, 21-4
f.89^r: *127, 131*
f.89^v (marbled end paper)

Notes:
  Like T.MS, which it succeeds, L.MS was evidently also intended
from the beginning to be a fair-copy of the sequence and to represent
Tennyson's final intentions. Ninety per cent of the sections are fair
copies, and only seven sections (*46, 56, 58, 98, 99, 120, 124*) and the
Epilogue are heavily revised. With a few exceptions (notably the five

sections which come after the Epilogue) the arrangement of the sequence approximates that of the published order. The epithalamion (Epilogue) is a counterpart to 'On a Mourner' which was intended to conclude the T.MS sequence.

L.MS lacks nine of the sections which are in T.MS. Four sections, *The light that shone when Hope was born'* (Add. Poem ii), *88*, *125*, and *126*, are all marked with an 'X' in T.MS, evidently to indicate that they were to be omitted from the sequence henceforward. Although *'The light that shone'* was never published by Tennyson, *88*, *125*, and *126* were all reinstated in **Trial**. Three sections, *Young is the grief I entertain* (Add. Poem iii), *Are these the far-famed Victor Hours* (Add. Poem iv), and *I keep no more a lone distress* (Add. Poem v), were all omitted on the advice of Spedding. *128*.9-24 is omitted from both L.MS and **Trial** but is reinstated in the sequence in **1850A**, where it has 1-8 added. As for *91*, although it is not now in L.MS, it almost certainly was originally. The top third of f.61 (having *92*, *93*, *94*) has been cut out. Tennyson inserted an autograph MS of *91* in a copy of **1850A** which was exhibited in 1909. The MS has not been traced, but it seems likely that it derives from L.MS f.61^r.

L.MS has forty-two sections (in addition to *'O Sorrower for the faded leaf'* (Add. Poem vi) and *Let Death and Memory keep the face* (Add. Poem vii)) which do not appear in any earlier MS, although they were not necessarily composed after 1842.

Provenance:

L.MS was bequeathed to Hallam and Lionel Tennyson by their parents. On the death of Hallam in 1928, it was deposited (along with other manuscript material and printed books) in the vaults of Barclays Bank, Piccadilly. The existence of L.MS was made known to scholars when it was displayed at the Tennyson Exhibition, celebrating the 150th anniversary of the poet's birth, in the Usher Gallery, Lincoln, in 1959. In 1974, L.MS, the property of the Tennyson Trust, was transferred from the Usher Gallery to the Tennyson Research Centre.

[Moxon MS] Houghton Library, Harvard University MS Eng 601.66 (24)

Description:

An autograph album 22 cm × 18 cm belonging to Emma Isola Moxon, the wife of Tennyson's publisher.

Contents:

31 is on f.24 (1 p.) and is signed 'Alfred Tennyson'.

Notes:

A fair copy. It is not dated, but it is located between an autograph poem by Samuel Rogers (f.20) dated 9 March 1837 and an autograph poem by Wordsworth (f.25) dated 18 March 1837.

The text comes between Heath MS and H.Lpr.101. It introduces one significant variant (in line 1) which became the published reading.

[Prayer Book MS] Tennyson Research Centre, Lincoln Central Library

Description:

A loose-leaf notebook of blue imitation morocco-texture cloth with calf spine and corners, the spine lettered in gilt 'Elegies.', 22 cm X 13 cm. There is no necessary connection between the boards and the loose leaves which they now contain: 76 ff. folded over threads running down the inside of the spine. The laid paper is watermarked 1855. The hand is Emily Tennyson's. Inside the front board in pencil in Hallam Tennyson's hand is 'Daily Prayers by Emily Tennyson'.

Contents:

Inside the front board in Tennyson's hand is a version of the Introductory stanzas, 13–16.

Notes:

A fair copy. This is referred to by Hallam Tennyson in *Eversley*, III 224: 'An old version of this verse was left by my father in MS in a book of prayers written by my mother.' Hallam Tennyson prints the stanza but has substituted 'But' for 'Yet' and has altered punctuation and capitalization.

Emily was doubtless making use of a loose-leaf notebook for which Tennyson no longer had any use. That the notebook is coincidentally labelled 'Elegies.' indicates that at one time it probably contained loose leaves having sections of *In Memoriam*.

[Sparrow MS(*18*)] MS in the possession of John Sparrow, Oxford

Description:

1 f. (1 p.) 13.5 cm X 9.5 cm, the bottom edge having been cut off. The wove paper has no watermark. The leaf is pasted down along the left margin to a sheet of blank paper (14 cm X 10.5 cm) which is pasted along the left margin to a similar sheet containing Sparrow MS(*19*).

Contents:

18. A fair copy.

Notes:

Along with Sparrow MS(*19*), this leaf was originally part of T.MS where it doubtless came towards the front of the notebook.

[Sparrow MS(*19*)] MS in the possession of John Sparrow, Oxford
Description:
1 f. (1 p.) 10 cm X 9.5 cm, the bottom edge having been cut off. The wove paper has no watermark. The leaf is pasted down along the left margin to a sheet of blank paper (11.5 cm X 10.5 cm) which is pasted along the left margin to a similar sheet containing Sparrow MS(*18*).
Contents:
19. A fair copy which comes between Heath MS and L.MS.
Notes:
Along with Sparrow MS(*18*), this leaf was originally part of T.MS where it doubtless came towards the front of the notebook.

[Sparrow MS(*59*)] MS in the possession of John Sparrow, Oxford
Description:
1 f. (1 p.) 11 cm X 10 cm, the bottom edge having been cut off. The wove paper has no watermark.
Contents:
59.
Notes:
A fair copy with no significant variants from the published text. It is later than H.Lpr.99.

[T.MS] Trinity College, Cambridge MS 0.15.13.
Description:
52 ff.[1] (60 pp.) with some missing and some partially torn away or cut out; 32 cm X 9.5 cm. The wove paper is watermarked 'Downton Mill 1834'. Inside the front board is an inscription by Hallam Tennyson:
First Jottings of In Memoriam / This MS is / Given to ᴧ Catherine ᴧ Lady Simeon / for life / In Memory of her husband / Sir John Simeon / to whom / it was originally intrusted.
f.1[r] has another inscription by Hallam but signed by Tennyson:
Anniversary of Hallam's Wedding day. / June 25th 1886 / Given to Lady Simeon / for her life time / but the private notes (by Spedding[2] are not to be shown by her / to anyone — nor is any thing to be copied[3] / After her death this book / is to be given to Hallam Tennyson / or his heirs if H. is not living / Signed / Tennyson.

[1] Including eight leaves inserted when the MS was rebound about 1860.
[2] The parenthesis '(by Spedding' is in pencil in Hallam Tennyson's hand.
[3] This line is interlineated.

f.4^r (all but the top of which has been torn away) has Tennyson's signature: 'A Tennyson'. On f.8^v (the top third of which has been cut out) Tennyson has written the following: 'adelantado / VIII / 1842 / Novaitu / Nov', alongside which is drawn a man's face in profile. '1842' and 'Nov' surely indicate the same date as that inscribed in L.MS: 'November 3 4 5 1842', but as T.MS antedates L.MS, November 1842 must be the *terminus ad quem* for T.MS and the *terminus a quo* for L.MS.

Contents:

Including five leaves which have become detached (H.Lpr.100, H.Lpr.103, Sparrow MS(*18*), Sparrow MS(*19*)) T.MS contains 71 sections published in *In Memoriam*, five sections originally intended for inclusion but not published by Tennyson, and 'On a Mourner'. Excluding the contents of the detached leaves, T.MS contains 67 sections published in *In Memoriam*, four sections not published by Tennyson, and 'On a Mourner', in the following order:

f.1^r : second inscription by Hallam Tennyson, signed by Tennyson (described above)
f.1^v: blank
f.2: blank
f.3: blank
f.4^r : 'A Tennyson' (described above)
f.4^v: blank
f.5: blank
f.6^r : *1*.1-4
f.6^v: blank
f.7: (not numbered in existing foliation; partially cut out): blank
f.8^r (partially cut out): blank
f.8^v: (words, numerals, and drawing, as described above)
f.9^r : *38, 23*
f.9^v: *24, 25*
f.10^r : *13*
f.10^v: blank
f.11^r : *28*
f.11^v: false start deleted (one stanza), *29*
f.12^r : *30*

f.12^v : *'The light that shone when Hope was born'* (Add. Poem ii), marked with 'X'
f.13^r : *31*
f.13^v: blank
f.14^r : *32*
f.14^v: *35*.13-16, with caret indicating for insertion in *35* on f.15^r
f.15^r : *33, 34, 35*
f.15^v: *36, 37, 40*.1-20 a-d, having 20 a-d deleted
f.16^r : *41, 40*.21-32
f.16^v: blank
f.17^r : *42*
f.17^v: blank
f.18^r (partially cut out): *43*, notes by Spedding
f.18^v: blank
f.19^r (partially cut out): *44*, notes by Spedding
f.19^v: blank
f.20^r : *45*
f.20^v: blank
f.21^r : *46*
f.21^v: *48, 49*

f.22^r: *51, 52, 53*
f.22^v: *54*, having 12 a–d deleted
f.23^r: *60*
f.23^v: blank
f.24^r: *61, 62, 63*
f.24^v: *65*
f.25^r: *66*
f.25^v: *67*
f.26^r: *68*, two drafts
f.26^v: blank
f.27^r: *71*
f.27^v: blank
f.28^r: *73*
f.28^v: blank
f.29^r: *74*
f.29^v: blank
f.30^r: *75, 76*
f.30^v: *77*
f.31^r: *78*, notes by Spedding
f.31^v: blank
f.32^r: *80, 81*, notes by Spedding
f.32^v: *79*
f.33^r: *82*
f.33^v: blank
f.34^r: *83*, having stanzas ordered
    1–4, 9–12, 5–8, 13–16
f.34^v: blank
(Stub between f.34 and f.35)
f.35^r: *85*.93–120, adding 93–6,
    109–20 to Heath MS version
f.35^v: blank
f.36^r: *102*
f.36^v: *104*
f.37^r: *105*

f.37^v: blank
f.38^r: *91, 92, 93*
f.38^v: *94*
f.39^r (partially cut out): *88*,
    marked with 'X'
f.39^v: notes by Spedding
f.40^r (partially cut out): *108*
f.40^v: blank
f.41^r (partially cut out): *112*,
    notes by. Spedding
f.41^v: *111*.21–4
f.42^r (partially cut out): *Young
    is the grief I entertain* (Add.
    Poem iii), 1–8 deleted, notes
    of interrogation made by
    Spedding
f.42^v: blank
f.43^r: *Are these the far-famed
    Victor Hours* (Add. Poem iv),
    128.9–24, *117*
f.43^v: *126*, having 1–4 and 4 a–d
    deleted, marked with 'X'
f.44^r: *I keep no more a lone
    distress* (Add. Poem v)
f.44^v: *125*, marked with 'X'
f.45: blank
f.46^r: *57* including 8 a–d, notes
    by Spedding
f.46^v: (profile of man's head)
f.47^r: 'On a Mourner'
f.47^v: *123*, having 4 a–d deleted,
    8 a–d
f.48: torn away
ff.49–52: blank

Notes:
   ff. 18, 19, 39–42 have been partially cut out, probably by Hallam Tennyson in order to remove comments by Spedding.
   The 'X' against four sections was doubtless made by Tennyson, evidently to indicate sections which he intended to omit: *'The light that shone when Hope was born'* (Add. Poem ii) is not in L.MS and was not published by Tennyson; *88, 125, 126* are not in L.MS, but they were reinstated in the sequence in **Trial**.

The title 'On a Mourner' was added in 1865 or later to the poem (having stanzas of five lines rhyming *a b a b b*) on f.47^r. It is a counterpart to the epithalamion at the end of L.MS.

Most of the sections are headed by arabic numerals: the sections on ff.9^v-22^v have numerals corresponding to **1850A**; from f.23^r onwards the sections have numerals corresponding to **1851A**. This perhaps suggests that T.MS was consulted when these editions were being prepared for the press.

Of the seventy-one sections which were to be published, forty-one appear in no earlier MSS. Of the sections which T.MS has in common with Hn.Nbk. and H.Lpr.101, these MSS antedate T.MS. T.MS immediately precedes L.MS. Although they are inscribed with the same date, T.MS obviously represents an earlier stage than L.MS in the development of the sequence: it has forty-three fewer sections than L.MS; the order of the sections is not so close to the published order as is that of L.MS; and the texts of the sections are not so close to the texts published in **1850A** as are those of L.MS. Of the sections which were to be published, all but five (*88, 91, 125, 126, 128.9*-12) appear in L.MS.

Ninety per cent of the sections are fair copies. Only three (*37, 111, 126*) are heavily revised. The order in which they appear generally approximates to the published order. There are, however, two obvious differences.

In the first place, most of the sections between *2* and *23* are absent, including seven (*3, 9, 17, 18, 19, 21, 22*) of the thirty-one sections which appear in MSS which antedate T.MS. This suggests that several leaves are missing from the front of T.MS. There is no doubt that five of the missing leaves are H.Lpr.100 (having *3* and *9*), H.Lpr.103 (having *The path by which I walkt alone, 22*, and *21*), Sparrow MS(*18*) (having *18*), and Sparrow MS(*19*) (having *19*).

In the second place, most of the sections between *86* and *131* are absent. After *85* the order of the sections begins to differ significantly from the published order, but the sections from *85* onwards are nevertheless ordered with care and most fall into distinct groups.

The arrangement of the sections in T.MS, as well as the inclusion of an envoy ('On a Mourner'), and the choice of *57* as the final section of the sequence (preceding the envoy) all suggest that during the years T.MS was in use, it was intended to be a fair copy of a sequence complete in itself and so to represent Tennyson's final intention with respect to a tribute to Arthur Hallam. Just as L.MS for the most part represents the poem published in 1850, T.MS represents the poem Tennyson might have published in, for example, 1843 (see pp. 12-13 for a fuller discussion).

Provenance:

Tennyson gave T.MS to his friend Sir John Simeon in 1859 or 1860, at which time it was rebound.[1] After Simeon's death in 1870, the MS was returned to Tennyson at his request.[2] Sometime later it was given to Lady Simeon for her lifetime in memory of her husband, but she prematurely returned it to Hallam Tennyson. In 1897, fulfilling his father's wishes, Hallam presented it to Trinity College.

[T.Nbk.] Trinity College, Cambridge MS 0.15.17

Description:

58 ff. survive, with numerous stubs; 20 cm X 12.5 cm. The wove paper is watermarked 'Ruse & Turners 1826'. Inside the front board is the label 'Rees Davies / Bookseller &c / 29 Lowgate / Hull'. Hallam Tennyson has written inside the front board: '1833-35' and 'Read to Fitz & Spedding – 35'. (Tennyson and FitzGerald visited Spedding at Mirehouse in 1835.)

Contents:

f.6: *30*

f.33^r: *9*, a fair copy

f.33^v: *17*, headed 'II', a fair copy

f.34^r: *18*, headed 'III', a fair copy

ff.34^v-35^r: *31* and *32* written as one poem drafted twice (T.Nbk.a, T.Nbk.b): T.Nbk.a (f.34^v) contains *31*.1-8, *32*.5-16, deleted; T.Nbk.b (f.35^r) contains *31*.1-8, *32*.9-12, adding *32*.1-4 and omitting *32*.13-16, a fair copy.

ff.36-37^r: *85*.1-4, 49-52, 57-76, 97-104, 61-4 (deleted), 105-8, 61-4. This draft, except for lacking 41-4, agrees with Heath MS (which, however, has 61-4 in its published location and not repeated).

f.37^r: *28*, a fair copy, having 8-9 missing because part of leaf is cut out.

Notes:

The earliest surviving MS of a group of sections. It is what Hallam Tennyson referred to as containing 'the first written sections of *In*

---

[1] Letter from Catherine Simeon to Hallam Tennyson, 9 December 1897, Beinecke MS. For an account of the Simeon family's connection with T.MS, and of Lady Simeon's erroneously describing T.MS (in the letter of 9 December) as once having been 'scraps of paper, of all sizes & shapes', see Joseph Sendry, 'The *In Memoriam* Manuscripts: Some Solutions to the Problems', *Harvard Library Bulletin*, XXI (April 1973), 205-7, and also his 'The *In Memoriam* Manuscripts: Additional Evidence', *Harvard Library Bulletin*, XXII (January 1974), 47-8.

[2] *Tennyson and His Friends*, 309.

Memoriam', although his several attempts to identify the sections (loose sheet in TRC; MS *Materials*, I 152; *Materials*, I 127-8; *Memoir*, I 109; *Eversley*, III 187) have errors and discrepancies and none is reliable (see Shatto, '"The first written sections of *In Memoriam*"', *Notes and Queries*, n.s. 25 (June 1978), 233-7).

9, *17*, and *18* are numbered sequentially, and so are the first example of Tennyson arranging his sections with respect to each other. These are the only sections in T.Nbk. which appear in earlier MSS, but only *9* descends from one of them (H.Lpr.98).

All the sections except *28* are in Heath MS, which antedates T.Nbk. in respect to *9*. In respect to the other sections, T.Nbk. antedates Heath MS, although Heath MS does not descend from T.Nbk.

Of the other poems in T.Nbk., most were composed 1833-4. There are also many drawings typical of Tennyson: portraits in profile and in full-face, hands, feet, etc.

[Beinecke MS] Beinecke Rare Book and Manuscript Library, Yale University MS Tinker 2044

Description:
An envelope 15 cm × 9.5 cm.

Contents:
39 is on the face.

Notes:
A fair copy with no significant variants from the published text. The section was composed in April 1868 (*Memoir*, II 53), but it was not published until 1870 because the MS of it had slipped into the back of a writing desk and so had become lost or forgotten (note by Sir Charles Tennyson in volume 8 of his notebooks (TRC) in preparation for *Alfred Tennyson*). It is possible that this mislaid MS may be the envelope now at Yale.

2. Descriptions of the Printed Texts

[Trial] The private printing which appeared in March 1850
Three copies (out of a probable total of twenty-five) survive: The Tennyson Research Centre (4060); The Bodleian Library (Don. f.290); The Beinecke Rare Book and Manuscript Library (Tinker 2065).

Formula:
Foolscap 8°: A^2 B-F^8 G^8 H-N^8 O^6; 96 leaves, pp. *i* ii iii *iv*, *1* 2-183 *184* 185-92.

(Note: TRC copy contains π^2 tipped in when the copy was rebound in 1891.)

Contents:

Introductory stanzas, pp. *i* ii iii; dedication 'IN MEMORIAM | A.H.H. | OBIIT SEPT. MDCCCXXXIII.', p. *iv*; 119 sections, pp. *1* 2-183; p. *184* blank; Epilogue, pp. 185-92.

(Note: TRC copy contains a half-title and title which are facsimiles of those in **1850A,** π^2.)

Notes:

It introduces nine sections not in L.MS: *1*.5-16, *88*, *91*, *106*, *114*, *116*, *125*, *126*, *129*, and the Introductory stanzas. Of these, the following are added to the sequence for the first time: Introductory stanzas, *1*.5-16, *106*, *114*, *116*, *129*. (*88*, *91*, *125*, *126* are in T.MS.) It omits three sections which are in L.MS: *Let Death and Memory keep the face* (Add. Poem vii), *56*, and *69*. Of the total number of 131 sections published in **1870**, it lacks *7*, *8*, *39*, *56*, *59*, *69*, *96*, *97*, *119*, *120*, *121*, *128*, and *124*.1-8, 17-20.

It was set from the fair copy (no longer extant) of L.MS made by Mrs Coventry Patmore (Allingham's *Diary*, 55). As **Trial** has many significant changes from L.MS, Tennyson must have revised Mrs Patmore's fair copy before it was sent to the printer, and he doubtless also revised the proofs (no longer extant). There are slight alterations in the order of sections *111-18* (L.MS has *112*, *113*, *111*, *118*, *115*, *117*, respectively, but not *114* or *116*). The five sections which come after the Epilogue in L.MS (*123*, *130*, *124*, *127*, *131*) are located in the positions in which they appear in the published sequence (except that *129* and *130* are transposed), and *107* is transferred from between *83* and *84* to the position it occupies in the published sequence. There are forty-three substantive verbal revisions and, because L.MS is only lightly pointed, much punctuation is added. The careless pointing of **Trial**, and also the many imperfections in the impression of the type in the reissues of **Trial** are discussed by W.D. Paden, 'A Note on the Variants of *In Memoriam* and *Lucretius*', *The Library*, VIII (December 1953), 259-73.

The earliest mention of the existence of **Trial** is made by W.M. Rossetti, who saw a copy in the possession of Coventry Patmore on 21 March 1850 (*Præraphaelite Diaries and Letters* (1900), 227). Hallam Tennyson's assertion that **Trial** did not appear until May 1850 (*Eversley*, III 195) is incorrect.

The TRC copy is the one which, bound with similar sheets of *Maud*, was retrieved at a sale by G.L. Craik of Macmillans in 1891. He returned it to Tennyson, who replied: 'I thank you and the Macmillans for your chivalrous gift. I value this more especially as showing your abhorrence of the sale of proof-sheets' (*Memoir*, II 383). (Tennyson and his son referred to privately-printed issues as 'proofs'.)

The Beinecke copy is inscribed by Tennyson inside the front cover, 'A. de Vere'. Tennyson has made changes in punctuation, and there are other marginal marks and verbal revisions in the hand of de Vere. Tennyson responded to only a few of de Vere's twenty-five suggested changes. He made verbal revisions in seven places: *2*.13; *24*.8, 10; *26*.13; *67*.9 (de Vere spotted a misprint); *105*.1–2; *111*.3. And he altered punctuation and capitalization in four places: *3*.1; *13*.13; *18*.1; *41*.23. These changes were not immediately introduced into the published text. Most appeared before or in **1855**, but the others appeared as late as **1863**, **1870**, and **1875**.

The Bodleian copy has on a preliminary page the initials 'H.L.' (Henry Lushington) and 'G.S.V.' (George Stovin Venables). There are a few pencil marks emending **Trial** readings to the **1850A** text (this copy of **Trial** was presented to the Bodleian along with a copy of **1850A**).

The 'Editions':

Most of the so-called 'editions' of *In Memoriam* published by Tennyson are, in fact, reissues having some revisions or corrections. Only **1850A**, **1851A**, **1855**, and **1870** need be considered in detail. **1850B** and **1850C**, however, are of interest in having been published within a few months of **1850A**.

[1850A]

Formula:

Foolscap 8°: A^4 B–O^8 P^2; 102 leaves, pp. *i–v*, vi vii *viii, 1* 2–201 *202* 203–10 *211 212*.

Contents:

Half-title 'IN MEMORIAM.', p. *i*; p. *ii* blank; title (see p. 38), p. *iii*; the printer's imprint, p. *iv*; Introductory stanzas, pp. *v* vi vii; dedication 'IN MEMORIAM ǀ A.H.H. ǀOBIIT MDCCCXXXIII.', p. *viii*; 129 sections, pp. *1* 2–201; p. *202* blank except for double rule, centred; Epilogue, pp. 203–10; pp. *211 212* blank.

Notes:

The first edition, but strictly, a second issue of **Trial**. The addition of ten sections necessitated repagination after section *6*, and the pages have been reset in formes.

Published 1 June. The announcement in *Publisher's Circular*, XIII 190 revealed the identity of the author.

It adds to **Trial** ten sections: *7, 8, 56, 69, 96, 97, 119, 120, 121, 128*, and also *124*.1-8, 17-20. Of these, the following are added to the sequence for the first time: *7, 8, 96, 97, 119, 120, 121, 124*.1-8, 17-20. It lacks *39* and *59*. *129* now comes before *130* (**Trial** has them transposed). It introduces twenty-eight major changes in diction: *1*.16, *24*.3, *26*.14, *33*.6, *34*.1, *36*.1, 2, *40*.12, *43*.7, 8, 13, *52*.16, *53*.12, *71*.1-2, 4, *77*.6, 7, *79*.16, *87*.20, *89*.12, *127*.6, 18, 19, *129*.2, 3, 6, 8, 11-12. It has more than a hundred minor changes in punctuation. These are mostly corrections of errors in **Trial**. The spelling 'landskip' is replaced by 'landscape' in *46*.8, *89*.16, *100*.2, *101*.19.

The publisher's copies of **1850A** measure 18 cm X 11.2 cm and are bound in purple (nowadays usually faded to brown) linen-texture cloth with covers decorated in blind and the spine ruled in blind and lettered in gilt *In / Memoriam*. The endpapers are pale yellow and the front ones enclose a set of Moxon advertisements dated February 1850 (pp. *1* 2-8). All the editions up to and including **1863B** have the same binding and endpapers, and include a set of Moxon advertisements.

[1850B]

Notes:

Strictly, a third issue of **Trial**, but the title-page reads 'Second Edition'. Published in July.

It has five changes in diction: *118*.18, *122*.3, *127*.9, *128*.19, *131*.5. It has about fifty changes in punctuation, of which a dozen are substitutions of commas for exclamation marks.

[1850C]

Notes:

Strictly, a fourth issue of **Trial**, but the title-page reads 'Third Edition'. Published in August.

It has two changes in diction, *53*.5, 7, and a dozen minor changes. There is no double rule on p. *202*.

[1851A]

Formula:

Foolscap 8°: A^4 B-O^8 P^2; 102 leaves, pp. *i–v* vi vii *viii 1* 2-202 *203* 204-11 *212*.

Contents:

Half-title as in **1850A–C**, p. *i*; p. *ii* blank; title 'IN MEMORIAM. | FOURTH EDITION. | LONDON: | EDWARD MOXON, DOVER STREET. | 1851.', p. *iii*; the printer's imprint, p. *iv*; Introductory stanzas, pp.

v vi vii; dedication as in **1850A-1850C**, p. *viii*; 130 sections, pp. *1* 2-202; p. *203* blank except for double rule, centred; Epilogue, pp. 204-11; p. *212* blank.

Notes:
Strictly, the second edition.
Adds *59*. It introduces six changes in diction, *2*.13, *24*.10, *62*.3, *71*.6, 8, *127*.16, and almost eighty minor changes.

[1855]

Notes:
Strictly, the third edition, as **1851B** is a reissue of **1851A**; but the title-page reads 'Sixth Edition'. The collational formula and contents are the same as for **1851A**.
It introduces twenty-five changes in diction: *6*.10, *15*.1, *21*.25, 27, *26*.16, *37*.11, 19, *43*.10, 13, *67*.15, *71*.6, *72*.16, *78*.14, *88*.6, *89*.12, *100*.1, *110*.8, *111*.3, 13, *113*.17, *114*.27, *116*.11-12, *126*.10, 11, 12. There are almost seventy-five minor changes, some of which are substitutions of commas for exclamation marks.

[1870]

Formula:
Foolscap 8°: A^4 B–O^8 P^2; 102 leaves, pp. *i–v* vi vii *viii 1* 2-203 *204* 205-12.

Contents:
Half-title 'IN MEMORIAM', p. *i*; p. *ii* blank; title 'IN MEMORIAM | the publisher's device | STRAHAN AND CO., PUBLISHERS | 56 LUDGATE HILL, LONDON | 1870', p. *iii*; the printer's imprint, p. *iv*; Introductory stanzas, pp. *v* vi vii; dedication as in **1850A**, p. *viii*; 131 sections, pp. *1* 2-203; p. *204* blank except for double rule, centred; Epilogue, pp. 205-12.

Notes:
Strictly, the fourth edition, as **1856-1869** are reissues of **1855**. Adds *39*.
After **1870** the only further significant changes in the text up to and including **1884B** are changes in diction in eleven places: *95*.36, 37, Epilogue, 56 (**1872**); *24*.8, *110*.13, *115*.6, 7 (**1875**); *40*.19, *115*.6, 7 (**1877**); *29*.8 (**1880**).

APPENDIX B

Minor Variants in the Text

Introductory stanzas]
10 why,] **1884A-**; why; **Trial-1883**

1]
1 truth,] **Trial-**; truth H.Lpr.101-L.MS
2 tones,] H.Lpr.101, T.MS, **Trial-**; tones L.MS
3 stepping-stones] T.MS, **Trial-**; stepping stones H.Lpr.101, L.MS
4 things.] H.Lpr.101, **Trial-**; things T.MS, L.MS
6 match?] **1850A-**; match, **Trial**
10 gloss:] **1851A-**; gloss; **Trial-1850C**
12 death,] **1850A-**; death — **Trial**
ground,] **1851A-**; ground; **Trial-1850C**
14 boast,] **1855-**; boast: **Trial-1851B**

2]
1 Yew,] **Trial-**; yew L.MS
stones] **Trial-**; stones, L.MS
2 under-lying] **Trial-**; underlying L.MS
dead,] **Trial-**; dead: L.MS
3 head,] **1855-**; head: L.MS; head; **Trial-1851B**
5 again,] **Trial-**; again L.MS
6 flock;] **Trial-**; flock: L.MS
7 thee,] **Trial-**; thee L.MS
11 summer suns] **Trial-**; summer-suns L.MS
12 gloom:] **1851A-**; gloom. L.MS-1850C
14 hardihood,] **Trial-**; hardihood L.MS
15 blood] L.MS, **1851B-**; blood, **Trial-1851A**

3]
1 Sorrow,] H.Lpr.100, **1875-**; Sorrow L.MS; sorrow, **Trial-1872**
3 breath,] H.Lpr.100, **Trial-**; breath L.MS
5 'The stars,'] **Trial-**; 'The stars' H.Lpr.100; The stars' L.MS
whispers,] **Trial-**; whispers H.Lpr.100, L.MS
run;] **Trial-**; run: H.Lpr.100; run L.MS
6 sky;] **Trial-**; sky: H.Lpr.100; sky L.MS
7 cry,] H.Lpr.100, **Trial-**; cry L.MS
8 sun:] **Trial-**; Sun. H.Lpr.100, L.MS

10 tone,] **Trial**-; tone H.Lpr.100, L.MS
11 own, −] **Trial**-; own − H.Lpr.100, L.MS
12 hands.'] **Trial**-; hands' H.Lpr.100, L.MS
13 blind,] **1850A**-; blind,? H.Lpr.100; blind? L.MS; blind, − **Trial**
14 good;] **Trial**-; good? H.Lpr.100; good L.MS
15 her,] H.Lpr.100; **Trial**-; her L.MS
    blood,] **Trial**-; blood H.Lpr.100, L.MS

4]
 1 away;] **Trial**-; away L.MS
 2 dark;] **Trial**-; dark L.MS
 3 bark,] **Trial**-; bark L.MS
 4 say:] **Trial**-; say L.MS
 5-8 O heart,... 'What is it] **1850C**-; O heart... 'What is it L.MS;
     'O heart,... What is it **Trial, 1850A**; 'O heart,... 'What is it **1850B**
 5 now,] **Trial**-; now L.MS
 6 desire,] **Trial**-; desire − L.MS
 7 inquire,] **1855**-; enquire L.MS; inquire **Trial-1851B**
 8 low?'] **Trial**-; low.' L.MS
11 Break,] **Trial**-; Break L.MS
    tears,] **Trial**-; tears L.MS
14 eyes;] **Trial**-; eyes L.MS
15 will,] **Trial**-; will L.MS
    cries,] **Trial**-; cries L.MS
16 loss.'] **Trial**-; loss' L.MS

5]
 1 sin] **Trial**-; sin, L.MS
 2 feel;] **Trial**-; feel: L.MS
 3 words,] **Trial**-; words L.MS
    Nature,] **1851A**-; Nature L.MS; nature, **Trial-1850C**
 4 Soul] **1850A**-; soul L.MS, **Trial**
 5 But,] **Trial**-; But L.MS
 6 measured] L.MS, **1850C**-; measur'd **Trial-1850B**
 7 exercise,] **1850C**-; exercise L.MS-**1850B**
 8 narcotics,] **Trial**-; narcotics L.MS
 9 o'er,] **Trial**-; oer L.MS
10 cold:] L.MS, **1884A**-; cold; **Trial-1883**
12 more.] **Trial**-; more L.MS

6]
 1 writes,] **Trial**-; writes L.MS
    'Other] **Trial**-; 'other L.MS

2 'Loss] **Trial-**; 'loss L.MS
  race' —] **Trial-**; race,' L.MS
3 commonplace,] **Trial-**; commonplace L.MS
4 well meant] **Trial-**; well-meant L.MS
6 more:] **Trial-**; more. L.MS
7 Never] **Trial-**; never L.MS
8 evening,] **Trial-**; evening L.MS
10 son;] **Trial-**; son, L.MS
11 done,] **1850C-**; done L.MS-**1850B**
17 I] **Trial-**; I, L.MS
18 well;] **Trial-**; well, L.MS
20 thought;] L.MS, **1850A-**; thought, **Trial**
21 home;] **Trial-**; home, L.MS
23 wishes,] L.MS, **1850A-**; wishes **Trial**
   thinking,] **Trial-**; thinking L.MS
23-4 'here to-day,' / Or 'here to-morrow will he come'] **1884A-**; 'here
   to-day / Or here to-morrow will he come. L.MS; here to-day, / Or
   here to-morrow will he come. **Trial-1883**
25 meek,] **1884A-**; meek L.MS-**1883**
26 hair;] **Trial-**; hair, L.MS
28 child,] **Trial-**; child L.MS
30 guest;] **Trial-**; guest, L.MS
31 best,'] **Trial-**; best' L.MS
32 rose;] **1850A-**; rose L.MS; rose. **Trial**
33 to-night;] **1850A-**; to night, L.MS; to-night, **Trial**
34 burns;] **Trial-**; burns, L.MS
36 right;] L.MS, **1850A-**; right. **Trial**
37 And, even] **Trial-**; And even, L.MS
38 fallen,] **Trial-**; fallen L.MS
41 O] L.MS, **1850B-**; O, **Trial-1850A** L.MS *has* be *interlineated in
   pencil by T. Hasty transcription caused the line to read originally*
   O what to her shall the end?
43 her,] **1850A-**; her L.MS, **Trial**
   maidenhood,] L.MS, **1850A-**; maidenhood, — **Trial**
44 me] L.MS, **Trial, 1855-**; me, **1850A-1851B**

7]
  5 clasp'd] **1850A-**; claspt H.Lpr.104
  6 me,] **1850A-**; me H.Lpr.104
    sleep,] **1850A-**; sleep H.Lpr.104
  8 door.] **1850A-**; door H.Lpr.104
  10 again,] **1850A-**; again H.Lpr.104
  12 day.] **1850A-**; day H.Lpr.104

8]
4 home;] **1851A-**; home, **1850A-C**
8 delight:] **1851A-**; delight; **1850A-C**
21 eye,] **1851A-**; eye **1850A-C**
24 dying,] **1851A-**; dying **1850A-C**

9]
1 ship,] H.Nbk.16, H.Nbk.17, **Trial-**; Ship, H.Lpr.98, Heath MS; Ship Hn.Nbk.; ship T.Nbk., H.Lpr.101-L.MS
shore] H.Nbk.16-L.MS, **1851A-**; shore, **Trial-1850C** (H.Nbk.17 *has part of leaf torn off*)
2 ocean-plains] H.Lpr.98, T.Nbk., H.Lpr.100, **Trial-**; oceanplains, H.Nbk.16; Ocean-plains Heath MS, Hn.Nbk.; ocean plains H.Lpr.101; Ocean plains L.MS (H.Nbk.17 *has part of leaf torn off*)
3 remains,] H.Nbk.16, Heath MS, H.Lpr.101, **Trial-**; remains H.Lpr.98, T.Nbk., Hn.Nbk., H.Lpr.100, L.MS (H.Nbk.17 *has part of leaf torn off*)
4 wings,] Heath MS, **Trial-**; wings H.Nbk.16-H.Lpr.98, T.Nbk.-L.MS
o'er.] H.Nbk.16, Heath MS, Hn.Nbk., **Trial-**; o'er H.Lpr.98; oer H.Lpr.101, H.Lpr.100; oer. T.Nbk., L.MS (H.Nbk.17 *has part of leaf torn off*)
6 In vain; a favourable] **Trial-**; . . . vain. A . . . H.Nbk.17-T.Nbk., H.Lpr.101, H.Lpr.100; . . . vain. A favorable . . . Hn.Nbk., L.MS
7] **1850A-**; . . . mirrored mast . . . H.Lpr.98, T.Nbk.; . . . mirror'd mast . . . Heath MS, Hn.Nbk.-L.MS; **Trial** (. . . mast, . . .) *has the for thy* (*error*)
8 urn.] H.Lpr.98, Heath MS, Hn.Nbk.-; urn! H.Nbk.16; urn T.Nbk.
10 keel,] H.Nbk.16, Heath MS-Hn.Nbk., **Trial-**; keel H.Lpr.98, H.Lpr.101-L.MS
Phosphor,] H.Nbk.16-Heath MS, **Trial-**; Phosphor T.Nbk.-L.MS
11 love,] H.Nbk.16-Heath MS, **Trial-**; love T.Nbk.-L.MS
thro'] H.Nbk.16, H.Lpr.98, T.Nbk., Hn.Nbk., L.MS-; thro Heath MS, H.Lpr.101, H.Lpr.100
12 decks.] H.Lpr.98, Hn.Nbk.-; decks H.Nbk.16, Heath MS, T.Nbk.
13 around,] H.Nbk.16-H.Lpr.100, **Trial-**; around L.MS
above;] **Trial-**; above, H.Nbk.16, H.Lpr.101, H.Lpr.100; above: H.Lpr.98; above. Heath MS, T.Nbk.; above! Hn.Nbk.; above L.MS
14 Sleep,] H.Nbk.16-Heath MS, H.Lpr.101, H.Lpr.100, **Trial-**; Sleep T.Nbk., Hn.Nbk., L.MS
heavens,] H.Nbk.16, H.Lpr.101, H.Lpr.100, **Trial-**; Heavens, H.Lpr.98, Heath MS; Heavens Hn.Nbk.; heavens T.Nbk., L.MS
prow;] **Trial-**; prow. H.Nbk.16, Heath MS, Hn.Nbk.; prow H.Lpr.98, T.Nbk., H.Lpr.101-L.MS

15 Sleep,] H.Nbk.16-Heath MS, Hn.Nbk.-H.Lpr.100, **Trial-**; Sleep
   T.Nbk., L.MS
   now,] H.Nbk.16-Heath MS, Hn.Nbk.-H.Lpr.100, **Trial-**; now
   T.Nbk., L.MS
16 friend,] H.Nbk.16-H.Lpr.100, **Trial-**; friend L.MS
   love;] **1850B-**; love − H.Nbk.16, H.Lpr.98, Hn.Nbk.-H.Lpr.100;
   love, Heath MS; love T.Nbk., L.MS; love. Trial, **1850A**
18 widow'd] Heath MS, Hn.Nbk.-; widowed H.Nbk.16, H.Lpr.98,
   T.Nbk.
   be] *In* Heath MS *John Heath wrote* is *Tennyson deleted this error
   in transcription and substituted* be
   run;] **Trial-**; run − H.Nbk.16, H.Lpr.98, Hn.Nbk.; run, Heath MS;
   run T.Nbk., H.Lpr.101-L.MS
19 mother] Heath MS *has* Mother
   son,] H.Nbk.16, H.Lpr.98, Hn.Nbk., **Trial-**; Son, Heath MS; Son
   H.Lpr.101; son T.Nbk., H.Lpr.100, L.MS

10]
   1 keel;] **Trial-**; keel: L.MS
   3 bright;] **Trial-**; bright: L.MS
   5 bring'st] **1850C, 1875-**; bringest L.MS-**1850B, 1851A-1874**
   6 lands;] **Trial-**; lands, L.MS
   7 hands;] **Trial-**; hands, L.MS
   8 And,] **Trial-**; And L.MS
   vanish'd] **Trial-**; vanisht L.MS
   11 fancies:] **Trial-**; fancies; L.MS
   13 sod,] **Trial-**; sod L.MS
   14 rains,] **Trial-**; rains L.MS
   16 God;] **Trial-**; God L.MS
   18 brine;] **Trial-**; brine L.MS
   19 clasp'd] **Trial-**; claspt L.MS
   mine,] **Trial-**; mine L.MS

11]
   2 grief,] **Trial-**; grief; L.MS
   6 furze,] **Trial-**; furze L.MS
   7 gossamers] **Trial-**; gossamers, L.MS
   10 its] **Trial-**; it's L.MS
   autumn bowers,] **Trial-**; Autumn-bowers L.MS
   11 towers,] **Trial-**; towers L.MS
   17 seas,] **Trial-**; seas L.MS
   sleep,] **Trial-**; sleep L.MS
   breast] **Trial-**; breast, L.MS

12]
2 Heaven] **Trial–**; heaven L.MS
  woe,] **Trial–**; woe L.MS
4 wings;] **Trial–**; wings – L.MS
5 go;] **1850B–**; go. L.MS; go: **Trial-1850A**
  stay;] **Trial–**; stay L.MS
6 ark] L.MS *has* are *revised to* ark
  behind,] **Trial–**; behind L.MS
7 mind,] **Trial–**; mind L.MS
8 cliffs,] **Trial–**; cliffs L.MS
9 O'er] **Trial–**; Oer L.MS
  ocean-mirrors] **1850B–**; Ocean-mirrors L.MS; ocean mirrors **Trial**, **1850A**
10 southern] **Trial–**; Southern L.MS
  skies,] **Trial–**; skies L.MS
11 rise,] **Trial–**; rise L.MS
12 marge,] **Trial–**; marge L.MS
13 saying;] **Trial–**; saying L.MS
  thus,] **Trial–**; thus – L.MS
14 care?'] **Trial–**; care' L.MS
15 air:] **Trial–**; air L.MS
16 'Is] **Trial–**; is L.MS
17 again,] **Trial–**; again L.MS
18 prow,] **Trial–**; prow L.MS
19 sits,] **Trial–**; sits L.MS
  learn] L.MS, **1882–**; learn, **Trial-1881**

13]
1 widower,] L.MS–; widower T.MS
2 sleep] **Trial–**; Sleep T.MS, L.MS
  reveals,] L.MS–; reveals T.MS
3 arms,] **Trial–**; arms T.MS, L.MS
4 empty,] L.MS–; empty T.MS
  these;] L.MS–; these T.MS
6 reposed;] **Trial–**, reposed, T.MS, L.MS
7 And,] **Trial–**; And T.MS, L.MS
8 too.] **Trial–**; too – T.MS, L.MS
9 choice,] **Trial–**; choice T.MS, L.MS
10 removed,] **Trial–**; removed, – T.MS; removed; L.MS
12 Spirit,] **1851A–**; Spirit T.MS; spirit L.MS; spirit, **Trial-1850C**
13 Come] L.MS–; Come, T.MS
  Time,] T.MS, **Trial–**; Time L.MS
  me,] T.MS, **1855–**; me L.MS-1851B
  years,] T.MS, **1855–**; years L.MS-1851B

14 dream;] **Trial-**; dream T.MS; dream: L.MS
15 seem,] **Trial-**; seem T.MS, L.MS
16 tears;] L.MS-; tears. T.MS
19 bales,] **Trial-**; bales L.MS

14]
  2 hadst] **Trial-**; had'st L.MS
    to-day,] **Trial-**; to day L.MS
  3 quay,] **Trial-**; quay L.MS
  5 standing,] **Trial-**; standing L.MS
    woe,] **Trial-**; woe L.MS
  7 plank,] **Trial-**; plank L.MS
10 half-divine;] **Trial-**; half-divine, L.MS
11 mine,] **Trial-**; mine L.MS
13 pain,] **Trial-**; pain L.MS
14 droop'd] **Trial-**; droopt L.MS
16 possess'd] **1850A-**; possest L.MS; posses'd **Trial**
17 change,] **Trial-**; change L.MS
18 frame,] **Trial-**; frame L.MS
19 all in all] **Trial-**; all-in-all L.MS

15]
  1 To-night] L.MS, **1851A-**; To night **Trial-1850C**
  2 day:] **1850A-**; day, L.MS; day. **Trial**
  5 crack'd,] **Trial-**; crackt, L.MS
  9 fancies,] **Trial-**; fancies L.MS
12 stir] **Trial-**; stir, L.MS
16 dote] **Trial-**; doat L.MS
    cloud] **Trial-**; cloud, L.MS
17 higher,] **Trial-**; higher L.MS
18 breast,] **Trial-**; breast L.MS
19 west,] **Trial-**; west L.MS

16]
  3 breast,] **Trial-**; breast? L.MS
  6 storm;] **Trial-**; storm L.MS
  8 self,] **Trial-**; self L.MS
10 heaven?] **Trial-**; heaven L.MS
11 shock,] **Trial-**; shock L.MS
    given,] **Trial-**; given L.MS
13 shelf,] **Trial-**; shelf L.MS
14 sink?] **Trial-**; sink; L.MS
16 myself;] **Trial-**; myself, L.MS

18 new,] **Trial–**; new L.MS
19 true,] **Trial–**; true L.MS
20 plan?] **Trial–**; plan. L.MS

17]
  1 comest,] H.Nbk.17–Hn.Nbk., **Trial–**; comest L.MS
    much wept for:] **Trial–**; much-wept-for: H.Nbk.17, T.Nbk., Hn.Nbk.,
    L.MS; much-wept-for. Heath MS
  4 seas.] H.Nbk.17, Hn.Nbk., **Trial–**; seas T.Nbk., Heath MS, L.MS
  6 sky,] **1851A–**; sky H.Nbk.17–L.MS; sky; **Trial–1850C**
  7 week:] L.MS–; week – H.Nbk.17–Heath MS; week. Hn.Nbk.
    by:] **Trial–**; by H.Nbk.17–Heath MS, L.MS; by, Hn.Nbk.
  8 quick,] Hn.Nbk., **Trial–**; quick – H.Nbk.17; quick: T.Nbk., L.MS;
    quiet: Heath MS (*error in transcription*)
  9 Henceforth,] H.Nbk.17–Heath MS, **Trial–**; Henceforth Hn.Nbk., L.MS
    may'st] H.Nbk.17–Hn.Nbk., **Trial–**; mayst L.MS
    roam,] **Trial–**; roam H.Nbk.17–L.MS
 10 blessing,] **Trial–**; blessing H.Nbk.17–L.MS
    light,] **Trial–**; light H.Nbk.17–L.MS
 11 waters] H.Nbk.17–Heath MS, L.MS–; waters, Hn.Nbk.
    night,] Hn.Nbk., **Trial–**; night H.Nbk.17–Heath MS, L.MS
 12 home.] H.Nbk.17, Heath MS–; home T.Nbk.
 14 Mid-ocean,] **1850A–**; Mid-ocean T.Nbk.–Hn.Nbk.; Mid-Ocean,
    L.MS; Mid ocean, **Trial**
    bark;] **Trial–**; bark T.Nbk.–L.MS
 15 drops] T.Nbk.–Heath MS, L.MS–; drops, Hn.Nbk.
 16 stars.] Hn.Nbk.–; stars T.Nbk., Heath MS
 17 done,] **Trial–**; done H.Nbk.17–L.MS
 18 precious] H.Nbk.17–Heath MS, L.MS–; pretious Hn.Nbk.
    thee;] **Trial–**; thee – H.Nbk.17; thee, Hn.Nbk.; thee T.Nbk., Heath
    MS, L.MS

18]
  1] **1851A–**; Tis well: tis something. . . . T.Nbk., Heath MS; Tis well:
    tis something: . . . Hn.Nbk., L.MS; 'Tis well, 'tis something, . . .
    Sparrow MS(*18*), **Trial–1850C**
  2 laid,] **Trial–**; laid H.Nbk.10, Heath MS–L.MS; laid – H.Nbk.17;
    laid. T.Nbk.
  3 his] Heath MS *reads* ~~the~~ his (*error in transcription*)
  4 land.] H.Nbk.10, H.Nbk.17, Hn.Nbk.–; land T.Nbk., Heath MS
  5 'Tis little;] **Trial–**; Tis little: T.Nbk.–L.MS
    it looks in truth] L.MS *reads* ~~in truth~~ it looks in truth (*error in*
    transcription)

6 blest] T.Nbk., Heath MS, Sparrow MS(*18*)-; blest, Hn.Nbk.
8 youth.] T.Nbk., Hn.Nbk.-; youth Heath MS
9 hands,] T.Nbk.-Sparrow MS(*18*), 1850A-; hands L.MS; hands! Trial
10 mask] T.Nbk., Hn.Nbk.-L.MS, 1850A-; masks Heath MS (*error in transcription*); mark Trial (*error*)
sleep,] Trial-; sleep. T.Nbk.; sleep Heath MS-L.MS
11 come,] T.Nbk.-Hn.Nbk., Trial-; come Sparrow MS(*18*), L.MS
weep,] Trial-; weep T.Nbk.-L.MS
12 dead.] T.Nbk., Hn.Nbk.-; dead Heath MS
14 I,] Trial-; I H.Nbk.10-L.MS
heart,] Trial-; heart H.Nbk.10-L.MS
15 lips] H.Nbk.10, L.MS-; lips, T.Nbk.-Sparrow MS(*18*)
16 me;] 1851A-; me H.Nbk.10, Heath MS, L.MS; me – T.Nbk., Hn.Nbk., Sparrow MS(*18*); me: Trial-1850C
17 not,] H.Nbk.10-Hn.Nbk., L.MS-; not Sparrow MS(*18*)
pain,] Trial-; pain H.Nbk.10-L.MS
18 mind,] T.Nbk., Hn.Nbk., Trial-; mind H.Nbk.10, Sparrow MS(*18*), L.MS; ~~life~~ mind Heath MS (*error in transcription*)
19 find,] T.Nbk., Hn.Nbk., Trial-; find H.Nbk.10, Heath MS, Sparrow MS(*18*), L.MS
20 again.] H.Nbk.10, T.Nbk., Hn.Nbk., Sparrow MS(*18*), Trial-; again Heath MS, L.MS

19]
1 darken'd] Sparrow MS(*19*)-; darkened Heath MS
2 more;] Trial-; more: Heath MS, Sparrow MS(*19*); more L.MS
3 shore,] Heath MS, Trial-; shore Sparrow MS(*19*), L.MS
4 wave.] Heath MS, Sparrow MS(*19*), Trial-; wave L.MS
5 fills;] 1850B-; fills: Heath MS, Sparrow MS(*19*), fills L.MS; fills, Trial, 1850A
6 sea-water] Sparrow MS(*19*)-; sea water Heath MS
by,] Trial-; by Heath MS-L.MS
7 Wye,] Trial-; Wye Heath MS-L.MS
8 hills.] Trial-; hills Heath MS-L.MS
9 hush'd] 1850A-; hush ed t Heath MS; husht Sparrow MS(*19*), L.MS; husht, Trial
along,] Heath MS, 1851A-; along Sparrow ｜MS(*19*), L.MS; along; Trial-1850C
10 hush'd] 1850A-; husht Heath MS-Trial
all,] Trial-; all Heath MS-L.MS
11 fill'd] Sparrow MS(*19*)-; filled Heath MS
fall,] Trial-; fall Heath MS-L.MS
12 sorrow] Heath MS, Sparrow MS(*19*), Trial-; Sorrow L.MS
song.] Heath MS, Sparrow MS(*19*), Trial-; song L.MS

13 down,] **Trial–**; down: Heath MS, Sparrow MS(*19*); down L.MS
14 its] Heath MS, **Trial–**; it's Sparrow MS(*19*); L.MS
    walls;] **1851A–**; walls: Heath MS, Sparrow MS(*19*), **Trial–1850C**;
    walls L.MS
15 falls,] **Trial–**; falls Heath MS–L.MS

20]
  1 griefs] **Trial–**; griefs, L.MS
    said,] **Trial–**; said — L.MS
  2 vows,] **Trial–**; vows — L.MS
  4 master] **Trial–**; Master L.MS
    dead;] **Trial–**; dead. L.MS
  5 is,] **Trial–**; is L.MS
  6 fulness] **Trial–**; fullness L.MS
    mind:] **Trial–**; mind L.MS
  7-8 'It . . . hard,' . . . 'to find / Another . . . this.'] **1870–**; *no quotation
    marks in* L.MS; 'It . . . hard' . . . 'to find / 'Another . . . this.' **Trial**;
    'It . . . hard' . . . 'to find / Another . . . this.' **1850A–1869**
  7 say,] **1870–**; say L.MS–1869
  9 these,] **Trial–**; these L.MS
  10 win;] **Trial–**; win L.MS
  11 within,] **Trial–**; within L.MS
  12 freeze;] **Trial–**; freeze. L.MS
  14 Death,] **Trial–**; Death L.MS
  15 breath,] **Trial–**; breath L.MS
  16 flit:] **Trial–**; flit L.MS
  17 none,] **Trial–**; none L.MS
  19 chair,] **Trial–**; chair L.MS
    think,] **Trial–**; think L.MS

21]
  1 below,] **Trial–**; below Hn.Nbk.–L.MS
  2 And,] **Trial–**; And Hn.Nbk.–L.MS
    wave,] **Trial–**; wave Hn.Nbk.–L.MS
  3 grave,] **Trial–**; grave Hn.Nbk.–L.MS
  5 then,] **Trial–**; then Hn.Nbk.–L.MS
  6 speak:] **1884A–**; speak Hn.Nbk.–L.MS; speak; **Trial–1883**
  7-8 'This . . . men.'] H.Lpr.103, **Trial–**; 'This . . . men Hn.Nbk.; This . . .
    men. L.MS
  7 weak,] **Trial–**; weak Hn.Nbk.–L.MS
  9-12 'Let . . . constancy.'] **Trial–**; 'let . . . constancy H.Lpr.103; let
    . . . constancy L.MS
  9 answers,] **Trial–**; answers H.Lpr.103, L.MS
    be,] **Trial–**; be H.Lpr.103, L.MS

10 pain,] **Trial–**; pain H.Lpr.103, L.MS
13 wroth:] **1875–**; wroth H.Lpr.103, L.MS; wroth, **Trial–1874**
13-20 'Is . . . 'A . . . moon?'] **1884A–**; 'Is . . . A . . . moon.' H.Lpr.103;
   'Is . . . A . . . moon? L.MS; 'Is . . . A . . . moon?' **Trial–1883**
13 hour] L.MS–; hour, H.Lpr.103
14 sorrow's] H.Lpr.103, **Trial–**; sorrows L.MS
   song,] H.Lpr.103, **Trial–**; song L.MS
17 swoon,] L.MS–; swoon? – H.Lpr.103
19 world,] **Trial–**; world H.Lpr.103, L.MS
21 Behold,] **Trial–**; Behold H.Lpr.103, L.MS
   thing:] **Trial–**; thing H.Lpr.103, L.MS
22 dust:] **Trial–**; dust H.Lpr.103; dust. L.MS
23 must,] **Trial–**; must H.Lpr.103, L.MS
24 sing:] **Trial–**; sing H.Lpr.103; sing. L.MS
25 gay,] **Trial–**; gay H.Lpr.103, L.MS
26 ranged;] **Trial–**; ranged: H.Lpr.103; ranged L.MS
27 changed,] **Trial–**; changed H.Lpr.103, L.MS

22]
 2 well,] **Trial–**; well H.Lpr.103, L.MS
 3 fell,] **Trial–**; fell H.Lpr.103, L.MS
 4 flower,] H.Lpr.103, **Trial–**; flower L.MS
   snow:] **1850A–**; snow L.MS; snow. H.Lpr.103, **Trial**
 5 way,] **Trial–**; way H.Lpr.103, L.MS
 6 And,] **1864–**; And H.Lpr.103**–1863**
 7 went,] **Trial–**; went H.Lpr.103, L.MS
 8 May:] **1850A–**; May H.Lpr.103, L.MS; May. **Trial**
 9 path] L.MS–; path, H.Lpr.103
   walk'd] **Trial–**; walkt, H.Lpr.103; walkt L.MS
10 autumnal] H.Lpr.103, **Trial–**; Autumnal L.MS
   slope,] **Trial–**; slope H.Lpr.103, L.MS
12 Shadow] **Trial–**; shadow H.Lpr.103, L.MS
   man;] **1850A–**; man H.Lpr.103; man – L.MS; man. **Trial**
13 companionship,] **Trial–**; companionship H.Lpr.103, L.MS
14 cold,] **1855–**; cold H.Lpr.103, L.MS; cold: **Trial**; cold; **1850A–1851B**
15 wrapt] H.Lpr.103, L.MS, **1850A–**; wrapped **Trial**
15 fold,] **Trial–**; fold H.Lpr.103, L.MS
16 lip,] **1855–**; lip H.Lpr.103, L.MS; lip. **Trial**; lip; **1850A–1851B**
18 follow,] H.Lpr.103, **Trial–**; follow L.MS
   tho'] L.MS–; tho H.Lpr.103
   haste,] **1855–**; haste H.Lpr.103, L.MS; haste; **Trial–1851B**
19 think,] **1851A–**; think H.Lpr.103**–1850C**
   that] H.Lpr.103, L.MS, **1851A–**; that, **Trial–1850C**
   waste] H.Lpr.103, L.MS, **1851A–**; waste, **Trial–1850C**

20 Shadow] **Trial–**; shadow H.Lpr.103, L.MS

23]
1 shut,] **Trial–**; shut T.MS, L.MS
2 fits,] **1855–**; fits T.MS, L.MS; fits; **Trial–1851B**
3 sits,] **Trial–**; sits T.MS, L.MS
4 Shadow] **Trial–**; shadow T.MS, L.MS
  cloak'd] **Trial–**; cloakt T.MS, L.MS
  foot,] L.MS, **1851A–**; foot T.MS, **Trial–1850C**
5 creeds,] L.MS–; creeds, – T.MS
7 looking] T.MS *has* lookings
  came,] **Trial–**; came T.MS, L.MS
  leads;] **Trial–**; leads T.MS, L.MS
9-24 How . . . Arcady.] **1870–**; how . . . Arcady. L.MS–1851B; 'how
  . . . Arcady.' **1855-1865B**; 'how . . . Arcady. T.MS, **1866-1869**
9 crying,] **Trial–**; crying T.MS, L.MS
10 dumb;] **Trial–**; dumb T.MS, L.MS
12 Pan:] **Trial–**; Pan – T.MS, L.MS
  caught,] **Trial–**; caught T.MS, L.MS
15 Thought . . . Thought] T.MS, **1865A–**; thought . . . thought L.MS;
  Thought . . . Thought; **1851A, B**; Thought . . . Thought, **Trial–1850C**,
  1855-1864
16 Thought] T.MS, **1850C–**; thought L.MS–**1850B**
  Speech;] **1855–**; speech T.MS, L.MS; Speech. **Trial**; Speech: **1850A–1851B**
17 good,] **Trial–**; good T.MS, L.MS
18 bring,] **Trial–**; bring T.MS, L.MS
19 Spring] **Trial–**; spring L.MS
20 Moved] T.MS, L.MS, **1850A–**; Mov'd **Trial**
  blood;] **1855–**; blood. T.MS, **Trial**; blood L.MS; blood: **1850A–1851B**
21 philosophy] L.MS–; 'Philosophy T.MS
22 sang,] **Trial–**; sang T.MS, L.MS

24]
2 say?] **Trial–**; say. T.MS; say L.MS
3 Day] T.MS, **Trial–**; day L.MS
4 dash'd] **Trial–**; dasht T.MS, L.MS
5 met,] T.MS, **Trial–**; met L.MS
6 earth] L.MS–; Earth T.MS
7 look'd] **Trial–**; lookt T.MS, L.MS
10 great?] **Trial–**; great – T.MS; great L.MS
11 state,] **Trial–**; state T.MS, L.MS

12 past] **Trial-**; Past T.MS, L.MS
   in] T.MS, L.MS, **1850A-**; on **Trial** [*error*]
   relief?] T.MS, **Trial-**; relief L.MS
13 past] **Trial-**; Past T.MS, L.MS
14 its] T.MS, **Trial-**; it's L.MS
   far;] **Trial-**; far T.MS, L.MS
16 not,] T.MS, **Trial-**; not L.MS
   therein?] T.MS, **Trial-**; therein. L.MS

25]
  1 Life, —] **Trial-**; Life — T.MS, L.MS
  2 fared;] **Trial-**; fared T.MS, L.MS
  3 then, as now,] **Trial-**; then as now T.MS, L.MS
  4 back.] T.MS, **Trial-**; back L.MS
  5 T.MS *has* me *interlineated by T. Hasty transcription caused the line*
    to read originally But this it was that made move
  6 air;] **Trial-**; air — T.MS; air L.MS
  7 bear,] **Trial-**; bear T.MS, L.MS
  8 Love:] T.MS, **1850A-**; Love. L.MS, **Trial**
  9 weary,] T.MS, **Trial-**; weary L.MS
   limb,] **Trial-**; limb T.MS, L.MS
11 pain,] **Trial-**; pain T.MS, L.MS
12 it,] T.MS, **Trial-**; it L.MS

26]
  1 way;] **Trial-**; way L.MS
  2 it;] **1850A-**; it, L.MS, **Trial**
  3 Love,] **Trial-**; Love L.MS
  5 guilt].**Trial-**; Guilt L.MS
  6 goodness,] **Trial-**; goodness L.MS
  7 tree,] **Trial-**; tree L.MS
  9 Oh,] **Trial-**; Oh L.MS
10 Him] **Trial-**; him L.MS
12 be,] **Trial-**; be — L.MS
13 find,] **Trial-**; find L.MS
14 seas,] **Trial-**; seas L.MS
15 Shadow] **Trial-**; shadow L.MS
   keys,] **Trial-**; keys L.MS

27]
  3 cage,] **1851A-**; cage — L.MS; cage **Trial-1850C**
  4 woods:] **1850A-**; woods L.MS; woods; **Trial**
  6 time,] **Trial-**; Time — L.MS

7 crime,] **Trial–**; crime L.MS
9 Nor,] **Trial–**; Nor L.MS
10 troth] **Trial–**; troth, L.MS
11 sloth;] L.MS, **1850A–**; sloth, **Trial**
13 befall;] **Trial–**; befall – L.MS
14 most;] **Trial–**; most: L.MS
15 'Tis] **Trial–**; Tis L.MS
   lost] **Trial–**; lost, L.MS
16 all.] **Trial–**; all L.MS

28]

1 Christ:] T.MS, **Trial–**; Christ T.Nbk., L.MS
2 hid;] **Trial–**; hid, T.Nbk.; hid: T.MS, L.MS
   still;] **Trial–**; still T.Nbk., L.MS; still: T.MS
3 Christmas bells] T.Nbk., L.MS–; Christmas-bells T.MS
4 mist.] T.Nbk., T.MS, **Trial–**; mist L.MS
5 round,] **Trial–**; round T.Nbk.-L.MS
6 near,] **Trial–**; near T.Nbk.-L.MS
   moor,] **Trial–**; moor T.Nbk., L.MS; moor. T.MS
7 fail,] **Trial–**; fail T.Nbk.-L.MS
8 sound:] **1850A–**; sound T.MS, L.MS; sound. **Trial**
9 wind,] **Trial–**; wind T.MS, L.MS
10 dilate,] **Trial–**; dilate T.Nbk.-L.MS
   decrease,] **Trial–**; decrease – T.Nbk.; decrease T.MS, L.MS
11 goodwill,] T.MS, **Trial–**; Goodwill – T.Nbk.; goodwill L.MS
   goodwill] T.MS–; Goodwill T.Nbk.
   peace,] **Trial–**; Peace T.Nbk., T.MS; peace L.MS
12 goodwill,] **Trial–**; Goodwill – T.Nbk.; goodwill T.MS, L.MS
   mankind.] T.MS, **Trial–**; mankind T.Nbk., L.MS
13 pain,] **Trial–**; pain T.Nbk.-L.MS
14 wish'd] **Trial–**; wisht T.Nbk.-L.MS
   wake,] **Trial–**; wake T.Nbk.-L.MS
17 rule,] **Trial–**; rule T.Nbk.-L.MS
18 controll'd] T.MS, L.MS, **1850A–**; controlled T.Nbk.; control'd **Trial**
   boy;] **Trial–**; boy T.Nbk.-L.MS
19 touch'd] L.MS–; toucht T.Nbk.; touch't T.MS
   joy,] **Trial–**; joy T.Nbk.-L.MS

29]

2 peace,] **Trial–**; peace T.MS, L.MS
3 decease,] **Trial–**; decease T.MS, L.MS
4 Christmas-eve;] **1850A–**; Christmas eve T.MS; Christmas-eve L.MS;
   Christmas-eve? **Trial**
7 delight] L.MS, **1884A–**; delight, **Trial–1883**

8 jest?] L.MS, **Trial**, **1880–**; jest. T.MS, **1850A–1878**
10 font,] T.MS, **Trial–**; font L.MS
11 Wont,] **1851A–**; Wont T.MS-**1850C**
12 house;] **Trial–**; house. T.MS; house L.MS
13 sisters] **Trial–**; Sisters T.MS, L.MS
14 nurses,] **Trial–**; nurses T.MS, L.MS
   new;] **1850A–**; new T.MS; new. L.MS; new, **Trial**
16 time?] L.MS–; time – T.MS
   They] **Trial–**; they T.MS, L.MS
   die.] L.MS–; die: T.MS

30]
2 Christmas hearth;] Heath MS, **1850A–**; Christmas-hearth: T.Nbk.;
   Christmas-hearth. Hn.Nbk.; Christmas hearth H.Lpr.101-L.MS;
   Christmas hearth, **Trial**
3 possess'd] **Trial–**; possest T.Nbk., Hn.Nbk.-T.MS; possessed Heath
   MS; possesst L.MS
   earth,] **Trial–**; Earth. T.Nbk.; Earth, Heath MS; Earth Hn.Nbk.;
   earth H.Lpr.101-L.MS
4 Christmas-eve.] L.MS–; Christmas-Eve. T.Nbk., Hn.Nbk.; Christmas
   eve. Heath MS, H.Lpr.101; Christmas-eve T.MS
5 hall] T.Nbk., L.MS–; Hall Heath MS-T.MS
6 gambol'd,] Heath MS, T.MS, **Trial–**; gamboled, T.Nbk.; gambol'd
   Hn.Nbk., H.Lpr.101, L.MS
8 Shadow] **Trial–**; shadow T.Nbk.-L.MS
   all.] Heath MS-T.MS, **Trial–**; all T.Nbk., L.MS
9 paused:] Heath MS *reads* ceased:
   beech:] T.Nbk.-Hn.Nbk., T.MS, **Trial–**; beech. H.Lpr.101; beech L.MS
10 land;] Heath MS, **Trial–**; land T.Nbk., Hn.Nbk.-L.MS
11 circle] T.Nbk., Heath MS, H.Lpr.101–; circle, Hn.Nbk.
   hand-in-hand] T.Nbk., Hn.Nbk.-T.MS, **Trial–**; hand in hand Heath
   MS, L.MS
12 silent,] Heath MS, **Trial–**; silent T.Nbk., Hn.Nbk.-L.MS
   each.] Heath MS-T.MS, **Trial–**; each T.Nbk., L.MS
13 echo-like] Heath MS-T.MS, **Trial–**; echolike T.Nbk.; echo like L.MS
   rang;] **Trial–**; rang. T.Nbk.; rang: Hn.Nbk.-T.MS; rang Heath MS. L.MS
14 sung,] T.Nbk.-Hn.Nbk., T.MS, **Trial–**; sung. H.Lpr.101; sung L.MS
   tho'] T.Nbk., H.Lpr.101–; though Heath MS; tho Hn.Nbk.
   dim,] T.Nbk.-T.MS, **Trial–**; dim L.MS
16 year:] T.Nbk., Hn.Nbk.–; year: – Heath MS
   sang:] **Trial–**; sang. T.Nbk.-L.MS
17 ceased:] T.Nbk., Hn.Nbk., **Trial–**; paused. – Heath MS; ceas'd:
   H.Lpr.101; cease't: T.MS, L.MS
   a] T.Nbk., Hn.Nbk.–; A Heath MS

18 surely] Heath MS–; Surely T.Nbk.
   meet:] Heath MS, H.Lpr.101–; meet. T.Nbk., Hn.Nbk.
19] **Trial**–; They rest, . . . their . . . sweet T.Nbk. *and* L.MS; They ~~sleep~~
   rest, we said, their ~~rest~~ sleep is sweet – Heath MS; They rest, . . .
   said; their . . . sweet: Hn.Nbk.; They rest, . . . said: their . . . sweet
   H.Lpr.101, T.MS (. . . sweet.)
21 range,] **Trial**–; range T.Nbk., Hn.Nbk., L.MS; range – Heath MS;
   range: H.Lpr.101, T.MS
22 Once more] Heath MS *reads* ~~Again~~ Once more
   sang:] Hn.Nbk.–; sang. T.Nbk.; sang Heath MS
   die] T.Nbk., Heath MS, L.MS–; die: Hn.Nbk.-T.MS
23 sympathy,] Hn.Nbk., **Trial**–; sympathy T.Nbk., Heath MS, L.MS;
   sympathy: H.Lpr.101, T.MS
24 us,] Hn.Nbk., **Trial**–; us T.Nbk. *2nd reading*, Heath MS, H.Lpr.101–
   L.MS
   although] **Trial**–; altho T.Nbk. *2nd reading*, Heath MS; altho'
   Hn.Nbk.-L.MS
   change;] **Trial**–; change T.Nbk. *2nd reading*, L.MS; change. Heath
   MS-T.MS
25 'Rapt] **1850A**–; Rapt T.Nbk.-**Trial**
   frail] Heath MS, H.Lpr.101–; frail, T.Nbk., Hn.Nbk.
26 gather'd] Hn.Nbk.–; gathered T.Nbk., Heath MS
   power,] T.Nbk., **Trial**–; power Heath MS-L.MS
   yet] Heath MS *reads* ~~still~~ yet
27 Pierces] Heath MS *reads* Pierceth
   seraphic] T.Nbk., Hn.Nbk., H.Lpr.101, L.MS–; Seraphic Heath MS,
   T.MS
28 orb,] T.Nbk., Heath MS, **Trial**–; orb Hn.Nbk.-L.MS
29] **1851A**–; Rise . . . morn! rise . . . morn T.Nbk.; Rise . . . rise . . .
   morn Heath MS; Rise . . . morn! rise . . . morn! Hn.Nbk.-T.MS;
   L.MS *has no punctuation*; . . . rise . . . **Trial-1850C**
30 night:] **Trial**–; night T.Nbk., Heath MS, H.Lpr.101, T.MS; night.
   Hn.Nbk., L.MS
31 Father,] H.Lpr.101, T.MS, **1851A**–; Father T.Nbk.-Hn.Nbk., L.MS;
   Father! **Trial-1850C**
   east,] **Trial**–; East T.Nbk.-L.MS

31]
  1 Lazarus] Heath MS –; Lazaras T.Nbk.b.
    charnel-cave,] Moxon MS, **Trial**–; charnel cave Heath MS, H.Lpr.101,
    T.MS; charnel-cave T.Nbk.b, L.MS
  2 return'd,] Moxon MS, **Trial**–; returned T.Nbk.b; returned, Heath
    MS; return'd H.Lpr.101-L.MS

3 demanded −] Heath MS, Moxon MS, **Trial−**; demanded, T.Nbk.b,
H.Lpr.101, T.MS; demanded L.MS
if] T.Nbk.b, Moxon MS −; If Heath MS
yearn'd] Moxon MS−; yearned T.Nbk.b, Heath MS
4 grave?] T.Nbk.a−Moxon MS, L.MS−; grave. H.Lpr.101, T.MS
5 'Where . . . days?'] Heath MS, **Trial−**; "Where . . . days"? Moxon MS;
Where . . . days.' H.Lpr.101; Where . . . days? T.Nbk.b, T.MS; Where
. . . days L.MS
thou, brother,] T.Nbk.b−Moxon MS, **Trial−**; thou brother H.Lpr.101−
L.MS
6 reply,] T.Nbk.b, Moxon MS, **Trial−**; reply Heath MS, H.Lpr.101−
L.MS
7 Which] T.Nbk.b, H.Lpr.101−; Which, Heath MS, Moxon MS
telling] T.Nbk.b, Heath MS, H.Lpr.101−; telling, Moxon MS
die] T.Nbk.b, H.Lpr.101−; die, Heath MS, Moxon MS
9 met,] **Trial−**; met Heath MS, H.Lpr.101, T.MS; met. Moxon MS;
met: L.MS
10 sound,] Heath MS, **Trial−**; sound. Moxon MS; sound H.Lpr.101−
L.MS
11 crown'd] Moxon MS−; crowned Heath MS
12 Olivet.] Heath MS−T.MS, **Trial−**; Olivet L.MS
13 Christ!] Heath MS−T.MS, **Trial−**; Christ L.MS
14 unreveal'd;] **Trial−**; unreveal'd. Moxon MS; unrevealed *revised to*
unreveal'd H.Lpr.101; unrevealed Heath MS, L.MS; unreveal'd T.MS
15 not;] **Trial−**; not: Heath MS, H.Lpr.101, T.MS; not: − Moxon MS;
not L.MS
seal'd] Moxon MS−; sealed Heath MS
16 Evangelist.] Heath MS−T.MS, **Trial−**; Evangelist L.MS

32]
1 prayer,] **Trial−**; prayer: T.Nbk.b; prayer. T.MS; prayer H.Lpr.101,
L.MS
3-4 he . . . there.] **Trial−**; he . . . there H.Lpr.101; 'he . . . there' T.Nbk.b,
T.MS, L.MS (there'.)
3 dead,] **Trial−**; dead T.Nbk.b−L.MS
6 other,] T.Nbk.b, L.MS−; other T.Nbk.a, H.Lpr.101, T.MS
7 face,] T.Nbk.b, **Trial−**; face T.Nbk.a, H.Lpr.101−L.MS
8 Life] H.Lpr.101−; life T.Nbk.a, b
9 thought,] T.Nbk.a, b, L.MS−; thought H.Lpr.101, T.MS
fears,] **Trial−**; fears T.Nbk.a−L.MS
10 complete,] T.Nbk.a, **Trial−**; complete T.Nbk.b−L.MS
12 tears.] H.Lpr.101−; tears T.Nbk.a, b
13 prayers,] T.Nbk.a, **Trial−**; prayers H.Lpr.101−L.MS

14 endure;] **1850A–**; endure! T.Nbk.a; endure H.Lpr.101–L.MS;
   endure, **Trial**
15 pure,] T.Nbk.a, H.Lpr.101, **1850A–**; pure T.MS–**Trial**
16 theirs?] H.Lpr.101–; their's. T.Nbk.a

33]
  2 Mayst] H.Lpr.101, **Trial–**; May'st T.MS, L.MS
    have] H.Lpr.101, T.MS, **Trial–**; 'ave L.MS
    reach'd] H.Lpr.101, **Trial–**; reach't T.MS, L.MS
    air,] **Trial–**; air H.Lpr.101–L.MS
  3 centre] H.Lpr.101, **Trial–**; center T.MS, L.MS
    everywhere,] **Trial–**; everywhere H.Lpr.101–L.MS
  4 form,] **1850A–**; form – T.MS; form L.MS; form. H.Lpr.101, **Trial**
  5 prays,] **Trial–**; prays H.Lpr.101–L.MS
  6 Heaven,] **Trial–**; heaven, H.Lpr.101–L.MS
    views;] **Trial–**; views H.Lpr.101–L.MS
  7 thou] H.Lpr.101–L.MS, **1850A–**; thou, **Trial**
    hint] H.Lpr.101–L.MS, **1850A–**; hint, **Trial**
  8 days.] H.Lpr.101, T.MS, **Trial–**; days L.MS
  9 faith] L.MS–; faith, H.Lpr.101, T.MS
    form] L.MS–; form, H.Lpr.101, T.MS
    thine,] **Trial–**; thine H.Lpr.101–L.MS
 10 good:] **1851A–**; good L.MS; good. H.Lpr.101, T.MS, **Trial–1850C**
 13 See thou,] **1850B–**; See thou H.Lpr.101–L.MS; See, thou **Trial,**
    1850A
    reason] L.MS–; Reason H.Lpr.101, T.MS
    ripe] H.Lpr.101–L.MS, **1850A–**; ripe, **Trial**
 14 within,] **1850A–**; within H.Lpr.101–**Trial**
 15 sin,] **Trial–**; sin H.Lpr.101–L.MS

34]
  2 evermore,] **Trial–**; evermore. H.Lpr.101, T.MS; evermore L.MS
  3 earth] H.Lpr.101, L.MS–; Earth T.MS
    core,] **Trial–**; core H.Lpr.101–L.MS
  4 is;] **1850A–**; is. H.Lpr.101; is, T.MS; is L.MS; is: **Trial**
  5 flame,] **Trial–**; flame H.Lpr.101–L.MS
  6 beauty;] **Trial–**; beauty, H.Lpr.101, T.MS; beauty L.MS
  7 Poet,] **Trial–**; Poet H.Lpr.101–L.MS
  8 aim.] H.Lpr.101, T.MS., **Trial–**; aim L.MS
 10 'Twere] **Trial–**; Twere H.Lpr.101–L.MS
    choose] H.Lpr.101, T.MS, **Trial–**; chuse L.MS
 11 mortal,] **Trial–**; mortal H.Lpr.101–L.MS
 12 die;] **Trial–**; die. H.Lpr.101–L.MS

13 'Twere] H.Lpr.101, **Trial-**; Twere T.MS, L.MS
 peace,] **Trial-**; peace H.Lpr.101-L.MS
14 draws,] **Trial-**; draws H.Lpr.101-L.MS
15 head-foremost] **Trial-**; head foremost H.Lpr.101-L.MS

35]
 2 house,] **1855-**; house T.MS, L.MS; house: **Trial-1851B**
 3-4 'The . . . dust:'] **1855-**; 'The . . . dust.' T.MS; The . . . dust L.MS;
 The . . . dust: **Trial-1851B**
 3 in;] **Trial-**; in: T.MS; in L.MS
 bows;] **Trial-**; bows: T.MS; bows L.MS
 4 dies:] **Trial-**; dies, T.MS; dies L.MS
 5 say?] **1855-**; say T.MS, L.MS; say, **Trial-1851B**
 5-7 'Yet . . . alive:'] **1855-**; 'Yet . . . alive' T.MS; 'Yet . . . alive L.MS;
 yet . . . alive – **Trial**; yet . . . alive? **1850A-1851B**
 5 here,] **Trial-**; here T.MS, L.MS
12 be;] **Trial-**; be. T.MS, L.MS
13 sigh,] **Trial-**; sigh T.MS, L.MS
14-16 'The . . . die.'] **Trial-**; The . . . die T.MS; The . . . die. L.MS
15 more,] **Trial-**; more T.MS, L.MS
16 Half-dead] T.MS, L.MS, **1851A-**; Half dead **Trial-1850C**
18 If] **Trial-**; if T.MS, L.MS
19 been,] T.MS, **Trial-**; been L.MS
20 shut,] **Trial-**; shut T.MS, L.MS
21 moods,] T.MS, **Trial-**; moods L.MS
23 crush'd] **Trial-**; crusht T.MS, L.MS
 grape,] **Trial-**; grape T.MS, L.MS
24 bask'd] **Trial-**; baskt T.MS, L.MS

36]
 1 Tho'] T.MS-; Tho H.Lpr.101
 join,] **Trial-**; join H.Lpr.101-L.MS
 2 Deep-seated] T.MS-; Deep seated H.Lpr.101
 frame,] **Trial-**; frame H.Lpr.101-L.MS
 4 Him] H.Lpr.101, **Trial-**; him T.MS, L.MS
 coin;] **Trial-**; coin T.MS; coin. H.Lpr.101, L.MS
 5 Wisdom] L.MS, **1851A-**; wisdom **Trial-1850C**
 powers,] **Trial-**; powers L.MS
 6 truth] **1851A-**; Truth L.MS-1850C
 fail,] **Trial-**; fail L.MS
 7 truth] H.Lpr.101, T.MS, **1851A-**; Truth L.MS-1850C
 8 doors.] L.MS-; doors H.Lpr.101, T.MS
11 deeds,] **Trial-**; deeds H.Lpr.101-L.MS

12 thought;] **Trial–**; thought H.Lpr.101, T.MS; thought. L.MS
13 sheaf,] **Trial–**; sheaf H.Lpr.101–L.MS
14 house,] **Trial–**; house H.Lpr.101–L.MS
　　grave,] **Trial–**; grave – T.MS; grave H.Lpr.101, L.MS
16 coral reef.] L.MS–; coral-reef. H.Lpr.101, T.MS

37]
　1 brow:] **Trial–**; brow T.MS, L.MS
　2–8] 'Thou . . . hill.'] **Trial–**; 'Thou . . . hill' T.MS; Thou . . . hill. L.MS
　2 least;] **Trial–**; least T.MS, L.MS
　3 priest,] **Trial–**; priest T.MS, L.MS
　4 thou.] T.MS, L.MS, **1855–**; thou: **Trial–1851B**
　5, 13, 17, 21] *Inverted commas introduced in* **1884A**
　5 rill,] **Trial–**; rill T.MS, L.MS
　6 feet,] **Trial–**; feet T.MS, L.MS
　9 replies,] **Trial–**; replies T.MS, L.MS
　10 cheek:] **Trial–**; cheek T.MS, L.MS
　11–24] 'I . . . song.'] **Trial–**; I . . . song. T.MS, L.MS
　12 mysteries;] **Trial–**; mysteries. T.MS, L.MS
　13 Muse,] **Trial–**; Muse T.MS; muse L.MS
　15 heart,] **Trial–**; heart T.MS, L.MS
　16 dues;] **Trial–**; dues. T.MS; dues L.MS
　17 dead,] **Trial–**; dead T.MS, L.MS
　18 divine,] **Trial–**; divine T.MS, L.MS
　20 said),] **Trial–**; said) T.MS, L.MS
　21 murmur'd,] **Trial–**; murmur'd T.MS, L.MS
　　along,] **Trial–**; along T.MS, L.MS
　22 clasp'd] **Trial–**; claspt T.MS, L.MS
　　reveal'd;] **Trial–**; reveal'd. T.MS; reveal'd L.MS
　23 master's] **Trial–**; Master's T.MS, L.MS
　　field,] T.MS, **Trial–**; field L.MS

38]
　1 on,] **Trial–**; on T.MS, L.MS
　2 Tho'] L.MS–; Tho T.MS
　3 dies,] **Trial–**; dies T.MS, L.MS
　4 gone.] T.MS, **Trial–**; gone L.MS
　5 gives,] T.MS, **Trial–**; gives L.MS
　6 herald melodies] L.MS–; herald-melodies T.MS
　　spring,] **Trial–**; spring: T.MS; spring L.MS
　8 lives.] **Trial–**; lives T.MS, L.MS
　10 free,] **Trial–**; free T.MS, L.MS

39]
8 Sorrow –] **1872–**; Sorrow Beinecke MS, **1870**
9 men, –] **1872–**; men, Beinecke MS, **1870**
12 again.] **1870–**; again Beinecke MS

40]
2 Spirits] L.MS–; spirits, T.MS
  away,] T.MS, **Trial–**; away L.MS
4 orange-flower!] **Trial–**; orange-flower; T.MS; orange-flower L.MS
6 home,] **Trial–**; home T.MS, L.MS
8 eyes;] **Trial–**; eyes T.MS, L.MS
9 move,] **Trial–**; move T.MS, L.MS
10 face,] T.MS, **Trial–**; face L.MS
12 love;] **Trial–**; love. T.MS, L.MS
13 rear,] T.MS, **Trial–**; rear L.MS
  teach,] **Trial–**; teach – T.MS; teach L.MS
14 Becoming] L.MS–; Becoming, T.MS
15 days,] T.MS, **Trial–**; days L.MS
16 each;] **Trial–**; each. T.MS, L.MS
17 And, doubtless,] **Trial–**; And doubtless T.MS, L.MS
20 heaven.] **Trial–**; Heaven. T.MS, L.MS
21 discern!] L.MS–; discern – T.MS
23 bride,] **Trial–**; bride T.MS, L.MS
24 return,] **Trial–**; return T.MS, L.MS
25 told,] L.MS–; told T.MS
26 babe,] **Trial–**; babe T.MS, L.MS
  boast,] **Trial–**; boast T.MS, L.MS
27 miss'd] **Trial–**; misst T.MS, L.MS
  most] T.MS, L.MS, **1884A–**; most, **Trial-1883**
28 old:] **1850A–**; old T.MS, L.MS; old. **Trial**
29 hands,] **Trial–**; hands T.MS, L.MS
30 low;] **Trial–**; low T.MS, L.MS
31 know,] **Trial–**; know T.MS, L.MS
32 lands.] L.MS–; lands T.MS

41]
1 spirit] L.MS, **Trial–**; spirit, Hn.Nbk., T.MS
2 higher;] **Trial–**; higher Hn.Nbk., L.MS; higher, T.MS
3 altar-fire,] T.MS, **Trial–**; altar-fire Hn.Nbk.; altar fire L.MS
4 gross.] T.MS, **Trial–**; gross: Hn.Nbk.; gross L.MS
5 thou] Hn.Nbk., L.MS–; Thou T.MS
  strange,] **Trial–**; strange Hn.Nbk.-L.MS
7 changes;] **1850A–**; changes, Hn.Nbk.; changes – T.MS; changes L.MS, **Trial**

ground,] T.MS, 1851A-; ground Hn.Nbk., L.MS; ground; **Trial-1850C**
9 be —] **Trial-**; be Hn.Nbk.-L.MS
11 light,] **Trial-**; light Hn.Nbk.-L.MS
12 once,] T.MS, **Trial-**; once Hn.Nbk., L.MS
    friend,] T.MS, **Trial-**; friend Hn.Nbk., L.MS
    thee.] T.MS, 1872-; thee! Hn.Nbk.; thee L.MS, **1870** (*misprint*);
    thee: **Trial-1869**
13 tho'] Hn.Nbk.-L.MS, 1851A-; though **Trial-1850C**
14 death;] **Trial-**; Death, Hn.Nbk.; death T.MS, L.MS
15 beneath,] **Trial-**; beneath Hn.Nbk.-L.MS
16 fields;] **Trial-**; fields — Hn.Nbk.; fields T.MS, L.MS
18 behold,] T.MS, **Trial-**; behold Hn.Nbk., L.MS
19 cold,] T.MS, **Trial-**; cold Hn.Nbk., L.MS
20 more,] **Trial-**; more Hn.Nbk.-L.MS
22 thee,] **Trial-**; thee Hn.Nbk.-L.MS
23 to-be,] 1851A-; to-be Hn.Nbk., L.MS; To-be T.MS; to be, **Trial-1850C**

42]
1 dim:] **1850A-**; dim L.MS; dim. Hn.Nbk., T.MS, **Trial**
2 outstript] Hn.Nbk.-L.MS, **1850A-**; outstripp'd **Trial**
    race;] **Trial-**; race. T.MS; race Hn.Nbk., L.MS
4 rank'd] **Trial-**; rankt Hn.Nbk.-L.MS
    him.] Hn.Nbk., T.MS, **Trial-**; him L.MS
5 still,] T.MS, **Trial-**; still. Hn.Nbk.; still L.MS
6 he the much-beloved] T.MS-; he, the much-beloved, Hn.Nbk.
    again,] Hn.Nbk., **Trial-**; again T.MS, L.MS
7 lord] Hn.Nbk., **Trial-**; Lord T.MS, L.MS
    experience,] Hn.Nbk., **Trial-**; experience T.MS, L.MS
8 will:] **1850A-**; will. Hn.Nbk.; will T.MS, L.MS; will; **Trial**
11] **Trial-**; When one, that loves, but knows not, reaps T.MS; *no*
    punctuation in Hn.Nbk. *and* L.MS
12 knows?] Hn.Nbk., **Trial-**; knows. T.MS; knows L.MS

43]
1 one,] **Trial-**; one T.MS, L.MS
3 its] L.MS-; its' T.MS
4 on;] **Trial-**; on. T.MS; on, L.MS
6 body,] **Trial-**; body T.MS, L.MS
    last,] L.MS-; last T.MS
7 past] **Trial-**; Past T.MS, L.MS
8 flower:] **Trial-**; flower T.MS; flower. L.MS
9 man;] **Trial-**; man L.MS
10 souls] **Trial-**; Souls L.MS
12 began;] **1855-**; began: L.MS, **1850A-1851B**; began. **Trial**

44]
1 dead?] H.Lpr.101, **Trial-**; dead Hn.Nbk., T.MS, L.MS
2 more;] **Trial-**; more Hn.Nbk.-L.MS
5 vanish'd,] **Trial-**; vanisht H.Lpr.101-L.MS
   tint,] **Trial-**; tint H.Lpr.101-L.MS
8 hint;] **Trial-**; hint H.Lpr.101, T.MS; hint. L.MS
9 years] Hn.Nbk., L.MS-; years, H.Lpr.101, T.MS
10] **1884A-**; If . . . springs Hn.Nbk.-T.MS: (If . . . springs) L.MS-**1874,**
   1877, 1878; (If . . . springs, **1875** (*bracket omitted in error*); (If . . .
   springs,) **1880-83**
12 peers.] Hn.Nbk., **Trial-**; peers H.Lpr.101-L.MS
13 fall,] **Trial-**; fall Hn.Nbk.-L.MS
14 round,] Hn.Nbk.-T.MS, **Trial-**; round L.MS
   doubt;] **1855-**; doubt. Hn.Nbk.; doubt H.Lpr.101-L.MS; doubt,
   Trial-1851B
15 angel] H.Lpr.101-; Angel Hn.Nbk.
16 place,] **Trial-**; place Hn.Nbk.-L.MS
   all.] H.Lpr.101, **Trial-**; all Hn.Nbk., T.MS, L.MS

45]
1 sky,] **Trial-**; sky Hn.Nbk.-L.MS
3 breast,] **Trial-**; breast Hn.Nbk.-L.MS
4 'this is I:'] **Trial-**; this is I Hn.Nbk.; this is I. T.MS, L.MS
5 much,] **Trial-**; much Hn.Nbk.-L.MS
6 'I,' and 'me,'] **Trial-**; I and me Hn.Nbk.-L.MS
7-8 'I . . . touch.'] **1855-**; I . . . touch Hn.Nbk., T.MS; I . . . touch.
   L.MS; I . . . touch; Trial; 'I . . . touch:' **1850A-1851B**
7 see,] **Trial-**; see Hn.Nbk.-L.MS
10 begin,] **Trial-**; begin Hn.Nbk.-L.MS
12 defined.] **Trial-**; defin'd. Hn.Nbk.; defin'd T.MS; defined L.MS
13 breath,] **Trial-**; breath Hn.Nbk.-L.MS

46]
1 track,] **Trial-**; track L.MS *2nd reading*
2 by,] L.MS *2nd reading*, **1850A-**; by **Trial**.
   flower,] **Trial-**; flower L.MS *2nd reading*
3 shadow'd] L.MS *2nd reading*, **1850A-**; shadowed **Trial**
   hour,] **Trial-**; hour L.MS *2nd reading*
4 life] **Trial-**; Life L.MS *2nd reading*
6 tomb,] **Trial-**; tomb H.Lpr.101-L.MS *2nd reading*
8 past;] **1850A-**; Past. H.Lpr.101; Past T.MS, L.MS *2nd reading*; past,
   Trial
9 tract] H.Lpr.101-L.MS, **1850A-**; track **Trial**

time] **Trial–**; Time H.Lpr.101–L.MS
reveal'd;] **1850A–**; reveal'd H.Lpr.101–L.MS; reveal'd, **Trial**
10 increase;] **Trial–**; increase H.Lpr.101, T.MS; increase, L.MS
11 Days] **Trial–**; Days, H.Lpr.101–L.MS
order'd] T.MS–; ordered H.Lpr.101
peace,] L.MS–; peace H.Lpr.101, T.MS
12 years] L.MS–; years, H.Lpr.101, T.MS
its] H.Lpr.101, L.MS–; it's T.MS
13 large,] L.MS–; large H.Lpr.101, T.MS
14 field,] **Trial–**; field H.Lpr.101–L.MS
far;] **1855–**; far. H.Lpr.101, T.MS; far: L.MS; far, **Trial–1851B**
16 marge.] T.MS–; marge H.Lpr.101

47]
1 each,] **Trial–**; each L.MS
whole,] **Trial–**; whole L.MS
2 rounds,] **Trial–**; rounds L.MS
and] **Trial–**; and, L.MS
7 beside;] **Trial–**; beside L.MS
8 meet:] **1850A–**; meet. L.MS, **Trial**
9 feast,] **Trial–**; feast L.MS
10 other's] **Trial–**; others L.MS
good:] **1855–**; good. L.MS; good; **Trial–1851B**
12 He] **Trial–**; he L.MS
15 landing-place,] **Trial–**; landing-place L.MS
say,] **Trial–**; say L.MS
16 We] **Trial–**; we L.MS

48]
1 lays,] H.Lpr.101, T.MS, **Trial–**; lays L.MS
born,] H.Lpr.101, T.MS, **Trial–**; born L.MS
3 proposed,] **Trial–**; proposed H.Lpr.101–L.MS
4 scorn:] **Trial–**; scorn. H.Lpr.101, T.MS; scorn L.MS
5 prove;] **Trial–**; prove. H.Lpr.101, T.MS; prove L.MS
6 takes,] T.MS, **Trial–**; takes H.Lpr.101, L.MS
remit,] H.Lpr.101, T.MS, **Trial–**; remit L.MS
7 flit,] **Trial–**; flit H.Lpr.101–L.MS
8 love:] **1850A–**; love H.Lpr.101–L.MS; love. **Trial**
9 hence, indeed,] **Trial–**; hence indeed H.Lpr.101–L.MS
words,] **1851A–**; words H.Lpr.101–L.MS; words; **Trial–1850C**
10 law,] **Trial–**; law H.Lpr.101–L.MS
12 chords:] **Trial–**; chords; H.Lpr.101, T.MS; chords L.MS
13 lay,] **1850A–**; lay H.Lpr.101–L.MS; lay; **Trial**

15 swallow-flights] T.MS, **Trial–**; swallow flights H.Lpr.101, L.MS
   song,] **Trial–**; song H.Lpr.101–L.MS
16 tears,] **Trial–**; tears H.Lpr.101–L.MS

49]
  1 art,] **Trial–**; Art, T.MS; Art L.MS
   nature,] **Trial–**; Nature, T.MS; Nature L.MS
   schools,] **Trial–**; schools T.MS, L.MS
  2 glance,] **Trial–**; glance T.MS, L.MS
  4 pools:] **1850A–**; pools. T.MS; pools L.MS; pools; **Trial**
  9 look,] **Trial–**; look T.MS, L.MS
   way,] **Trial–**; way T.MS, L.MS
11 break,] **Trial–**; break T.MS, L.MS
12 play.] **Trial–**; play T.MS, L.MS
14 Ay me,] **1851A–**; Aye me! T.MS; Ay me L.MS; Ay me! **Trial–1850C**
   down,] **Trial–**; down T.MS, L.MS

50]
  2 creeps,] **Trial–**; creeps L.MS
  3 tingle;] **Trial–**; tingle L.MS
  6 trust;] **1855–**; trust L.MS; trust, **Trial–1851B**
  7 Time,] **1851A–**; Time L.MS; time, **Trial–1850C**
   maniac] L.MS, **1855–**; maniac, **Trial–1851B**
   dust,] **Trial–**; dust L.MS
  8 Life,] **1851A–**; Life L.MS; life, **Trial–1850C**
   Fury] L.MS, **1855–**; Fury, **Trial–1851B**
  9 dry,] **Trial–**; dry L.MS
10 spring,] **Trial–**; Spring L.MS
11 eggs,] **Trial–**; eggs L.MS
   sing] L.MS, **1884A–**; sing, **Trial–1883**
13 away,] **Trial–**; away L.MS
14 strife,] **Trial–**; strife L.MS
15 life] **Trial–**; Life L.MS

51]
  1 dead] L.MS–; Dead H.Lpr.101, T.MS
  2 side?] H.Lpr.101, T.MS, **Trial–**; side L.MS
  3 hide?] H.Lpr.101, T.MS, **Trial–**; hide L.MS
  4 dread?] H.Lpr.101, T.MS, **Trial–**; dread L.MS
  5 strove,] **Trial–**; strove – H.Lpr.101, T.MS; strove L.MS
  6 blame,] **Trial–**; blame H.Lpr.101, L.MS; blame – T.MS
  8 love?] H.Lpr.101, T.MS, **Trial–**; love L.MS
  9 untrue:] **Trial–**; untrue. H.Lpr.101, T.MS; untrue L.MS

10 love] H.Lpr.101, L.MS–; Love T.MS
   faith?] H.Lpr.101, T.MS, Trial–; faith L.MS
11 Death:] Trial–; Death. H.Lpr.101, T.MS; death L.MS
12 dead] T.MS–; Dead H.Lpr.101
13 fall:] Trial–; fall. H.Lpr.101, T.MS; fall L.MS
14 watch, like God,] Trial–; watch like God H.Lpr.101–L.MS
15 ours,] Trial–; our's H.Lpr.101, T.MS; ours L.MS

52]
1–4 I . . . thought.] Trial–; 'I . . . thought' T.MS; I . . . thought L.MS
 1 ought,] T.MS, Trial–; ought L.MS
 2 love] T.MS, Trial–; Love L.MS
   beloved;] Trial–; beloved T.MS, L.MS
 5 'Yet . . . song,'] Trial–; Oh . . . song T.MS; 'Yet . . . song' L.MS
   plaintive] T.MS *reads* plantive
 6 Spirit] Trial–; spirit T.MS, L.MS
   love] T.MS, Trial–; Love L.MS. (T.MS *has* love *interlineated due to hasty transcription*)
   replied;] Trial–; replied T.MS, L.MS
7, 9, 13, 16 'Thou . . . 'What . . . 'So . . . pearl.'] Trial–; *no inverted commas in* T.MS, L.MS
 7 canst] L.MS–; can'st T.MS
   side,] Trial–; side T.MS, L.MS
 8 wrong.] T.MS, Trial–; wrong L.MS
 9 'What] Trial–; What L.MS
10 bears?] Trial–; bears L.MS
11 record? not] L.MS, 1850A–; record? – not Trial
12 blue:] 1851A–; blue. T.MS, L.MS; blue; Trial–1850C
13 not,] Trial–; not T.MS, L.MS
   girl,] Trial–; girl T.MS, L.MS
14 life] T.MS, Trial–; Life L.MS
   dash'd] Trial–; dasht T.MS, L.MS
   sin.] T.MS, Trial–; sin L.MS
15 Abide:] L.MS–; Abide T.MS
   gather'd] T.MS, L.MS, 1851A–; gathered Trial–1850C
   in,] Trial–; in T.MS, L.MS

53]
 1 seen,] T.MS, Trial–; seen L.MS
 2 man,] Trial–; man T.MS, L.MS
   boys,] T.MS, Trial–; boys L.MS
 3 noise,] T.MS, Trial–; noise L.MS
 4 green:] 1850B–; green. T.MS; green L.MS; green; Trial–1850A

5 give,] T.MS, 1851A-; give L.MS-1850C
6 That] L.MS-; That, T.MS
   sown,] T.MS, Trial-; sown L.MS
7 The soil, left barren,] Trial-; The soil left barren T.MS, L.MS
8 live?] Trial-; live. T.MS; live L.MS
10 life] T.MS, Trial-; Life L.MS
   youth,] Trial-; youth T.MS, L.MS
12 round?] Trial-; round. T.MS; round L.MS
13 good:] L.MS-; good! T.MS
   well:] Trial-; well T.MS; well, L.MS
14 Philosophy.] L.MS, 1851A-; philosophy T.MS, Trial-1850C
15 mark,] Trial-; mark T.MS, L.MS
16 Hell.] L.MS-; Hell T.MS

54]
1 Oh] T.MS, Trial-; O L.MS
   that somehow] Trial-; that, somehow, T.MS, L.MS
2 ill,] Trial-; ill T.MS, L.MS
3 nature,] Trial-; Nature, T.MS, L.MS
4 doubt,] L.MS-; doubt T.MS
   blood;] L.MS-; blood – T.MS
5 feet;] L.MS-; feet T.MS
6 destroy'd,] Trial-; destroy'd T.MS, L.MS
7 void,] L.MS-; void T.MS
9 cloven] Trial-; clov'n T.MS, L.MS
11 shrivell'd] L.MS, 1884A-; shrivel'd T.MS, Trial-1883
   fire,] L.MS-; fire T.MS
13 anything;] Trial-; anything T.MS; anything. L.MS
15 far off] T.MS, Trial-; far-off L.MS
   last,] Trial-; last – T.MS; last L.MS
   all,] Trial-; all T.MS, L.MS
17 dream:] L.MS-; dream – T.MS
   I?] Trial-; I. T.MS, L.MS
18 night:] Trial-; night T.MS; night, L.MS
19 light:] Trial-; light T.MS; light, L.MS

55]
1 wish,] Trial-; wish L.MS
2 grave,] L.MS, 1855-; grave; Trial-1851B
5 strife,] Trial-; strife L.MS
6 dreams?] Trial-; dreams, L.MS
9 I,] Trial-; I L.MS
12 bear,] 1855-; bear; L.MS-1851B

13 trod,] **Trial–**; trod; L.MS
16 God,] L.MS, **1855–**; God; **Trial–1851B**
17 faith,] **Trial–**; faith L.MS
   grope,] **Trial–**; grope L.MS
18 chaff,] **Trial–**; chaff; L.MS
19 all,] **Trial–**; all L.MS
20 hope.] **Trial–**; hope L.MS

56]
 1 type?'] **1850A–**; type'! L.MS
 3 cries,] **1870–**; cries L.MS–1869
 3-8 'A . . . more.'] **1870–**; a . . . more' L.MS; 'a . . . more.' **1850A–1869**
 3 gone:] **1850A–**; gone L.MS
 4 nothing,] **1850A–**; nothing: L.MS
   go.] **1850A–**; go: L.MS
 5 'Thou] **1860–**; Thou L.MS–1859
   me:] **1850A–**; me. L.MS
 6 life,] **1850A–**; life: L.MS
   death:] **1850A–**; Death. L.MS
 7 breath:] **1850A–**; breath L.MS
 8 And] **1850A–**; and L.MS
   shall he,] **1850A–**; shall he L.MS
10 eyes,] **1850A–**; eyes L.MS
11 skies,] **1850A–**; skies L.MS
12 prayer,] **1850A–**; prayer L.MS
13 love] **1850A–**; Love L.MS
   indeed] **1850A–**; indeed. L.MS
14 love] **1850A–**; Love L.MS
   Creation's] **1850A–**; Creations L.MS
15 Tho'] **1850A–**; Tho L.MS
   Nature,] **1850A–**; Nature L.MS
16 creed –] **1850A–**; creed. – L.MS
17 loved,] **1850A–**; loved L.MS
   ills,] **1850A–**; ills L.MS
19 dust,] **1850A–**; dust L.MS
20 hills?] **1850A–**; hills – L.MS
21 A] **1850A–**; a L.MS
   dream,] **1850A–**; dream. L.MS
22 discord.] **1850A–**; discord: L.MS
   prime,] **1850A–**; prime L.MS
23 slime,] **1850A–**; slime L.MS
24 match'd] **1850A–**; matchd L.MS
   him.] **1850A–**; him L.MS
25 life] **1850A–**; Life L.MS

57]

1 Peace;] **1855-**; Peace — T.MS; Peace! **Trial**; Peace, L.MS, **1850A-1851B**
 away:] **1850A-**; away! T.MS; away. L.MS; away — **Trial**
2 song:] **Trial-**; song. T.MS, L.MS
3 Peace;] **1855-**; Peace — T.MS; Peace, **L.MS-1851B**
 away:] **1855-**; away! T.MS; away. L.MS; away; **Trial-1851B**
4 wildly:] L.MS, **1855-**; wildly. T.MS; wildly; **Trial-1851B**
5 go:] L.MS, **1855-**; go. T.MS; go, **Trial-1851B**
 your] **L.MS-**; Your T.MS
 pale;] **1855-**; pale. T.MS; pale L.MS; pale, **Trial-1851B**
6 behind:] **1851A-**; behind. T.MS, L.MS; behind; **Trial-1850C**
7 shrined;] **1855-**; shrined: T.MS; shrined L.MS; shrined, **Trial-1851B**
8 pass;] **Trial-**; pass. T.MS; pass: L.MS
9 ears,] T.MS, **1855-**; ears **L.MS-1851B**
 hearing] **Trial-**; Hearing T.MS, L.MS
 dies,] T.MS, **Trial-**; dies L.MS
12 look'd] L.MS, **1851A-**; lookt T.MS; looked **Trial-1850C**
 eyes.] T.MS, **Trial-**; eyes L.MS
13 now,] T.MS, **Trial-**; now L.MS
 o'er and o'er,] **Trial-**; oer and oer T.MS, L.MS
14 dead;] **Trial-**; dead, T.MS; dead L.MS
15 'Ave, Ave, Ave,'] **Trial-**; 'Ave, Ave, Ave' T.MS; Ave, Ave, Ave L.MS
 said,] T.MS, **Trial-**; said L.MS
16 'Adieu,] T.MS, **Trial-**; Adieu, L.MS
 adieu'] **Trial-**; Adieu' T.MS; Adieu L.MS
 evermore.] T.MS, L.MS, **1855-**; evermore! **Trial-1851B**

58]

1 farewell:] **Trial-**; farewell. L.MS
2 halls,] **Trial-**; halls L.MS
5 And, falling, idly] **1850A-**; And falling idly L.MS; And falling idly, **Trial**
6 day,] **Trial-**; day L.MS
7 Half-conscious] **Trial-**; Half conscious L.MS
 clay,] **Trial-**; clay L.MS
9 answer'd:] **Trial-**; answerd L.MS
11 here,] **Trial-**; here L.MS

59]

1 Sorrow,] **1851A-**; Sorrow H.Lpr.99, Sparrow MS(*59*)
2 mistress,] **1851A-**; mistress H.Lpr.99, Sparrow MS(*59*)
 wife,] **1851A-**; wife H.Lpr.99, Sparrow MS(*59*)

3 bosom-friend] **1851A-**; bosom friend H.Lpr.99; bosomfriend
Sparrow MS(*59*)
  life;] **1851A-**; life H.Lpr.99, Sparrow MS(*59*)
4 be;] **1851A-**; be H.Lpr.99, Sparrow MS(*59*)
5 Sorrow,] **1851A-**; Sorrow H.Lpr.99, Sparrow MS(*59*)
  blood,] **1851A-**; blood H.Lpr.99, Sparrow MS(*59*)
6 bride,] **1851A-**; bride H.Lpr.99, Sparrow MS(*59*)
7 aside,] **1851A-**; aside H.Lpr.99, Sparrow MS(*59*)
8 good.] Sparrow MS(*59*)-; good H.Lpr.99
9 move,] **1851A-**; move H.Lpr.99, Sparrow MS(*59*)
10 to-day;] **1855-**; today Sparrow MS(*59*); to-day, **1851A, 1851B**
12 love;] **1851A-**; love H.Lpr.99, Sparrow MS(*59*)
13 forth,] **1851A-**; forth H.Lpr.99, Sparrow MS(*59*)
14 come,] **1851A-**; come H.Lpr.99, Sparrow MS(*59*)

60]
1 past;] **1850A-**; past — H.Lpr.101, T.MS; past L.MS; past: **Trial**
  tone:] **Trial-**; tone. H.Lpr.101, T.MS; tone L.MS
2 yet,] **Trial-**; yet. H.Lpr.101, T.MS; yet L.MS
4 own.] **Trial-**; own H.Lpr.101-L.MS
5 sphere,] **Trial-**; sphere H.Lpr.101-L.MS
6 lot,] H.Lpr.101, T.MS, **1855-**; lot L.MS; lot; **Trial-1851B**
7 Half jealous] **Trial-**; Half-jealous H.Lpr.101-L.MS
  what,] **Trial-**; what H.Lpr.101-L.MS
8 there.] **Trial-**; there H.Lpr.101-L.MS
9 forlorn;] **Trial-**; forlorn. H.Lpr.101, T.MS; forlorn L.MS
10 days,] **Trial-**; days: H.Lpr.101; days; T.MS; days L.MS
11 ways,] **Trial-**; ways H.Lpr.101-L.MS
13 go,] **Trial-**; go H.Lpr.101-L.MS
14 by:] **1855-**; by. H.Lpr.101-L.MS; by; **Trial-1851B**
15 weeps, 'How] **Trial-**; weeps 'how H.Lpr.101-L.MS
  I!] H.Lpr.101-L.MS, **1850A-**; I, — **Trial**
16 low?'] **Trial-**; low:' H.Lpr.101; low' T.MS; low L.MS

61]
1 If,] **1850A-**; If Hn.Nbk.-**Trial**
  state] Hn.Nbk.-L.MS, **1850A-**; state, **Trial**
  sublime,] **Trial-**; sublime Hn.Nbk.-L.MS
3 wise,] **Trial-**; wise Hn.Nbk.-L.MS
5 below,] **Trial-**; below Hn.Nbk.-L.MS
6 dimly character'd] T.MS-; dimly-character'd Hn.Nbk.
  slight,] **Trial-**; slight. Hn.Nbk.; slight T.MS, L.MS
7 dwarf'd] **Trial-**; dwarft Hn.Nbk.-L.MS
  night,] **Trial-**; night Hn.Nbk.-L.MS

.8 blanch'd] **Trial**-; blancht Hn.Nbk.-T.MS; blanch't L.MS
grow!] Hn.Nbk., **1850A**-; grow T.MS, L.MS; grow? **Trial**
9 shore,] **Trial**-; shore Hn.Nbk.-L.MS
10 man;] **Trial, 1850B**-; man Hn.Nbk.-L.MS; man: **1850A**
11 thee,] Hn.Nbk., L.MS-; thee T.MS
Spirit,] Hn.Nbk., L.MS-; spirit T.MS
love,] T.MS-; love: Hn.Nbk.

62]
2 fail,] **Trial**-; fail T.MS, L.MS
3 tale,] **Trial**-; tale T.MS, L.MS
4 past;] **Trial**-; Past T.MS; past. L.MS
5 thou,] **Trial**-; thou T.MS, L.MS
one] L.MS-; one, T.MS
declined,] T.MS, **Trial**-; declined L.MS
6 boy,] T.MS, **Trial**-; boy L.MS
7 joy,] **Trial**-; joy T.MS, L.MS
8 mind;] **Trial**-; mind T.MS, L.MS
9 world,] L.MS-; world T.MS
10 dies,] **Trial**-; dies T.MS, L.MS

63]
1 o'er-driven,] **Trial**-; oerdriven, T.MS; oerdriven L.MS
2 part,] T.MS, **Trial**-; part L.MS
4 its] L.MS-; it's T.MS
heaven;] **Trial**-; Heaven. T.MS, L.MS
5 these,] **Trial**-; these T.MS, L.MS
6 thou, perchance,] **Trial**-; thou perchance T.MS, L.MS
I,] **Trial**-; I T.MS, L.MS
7 sympathy,] **1872**-; sympathy T.MS-1870
8 ease.] T.MS, **Trial**-; ease L.MS
9 mayst] L.MS, **1872**-; may'st T.MS, **Trial**-1870
weep,] **Trial**-; weep T.MS, L.MS
10 As,] T.MS, **Trial**-; As L.MS
bound,] T.MS, **Trial**-; bound L.MS
12 height,] **Trial**-; height T.MS, L.MS

64]
2 divinely gifted] **Trial**-; divinely-gifted L.MS
man,] **Trial**-; man L.MS
4 village green;] **Trial**-; village-green; L.MS
9 known] **Trial**-; known, L.MS
13 higher,] **Trial**-; higher L.MS

18 still,] **Trial-**; still L.MS
23 play'd] L.MS, **1851A-**; played **Trial-1850C**
kings,] **Trial-**; kings L.MS
24 mate;] **Trial-**; mate, L.MS
27 furrow musing] **Trial-**; furrow, musing, L.MS
stands;] **Trial-**; stands. L.MS

65]
1 soul,] **1851A-**; soul T.MS, L.MS; soul! **Trial-1850C**
wilt;] **Trial-**; wilt T.MS, L.MS
3-4 'Love's . . . spilt.'] T.MS, **Trial-**; "Love's . . . spilt" L.MS
3 lost,] **Trial-**; lost T.MS; lost: L.MS
6 wrought] T.MS, **Trial-**; wrought, L.MS
7 thought,] **Trial-**; thought T.MS, L.MS
8 Self-balanced] **Trial-**; Self balance't T.MS; Self-balance't L.MS
wing:] L.MS-; wing. T.MS
9 friends,] **Trial-**; friends T.MS, L.MS
10 me,] **Trial-**; me T.MS, L.MS
11 thee] T.MS, L.MS, **1867-**; thee, **Trial-1866**
12 ends.] T.MS, **Trial-**; ends L.MS

66]
1 diseased;] **Trial-**; diseased. Hn.Nbk.; diseased: T.MS; diseased L.MS
2 wonder] T.MS-; wonder, Hn.Nbk.
play] T.MS-; play, Hn.Nbk.
3 gay,] **Trial-**; gay Hn.Nbk.-L.MS
4 pleased.] Hn.Nbk., **Trial-**; pleased — T.MS; pleased L.MS
5 crost,] **Trial-**; crost — Hn.Nbk., T.MS; crost L.MS
6 mind,] **Trial-**; mind — Hn.Nbk., T.MS; mind L.MS
7 kind,] **Trial-**; kind Hn.Nbk.-L.MS
8 lost;] **Trial-**; lost. Hn.Nbk.; lost — T.MS; lost L.MS
10 free,] **Trial-**; free: Hn.Nbk., T.MS; free L.MS
11 knee,] **Trial-**; knee Hn.Nbk-L.MS
12 hand:] T.MS, **Trial-**; hand Hn.Nbk., L.MS
13 threads,] **Trial-**; threads: Hn.Nbk.-L.MS
14 pastime,] Hn.Nbk., T.MS, **Trial-**; pastime L.MS
sky;] **Trial-**; sky. Hn.Nbk., T.MS; sky L.MS
15 die,] **Trial-**; die: Hn.Nbk., T.MS; die L.MS

67]
1 falls,] **Trial-**; falls T.MS, L.MS
2 rest] L.MS-; rest — T.MS
3 west,] **Trial-**; west — T.MS; west L.MS

4 walls:] **1850A–**; walls. T.MS; walls L.MS; walls; **Trial**
5 appears,] **Trial–**; appears T.MS, L.MS
7 name,] **Trial–**; name T.MS, L.MS
8 o'er] T.MS, **Trial–**; oer L.MS
  years.] **Trial–**; years T.MS, L.MS
9 The] T.MS, L.MS, **1850A–**; Thy **Trial** (*error*)
  away;] **Trial–**; away: T.MS, L.MS
10 dies;] **Trial–**; dies, T.MS; dies L.MS
11 And] L.MS–; And, T.MS
  eyes] L.MS–; eyes, T.MS
12 gray:] **Trial–**; gray T.MS; gray. L.MS
14 coast,] **Trial–**; coast T.MS, L.MS

68]

1 head,] T.MS b, **Trial–**; head Hn.Nbk., T.MS a, L.MS
2 Sleep,] T.MS a–; Sleep Hn.Nbk.
  twin-brother,] T.MS b, **Trial–**; twin-brother Hn.Nbk., T.MS a, L.MS
  breath;] **Trial–**; breath. Hn.Nbk.; breath T.MS a, L.MS; breath: T.MS b
3 Sleep,] T.MS b, **Trial–**; Sleep Hn.Nbk., T.MS a, L.MS
  twin-brother,] **Trial–**; twin-brother Hn.Nbk.–L.MS
  Death,] **Trial–**; Death: T.MS b; Death Hn.Nbk., T.MS a, L.MS
4 dead:] **Trial–**; dead. Hn.Nbk.–T.MS b; dead L.MS
5 walk'd] **Trial–**; walkt T.MS b, L.MS
  forlorn,] T.MS b, **Trial–**; forlorn L.MS
6 dew,] **Trial–**; dew; T.MS b; dew L.MS
8 Reveillée] **1850A–**; Reveilleé T.MS b, L.MS; Reveillee **Trial**
  morn.] T.MS b, **Trial–**; morn L.MS
10 eye,] T.MS a, b, **1855–**; eye Hn.Nbk., L.MS–1851B
11 why,] T.MS b, **Trial–**; why Hn.Nbk., T.MS a, L.MS
12 doubt:] **Trial–**; doubt Hn.Nbk., T.MS b; doubt. T.MS a, L.MS
14 wake,] **Trial–**; wake Hn.Nbk.–L.MS
  truth;] **Trial–**; truth. Hn.Nbk.; truth T.MS a, L.MS; truth: T.MS b
15 youth] Hn.Nbk., T.MS a, L.MS–; youth, T.MS b
16 thee.] Hn.Nbk., T.MS a, b, **Trial–**; thee L.MS

69]

1 more,] **1850A–**; more L.MS
2 lost:] **1850A–**; lost. L.MS
3 frost,] **1850A–**; frost L.MS
4 door:] **1851A–**; door. L.MS–1850C
5 wander'd] **1850A–**; wanderd L.MS
  town,] **1850A–**; town L.MS
6 boughs:] **1850A–**; boughs L.MS

7 brows,] **1850A–**; brows L.MS
8 crown:] **1851A–**; crown. L.MS–**1850C**
9 scoffs,] **1850A–**; scoffs: L.MS
10 hairs:] **1850A–**; hairs L.MS
12 thorns:] **1851A–**; thorns. L.MS–**1850C**
13 fool,] **1850A–**; fool: L.MS
   child:] **1850A–**; child. L.MS
14 night;] **1855–**; night L.MS; night: **1850A–1851B**
15 low,] **1850A–**; low: L.MS
   bright;] **1855–**; bright L.MS; bright, **1850A–1851B**
16 smiled:] **1850A–**; smiled. L.MS
17 hand,] **1850A–**; hand L.MS
18 leaf:] **1850A–**; leaf L.MS
19 grief,] **1862A–**; grief L.MS, **1861**; grief; **1850A–1860**

70]
 1 the] L.MS a, b, **1850A–**; thy **Trial** (*error*)
   right,] L.MS a, **Trial–**; right L.MS b
 4 night;] L.MS b, **1855–**; night: L.MS a, **Trial–1851B**
 6 gapes,] L.MS a, **Trial–**; gapes L.MS b
 8 thought;] L.MS a, **Trial–**; thought, L.MS b
10 drive;] L.MS a, **Trial–**; drive L.MS b
11 half alive,] **Trial–**; half-alive, L.MS a; half-alive L.MS b
12 shores;] L.MS a, **1867–**; shores L.MS b; shores: **Trial–1866**
14 roll,] L.MS a, **Trial–**; roll L.MS b

71]
 3 night-long] **Trial–**; nightlong T.MS, L.MS
   Past] T.MS, **Trial–**; past L.MS
 4 thro'] T.MS, L.MS, **1851A–**; through **Trial–1850C**
 9 talk'd] **Trial–**; talkt T.MS, L.MS
10 change,] **Trial–**; change – T.MS, L.MS
11 strange,] **Trial–**; strange – T.MS, L.MS
12 walk'd] **1850A–**; walkt, T.MS; walkt L.MS; walk'd; **Trial**
13 reach,] T.MS, **Trial–**; reach L.MS

72]
 1 again,] **Trial–**; again L.MS
 2 howlest,] **Trial–**; howlest L.MS
   night,] **Trial–**; night L.MS
 3 white,] **Trial–**; white L.MS
 4 pane?] **Trial–**; pane, L.MS
 6 doom,] **Trial–**; doom L.MS

7 sicken'd] L.MS, **1850B**-; sickened **Trial, 1850A**
8 sun;] **Trial**-; Sun − L.MS
11 sideways,] **Trial**-; sideways L.MS
12 shower;] **Trial**-; shower − L.MS
14 East,] **Trial**-; East L.MS
   or,] **Trial**-; or L.MS
   whispering,] **Trial**-; whispering L.MS
15 chequer-work] **Trial**-; chequerwork L.MS
16 look'd] **Trial**-; lookt L.MS
   same.] **1884A**-; same L.MS; same, **Trial**-1883
17 wan,] **Trial**-; wan L.MS
   chill,] **Trial**-; chill L.MS
   now;] **Trial**-; now L.MS
18 Day,] **Trial**-; Day L.MS
   crime,] **Trial**-; crime L.MS
19 time,] **Trial**-; Time, L.MS
20 nature's] **Trial**-; Nature's L.MS
   best:] **1850A**-; best; L.MS, **Trial**
   thou,] **Trial**-; thou L.MS
21 may'st] **Trial**-; mayst L.MS
22 star,] **Trial**-; star L.MS
23 afar,] **Trial**-; afar L.MS
24 boughs,] **Trial**-; boughs L.MS
26 day;] **Trial**-; day: L.MS
27 gray,] **Trial**-; gray L.MS

73]
   1 worlds,] **Trial**-; worlds − H.Lpr.101, T.MS; worlds L.MS
   do,] **Trial**-; do. H.Lpr.101; do − T.MS; do L.MS
   2 done,] **Trial**-; done − H.Lpr.101, T.MS; done L.MS
   be,] **Trial**-; be H.Lpr.101-L.MS
   3 thee,] **Trial**-; thee H.Lpr.101-L.MS
   4 true?] **Trial**-; true. H.Lpr.101-L.MS
   5 quench'd] H.Lpr.101, **Trial**-; quench't T.MS, L.MS
   foresaw,] H.Lpr.101, **Trial**-; foresaw: T.MS; foresaw. L.MS
   6 miss'd] H.Lpr.101, **Trial**-; misst T.MS, L.MS
   wreath:] H.Lpr.101, T.MS, **1850A**-; wreath L.MS; wreath; **Trial**
   7 nature,] H.Lpr.101, **1851A**-; Nature, T.MS; Nature − L.MS; nature;
   Trial-1850C
   no,] **Trial**-; no H.Lpr.101-L.MS
   death;] **1851A**-; Death H.Lpr.101-L.MS; death, **Trial-1850C**
   8 law.] H.Lpr.101, T.MS, **Trial**-; law L.MS
   9 pass;] **1855**-; pass: H.Lpr.101-**1851B**

10 dim,] **Trial–**; dim H.Lpr.101–L.MS
  dim,] **Trial–**; dim H.Lpr.101–L.MS
  weeds:] **1850A–**; weeds H.Lpr.101–L.MS; weeds; **Trial**
12 age?] **Trial–**; age H.Lpr.101; age. T.MS, L.MS
13 fame,] **Trial–**; fame H.Lpr.101, T.MS; Fame L.MS
14 exults,] **Trial–**; exults H.Lpr.101–L.MS
15 self-infolds] T.MS–; self infolds H.Lpr.101

74]
  1 face,] T.MS, **Trial–**; face Hn.Nbk., L.MS
  2 it] Hn.Nbk., L.MS, **Trial–**; it, T.MS
  more,] T.MS, **Trial–**; more Hn.Nbk., L.MS
  3 likeness,] **1855–**; likeness T.MS–1851B
  before,] **1855–**; before T.MS–1851B
  4 out –] L.MS–; out T.MS
  race:] **Trial–**; race. T.MS, L.MS
  7 below,] L.MS–; below Hn.Nbk., T.MS
  9 see,] **Trial–**; see Hn.Nbk., T.MS; see; L.MS
  10 unsaid,] L.MS–; unsaid Hn.Nbk., T.MS
  11 it,] Hn.Nbk., **Trial–**; it T.MS, L.MS

75]
  1 unexpress'd] **Trial–**; unexpresst Hn.Nbk., T.MS; unexprest L.MS
  2 relief,] **Trial–**; relief Hn.Nbk.–L.MS
  4 guess'd;] **Trial–**; guesst Hn.Nbk. (*revised from* guest), L.MS; guesst. T.MS
  6 things,] **Trial–**; things – Hn.Nbk.; things T.MS, L.MS
  7 voice] T.MS–; voice, Hn.Nbk.
  sings,] **Trial–**; sings Hn.Nbk.–L.MS
  8 wert?] Hn.Nbk., **Trial–**; wert. T.MS, L.MS
  10 long,] T.MS, **Trial–**; long: Hn.Nbk.; long L.MS
  12 praise.] Hn.Nbk., **Trial–**; praise T.MS, L.MS
  13 perish'd] **Trial–**; perisht Hn.Nbk.–L.MS
  green,] **Trial–**; green Hn.Nbk.–L.MS
  14 And,] **Trial–**; And Hn.Nbk.–L.MS
  sun,] **Trial–**; Sun Hn.Nbk.–L.MS
  16 been.] Hn.Nbk., T.MS, **Trial–**; been L.MS
  17 silence] T.MS–; Silence Hn.Nbk. (*deleted and revised stanzas*)
  fame;] Hn.Nbk. (*revised stanza*), **Trial–**; fame Hn.Nbk. (*deleted stanza*), L.MS; fame, T.MS
  18 But] Hn.Nbk. (*deleted stanza*), T.MS–; But, Hn.Nbk. (*revised stanza*)
  somewhere,] **Trial–**; somewhere Hn.Nbk. (*deleted and revised stanzas*) –L.MS

view,] Hn.Nbk. (*revised stanza*), **Trial-**; view Hn.Nbk. (*deleted stanza*), T.MS, L.MS

76]
1 fancy,] **Trial-**; fancy T.MS, L.MS
  ascend,] **Trial-**; ascend T.MS, L.MS
4 end;] **Trial-**; end. T.MS, L.MS
5 foresight;] **1855-**; foresight: T.MS-**1851B**
6 to come,] **Trial-**; to-come. T.MS; to come L.MS
7 lo,] **1850B-**; lo! T.MS, **Trial, 1850A**; lo L.MS
8 yew;] **Trial-**; yew. T.MS; yew L.MS
9 matin songs,] **Trial-**; matin-songs T.MS; matin songs L.MS
10 planet,] T.MS, **Trial-**; planet L.MS
  last,] T.MS, **Trial-**; last L.MS
11 vast,] **Trial-**; Vast T.MS, L.MS
12 oak.] T.MS, **Trial-**; oak L.MS
14 Mays,] T.MS, **Trial-**; Mays L.MS
  vain;] **Trial-**; vain T.MS, L.MS
15 they] L.MS-; they, T.MS
16 towers?] T.MS, **Trial-**; towers. L.MS

77]
2 him,] **Trial-**; him T.MS, L.MS
3 songs, and deeds, and lives,] **Trial-**; songs and deeds and lives T.MS, L.MS
4 time?] **Trial-**; Time? T.MS; Time L.MS
7 locks;] **1850A-**; locks: T.MS; locks L.MS; locks, **Trial**
8 wane] L.MS-; wane, T.MS
9 find,] **Trial-**; find T.MS, L.MS
10 And,] T.MS, **Trial-**; And L.MS
  passing,] T.MS, **Trial-**; passing L.MS
  page] L.MS-; page, T.MS
11 grief,] **1855-**; grief, − T.MS; grief − L.MS-**1851B**
  else,] **Trial-**; else − T.MS; else L.MS
12 long-forgotten] T.MS, L.MS, **1855-**; long forgotten **Trial-1851B**
  mind.] T.MS, **Trial-**; mind L.MS
13 My] **Trial-**; my T.MS, L.MS
14 same;] **Trial-**; same. T.MS; same L.MS
15 fame,] **Trial-**; fame T.MS, L.MS

78]
2 Christmas hearth;] **1855-**; Christmas-hearth: Hn.Nbk.; Christmas hearth. T.MS; Christmas hearth L.MS; Christmas hearth, **Trial-1851B**

3 possess'd] **Trial-**; possest Hn.Nbk., T.MS; possesst L.MS
 earth,] Hn.Nbk., **Trial-**; earth T.MS, L.MS
4 Christmas-eve:] **1850B-**; Christmas-eve. Hn.Nbk., T.MS; Christmas-eve L.MS; Christmas-eve; **Trial, 1850A**
5 yule-clog] T.MS, **Trial-**; yule clog Hn.Nbk., L.MS
 frost,] L.MS-; frost: Hn.Nbk., T.MS
6 swept,] L.MS-; swept; Hn.Nbk.; swept T.MS
8 lost.] Hn.Nbk., L.MS, **Trial-**; lost T.MS
9 behind,] Hn.Nbk., **Trial-**; behind T.MS, L.MS
10 place,] **Trial-**; place: Hn.Nbk.; place T.MS, L.MS
11 picture's] Hn.Nbk.-L.MS, **1850B-**; pictures **Trial, 1850A** (*error*)
 grace,] Hn.Nbk., **Trial-**; grace T.MS, L.MS
12 hoodman-blind.] **Trial-**; hoodmanblind. Hn.Nbk.-L.MS
13 distress?] T.MS-; distress, Hn.Nbk.
14 tear,] Hn.Nbk.-L.MS, **1850A-**; tears, **Trial** (*error*)
 pain:] **Trial-**; pain. Hn.Nbk.-L.MS
15 sorrow, then] **Trial-**; sorrow then, Hn.Nbk., T.MS; Sorrow then L.MS
 sorrow] Hn.Nbk., T.MS, **Trial-**; Sorrow L.MS
16 grief,] Hn.Nbk., T.MS, **Trial-**; Grief, L.MS
 grief] T.MS, **Trial-**; Grief Hn.Nbk., L.MS
 less?] T.MS-; less Hn.Nbk.
17 regret, regret] **1851A-**; Regret, Regret T.MS; Regret! Regret L.MS;
 regret, Regret **Trial-1850C**
 die!] **Trial-**; die. T.MS, L.MS
18 frame,] T.MS, **Trial-**; frame L.MS
19 same,] **Trial-**; same T.MS, L.MS

79]
1 'More . . . me,' -] **1884A-**; More . . . me T.MS, L.MS; 'More . . . me' -
 Trial-1883
2 heart!] **Trial-**; heart T.MS; heart. L.MS
3 art] T.MS, L.MS, **1851A-**; art, **Trial-1850C**
5 kind,] T.MS, **Trial-**; kind L.MS
6 Nature's] T.MS, L.MS, **1884A-**; nature's **Trial-1883**
 mint;] **Trial-**; mint T.MS; mint: L.MS
8 mind.] L.MS-; mind T.MS
10 Thro'] T.MS, L.MS, **1855-**; Through **Trial-1851B**
 coves;] **Trial-**; coves: T.MS, L.MS
13 vows,] **Trial-**; vows T.MS, L.MS
14 learn'd,] **Trial-**; learn'd T.MS; learned L.MS
15 turn'd] T.MS, **Trial-**; turned L.MS
17 thine,] **Trial-**; thine T.MS, L.MS
18 poor,] **Trial-**; poor T.MS, L.MS
20 mine.] L.MS-; mine T.MS

80]

1 rise,] **Trial–**; rise T.MS, L.MS
2 Death] L.MS–; Death, T.MS
  died] L.MS–; died, T.MS
3 side,] **Trial–**; side T.MS, L.MS
4 eyes;] **Trial–**; eyes. T.MS; eyes L.MS
5 fancy] L.MS–; Fancy T.MS
  shapes,] T.MS, **Trial–**; shapes L.MS
  fancy] L.MS–; Fancy T.MS
  can,] T.MS, **Trial–**; can L.MS
6 wrought,] **Trial–**; wrought T.MS, L.MS
7 life] L.MS–; Life T.MS
  thought,] **Trial–**; Thought T.MS; thought L.MS
8 peace] L.MS–; Peace T.MS
  man.] T.MS, **Trial–**; man L.MS
9 brain;] **Trial–**; brain. T.MS; brain L.MS
10 speaks;] **Trial–**; speaks L.MS
11 weeks] L.MS, **1884A–**; weeks, **Trial–1883**
12 gain.] **Trial–**; gain T.MS, L.MS
13 free;] **Trial–**; free T.MS, L.MS
14 save,] **Trial–**; save T.MS, L.MS
15 grave] T.MS, L.MS, **1850B–**; grave, **Trial–1850A**

81]

1 said] L.MS–; said, T.MS
  here,] **1875–**; here – Trial; here T.MS, L.MS, **1850A–1874**
2-4 'My . . . ear.'] L.MS–; 'My . . . ear. T.MS
2 love] L.MS–; Love T.MS
  range;] **1850B–**; range. T.MS; range L.MS; range, **Trial, 1850A**
3 change,] **Trial–**; change T.MS, L.MS
4 love] **Trial–**; Love T.MS, L.MS
5 store:] **1850A–**; store T.MS; store. L.MS; store; **Trial**
7 faint,] **Trial–**; faint T.MS, L.MS
8 'More . . . more.'] **Trial–**; 'More . . . more. T.MS; 'More . . . more' L.MS
10 gain,] L.MS–; gain T.MS
11 grain,] L.MS–; grain T.MS

82]

2 face;] **Trial–**; face T.MS, L.MS
3 earth's] L.MS–; Earth's T.MS
4 him,] **Trial–**; him T.MS, L.MS
  faith.] T.MS, **Trial–**; faith L.MS
5 on,] L.MS–; on T.MS

6 spirit] **Trial–**; Spirit T.MS, L.MS
walks;] **Trial–**; walks T.MS, L.MS
7 stalks,] **1851B–**; stalks T.MS–**1851A**
9 Death,] **Trial–**; Death T.MS, L.MS
10 virtue] **Trial–**; Virtue T.MS, L.MS
earth:] **1850B–**; Earth. T.MS; Earth L.MS; earth; **Trial, 1850A**
12 profit,] L.MS–; profit T.MS
14 heart;] **Trial–**; heart T.MS, L.MS
16 speak.] T.MS, **Trial–**; speak L.MS

83]
1 northern] **Trial–**; Northern T.MS, L.MS
shore,] **Trial–**; shore T.MS, L.MS
2 new-year] **Trial–**; Newyear, T.MS; New-year L.MS
long;] **Trial–**; long. T.MS; long L.MS
3 nature] **Trial–**; Nature T.MS, L.MS
wrong;] **1851A–**; wrong T.MS, L.MS; wrong, **Trial–1850C**
4 long,] **Trial–**; long T.MS, L.MS
more.] T.MS, **Trial–**; more L.MS
7 days,] **Trial–**; days? T.MS; days L.MS
9 foxglove spire,] **1850B–**; foxglove-spire T.MS, L.MS; fox-glove spire, **Trial, 1850A**
10 blue,] **Trial–**; blue T.MS, L.MS
11 dash'd] **1850B–**; dasht T.MS–**1850A**
dew,] T.MS, **Trial–**; dew L.MS
13 new-year,] **Trial–**; Newyear, T.MS; New-year, L.MS
long,] **Trial–**; long T.MS, L.MS
14 blood,] **Trial–**; blood T.MS, L.MS
15 bud] T.MS, L.MS, **1872–**; bud, **Trial–1870**

84]
1 alone] L.MS, **1855–**; alone, **Trial–1851B**
2 below,] **Trial–**; below L.MS
4 grown;] **Trial–**; grown L.MS
5 good,] **Trial–**; good L.MS
7 smile,] **Trial–**; smile L.MS
kiss,] **Trial–**; kiss L.MS
9 mine;] **Trial–**; mine L.MS
10 on,] **Trial–**; on L.MS
12 house,] **Trial–**; house L.MS
15 orange flower,] **Trial–**; orangeflower L.MS
16 Hope,] **Trial–**; hope L.MS
21 guest,] **Trial–**; guest L.MS

23 table-talk,] **Trial**–; tabletalk L.MS
24 dispute,] **Trial**–; dispute L.MS
   jest;] **1855**–; jest: L.MS-**1851B**
29 fair;] **Trial**–; fair. L.MS
31 powers,] **Trial**–; powers L.MS
35 thought,] **Trial**–; thought L.MS
36 globe;] **Trial**–; globe L.MS
37 flee,] **Trial**–; flee L.MS
39 And,] **Trial**–; And L.MS
42 He] **1851A**–; he L.MS-**1850C**
   Holy Land] **Trial**–; holy land L.MS
43 hand,] **Trial**–; hand L.MS
44 soul.] **Trial**–; soul L.MS
46 Ah,] **Trial**–; Ah L.MS
   fancy,] **Trial**–; Fancy L.MS
47 again.] **Trial**–; again L.MS

85]
 1 pall,] **Trial**–; pall T.Nbk., Heath MS, L.MS
 2 it,] **Trial**–; it T.Nbk.-L.MS
   sorrow'd] L.MS–; sorrowed T.Nbk., Heath MS
   most,] **Trial**–; most T.Nbk., Heath MS, L.MS
 3 'Tis] **Trial**–; Tis T.Nbk., Heath MS, L.MS
   lost,] **Trial**–; lost T.Nbk.-L.MS
 4 all –] L.MS–; all. T.Nbk.; all Heath MS
 5 word,] **Trial**–; word L.MS
   deed,] **Trial**–; deed L.MS
 7 grief,] **Trial**–; grief L.MS
 8 lead;] **Trial**–; lead – L.MS
 9 above] L.MS, **1855**–; above, **Trial-1851B**
10 sorrow,] **Trial**–; sorrow L.MS
   sustain'd;] **Trial**–; sustain'd L.MS
12 love;] **Trial**–; love – L.MS
14 breast,] **Trial**–; breast L.MS
15 reproaches,] **Trial**–; reproaches L.MS
   exprest,] **Trial**–; exprest L.MS
16 laws.] **Trial**–; laws L.MS
17 kept,] **Trial**–; kept L.MS
   falls,] **Trial**–; falls L.MS
20 touch'd] **Trial**–; touched L.MS
   him,] **Trial**–; him L.MS
   slept.] **Trial**–; slept L.MS
22 state,] **Trial**–; state L.MS

23 gate,] **Trial-**; gate L.MS
24 there;] **1850A-**; there L.MS; there. **Trial.**
25 thro'] L.MS, **1850B-**; through **Trial, 1850A**
 climes,] **Trial-**; climes L.MS
27 knowledge] L.MS *has* knowlege
28 times.] **Trial-**; times L.MS
29 remain'd,] **Trial-**; remain'd L.MS
 dim,] **Trial-**; dim L.MS
30 life,] **Trial-**; life L.MS
 little worth,] **Trial-**; little-worth L.MS
31 earth,] **Trial-**; earth L.MS
32 him.] **Trial-**; him L.MS
33 friendship,] **Trial-**; friendship L.MS
 control,] **Trial-**; control L.MS
34 heart,] **Trial-**; heart L.MS
 warm,] **Trial-**; warm L.MS
35 essence,] **Trial-**; Essence! L.MS
 form,] **Trial-**; form L.MS
36 ghost,] **1855-**; ghost! L.MS-**1851B**
 soul!] **Trial-**; soul L.MS
37 I,] **Trial-**; I L.MS
39 demands] L.MS, **1864-**; demands, **Trial-1863**
40 die.] **Trial-**; die L.MS
42 feel,] **Trial-**; feel Heath MS, L.MS
 tho'] Heath MS, L.MS, **1850B-**; though **Trial, 1850A**
 alone,] **Trial-**; alone Heath MS-L.MS
43 being] L.MS-; Being Heath MS
 own,] **Trial-**; own Heath MS-L.MS
44 mine;] **1850A-**; mine Heath MS, L.MS; mine. **Trial**
45 deck'd] **1850A-**; deckt L.MS, **Trial**
46 grace,] **1850B-**; grace L.MS-**1850A**
47 tenderness,] **Trial-**; tenderness L.MS
48 All-subtilising] **Trial-**; All-subtilizing L.MS
 intellect:] **1850A-**; intellect L.MS; intellect. **Trial**
50 weakness,] Heath MS, **Trial-**; weakness T.Nbk., L.MS
51 mind,] **Trial-**; mind T.Nbk., Heath MS, L.MS
52 reserved.] T.Nbk., Heath MS, **Trial-**; reserved L.MS
53 woe,] **Trial-**; woe L.MS
54 strife,] **Trial-**; strife L.MS
55 thro'] L.MS, **1850B-**; through **Trial, 1850A**
 life,] **Trial-**; life L.MS
58 met;] **Trial-**; met: T.Nbk., Heath MS; met L.MS
60 men.] T.Nbk., **Trial-**; men Heath MS, L.MS

61 love:] **Trial–**; love; Heath MS; love L.MS
62 overmuch;] **Trial–**; overmuch T.Nbk. (*all drafts*), Heath MS, L.MS
63 I,] Heath MS, **Trial–**; I T.Nbk. (*all drafts*), L.MS
64 master'd] L.MS–; mastered T.Nbk. (*all drafts*), Heath MS
    Time;] **Trial–**; time T.Nbk. (*draft following* 60), Heath MS; time.
    T.Nbk. (*drafts following* 104 *and* 108); Time L.MS
65 Time] L.MS–; time T.Nbk., Heath MS
    indeed,] **Trial–**; indeed T.Nbk., Heath MS, L.MS
66 fears:] **1855–**; fears Heath MS, L.MS; fears. T.Nbk., **Trial–1851B**
68 this:] **Trial–**; this. T.Nbk.; this Heath MS, L.MS
69 Summer] T.Nbk., **Trial–**; summer Heath MS, L.MS
    floods,] **Trial–**; floods T.Nbk., Heath MS, L.MS
70 Spring] T.Nbk., L.MS–; spring Heath MS
    brooks,] **Trial–**; brooks T.Nbk., Heath MS, L.MS
71 Autumn,] **Trial–**; Autumn T.Nbk., Heath MS, L.MS
    rooks,] **Trial–**; rooks T.Nbk., Heath MS, L.MS
72 woods,] **Trial–**; woods T.Nbk., Heath MS, L.MS
74 Recalls,] **Trial–**; Recalls T.Nbk., Heath MS; Recall L.MS
    gloom,] **Trial–**; gloom T.Nbk., Heath MS, L.MS
75 tomb,] **Trial–**; tomb T.Nbk., Heath MS, L.MS
76 grave:] **Trial–**; grave T.Nbk., Heath MS; grave. L.MS
77 tomb,] **Trial–**; tomb L.MS
78 stillness,] **Trial–**; stillness L.MS
    speak:] **1851A–**; speak L.MS; speak; **Trial–1850C**
79–84 'Arise, . . . more.'] **Trial–**; Arise . . . more. L.MS
80 come.] **Trial–**; come L.MS
81 'I] **1884A–**; I L.MS–1883
    shore;] **Trial–**; shore L.MS
82 reach;] **Trial–**; reach L.MS
85 I,] **1850B–**; I L.MS–1850A
85–8] 'Can . . . pain?'] **Trial–**; 'can . . . pain L.MS
85 nature] **Trial–**; Nature L.MS
86 free?] **Trial–**; free L.MS
87 Canst] **Trial–**; can'st L.MS
89 fall;] **Trial–**; fall L.MS
90–92 ''Tis . . . all.'] **Trial–**; 'Tis . . . all L.MS
90 this;] **Trial–**; this L.MS
91 bliss,] **Trial–**; bliss L.MS
93 dead;] **Trial–**; dead T.MS, L.MS
94 say;] **Trial–**; say T.MS, L.MS
95 grief] **Trial–**; Grief T.MS, L.MS
    play] T.MS, L.MS, **1884A–**; play, **Trial–1883**
97 end,] L.MS–; end T.Nbk.–T.MS

98 pass,] **Trial-**; pass T.Nbk.-L.MS
100 friend;] **1850A-**; friend – T.Nbk.-T.MS; friend, L.MS, **Trial**
101 fresh,] T.Nbk., Heath MS, L.MS-; fresh T.MS
    true,] **Trial-**; true T.Nbk.-L.MS
102 I,] Heath MS, T.MS-; I T.Nbk.
    brother-hands,] Heath MS, T.MS-; brother-hands T.Nbk.
103 not,] T.MS, **Trial-**; not T.Nbk., Heath MS, L.MS
    would,] T.MS, **Trial-**; would T.Nbk., Heath MS, L.MS
104 for] Heath MS *has* from *revised to* for (*error in transcription*)
    him] T.MS-; him, T.Nbk., Heath MS
    you.] Heath MS, **Trial-**; you T.Nbk., T.MS, L.MS
106 hours?] T.Nbk.-T.MS, **Trial-**; hours. L.MS
107 love,] T.Nbk., Heath MS, L.MS-; Love, T.MS
    friendship,] T.Nbk., Heath MS, L.MS-; Friendship, T.MS
    powers,] T.MS, **1851A-**; powers T.Nbk., Heath MS, L.MS-**1850C**
108 heart.] T.Nbk.-T.MS, **Trial-**; heart L.MS
109 mine,] T.MS, L.MS, **1855-**; mine **Trial-1851B**
    deplore,] **Trial-**; deplore T.MS, L.MS
110 place,] **Trial-**; place T.MS, L.MS
111 embrace,] **Trial-**; embrace T.MS, L.MS
112 more,] **Trial-1855, 1860-**; more – T.MS, L.MS; more. **1856, 1859**
113 heart,] T.MS, **Trial-**; heart L.MS
    widow'd,] T.MS, **Trial-**; widow'd L.MS
114 gone,] **Trial-**; gone T.MS, L.MS
116 breast.] T.MS, **Trial-**; breast L.MS
117 Ah,] **Trial-**; Ah! T.MS; Ah L.MS
    bring,] **Trial-**; bring T.MS, L.MS
118 dear,] **Trial-**; dear T.MS, L.MS
119 year,] **Trial-**; year T.MS, L.MS
120 Spring.] T.MS, **Trial-**; spring. L.MS

86]
  1 showers,] **Trial-**; showers L.MS
    air,] **Trial-**; air L.MS
  6 Thro'] L.MS, **1850A-**; Through **Trial**
    dewy-tassell'd] **Trial-**; dewy-tassel'd L.MS
    wood,] **Trial-**; wood L.MS
  9 cheek,] **Trial-**; cheek L.MS
11 frame,] **Trial-**; frame L.MS
    Doubt and Death,] L.MS, **1850A-**; doubt and death, **Trial**
14 far,] **Trial-**; far L.MS

87]

1 walls] **Trial–**; walls, L.MS
2 gown;] **Trial–**; gown: L.MS
3 thro'] L.MS, **1855–**; through **Trial–1851B**
  town,] **Trial–**; town L.MS
11 willows;] **Trial–**; willows, L.MS
14 same,] **Trial–**; same L.MS
  same;] **Trial–**; same, L.MS
16 dwelt.] **Trial–**; dwelt L.MS
17 door:] **Trial–**; door. L.MS
18 linger'd;] **Trial–**; linger'd: L.MS
19 songs,] **Trial–**; songs L.MS
  hands,] **Trial–**; hands L.MS
20 floor;] **Trial–**; floor: L.MS
22 art,] **Trial–**; Art L.MS
23 labour,] **Trial–**; labour L.MS
  mart,] **Trial–**; mart L.MS
24 land;] **Trial–**; land: L.MS
26 string;] **Trial–**; string L.MS
27 ring,] **Trial–**; ring L.MS
29 master-bowman,] **Trial–**; Master-bowman, L.MS
  he,] **1851A–**; he L.MS-**1850C**
31 him.] **Trial–**; him: L.MS
  Who,] **Trial–**; who, L.MS
33 point,] **1855–**; point L.MS-**1851B**
  grace] L.MS, **1855–**; grace, **Trial–1851B**
34 law,] **Trial–**; law L.MS
36 face,] **Trial–**; face L.MS
37 form,] **Trial–**; form L.MS
40 Michael] **Trial–**; Michel L.MS

88]

1 warble,] **Trial–**; warble T.MS
  liquid sweet,] **Trial–**; liquid-sweet T.MS
2 thro'] T.MS, **1855–**; through **Trial–1851B**
  quicks,] **Trial–**; quicks T.MS
3 mix,] **Trial–**; mix T.MS
4 meet,] **Trial–**; meet? T.MS
5 radiate:] **Trial–**; radiate? T.MS
6 leaf,] **Trial–**; leaf T.MS
8 joy:] **Trial–**; joy. T.MS
10 strings;] **Trial–**; strings T.MS

89]

2 bright;] **1851A–**; bright L.MS; bright: **Trial–1850C**
3 thou,] **Trial–**; thou L.MS
4 foliage,] **Trial–**; foliage L.MS
  sycamore;] **Trial–**; sycamore, L.MS
5 often,] **Trial–**; often L.MS
  down,] **Trial–**; down L.MS
6 fair,] **Trial–**; fair L.MS
8 town:] **Trial–**; town. L.MS
9 saw;] **Trial–**; saw: L.MS
10 sports;] **Trial–**; sports: L.MS
11 him,] **Trial–**; him L.MS
13 retreat,] **Trial–**; retreat L.MS
14 dark,] **Trial–**; dark L.MS
16 thro'] L.MS, **1855–**; through **Trial–1851B**
  heat:] **Trial–**; heat! L.MS
17 sound] **Trial–**; sound, L.MS
18 dew,] **Trial–**; dew L.MS
19 flew,] **Trial–**; flew L.MS
21 when] **Trial–**; when, L.MS
23 him,] **Trial–**; him L.MS
24 Tuscan poets] **Trial** *has* Tuscanpoets
  lawn:] **Trial–**; lawn. L.MS
26 guest,] **Trial–**; guest L.MS
  sister,] **Trial–**; sister L.MS
  sung,] **Trial–**; sung: L.MS
28 moon:] **Trial–1855, 1859–**; moon. L.MS; moon **1856** (*error*)
29 moods,] **Trial–**; moods L.MS
31 livelong] L.MS–**1883, 1884B–**; lifelong **1884A** (*error*)
33 theme,] **Trial–**; theme L.MS
34 hate,] **Trial–**; hate L.MS
35 state,] **Trial–**; state L.MS
37 town,] **Trial–**; town L.MS
38 still,] **Trial–**; still; L.MS
39–42 'ground . . . man.'] **1850A–**; ground . . . man. L.MS; 'ground . . . man:' **Trial**
40 down,] **Trial–**; down L.MS
41 'And merge' . . . 'in] **1884A–**; And merge . . . in L.MS, **1851A, B** (*error*); And merge' . . . 'in **Trial–1850C, 1855–83**
43 ran,] **Trial–**; ran L.MS
44 wine-flask] **Trial–**; wineflask L.MS
  moss,] **Trial–**; moss L.MS
45 wave;] **Trial, 1850B–**; wave L.MS; wave **1850A** (*error*)

46 last,] **Trial**-; last L.MS
  afar,] **Trial**-; afar L.MS
48 Had] L.MS, **1850A**-; Has **Trial** (*error*)
  grave,] **Trial**-; grave L.MS
49 ankle-deep] **Trial**-; ankle deep L.MS
  flowers,] **Trial**-; flowers L.MS
51 pail,] **Trial**-; pail L.MS

90]
 1 love] **Trial**-; Love L.MS
  mind,] **Trial**-; mind L.MS
 3 heaven,] **Trial**-; Heaven, L.MS
 4 mankind;] **Trial**-; mankind: L.MS
 6 life,] **Trial**-; life L.MS
 8 rise:] **Trial**-; rise. L.MS
 9 'Twas] **Trial**-; Twas L.MS
  well,] **Trial**-; well L.MS
  indeed,] **Trial**-; indeed L.MS
  wine,] **Trial**-; wine L.MS
10 tear,] **1855**-; tear; L.MS; tear: **Trial–1851B**
12 half divine;] **Trial**-; half-divine; L.MS
14 hands;] L.MS, **1855**-; hands: **Trial–1851B**
17 Yea,] **Trial**-; Yea L.MS
  these,] **Trial**-; these L.MS
18 yet-loved] L.MS, **1850B**-; yet-lov'd **Trial, 1850A**
  sire] **Trial**-; Sire L.MS
19 death,] **Trial**-; death L.MS
21 dear,] **Trial**-; dear L.MS
  me:] **Trial**-; me, L.MS
22 wrought,] **Trial**-; wrought L.MS

91]
 1 larch,] **Trial**-; larch H.Lpr.101, T.MS
 2 thrush;] **Trial**-; thrush, H.Lpr.101, T.MS
 4 sea-blue] **Trial**-; seablue H.Lpr.101, T.MS
  March;] **Trial**-; March H.Lpr.101, T.MS
 5 Come,] **Trial**-; Come! H.Lpr.101; Come: T.MS
  know] T.MS-; knew H.Lpr.101 (*error in transcription*)
 6 time] **Trial**-; Time H.Lpr.101, T.MS
  peers;] **Trial**-; Peers H.Lpr.101; peers T.MS
 7 unaccomplish'd] H.Lpr.101, **Trial**-; unaccomplisht T.MS
10 breathe,] **1855**-; breathe H.Lpr.101–**1851B**
  sweet,] **1855**-; sweet H.Lpr.101–**1851B**

11 wheat,] **Trial–**; wheat H.Lpr.101, T.MS
12 grange;] **Trial–**; grange H.Lpr.101, T.MS
13 Come:] H.Lpr.101, **Trial–**; Come; T.MS
   night,] **Trial–**; night H.Lpr.101, T.MS
14 warm,] **Trial–**; warm H.Lpr.101, T.MS
15 Come,] **Trial–**; Come H.Lpr.101, T.MS
   after form,] **Trial–**; After-form H.Lpr.101; after-form T.MS

92]

 2 likeness,] **Trial–**; likeness – T.MS; likeness L.MS
   vain] L.MS–; vain, T.MS
 4 Yea,] T.MS, **Trial–**; Yea L.MS
   tho'] T.MS, **1855–**; tho L.MS; though **Trial–1851B**
 6 behind,] **Trial–**; behind; T.MS; behind L.MS
 7 say,] **Trial–**; say T.MS, L.MS
7-8 I hear . . . past.] **Trial–**; 'I hear . . . past' T.MS; I hear . . . Past L.MS
 8 memory] T.MS, **Trial–**; Memory L.MS
 9 Yea,] **Trial–**; Yea T.MS, L.MS
   tho'] L.MS–; tho T.MS
10 year;] **Trial–**; year T.MS, L.MS
11 months,] **Trial–**; months T.MS, L.MS
   near,] **Trial–**; near T.MS, L.MS
12 phantom-warning] **Trial–**; phantom-warnings T.MS; phantom warning L.MS
   true,] **Trial–**; true; T.MS; true L.MS
13 prophecies,] **Trial–**; prophecies T.MS, L.MS
14 presentiments,] T.MS, **Trial–**; presentiments L.MS

93]

 3 land] T.MS, L.MS, **1884A–**; land, **Trial–1883**
 4 walk'd] **Trial–**; walkt T.MS, L.MS
   clay?] T.MS, **Trial–**; clay L.MS
 5 lost,] **Trial–**; lost – T.MS; lost L.MS
 6 he,] L.MS–; he T.MS
   Spirit] **Trial–**; spirit T.MS, L.MS
   himself,] **Trial–**; himself T.MS, L.MS
 7 numb;] **1850A–**; numb T.MS, L.MS; numb: **Trial**
 8 Spirit to Spirit,] **Trial–**; Spirit to spirit – T.MS; Spirit to Spirit L.MS
   Ghost to Ghost.] **Trial–**; ghost to ghost. T.MS; Ghost to Ghost L.MS
 9 O,] **Trial–**; Oh T.MS, L.MS
10 gods] **Trial–**; Gods T.MS, L.MS
   bliss,] **Trial–**; bliss – T.MS; bliss L.MS
11 O,] **Trial–**; Oh T.MS, L.MS
   abyss] **Trial–**; Abyss T.MS, L.MS

12 tenfold-] L.MS-; Tenfold- T.MS
   change,] **Trial-**; change T.MS, L.MS
14 name;] **Trial-**; name T.MS, L.MS
15 frame] T.MS, **Trial-**; frame, L.MS

94]
  1 head,] T.MS, **Trial-**; head L.MS
  5 thou,] **Trial-**; thou T.MS, L.MS
   any,] **Trial-**; any T.MS, L.MS
  6 day,] **Trial-**; day T.MS, L.MS
  7 Except,] T.MS, **Trial-**; Except L.MS
   them,] T.MS, **Trial-**; them L.MS
   canst] L.MS-; can'st T.MS
   say,] **1855-**; say T.MS-1851B
  9 breast,] **Trial-**; breast T.MS, L.MS
10 fair,] T.MS, **Trial-**; fair L.MS
11 air,] **Trial-**; air T.MS, L.MS
12 rest:] **Trial-**; rest. T.MS; rest L.MS
13 din,] T.MS, **Trial-**; din L.MS
14 doubt] **Trial-**; Doubt T.MS, L.MS
   waits,] **Trial-**; waits T.MS, L.MS
15 gates,] **1855-**; gates T.MS-1851B
16 within.] **Trial-**; within T.MS, L.MS

95]
  1 lawn,] **Trial-**; lawn L.MS
  2 dry;] **Trial-**; dry L.MS
  3 warmth;] **Trial-**; warmth, L.MS
   o'er] **Trial-**; oer L.MS
  4 drawn;] **Trial-**; drawn, L.MS
  7 heard,] **1855-**; heard L.MS-1851B
  9 skies,] **Trial-**; skies L.MS
11 dusk,] **1850A-**; dusk L.MS, **Trial**
12 eyes;] **Trial-**; eyes: L.MS
14 knoll,] **Trial-**; knoll L.MS
   where,] **Trial-**; where L.MS
   ease,] **Trial-**; ease L.MS
15 glimmer'd,] **1851A-**; glimmerd L.MS; glimmer'd **Trial-1850C**
16 field.] **Trial-**; field: L.MS
17 others,] **Trial-**; others L.MS
   one,] **Trial-**; one L.MS
20 out,] **Trial-**; out L.MS
21 seized] **Trial-**; seiz'd L.MS

heart;] **Trial–**; heart: L.MS
been,] **Trial–**; been L.MS
26 silent-speaking] **Trial–**; silent speaking L.MS
  words,] **Trial–**; words; L.MS
29 vigour,] **Trial–**; vigour L.MS
33 word,] **Trial–**; word L.MS
  line,] **Trial–**; line L.MS
35 seem'd] **Trial–**; seemd L.MS
36 flash'd] **Trial–**; flasht L.MS
  mine,] **Trial–**; mine L.MS
37 wound,] **Trial–**; wound L.MS
38 heights] **Trial–**; heigths L.MS
  is,] **Trial–**; is L.MS
42 Time –] **Trial–**; Time, L.MS
  Chance –] **Trial–**; Chance L.MS
44 cancell'd,] **Trial–**; cancell'd L.MS
45 words!] **Trial–**; words L.MS
  ah,] **Trial–**; ah L.MS
46 speech,] **Trial–**; speech L.MS
47 intellect] **Trial–**; Intellect L.MS
48 became:] **Trial–**; became. L.MS
50 where,] **Trial–**; where L.MS
  couch'd] **Trial–**; couchd L.MS
  ease,] **Trial–**; ease L.MS
51 glimmer'd,] **Trial–**; glimmer'd L.MS
52 field:] **Trial–**; field L.MS
55 sycamore,] **Trial–**; sycamore L.MS
56 perfume,] **1855–**; perfume; L.MS-**1851B**
57 overhead,] **Trial–**; overhead L.MS
58 elms,] **Trial–**; elms L.MS
59 rose,] **Trial–**; rose L.MS
60 fro,] **Trial–**; fro L.MS
61 dawn,'] **Trial–**; dawn' L.MS
  away;] **Trial–**; away: L.MS
62 West,] **Trial–**; West L.MS
  breath,] **Trial–**; breath L.MS
63 lights,] **Trial–**; lights L.MS
  life] **Trial–**; Life L.MS
  death,] **Trial–**; Death L.MS

96]
2 light-blue] **1850A–**; lightblue H.Nbk.19
5 one indeed] **1850A–**; one, indeed, H.Nbk.19

7 touch'd] H.Nbk., **1850C-**; touched **1850A, B**
  first,] **1850A-**; first H.Nbk.19
8 true:] H.Nbk.19 *has* true — *revised to* true:
13 strength,] **1850A-**; strength H.Nbk.19
14 judgment] **1850A, 1862A-**; Judgement H.Nbk.19; judgement
  1851A-1861
  blind,] **1850A-**; blind: H.Nbk.19
15 spectres] **1850A-**; Spectres H.Nbk.19
  mind] **1850A-**; Mind H.Nbk.19
18 night,] **1850A-**; night H.Nbk.19
22 Sinaï's] **1850A-**; Sinai's H.Nbk.19
23 gods] **1850A-**; Gods H.Nbk.19
  gold,] H.Nbk.19, **1855-**; gold **1850A-1851B**

97]
  1 trees;] **1851A-**; trees, **1850A-C**
  3 crown'd;] **1851A-**; crown'd, **1850A-C**
  5 life —] **1850A-**; life H.Nbk. b
  7 mystery,] **1850A-**; mystery H.Nbk. b
11 June,] **1850A-1883**, *this edition*; June **1884A, B** (*error*)
13 away;] **1850A-**; away H.Nbk. a; away. H.Nbk. b
15 yet,] **1850A-**; yet H.Nbk. a, b
16 Whate'er] H.Nbk. b-; Whateer H.Nbk. a
  say.] H.Nbk. b-; say H.Nbk. a
18 yet,] **1850A-**; yet: H.Nbk. a, b
  weep,] **1850A-**; weep H.Nbk. a, b
21 mind,] **1850A-**; mind; H.Nbk. a; mind H.Nbk. b
22 star,] **1850A-**; star: H.Nbk. a; star H.Nbk. b
23 far,] **1850A-**; far H.Nbk. a; far: H.Nbk. b
24 cold:] **1850A-**; cold H.Nbk. a; cold; H.Nbk. b
25 before,] **1850A-**; before H.Nbk. a, b
26 bliss:] **1864-**; bliss H.Nbk. a; bliss. H.Nbk. b; bliss; **1850A-1863**
27 is,] **1884A-**; is H.Nbk. a, b; is; **1850A-1883**
28 more.] H.Nbk. b-; more H.Nbk. a
29 plays,] **1850A-**; plays; H.Nbk. a; plays H.Nbk. b
31 house,] **1850A-**; house H.Nbk. a, b
32 things.] **1850A-**; things H.Nbk. a, b
34 wise,] **1850A-**; wise H.Nbk. a, b
35 eyes,] **1850A-**; eyes H.Nbk. a, b

98]
  1 Rhine,] **Trial-**; Rhine L.MS
  4 vine] L.MS, **1850A-**; vine, **Trial**

5 breath,] **Trial–**; breath L.MS
6 City.] **Trial–**; city. L.MS
9 fair] L.MS, **1850A–**; fair, **Trial**
10 unmark'd] **1850B–**; unmarked L.MS–**1850B**
　me:] **Trial–**; me. L.MS
13 Evil] **1855–**; evil L.MS–**1851B**
14 bridal;] **1850A–**; bridal, L.MS; bridal: **Trial**
17 men,] **Trial–**; men L.MS
19 kings:] **Trial–**; kings, L.MS
21 mother town] **1850A–**; mother-town L.MS; mother-town, **Trial**
27 lamps,] **Trial–**; lamps L.MS
28 song,] **Trial–**; song L.MS
30 dance,] **Trial–**; dance L.MS
32 crimson] **Trial–**; crimson, L.MS

99]
1 dawn,] L.MS b, **1850B–**; dawn L.MS a, **Trial**, **1850A**
2 birds,] L.MS a, **Trial–**; birds L.MS b
4 Day,] L.MS a, **Trial–**; Day L.MS b
7 past,] **Trial–**; Past L.MS b
12 leaves;] L.MS b–; leaves – L.MS a
14 earth,] **Trial–**; earth L.MS a, b
15 bridal,] **Trial–**; bridal L.MS a, b
　birth,] **Trial–**; birth – L.MS a; birth L.MS b
16 death.] **Trial–**; death – L.MS a, b
17 O] L.MS a, b, **1865A–**; O, **Trial**–**1864**
　be,] **Trial–**; be L.MS a, b
19 To-day] L.MS b–; Today L.MS a
　souls;] **Trial–**; souls: L.MS a, b

100]
1 end to end] L.MS, **1851A–**; end to end, **Trial**–**1850C**
2 underneath,] L.MS, **1851A–**; underneath **Trial**–**1850C**
4 friend;] **1851A–**; friend. L.MS, **Trial**; friend: **1850A–C**
8 wold;] **Trial–**; wold. L.MS
10 trill,] **Trial–**; trill; L.MS
19 these,] **Trial–**; these L.MS

101]
1 Unwatch'd,] **1855–**; Unwatch'd L.MS–**1851B**
　sway,] **Trial–**; sway L.MS
2 down,] **Trial–**; down: L.MS
3 Unloved,] **1859–**; Unloved L.MS–**1856**

4 away;] **Trial-**; away. L.MS
5 Unloved,] **Trial-**; Unloved L.MS
  sun-flower,] **Trial-**; sunflower L.MS
  fair,] **Trial-**; fair L.MS
6 seed,] **Trial-**; seed; L.MS
8 air;] **Trial-**; air. L.MS
9 Unloved,] **Trial-**; Unloved L.MS
  bar,] **Trial-**; bar L.MS
10 plain,] **Trial-**; plain L.MS
12 star;] **1850A-**; star. L.MS, **Trial**
14 crake;] **Trial-**; crake L.MS
18 blow,] **Trial-**; blow L.MS
22 glebe,] **Trial-**; glebe L.MS
   glades;] **Trial-**; glades, L.MS

102]
1 place] L.MS *has error in transcription:* home place
2 sky;] **Trial-**; sky. T.MS; sky L.MS
3 roofs,] **Trial-**; roofs T.MS, L.MS
  cry,] **Trial-**; cry T.MS, L.MS
4 race.] T.MS, **Trial-**; race L.MS
5 go,] **Trial-**; go T.MS, L.MS
  home,] **Trial-**; home T.MS, L.MS
6 garden-walks] L.MS-; garden walks T.MS
  move,] **Trial-**; move T.MS, L.MS
8 masterdom.] T.MS, **Trial-**; masterdom L.MS
9-12 'Here . . . tassel-hung.'] **1884A-**; 'here . . . tassel-hung.' T.MS; here
   . . . tassel-hung L.MS; here . . . tassel-hung. **Trial-1883**
9 whispers,] **Trial-**; whispers T.MS, L.MS
10 matin song,] **Trial-**; matinsong, T.MS; matinsong L.MS
11 love-language] T.MS, **Trial-**; lovelanguage L.MS
12 hazels] L.MS-; hazels, T.MS
13 answers,] **Trial-**; answers. T.MS; answers L.MS
   'Yea,] T.MS, **Trial-**; 'Yea L.MS
14 after hours] T.MS, **Trial-**; after-hours L.MS
15 bowers,] **Trial-**; bowers T.MS, L.MS
16 dear.'] T.MS, **Trial-**; dear L.MS
17 day,] **Trial-**; day T.MS, L.MS
18 claim,] T.MS, **Trial-**; claim L.MS
19 game,] T.MS, **Trial-**; game L.MS
20 way.] T.MS, **Trial-**; way L.MS
21 go:] **Trial-**; go — T.MS; go. L.MS
22 farms;] **Trial-**; farms — T.MS; farms L.MS

103]
4 after-morn] L.MS, **1850B–**; after morn **Trial, 1850A**
6 me:] **Trial–**; me. L.MS
  distant] **Trial–**; Distant L.MS
12 veil'd,] **Trial–**; veil'd L.MS
13 which,] **Trial–**; which L.MS
  veil'd,] **Trial–**; veil'd L.MS
14 loved,] **Trial–**; loved L.MS
15 ever:] **Trial–**; ever. L.MS
  then] **Trial–**; Then L.MS
16 sea:] **Trial–**; sea. L.MS
17 go] **Trial–**; go, L.MS
18 wail'd,] **Trial–**; wail'd L.MS
20 below;] **Trial–**; below: L.MS
21 mead,] **Trial–**; mead L.MS
22 bluff] **Trial–**; bluff, L.MS
24 iris,] **Trial–**; Iris, L.MS
  reed;] **Trial–**; reed: L.MS
25 shore] L.MS, **1875–**; shore, **Trial–1874**
28 before;] **Trial–**; before: L.MS
30 wax'd] **1850B–**; waxt L.MS–**1850A**
  limb;] **Trial–**; limb. L.MS
33 death] **Trial–**; Death L.MS
  war,] **Trial–**; War, L.MS
34 history] **Trial–**; History L.MS
35 be,] **Trial–**; be; L.MS
36 one] **Trial–**; one, L.MS
38 foam,] **Trial–**; foam L.MS
39 deep,] **Trial–**; deep L.MS
42 But] **Trial–**; But, L.MS
  man] **Trial–**; man, L.MS
43 us.] **Trial–**; us: L.MS
  Up] **Trial–**; up L.MS
46 lot;] **Trial–**; lot: L.MS
47–48] **Trial–**; "We served thee here" they said "so long: / And wilt thou leave us now behind"? L.MS
49 was,] **Trial–**; was L.MS
51–52] **Trial–**; Replying "Enter likewise ye, / And go with us" they enter'd in: L.MS
53 And] **Trial–**; And, L.MS
55 cloud] **Trial–**; cloud, L.MS

104]
1 Christ;] **Trial-**; Christ T.MS, L.MS
2 still;] **Trial-**; still. T.MS; still L.MS
4 pealing,] L.MS-; pealing T.MS
5 below,] **Trial-**; below T.MS, L.MS
7 breast,] **Trial-**; breast T.MS, L.MS
8 know.] **Trial-**; know T.MS, L.MS
9 strangers'] **1850A-**; strangers T.MS, L.MS; stranger's Trial (*misprint*)
   sound,] **Trial-**; sound L.MS
10 strays,] **Trial-**; strays L.MS
11 days,] **Trial-**; days T.MS, L.MS

105]
3 land,] **Trial-**; land H.Lpr.101-L.MS
4 Christmas eve.] **Trial-**; Christmas-eve H.Lpr.101, T.MS; Christmas
   eve L.MS
6 snows:] **Trial-**; snows. H.Lpr.101, T.MS; snows L.MS
7 blows,] **Trial-**; blows H.Lpr.101-L.MS
8 comes,] **Trial-**; comes: H.Lpr.101, T.MS; comes L.MS
   gone.] H.Lpr.101, T.MS, **Trial-**; gone L.MS
9 grief] **Trial-**; Grief H.Lpr.101-L.MS
10 mime;] **Trial-**; mime H.Lpr.101-L.MS
11 place,] **Trial-**; place H.Lpr.101-L.MS
   time,] **Trial-**; Time H.Lpr.101-L.MS
12 use.] H.Lpr.101, **Trial-**; Use. T.MS; Use L.MS
13 cast,] **Trial-**; cast H.Lpr.101-L.MS
14 proved,] **Trial-**; proved H.Lpr.101-L.MS
15 loved,] **Trial-**; loved H.Lpr.101-L.MS
16 past.] **Trial-**; Past. H.Lpr.101, T.MS; Past L.MS
17 floor,] **Trial-**; floor H.Lpr.101-L.MS
18 warm;] **Trial-**; warm H.Lpr.101-L.MS
20 Thro'] H.Lpr.101-L.MS, **1855-**; Through **Trial-1851B**
   more?] H.Lpr.101, T.MS, **Trial-**; more L.MS
21 song,] H.Lpr.101, T.MS, **Trial-**; song L.MS
   game,] H.Lpr.101, T.MS, **Trial-**; game L.MS
   feast;] **1855-**; feast! H.Lpr.101, T.MS; feast L.MS; feast, **Trial-1851B**
22 touch'd,] **Trial-**; touch'd H.Lpr.101; touch't, T.MS; touch't L.MS
   blown;] **Trial-**; blown! H.Lpr.101, T.MS; blown L.MS
23 motion,] H.Lpr.101, **Trial-**; motion; T.MS; motion: L.MS
24 east] **Trial-**; East. H.Lpr.101; East T.MS, L.MS
25 wood.] L.MS-; wood – H.Lpr.101, T.MS
26 seed;] **Trial-**; seed – H.Lpr.101; seed. T.MS; seed L.MS
27 measured] H.Lpr.101-L.MS, **1850C-**; measur'd **Trial-1850B**
   arcs,] **Trial-**; arcs H.Lpr.101-L.MS

106]
25 disease;] **1855–**; disease, **Trial–1851B**

107]
1 born,] **Trial–**; born L.MS
10 crescent,] **1850A–**; crescent L.MS, **Trial**
   hangs] L.MS, **1850A–**; hangs, **Trial**
13 Together,] **Trial–**; Together L.MS
   pass] L.MS, **1850B–**; pass, **Trial, 1850A**
15 coast.] **Trial–**; coast: L.MS
   But] **Trial–**; but L.MS
   wine,] **Trial–**; wine L.MS
16 glass;] **Trial–**; glass: L.MS
17 lie,] **Trial–**; lie L.MS
18 heat;] **Trial–**; heat: L.MS
19 talk] **Trial–**; talk, L.MS
20 by;] L.MS, **1855–**; by: **Trial–1851B**
23 him,] **1862A–**; him L.MS-**1861**
   be,] **Trial–**; be L.MS

108]
1 kind,] **Trial–**; kind T.MS, L.MS
2 And,] **Trial–**; And T.MS, L.MS
   stone,] **Trial–**; stone T.MS, L.MS
3 alone,] **Trial–**; alone. T.MS; alone L.MS
4 wind:] **Trial–**; wind. T.MS; wind L.MS
5 faith,] **Trial–**; faith T.MS, L.MS
7 height,] **Trial–**; height T.MS; hight L.MS
8 Death?] **Trial–**; death? T.MS; Death L.MS
9 place,] **Trial–**; place T.MS, L.MS
10 hymns?] **Trial–**; hymns T.MS, L.MS
12 death] **Trial–**; Death T.MS, L.MS
   face.] T.MS, **Trial–**; face L.MS
14 skies:] **Trial–**; skies T.MS; skies. L.MS
15 'Tis] **Trial–**; Tis T.MS, L.MS
   wise,] L.MS–; wise T.MS

109]
3 eye,] **Trial–**; eye L.MS
6 man;] L.MS–; man (*misprint in* Eversley)
7 Impassion'd] **Trial–**; Empassion'd L.MS
8 its] **Trial–**; it's L.MS
9 nature] **Trial–**; nature, L.MS

13 freedom] **Trial-**; freedom, L.MS
15 England;] **1855-**; England, L.MS-**1851B**
18 sort,] **Trial-**; sort L.MS
   twine] L.MS, **1851A-**; twine, **Trial-1850C**
19 thine,] **Trial-**; thine L.MS
   unask'd,] L.MS, **1850B-**; unasked, **Trial, 1850A**
21 been,] **Trial-**; been; L.MS *2nd reading*
22 vain,] **1855-**; vain L.MS *2nd reading*-**1851B**
23 remain,] **Trial-**; remain L.MS

110]
 2 years:] **Trial-**; years. L.MS
 3 fears,] **Trial-**; fears L.MS
 6 pride,] **Trial-**; pride. L.MS
11 thee,] **Trial-**; thee L.MS
13 apart,] **Trial-**; apart L.MS
17 skill,] **Trial-**; skill L.MS
18 tire,] **Trial-**; tire L.MS

111]
 1 spirit,] **1850B-**; spirit L.MS-**1850A**
   down] L.MS, **1850B-**; down, **Trial, 1850A**
 2 all,] **1850B-**; all L.MS-**1850A**
 3 ball,] **1855-**; ball L.MS-**1851B**
 5 spirit,] **Trial-**; spirit L.MS
 8 pale:] **Trial-**; pale; L.MS
14 hour] L.MS, **1855-**; hour, **Trial-1851B**
15 manners,] **Trial-**; manners L.MS
18 by,] **Trial-**; by L.MS
19 eye,] **Trial-**; eye L.MS
20 Nature] L.MS, **1850A-**; nature **Trial**
   light;] **1855-**; light L.MS; light, **Trial-1851B**
23 charlatan,] **Trial-**; charlatan T.MS, L.MS
24 use.] **Trial-**; use T.MS, L.MS

112]
 1 wisdom] H.Lpr.101, T.MS, **Trial-**; Wisdom L.MS
   less,] **Trial-**; less H.Lpr.101-L.MS
 2 I,] H.Lpr.101, T.MS, **Trial-**; I L.MS
 3 insufficiencies,] **Trial-**; insufficiencies H.Lpr.101-L.MS
 4 perfectness.] H.Lpr.101, T.MS, **Trial-**; perfectness L.MS
 5 thou,] **Trial-**; thou T.MS, L.MS
 6 love,] **Trial-**; love T.MS, L.MS

8 souls,] **Trial-**; souls T.MS, L.MS
  doom.] T.MS, **Trial-**; doom L.MS
9 thou?] L.MS-; thou: H.Lpr.101; Thou? T.MS
10 touch,] **Trial-**; touch H.Lpr.101-L.MS
11 hope] **Trial-**; Hope H.Lpr.101-L.MS
   much,] **Trial-**; much H.Lpr.101-L.MS
12 hour,] **Trial-**; hour H.Lpr.101-L.MS
13 brought,] **Trial-**; brought H.Lpr.101-L.MS
14 made,] **Trial-**; made H.Lpr.101-L.MS
15 world-wide] H.Lpr.101, T.MS, **Trial-**; worldwide L.MS
16 vassal tides] L.MS-; vassal-tides H.Lpr.101, T.MS
   thought.] **Trial-**; Thought. H.Lpr.101-L.MS

113]

1 'Tis] **Trial-**; Tis L.MS
  sorrow] **Trial-**; Sorrow L.MS
  wise;] **Trial-**; wise L.MS
3 me,] **Trial-**; me L.MS
4 rise;] **Trial-**; rise: L.MS
5 doubt,] **1864-**; doubt L.MS-1863
6 intellect,] **Trial-**; intellect L.MS
7 strive,] **Trial-**; strive L.MS
  fashion,] **Trial-**; fashion L.MS
8 wouldst] **Trial-**; would'st L.MS
  been:] **Trial-**; been L.MS
10 sent,] **Trial-**; sent L.MS
11 Parliament,] **Trial-**; Parliament L.MS
12 storm,] **Trial-**; storm — L.MS
13 force,] **Trial-**; force L.MS
14 Becoming,] **Trial-**; Becoming L.MS
   birth,] **Trial-**; birth L.MS
16 course,] **Trial-**; course L.MS
17 go,] **Trial-**; go L.MS
18 energies,] **Trial-**; energies L.MS
19 overthrowings,] **Trial-**; overthrowings L.MS

114]

1 Knowledge?] Heath MS, **1851A-**; knowledge? **Trial-1850C**
22 Wisdom] **1851A-**; wisdom **Trial-1850C**

115]

10 vale,] **Trial-**; vale L.MS
13 seamew] **Trial-**; sea mew L.MS
   pipes,] **Trial-**; pipes L.MS

14 gleam,] **Trial–**; gleam L.MS
19 violet,] **Trial–**; violet L.MS

117]
  1 hours,] **Trial–**; hours T.MS, L.MS
    this] **1884A–**; this, – **Trial**; this, T.MS, L.MS, **1850A–1883**
  2 place,] L.MS–; place T.MS
  3 embrace,] L.MS–; embrace T.MS
  4 bliss:] **1850A–**; bliss – T.MS; bliss; L.MS; bliss. **Trial**
  6 sweet;] **Trial–**; sweet T.MS; sweet, L.MS
  7 meeting] T.MS, L.MS, **1860–**; meeting, **Trial–1859**
    meet,] **Trial–**; meet T.MS, L.MS
  8 hundredfold] **Trial–**; hundred fold T.MS, L.MS
    accrue,] L.MS–; accrue T.MS
  9 runs,] L.MS–; runs T.MS
10 steals,] L.MS–; steals T.MS
11 wheels,] L.MS–; wheels T.MS
12 suns.] **Trial–**; Suns. T.MS, L.MS

118]
  2 giant] **Trial–**; Giant L.MS
  3 truth,] **Trial–**; truth L.MS
  4 lime;] **Trial–**; lime, L.MS
  5 dead] L.MS, **1855–**; dead, **Trial–1851B**
10 seeming-random] L.MS, **1850A–**; seeming random **Trial**
    forms,] **Trial–**; forms L.MS
11 storms,] **Trial–**; storms L.MS
12 man;] **Trial–**; man, L.MS
13 clime,] **Trial–**; clime L.MS
15 place,] **Trial–**; place; L.MS
17 himself,] **Trial–**; himself L.MS
    more;] **Trial–**; more, L.MS
21 gloom,] **Trial–**; gloom L.MS
23 dipt] L.MS, **1850B–**; dipp'd **Trial, 1850A**
26 Faun,] **Trial–**; faun, L.MS
    feast;] **1850A–**; feast. L.MS, **Trial**
27 upward,] **Trial–**; upward L.MS
    beast,] **Trial–**; beast L.MS

119]
  9 bland,] **1884A–**; bland **1850A–1883**

122]
1 Oh,] **Trial–**; O L.MS
  then,] **Trial–**; then L.MS
2 doom,] **Trial–**; doom L.MS
5 more,] **Trial–**; more L.MS
  awe,] **Trial–**; awe L.MS
7 soul,] **Trial–**; soul L.MS
8 law;] **Trial–**; law – L.MS
9 me,] **Trial–**; me L.MS
10 now,] **Trial–**; now L.MS
12 blood,] **Trial–**; blood L.MS
  wave,] **Trial–**; wave L.MS
14 boy,] **Trial–**; boy L.MS
15 joy,] **Trial–**; joy L.MS
16 life] **Trial–**; Life L.MS
  death;] **Trial–**; Death L.MS
18 dew-drop] **Trial–**; dewdrop L.MS
  bow,] L.MS, **1851A–**; bow; **Trial–1850C**
20 rose.] **Trial–**; rose L.MS

123]
2 earth,] **Trial–**; Earth, T.MS; Earth L.MS
  seen!] T.MS, **Trial–**; seen. L.MS
3 roars,] **Trial–**; roars T.MS, L.MS
5 shadows,] **Trial–**; shadows T.MS, L.MS
6 form,] **Trial–**; form T.MS, L.MS
  stands;] **Trial–**; stands. T.MS, L.MS
7 melt] **Trial–**; melt, T.MS, L.MS
  lands,] **Trial–**; lands T.MS; lands: L.MS
9 dwell,] L.MS–; dwell T.MS
10 dream,] **Trial–**; dream T.MS, L.MS
  true;] L.MS–; true T.MS

124]
2 faith;] **1850B–**; faith, H.Lpr.102, **1850A**
9 faith] L.MS, **1850A–**; Faith **Trial**, H.Lpr.102
  had] L.MS, H.Lpr.102, **1850A–**; hath **Trial** (*error?*)
  fall'n] L.MS, H.Lpr.102, **1850A–**; fallen **Trial**
  asleep,] L.MS, **Trial**, **1850A–**; asleep H.Lpr.102
10 voice] L.MS *2nd reading*, **1850A–**; voice, **Trial**
  'believe . . . more'] L.MS *2nd reading*, **1850A–**; 'Believe . . . more,' **Trial**
11 ever-breaking] **1850A–**; ever breaking L.MS *2nd reading*, **Trial**
  shore] L.MS *2nd reading*, **1850A**; shore, **Trial**

12 deep;] **1850A-**; deep. L.MS *2nd reading*, **Trial**
14 part,] L.MS, **1850A-**; part; **Trial**; part H.Lpr.102
15 And] L.MS, H.Lpr.102, **1850A-**; And, **Trial**
    wrath] L.MS, H.Lpr.102, **1850A-**; wrath, **Trial**
16 answer'd] L.MS, H.Lpr.102, **1850A-**; answer'd, **Trial**
    felt.'] **Trial, 1850A-**; felt' L.MS, H.Lpr.102
17 fear:] **Trial, 1850A-**; fear H.Lpr.102
18 wise;] **1850A-**; *punctuation illegible in* H.Lpr.102
19 cries,] **Trial, 1850A-**; cries H.Lpr.102 |
23 hands] L.MS, **H.Lpr.102-**; hands, **Trial**

125]
  1 sung,] **Trial-**; sung — T.MS
  3 Yea,] **Trial-**; Yea T.MS
  4 tongue,] **Trial-**; tongue: T.MS
  5 youth;] **Trial-**; youth, T.MS
  6 eyes;] **Trial-**; eyes T.MS
  7 lies,] **Trial-**; lies T.MS
  8 fix'd] **Trial-**; fixt T.MS
    truth:] **Trial-**; truth. T.MS
10 breathed] **1850A-**; breath'd T.MS, **Trial**
    song;] **Trial-**; song, T.MS
12 there;] **Trial-**; there, T.MS
14 deeps,] **Trial-**; deeps T.MS
15 force,] **Trial-**; force T.MS
16 dancing,] **Trial-**; dancing T.MS

126]
  3 friend,] **Trial-**; friend T.MS
  5 King] **Trial-**; king T.MS
    Lord,] **Trial-**; Lord T.MS
  6 tho'] T.MS, **1850A-**; though **Trial**
  7 earth,] **Trial-**; earth T.MS
  8 Encompass'd] **Trial-**; Encompasst T.MS
    guard,] **Trial-**; guard T.MS
10 place,] **Trial-**; place T.MS
11 space,] **1855-**; space T.MS-**1851B**

127]
  2 fear;] **Trial-**; fear. L.MS
  4 storm,] **Trial-**; storm L.MS
  5 Proclaiming] **Trial-**; Proclaiming, L.MS
    spread,] **Trial-**; spread L.MS

6 justice,] **1850A-**; justice − L.MS; justice; **Trial**
9 crown,] **Trial-**; crown L.MS
10 lazar,] **Trial-**; lazar L.MS
11 crags;] **Trial-**; crags, L.MS
12 down,] **Trial-**; down L.MS
13 flood;] **Trial-**; flood, L.MS
14 high,] **Trial-**; high L.MS
15 sky,] **Trial-**; sky L.MS
17 compass'd] **Trial-**; compassd L.MS
    Hell;] **Trial, 1855-**; Hell L.MS; Hell, **1850A-1851B**
18 spirit,] **Trial-**; spirit L.MS
19 tumult] L.MS, **1850A-**; tumult, **Trial**

128]

5 doubt] **1850A-**; doubt, H.Lpr.102
    flood] H.Lpr.102, **1850B-**; flood, **1850A**
6 time] **1850A-**; Time H.Lpr.102
    made,] **1850A-**; made H.Lpr.102
9 Hours] H.Lpr.102; hours, T.MS
    Fear,] H.Lpr.102-; Fear T.MS
11 new;] **1855-**; new, − T.MS; new H.Lpr.102; new, **1850A-1851B**
12 here,] **1850A-**; here − T.MS; here H.Lpr.102
16 word,] **1850A-**; word T.MS, H.Lpr.102
17 power,] T.MS, **1850A-**; power H.Lpr.102
18 desk,] T.MS, **1850A-**; desk H.Lpr.102
19 picturesque] H.Lpr.102-; picturesque, T.MS
20 tower;] **1850A-**; tower T.MS, H.Lpr.102
22 yours.] H.Lpr.102-; your's. T.MS
    part] H.Lpr.102-; part, T.MS
23 all,] **1850A-**; all T.MS, H.Lpr.102
    art,] **1850A-**; Art T.MS, H.Lpr.102

129]

5 unknown;] **1855-**; unknown, **Trial-1851B**
9 be;] **1855-**; be, **Trial-1851B**

130]

1 air;] **Trial-**; air: L.MS
2 run;] **Trial-**; run: L.MS
3 sun,] **Trial-**; sun; L.MS
5 then?] L.MS, **1850A-**; then? − **Trial**
    thou] **Trial-**; thou, L.MS
    guess;] **Trial-**; guess L.MS

7 thee] **1850B-**; thee, L.MS–**1850A**
8 less:] **Trial-**; less. L.MS
9 before;] **Trial-**; before, L.MS
10 now;] **Trial-**; now: L.MS
11 mix'd] **Trial-**; mixt L.MS
   thou,] **Trial-**; thou L.MS
13 nigh;] **Trial-**; nigh L.MS
14 still,] **Trial-**; still L.MS
   rejoice;] **Trial-**; rejoice L.MS
15 prosper,] **Trial-**; prosper L.MS
   voice;] **Trial-**; voice L.MS
16 die.] **Trial-**; die L.MS
   tho'] L.MS, **1850A-**; though **Trial**

131]
   1 will] H.Nbk.18, **Trial-**; will, L.MS
   3 rock,] **Trial-**; rock H.Nbk.18, L.MS
   4 pure,] **Trial-**; pure H.Nbk.18; pure. L.MS
   10 proved] H.Nbk.18, **Trial-**; proved, L.MS

[Epilogue]
   1 tried,] **Trial-**; tried L.MS
   4 music] **Trial-**; music, L.MS
   10 years:] **Trial-**; years; L.MS
   12 love] **Trial-**; Love L.MS
   17 love] **Trial-**; Love L.MS
   20 before;] **Trial-**; before: L.MS
   22 times,] **Trial-**; times L.MS
   23 rhymes,] **Trial-**; rhymes L.MS
   24 shade.] **Trial-**; shade: L.MS
   28 its] **Trial-**; it's L.MS
   bower:] **Trial-**; bower. L.MS
   29 eyes] **Trial-**; eyes, L.MS
   30 thee;] **Trial-**; thee: L.MS
   31 brighten] **Trial-**; brighten, L.MS
   32 paradise.] **Trial-**; Paradise. L.MS
   37 power;] **1850A-**; power, L.MS; power **Trial**
   40 lightly] **Trial-**; lightly, L.MS
   41 near,] **Trial-**; near: L.MS
   42 bride;] **Trial-**; bride L.MS
   43 or] **Trial-**; or, L.MS
   beside] **Trial-**; beside, L.MS

44 fear.] **1884A-**; fear: L.MS-**1883**
46 watch'd] L.MS, **1850A-**; watched **Trial**
47 harm] **Trial-**; harm, L.MS
50 dead;] **Trial-**; dead, L.MS
53 ear.] **Trial-**; ear: L.MS
　on,] **Trial-**; on; L.MS
54 answer'd,] **Trial-**; answer'd L.MS
57 read,] L.MS, **1851A-**; read **Trial-1850C**
58 morn,] L.MS, **1851A-**; morn **Trial-1850C**
59 unborn;] **Trial-**; unborn: L.MS
60 sign'd,] **Trial-**; sign'd L.MS
62 breeze;] **Trial-**; breeze. L.MS
66 Many] **Trial-**; many L.MS
72 to-day] **1851A-**; To day L.MS; to day **Trial-1850C**
　its] **1850C-**; it's L.MS-**1850B**
　side.] **Trial-**; side: L.MS
73 To-day] **1851A-**; To day L.MS-**1850C**
74 increased,] **1851A-**; increased L.MS; increas'd **Trial-1850C**
75 feast,] **1850A-**; feast L.MS, **Trial**
78 sun;] **Trial-**; sun. L.MS
81 round,] **Trial-**; round: L.MS
82 warm'd] **Trial-**; warm'd, L.MS
84 days.] **Trial-**; days: L.MS
90 wait;] **Trial-**; wait: L.MS
91 late;] **Trial-**; late: L.MS
92 Farewell,] **Trial-**; Farewell: L.MS
　kiss,] **Trial-**; kiss; L.MS
97 grew,] **Trial-**; grew: L.MS
99 look'd,] **Trial-**; look'd L.MS
100 dew.] **Trial-**; dew: L.MS
104 three-times-three,] **1851A-**; three-times-three. L.MS; three times three, **Trial-1850C**
105 dance; —] **Trial-**; dance; L.MS
106 loud,] **Trial-**; loud; L.MS
108 fire:] **Trial-**; fire. L.MS
112 silent-lighted] **Trial-**; silent lighted L.MS
114 mountain head,] **Trial-**; mountain-head, L.MS
115 o'er] **Trial-**; oer L.MS
116 hills;] **Trial-**; hills, L.MS
121 ocean] **Trial-**; Ocean L.MS
123 vast] **Trial-**; Vast L.MS
124 being] **Trial-**; Being L.MS
125 phase,] **Trial-**; phase L.MS

126 think,] **Trial–**; think L.MS
128 race] L.MS– (race⟨.⟩)
129 that,] **Trial–**; that L.MS
    eye,] **Trial–**; eye L.MS
130 knowledge;] **Trial–**; Knowledge; L.MS
132 Nature] **Trial–**; Nature, L.MS
134 did,] **Trial–**; did L.MS
135 hoped,] **Trial–**; hoped L.MS
    suffer'd,] **Trial–**; suffer'd L.MS
143 event,] **Trial–**; event L.MS
144 creation] **Trial–**; Creation L.MS

ADDITIONAL POEMS

i]

  5 warbled,] *Ricks*; warbled. H.Lpr.103
   'Make] *Ricks*; 'make H.Lpr.103
  6 Hear] *Ricks*; hear H.Lpr.103
   am.'] *Ricks*; am. H.Lpr.103
  8 chanted,] *Ricks*; chanted H.Lpr.103
   'Find . . . soul.'] *Ricks*; Find . . . soul. H.Lpr.103
  9 still'd.] *Ricks* (stilled.); still'd H.Lpr.103
11 breezes,] *Ricks*; breezes H.Lpr.103
12 unfulfill'd.] *Ricks* (unfulfilled.); unfulfill'd H.Lpr.103

ii]

  1 born':] *Ricks, TLS*; born' T.MS
  2 Melpomene,] *Ricks, TLS*; Melpomene T.MS
3-5 'It . . . this',] *Ricks, TLS*; It . . . this' T.MS
  3 thee,] *Ricks, TLS*; thee T.MS
  4 forlorn.] *Ricks, TLS*; forlorn T.MS
  5 cries,] *Ricks, TLS*; cries T.MS
  6 'That] *Ricks, TLS*; That T.MS
  9 boy:] *Ricks, TLS*; boy T.MS
12 – O the wonder –] *Ricks, TLS*; O the wonder T.MS
   joy;] *Ricks, TLS*; joy T.MS
13 that] T.MS; that, *Ricks, TLS*

iii]

  1 grief] *Memoir, Eversley*; Grief T.MS
   entertain,] *Memoir, Eversley*; entertain T.MS
  2 tells,] *Memoir, Eversley*; tells T.MS
  4 reason] *Memoir, Eversley*; Reason T.MS
   brain.] T.MS; brain: *Memoir, Eversley*

5 grief] *Memoir*, *Eversley*; Grief T.MS
name.] T.MS; name: *Memoir*; name, *Eversley*
6 will.] T.MS; will; *Memoir*, *Eversley*
7 'Tis] *Memoir*, *Eversley*; Tis T.MS
far] T.MS; far, *Memoir*, *Eversley*
8 shame,] *this edition*; shame T.MS; shame: *Memoir*; shame. *Eversley*
10 wast] T.MS, *Memoir*; wast, *Eversley*
11 past] *this edition*; Past T.MS; past, *Memoir*, *Eversley*
12 would'st] T.MS, *Eversley*; wouldst *Memoir*
been –] T.MS; been: *Memoir*, *Eversley*
13 mastermind] T.MS; master mind *Memoir*, *Eversley*
masterminds,] T.MS; master minds, *Memoir*, *Eversley*
15 fate,] *Memoir*, *Eversley*; Fate, T.MS
16 foursquare] T.MS; four-square *Memoir*, *Eversley*

iv]

3 not,] T.MS, *Eversley*; not; *Memoir*
5 Behold,] *Memoir*, *Eversley*; Behold T.MS
6 see] T.MS; see, *Memoir*, *Eversley*
truth,] *Memoir*, *Eversley*; truth T.MS
7 youth,] *Memoir*, *Eversley*; youth T.MS
10 yourselves,] T.MS, *Memoir*; yourselves *Eversley*
wisdom-led,] *Memoir*, *Eversley*; wisdom-led T.MS
13 forward:] T.MS; forward! *Memoir*, *Eversley*
throne,] *Memoir*, *Eversley*; throne T.MS
14 Dissolve] *Memoir*, *Eversley*; Dessolve T.MS
15 war,] *Memoir*, *Eversley*; War T.MS

v]

1 distress.] T.MS; distress, *Memoir*, *Eversley*
2 grave.] T.MS; grave, *Memoir*, *Eversley*
3 have,] *Memoir*, *Eversley*; have T.MS
6 way:] T.MS; way; *Memoir*, *Eversley*
7 say,] *this edition*; say T.MS, *Memoir*, *Eversley*
8 'The . . . be.'] T.MS; "The . . . be." *Memoir*, *Eversley*
9 whispers,] T.MS; whispers *Memoir*, *Eversley*
loss,] *this edition*; loss: T.MS, *Memoir*, *Eversley*
10 remain,] *this edition*; remain T.MS; remain! *Memoir*, *Eversley*
11 MERCY JESU] T.MS; 'Mercy Jesu' *Memoir*, *Eversley*
rain,] *this edition*; rain T.MS; rain! *Memoir*, *Eversley*
12 MISERERE] T.MS; 'Miserere' *Memoir*, *Eversley*
13 dew,] *Memoir*, *Eversley*; dew T.MS
14 Art!'] *this edition*; Art' T.MS; art!" *Memoir*, *Eversley*

15 friend,] *Memoir, Eversley*; friend T.MS
   heart,] *Memoir, Eversley*; heart T.MS
16 Nature] T.MS; nature *Memoir, Eversley*

vi]
  1 leaf',] *Ricks*; leaf' L.MS
  2 said,] *Ricks*; said L.MS
  3 'Why] *Ricks*; Why L.MS
    dead?] *Ricks*; dead L.MS
  5 thee,] *Ricks*; thee L.MS
  6 labour?] *Ricks*; labour. L.MS
10 sands,] *Ricks*; sands L.MS
15 soul] *Ricks*; souls L.MS (*error*)
16 tomb,] *Ricks*; tomb L.MS

vii]
  3 there,] *Ricks*; there. L.MS
  7 past,] *Ricks*; past L.MS
  9 bland,] *Ricks*; bland L.MS
10 eye,] *Ricks*; eye L.MS

viii]
  6 aloud,] *Materials, Ricks*; aloud Cambridge MS
  9 Truth-seeking] *Memoir, Ricks*; Truth seeking Cambridge MS, *Materials*
    afraid,] *Materials, Memoir, Ricks*; afraid — Cambridge MS
10 now —] *Materials, Memoir, Ricks*; now Cambridge MS
12 weigh'd?] *this edition*; weigh'd Cambridge MS; weighed? *Materials, Memoir, Ricks*
14 flame,] *Materials, Ricks*; flame Cambridge MS
15 London's] *Materials, Ricks*; Londons Cambridge MS
    shame —] *Materials, Ricks*; shame Cambridge MS
16 lust.] *Materials, Ricks*; lust Cambridge MS
18 despair,] *Memoir, Ricks*; despair Cambridge MS, *Materials*
20 God.] *Materials, Memoir, Ricks*; God Cambridge MS

ix]
  1 sky!] *Memoir*; sky H.Lpr.104
  2 hill.] H.Lpr.104; hill, *Memoir*
  3 still.] H.Lpr.104; still: *Memoir*
  4 die.] *Memoir*; die H.Lpr.104
  5 me:] H.Lpr.104; me, *Memoir*
  6 Alas,] *Memoir*; Alas H.Lpr.104
    weak.] H.Lpr.104; weak: *Memoir*

INDEX OF FIRST LINES